Muslims and Capitalism –
An Uneasy Relationship?

Edited by
Béatrice Hendrich

AF622762

KULTUR, RECHT UND POLITIK IN MUSLIMISCHEN GESELLSCHAFTEN

Herausgegeben von

Thomas Bauer, Stephan Conermann, Sabine Damir-Geilsdorf,
Gudrun Krämer, Anke von Kügelgen, Eva Orthmann,
Anja Pistor-Hatam, Irene Schneider, Reinhard Schulze

Band 39

ERGON VERLAG

Muslims and Capitalism – An Uneasy Relationship?

Edited by
Béatrice Hendrich

ERGON VERLAG

Gedruckt mit freundlicher Unterstützung der Fritz Thyssen Stiftung, Köln

Umschlagabbildung:
Claudia Bülbül, Feldforschung 2014,
AKM Şura, Ort: KA-MU-DER Vakfi Fatih İstanbul

Bibliografische Information der Deutschen Nationalbibliothek
Die Deutsche Nationalbibliothek verzeichnet diese Publikation in der Deutschen Nationalbibliografie; detaillierte bibliografische Daten sind im Internet über http://dnb.d-nb.de abrufbar.

© Ergon – ein Verlag in der Nomos Verlagsgesellschaft, Baden-Baden 2018
Das Werk einschließlich aller seiner Teile ist urheberrechtlich geschützt.
Jede Verwertung außerhalb des Urheberrechtsgesetzes bedarf der Zustimmung des Verlages.
Das gilt insbesondere für Vervielfältigungen jeder Art, Übersetzungen, Mikroverfilmungen und für Einspeicherungen in elektronische Systeme.
Gedruckt auf alterungsbeständigem Papier.
Umschlaggestaltung: Jan von Hugo
Satz: Thomas Breier

www.ergon-verlag.de

ISBN 978-3-95650-463-1 (Print)
ISBN 978-3-95650-464-8 (ePDF)
ISSN 1863-9801

Table of Contents

Béatrice Hendrich
Introduction:
Exalting the Past, Rebelling against the Present,
and Struggling for a (Better) Future? ... 7

Part One: The Past and the Future

Mouez Khalfaoui
Primary Islamic Texts on Land, Water, and Capital Ownership ... 23

Anas Malik
Beyond State and Market:
Institutional Diversity and Polycentricity in Islamic Contexts ... 33

Part Two: Marxism, Anti-Capitalism, Islam

Manfred Sing
The Tempestuous Affair between Marxism and Islam:
Attraction, Hostility, and Accommodation since 1917 ... 51

Leandros Fischer
Left-wing Perspectives on Political Islam:
A Mapping Attempt ... 103

Katajun Amirpur
Iranian Godfathers of Islamic Socialism –
"It is the Marxists Who Have Learned It from Islam" ... 121

Bayram Koca
The Emergence of Anti-Capitalist Muslims in Turkey:
"God, Bread, Freedom" ... 135

Tahir Kamran
Ubaidullah Sindhi as a Revolutionary:
A Study of Socialist Activism in Deobandi Islam ... 151

Part Three: Social Justice and Anti-Capitalism

Sabine Damir-Geilsdorf
"... So That It May Not Circulate Solely between
the Wealthy among You."
The Critique of Capitalism and the Vision of a "Balanced Society"
(*mujtamaʿ mutawāzin*) in the Writings of Sayyid Quṭb (1906–1966) ... 173

Elisheva Machlis
A Shiite Economic Model.
From Bāqir al-Ṣadr to Contemporary Iraq 191

Fabio Vicini
Between Islamism and Human Rights.
Mazlumder as a Third Way within Turkish Islamism? 207

Béatrice Hendrich
A Sufi Martyr and Harbinger of Anti-Capitalism.
Şeyh Bedreddin as an Emblematic Figure in 'Progressive' Publications 223

Part Four: Different Ways to Non-Capitalism

Hans Visser
The Lure of Gold and Silver Dinars and Dirhams for the 21st Century 249

Anthony T. Fiscella
Three Images of Anti-authoritarian Socialism within Islamic Contexts:
Isabelle Eberhardt/Mahmoud Essadi, Muammar Qaddafi's *Green Book*, and Heba Raouf Ezzat 271

Michelangelo Guida
Turkish Islamists' Enthusiasm for Versace:
Islamism between Rejection and Adoption of the West 295

The Authors 313

Introduction: Exalting the Past, Rebelling against the Present, and Struggling for a (Better) Future?

A Critical Approach towards Capitalist Modes of Production and Government by Islamically-Oriented Movements

Béatrice Hendrich

What is the relation between Islam and Capitalism? Is there any at all? Evidently, these very questions already contain pitfalls: In order to answer them in a conclusive manner, a fixed definition of 'Islam' and 'Capitalism' would be necessary as a first step. Obviously, those definitions could only be provided in the form of essentialist statements.

However, every now and then individuals and movements, academics and activists, endeavor to find an answer to these questions. In the 1960s, Maxime Rodinson published his *Islam et Capitalisme* (Rodinson 1966). Rodinson argued that the absence of a capitalist development in the Islamic world was a direct result of colonial exploitation and the structures of underdevelopment based thereupon. The main objectives of Rodinson's book were a critical analysis of Max Weber's *Die protestantische Ethik und der Geist des Kapitalismus* (1904) and of Marxist tenets regarding the reasons for economic (under-)development. It is telling that Rodinson based his work on an examination of outright Western concepts and authors. It tells us about the state of Oriental Studies in the 1960s–Rodinson was an *Orientalist–*, and it tells us about the related perspective taken even by a scholar who aimed to deconstruct "the argument attributed to Weber that the Islamic ethic is too antipathetic to rationality to have permitted the indigenous development of capitalism"[1] and whose attitudes towards the Islamic world were basically positive. Rodinson quotes from the Quran and hadiths, and every now and then he refers to Muslim scholars, although what really matters to him are Marx and Weber. As a matter of fact, when *Islam et Capitalisme* was published, 'Alī Sharī'ati (1933–1977) was only starting to become famous. But what about earlier Muslim reformers such as the Egyptian Sayyid Quṭb (1906–1966) and H. Oemar Said Tjokroaminoto (1882–1934) in Indonesia, or Muslim-socialist movements and parties in the early Soviet

1 Leonard Binder, "Islam and Capitalism. By Maxime Rodinson and Brian Pearce", *American Journal of Sociology* 87: 2 (1981), 492–495, 493.

Union or colonial India? Rodinson himself mentions Quṭb in the "Afterword", added to the book's first American edition in 1973; the very mode of the paragraph is however rather belittleling. Nor does it express further interest in Quṭb and the likes:

> I might have discussed more extensively the many contemporary Muslim writers who have taken up ... the theme of the applicability of the 'social' principles of Islam to present-day society and to the ideal community. These writers are numerous, to be sure, but their arguments are always the same as those advanced by the two or three writers whom I did mention and criticize. In view of the influence he had, and the important ... role played by his life and his death, I might have analysed the work of the ideologist of the Muslim Brotherhood, Sayyid Qutb, whom Nasser hanged for conspiracy in 1966.[2]

In the summer of 2013, in Turkey a movement called Anti-capitalist Muslims (Antikapitalist Müslümanlar, AKM) obtained a sudden and unexpected popularity. Without a doubt, this sudden popularity was to a broad extent the result of the technical means of modern mass communication. The AKM's slogans, together with a particular visual appearance and an extensive use of social media, aroused the curiosity of the audience within and beyond the Turkish borders. What is more important, however, is that their slogans and behavior obviously corresponded to the needs and expectations of those who had long since been asking and searching for a third way in (developing) Muslim countries in general, and in Turkey in particular.

The summer of 2013 was the time of the, as it would later be called, Gezi Resistance. The initial cause of the conflict was the planned destruction of the Gezi Park in one of the historical centers of Istanbul, in Taksim, as part an urban renewal plan. Environmental activists started sit-ins and other forms of protest at the end of May with the aim to save the trees. Disinclined to discuss a compromise, the local government took violent measures against the protesters, thus transforming a demonstration into a pluralistic movement which then spread nationwide. During June 2013, Turkey experienced new forms of dialogue and social solidarity among the protesters and their sympathizers, but the toll exacted for this short period of hope was heavy, with seven people dead and hundreds affected by teargas or more seriously injured.[3] Although the Anti-capitalist Muslims had not initiated the resistance, once they had set up their tents and banners in the protest camp, they turned into important actors in the resistance as they added, in every sense, an unexpected color to what had started as an urban, middle-class eco-protest. With their key slogan "Property belongs to God" (*Mülk Allah'ındır*) they easily entrenched themselves in the protest against the brutal

2 Maxime Rodinson, *Islam and Capitalism*, New York: Random House 1973, 237–238.

3 Leyla Önal, "Gezi Park and EuroMaidan: Social Movements at the Borders", *The European Journal of Social Science Research* 29: 1 (2016), 16–40, 21–22.

capitalism of the ruling class and their disrespect towards both nature and human rights and needs. Beyond catchy slogans, the AKM catered to the need and longing for a rapprochement between culturally and politically diverse segments of the society such as secular Kemalists, practicing Muslims, and all the other smaller or very small groups and communities in Turkey such as Alevis, queer people or non-Turkish ethnicities. The sudden increase of the Anti-capitalist Muslims' popularity was at least partly due to earlier activities aimed at dialogue between former 'adversary' groups, e.g. between Turkish and Armenian young people,[4] or 'secular' and 'religious' women.[5] These dialogical activities had demonstrated that it was possible to eliminate ideological borders (Entgrenzung[6]). The AKM who base their demand for social justice on a revised reading of the Quran became famous for their cooperation during the Gezi Resistance with groups detested by conservative Islam such as the queer community or leftist activists.

AKM is in the first instance a Turkish movement, the result of a distinctive national history of modernization and a recent massive socio-economical change which includes the emergence of a new, affluent and influential class of Muslim entrepreneurs coming from Anatolia instead of from established families in urban centers in the West. The new 'green' capitalism did not go unprotested by those Muslims who attach more significance to societal equality than to an economic growth which the masses do not profit from.

One may argue that it is inappropriate to compare Rodinson's approach to the relation between Islam and capitalism with the approach of the Anti-capitalist Muslims because of the general differences between an academic treatise–like Rodinson's–and the statements of a movement, such as the AKM. On the other hand, the main actors of the anti-capitalist and left-Islam field would also claim intellectual respectability, as it is demonstrated by their education and numerous journal and book publications. For this reason, a comparison between the two is not only possible but strongly recommended. The most significant difference we encounter in a comparison of the discourses is indeed that of the claimed cultural heritage of each. While Rodinson had explained away his omission of Muslim/Islamist reformists and revolutionaries as the quote above has shown, saying that they only repeat each other's words, it is precisely this modern chain of *Islamic* tradition which, in the eyes of the current Muslims of the third way, adds

---

4 Leyla Neyzi and Hranush Kharatyan-Araqelyan, *Speaking to One Another: Personal Memories of the Past in Armenia and Turkey*, Bonn: DVV International 2010.

5 Dilek Cindoğlu, *Headscarf Ban and Discrimination: Professional Headscarved Women in the Labor Market* (=TESEV Publication 11), Istanbul: Mega Basım 2011.

6 Cüneyt Dinç and Nazlı Çağın Bilgili, " 'Damit wir ein neues Vokabular erschaffen'. Der linksislamische Islami Sol in der Türkei", *Grenzräume, Grenzgänge, Entgrenzungen*, Wiebke Hohberger, Roy Karadag, Katharina Müller and Christoph Ramm, eds., Wiesbaden: Springer 2018, 127–145.

value to their teaching and activities. This chain consists of numerous names from Muslim history and modern political movements, names which appear repeatedly in this edited volume, no matter which concrete geography or historical period the articles deal with: Abū Ẕarr al-Ghifāri, 'the fourth convert to Islam' (d. 652); the outstanding Sufis Manṣūr al-Ḥallāj (857–922) and Şeyh Bedreddin (1359–1416), both executed by the state; or 'Alī Sharī'atī (1933–1977), the Iranian intellectual who introduced Islam in the leftist discourse of his time, and the religious scholar Ayātollah Maḥmūd Tāleghānī (1914–1979). This is not to say that movements such as the AKM have lost sight of the examples of non-Muslim reformers and revolutionaries. On the contrary, Karl Marx is a name one can refer to without hesitation, followed by that of Engels (and his *Peasant War in German*), accompanied by Walter Benjamin's and Jean Paul Sartre's, and other names drawn from the global history of religious-political movements, such as Jan Hus (1370-1415), Thomas Müntzer (1489–1525), and Mahatma Gandhi.

The invocation of non-Muslim exemplars serves two ends: It emphasizes the cultural border-transgressing and global character of the AKM and similar movements; more often, however, it opens up the opportunity to demonstrate the supremacy of the Muslim forefathers when it comes to the timeline: Şeyh Bedreddin and Thomas Müntzer share the same revolutionary vision, but the sheikh implemented his a hundred and fifty years earlier. While Marx provides some interesting features for socialist Muslims, the struggle for shared property and social equality had already started during the early years of Islam. The invocation of the chain of Muslim exemplary figures and ideas drawn from the past is a familiar strategy of legitimizing one's own behavior. It functions the same way as collecting the sayings of the prophet and his adherents, and the hadiths compilations do. It expresses consensus inside the community and demands loyalty to the same.[7] At the same time, to claim and appropriate this history as a genuine cultural heritage means to locate one's own movement in the contested field of Turkey's historical memory in this specific way and to insist on this position.

The Anti-capitalist Muslims are an element of a broader field of societal movements in Turkey which is known by its exonym, *İslami Sol*, Islamic Left. The players in this field are diverse individuals, movements and groups which address so-called 'classical issues of the political left' such as the realization of social equality and rights while basing their arguments on the Quranic text. Many of them would avoid labeling themselves as "left" because of the traditionally tense relations between Turkish leftists and Muslim activists, while others explicitly endeavor to re-structure the rela-

7 Abbas Barzegar, "'Adhering to the Community (*Luzūm al-Jamāʿa*)': Continuities between late Umayyad Political Discourse and 'Proto-Sunni' Identity", *Review of Middle East Studies* 49: 2 (2016), 140–158.

tions between leftists and Muslims, or leftist political concepts and the tenets of Islam.[8] A motive common to these diverse groups is the frustration that the fading away of the secular Kemalist political establishment has not lead to the establishment of a morally improved political and social system in Turkey.

An interesting example from the intersecting zones of *İslami Sol* and Muslim capitalism is an association of Muslim entrepreneurs with a moral claim, *Turkish Entrepreneurship and Business Ethics Association* (*Türkiye İktisadi Girişim ve İş Ahlakı Derneği*, İGİAD), not to be confused with the much larger association MÜSİAD (*Müstakil Sanayici ve İş Adamları Derneği*) which fosters a neoliberal system focusing on the demands of the Muslim consumer.[9] Özlem Madi-Sisman calls the members of İGİAD "reluctant capitalists",[10] since they have found their own 'third way'. They answer the question of appropriate economic behavior "within a capitalistic system without transgressing Islamic boundaries" by means of "introducing Islamic morality into capitalism".[11] While İGİAD stresses the *conservative* Muslim identity of its members, they come close to the Anti-capitalist Muslims with regard to the Islamic ownership concept: One should be "aware that all possessions and reputations are temporary. Everything belongs to Allah".[12]

Although capitalism-critical and/or leftist Islam does not seem to be at the forefront among Muslim movements at present, its importance for and influence on the Muslim world in modernity should not be underestimated. History has seen far more movements and individuals of significance than we were able to collect in this volume. Moreover, the current relations between capitalism–often conceived as the economic system of imperialism and colonialism–and Islam are not at all neatly and conclusively defined. Issues which should have been, but are not discussed (in detail) in this volume are e.g. the Tatar revolutionary Mir Said Sultan-Galiev (1892–1940) and his theory of Muslim national communism,[13] or the close friend and supporter of Mahatma Gandhi, Khan Abdul Ghaffar Khan, a Pashtoon fighter for independence, socialism, justice and peace (1890–1988), whose convictions were anchored in the Quran and in the sermons of his role

---

8 Dinç and Çağın Bilgili, " 'Damit wir ein neues Vokabular erschaffen' ", 129.

9 For further details on MÜSİAD see the article of Bayram Koca in this volume, "The Emergence of Anti-Capitalist Muslims in Turkey: 'God, Bread, Freedom' ".

10 Özlem Madi-Sisman, *Muslims, Money, and Democracy in Turkey: Reluctant Capitalists*, New York: Palgrave 2017.

11 Ibid., 6.

12 Ibid., 128.

13 Ben Fowkes and Bülent Gökay, "Unholy Alliance: Muslims and Communists. An Introduction", *Journal of Communist Studies and Transition Politics* 25: 1 (2009), 1–31, 5. Some remarks can be found in the articles of Leandros Fischer and Manfred Sing in this volume.

model, Prophet Muḥammad. Almost ignored by Turkish historiography, the Turkish War of Liberation (1919–1922) had its Muslim Socialist fighters, too; the Green Army (*Yeşil Ordu*) under Çerkez Ethem "was an anti-capitalist, anti-imperialist and anti-militarist organization, and aimed to establish a socialist union in the world of Islam by modifying the Russian Revolution"[14].

Likewise, we should have talked about the future of Eco-Islam which shares the concern for economic justice based on the inalienability of vital goods such as soil and water.[15] And finally, no paper deals explicitly with a feminist or a gender perspective, or with queer activists inside the Islamic non-capitalist movements. These are only a few examples from this broad field which provide countless aspects for future research. Last but not least the question of social and political *justice* must be mentioned. As the articles in this volume demonstrate, the realization of justice in this world is what most movements center on while the economic system is more a means to reach this goal than an ideological fetish.

The aforementioned Gezi Resistance and the emerging new movements aiming at social justice and equality legitimized by Quranic ideals were the initial impulse to organize an international workshop on non-capitalist or anti-capitalist Islam in 2014 at the University of Cologne. The blossoming of an anti-capitalist Islam in Turkey raised a great number of related questions: Are there similar movements in other countries? What are their ideological and theological principles? Are there historical predecessors? What is the relationship between the critique of capitalism, a rejection of the 'West' and the quest for democracy? What is the relation between democracy and a free market economy? Can democracy be realized in a non-capitalist system? Why does the Muslim world at present seem to be dominated by an unrestricted demand for wealth accumulation and close contact with Western capitalism? And why does the left in the Western world lack a proper response to the challenge of Islamist-left movements or parties? Charles Tripp discusses in his *Islam and the Moral Economy. The Challenge of Capitalism* the implementation, success and breakdown of the third way. Clearly, the concept of ownership relations ("Ownership is for God only") was of vital importance for reformists in the early 20th century, he argues, but Iran is the only country to date in which an anti-capitalist economy has been institutionalized. This system has nevertheless not been used as a model for other economies because firstly, it is a predominantly Shiite

---

14 Bülent Gökay, *Soviet Eastern Policy and Turkey, 1920–1991: Soviet Foreign Policy, Turkey and Communism*, London: Routledge 2012, 20.

15 Donatella Vincenti, "Sustainability Transitions in Arab-Islamic Countries: Egypt as a Case Study", *Agriculture and Agricultural Science Procedia* 8 (2016), 135–140.

country and secondly, it has not lead to the liberation of the people but instead has striven for a liberal market economy.[16]

This edited volume contains the revised workshop presentations. The authors, coming from different disciplinary backgrounds, accordingly use different approaches to tackle their topics, focusing on historical change, political circumstances, or theoretical concepts. The volume sets off with an analysis of "Primary Islamic Texts on Land, Water, and Capital Ownership" by Mouez Khalfaoui. The article aims at understanding how economic subjects were debated in the Islamic past and what impact those texts, originating from the 7th to 9th century, had on subsequent literature on the subject. Khalfaoui demonstrates that *work* is a largely ignored aspect in later literature on Islamic economy while in the texts under consideration it represents a key issue. Anas Malik opens the door towards the future of economic development potentials in the contemporary Islamic context. Malik shifts the focus from the relations between market and state which dominate literature on development, to the opportunities a sensitive appreciation of inherited institutional diversity provides. In "Beyond State and Market: Institutional Diversity and Polycentricity in Islamic Contexts", the author bases his examination on a theory of institutions inspired by Vincent and Elenor Ostrom. In a polycentric polity, the 'state' is rather an association of associations. Evidently, this structural plurality would be reflected in processes of government and decision taking; this entails also the difficulty of deciding on the legitimacy of each decision or action. Interestingly, from this point of view, polycentricity also challenges what Malik calls the "oddly atraditional marriage of the central state authority and religious law" when the post-colonial state defines and sanctions orthodoxy. A further advantage of polycentric institutionalism is that it supports and favors the local actors over intruders, entrepreneurs and foreign capital. Thus, sustainable development would become a core element of economic politics, instead of the usual strategies of foreign investors: exploitation, destruction and withdrawal. One must be aware, however, that local knowledge may not always suffice in order to respond to demands or provide help, so cooperation with external experts or consultation with institutions with a superior authority can be indispensable.

The relation between Marxism, anti-capitalism and Islam constitutes a main topic in the given framework. In "The Tempestuous Affair between Marxism and Islam: Attraction, Hostility, and Accommodation since 1917", Manfred Sing offers a thorough, historical examination of the often neglected relation of Marxism and *Islam*–and not just of 'religion' in the sense

16 Charles Tripp, *Islam and the Moral Economy: the Challenge of Capitalism*, Cambridge: Cambridge Univ. Press 2006.

of 'Christianity'. He treats Marxism as a global movement with regionally distinct but interdependent features. The impact of socialist ideas on the Middle East has resulted in "hybrid forms of Arab socialism and Islamic socialism as political rivals of communism". To question these hybrid forms also necessitates grappling with the post-colonial critique of Marxism as a foreign, Western ideology. What seems to be a convincing and appealing critique at first glance turns out to be a culturalist simplification. There have been numerous ways to adapt and implement Marxism into a preexisting cultural order, while many of these new readings aim for a compatible third way beyond capitalism and communism.

In his chapter "Left-wing Perspectives on Political Islam: A Mapping Attempt", Leandros Fischer turns Sing's perspective the other way around. The emergence of political Islam beginning in the late 1970s has confronted the Left with an unexpected challenge. Some 'classical issues' of leftist politics, particularly the support of the impoverished masses and the overcoming of an unjust economic system, had become the main issues of *religious* movements. The subsequent confusion inside the Left was channeled into two key questions: Is there something unique about 'Islamic culture' that hinders Marxist ideas from gaining a mass following in the Arab and Muslim world? And, similar to Sing's discussion of Marxism as a tool of Westernization, is Marxism 'Eurocentric'? Fischer's article covers the Left's perception of Islam from a variety of angles, including regional particularities and more general debates on Islamophobia and integration as well as Marx's and Engels', and the early Bolsheviks' attitudes towards religion. He concludes that the concrete historical and regional circumstances seem to override ideological and essentialist considerations when it comes to the formulation of political strategies for how to deal with Islamism.

Among the most eminent names which appear again and again in the chapters of this volume are those of ʿAlī Sharīʿatī and Sayyid Quṭb. Katajun Amirpur discusses the significance of Sharīʿatī, together with a second Iranian thinker, Jalāl Āl-i, for the Iranian Revolution specifically, and for later Islamic-leftist activists in and outside Iran generally. The reintroduction of religion into the political discourse of Iran is to a great extent the result of the efforts of these two men who were not clerics but had a leftist political background. Sharīʿatī coined the term "Red Shia" in the sense of the true, revolutionary Shia of Imam ʿAlī, and added the social dimension, justice, to the new, revolutionary Shiite discourse. The ideal world would be characterized by "virtue, joint struggle for justice, equality, brotherhood, joint ownership of the means of production, and above all, the desire to create a classless society on earth" (Amirpur). Amirpur also demonstrates how the issue of authenticity and cultural mimicry can be solved if the perspective is turned around: That no longer does the East imitate the West but rather the

West copies the intellectuals of the East. Thus, she titles her paper "Iranian Godfathers of Islamic Socialism–'It is the Marxists who have learned it from Islam' ".

The paper by Bayram Koca, "The Emergence of Anti-Capitalist Muslims in Turkey: 'God, Bread, Freedom' " deals with the ideological and theological background of the aforementioned AKM, focusing on its most vital period from 2012 to 2015. Usually, the name of İhsan Eliaçık appears together with that of the movement, although the AKM and Eliaçık parted ways when Eliaçık became too much of a 'leader' in public perception, which is irreconcilable with the understanding of equality among the AKM members. However, through the numerous publications and sermons of the trained theologian and activist, names of the Islamic past have re-entered the discourse of socialist or Anti-capitalist Muslims in Turkey, first and foremost 'Alī Sharī'atī and Sayyid Quṭb. Koca deals with the political and economic changes which triggered the emergence of the AKM and similar movements or associations. He aims to explain the paradox to outsiders that just when an Islamically-oriented party became the unchallenged ruler of the Turkish Republic for the first time ever, a Muslim opposition became so popular. In order to understand this cleavage inside the field of political Islam in Turkey, it is essential, according to Koca, to discern clearly the difference between Left-Islam and Market Islam.

In his chapter "Ubaidullah Sindhi as a Revolutionary: A Study of Socialist Activism in Deobandi Islam" Tahir Kamran provides another example of Islamic socialist activism, but takes us to a different geography including a different Islamic school, and to the very particular circumstances British colonialism had created in the Indian subcontinent. Ubaidullah Sindhi's biography resembles in many aspects the biographies of later activists with a so-called pluralistic identity. His case shows clearly how strongly colonialism has shaken and re-arranged political and religious affiliation and convictions. Ubaidullah Sindhi was born into a Sikh family. His activism and teaching stem from his deliberate conversion to Islam, a keen interest in Pan-Islamism, and a shifting if not shaky stand towards Europeanization. He was very disappointed when he saw Pan-Islamism vanishing in the newly established Republic of Turkey where he stayed from 1923–26, but he nevertheless later defended elements of a technical Europeanization such as the shift to Latin letters for Urdu, which was very similar to the top-down restructuring measures in Turkey. Ubaidullah equated Ibn al-'Arabi's philosophy with Vedantism and considered it capable of laying the political foundation for a united India. But most importantly, his political critique was informed by socialism. For him, wealth accumulation and impoverishment of the masses inevitably leads to moral and religious decline.

For anti-capitalist or left-Islam movements, the issue of social justice is a very strong incentive. The papers gathered in this volume under the subtitle "Social Justice and Anti-Capitalism" prove this statement convincingly. "'... So that it may not circulate solely between the wealthy among you'. The Critique of Capitalism and the Vision of a 'balanced society' (*mujtamaʿ mutawāzin*) in the Writings of Sayyid Quṭb (1906–1966)" is the title of the paper by Sabine Damir-Geilsdorf who documents how central the idea of social equality was for Quṭb. The article provides us with insights into this part of Quṭb's writing, based on an intense reading of the original sources. Nowadays, Quṭb is usually regarded as a provider of Islamist concepts supporting radical and violent action. As Damir-Geilsdorf shows, Quṭb's activities–which were similarly to the activities of Ubaidullah Sindhi' also decisively influenced by British colonial rule–aimed to a substantial degree at the establishment of a socially and economically 'balanced society' to be brought about by a revolutionary movement. Unlike aforementioned activists, Quṭb not only condemned capitalism as an element of colonial violence but also rejected communism. Notions similar to those of Quṭb are today part of the 'program' of radical Islamists even if these more recent groups publicly denounce the Muslim Brotherhood of which Quṭb was a leading member. Quṭb's concepts appear as adoptable and adaptable to a changing environment, and with regard to their fundamental messages today as topical as 50 years ago.

In her chapter "A Shiite Economic Model. From Bāqir al-Ṣadr to Contemporary Iraq", Elisheva Machlis tackles the Shiite understanding of *justice*, based on a case study of post-2003 Iraq. In contrast to Sunni Islam, Shiite Islam links justice to the divinely designated Imams, not to the scope of the elected ruler, and so justice can be realized to its full extent only with the return of the hidden Imam. Yet, the emergence of political Islam in the Sunni world also influenced Shiite scholars who started to ask how to realize a closer relation between religious concepts and issues of everyday life. Muḥammad Bāqir al-Ṣadr (1935–1980), the chief ideologist of the Daʿwa Party, can be considered a famous example of this development. He called for an Islamic state with a distinctive economic system. He provided an all-inclusive theory, placing his Islamic model as a middle way between communism and capitalism. With the growing fragmentation of Iraq in the post-2003 period, however, and the challenge of Sunni Jihadists, the Shiite state was fighting for survival. The state became less democratic, and any form of social justice became at this stage irrelevant for the political vision of Iraq. Machlis' chapter also raises the question whether a democratic system, as Iraq attempted to acquire after Saddam Husseyn's fall, is not rather prone to a more capitalist, liberal economic system, so that democratization would imply leaving the third way.

A Turkish version of the quest for justice is presented by Fabio Vicini in his study on an Islamist Human Rights organization, *Mazlumder* ("Between Islamism and Human Rights. *Mazlumder* as a Third Way within Turkish Islamism?"). The Organization for Human Rights and Solidarity for Oppressed People is part of the underground developments within Turkish Islamism, as Vicini puts it. While the driving forces of the political change in Turkey after 2002, the ruling Party for Justice and Development as well as its now fiercest opponent, the Gülen network, have been widely studied, research on Islamist groups and movements beyond the new Muslim establishment is still in its infancy. This is all the more deplorable as the dynamic and mercurical character of this scene represents an attractive field for cultural and social research. *Mazlumder* has operated since 1991 within the framework of civil-society organizations by gathering younger and older Muslims around the common goal of raising the standards of human rights in the country. Unlike other organizations that focus on issues of religious discrimination, *Mazlumder* has embraced a more open perspective on rights, including those of other religious and ethnic minorities in the country. In their rejection of a Westernized capitalist system and their proximity to a 'classical Islamist' reading of capitalism as the economic system of colonialism and imperialism, they constitute a link between those earlier Islamist movements and new developments in the form of the Anti-capitalist Muslims and similar groups. It is important to bear in mind that from *Mazlumder*'s perspective, sovereignty rests with God; thus, rights and justice do not exist independently and in the form of 'natural human rights'. Equality and brotherhood are consequences of the indisputable Oneness of God, since a hierarchical system produces servants and rulers, but the only true ruler is God. For the members of *Mazlumder*, equality and brotherhood have an elevated position in Islamic justice, while "the institutionalization of the capitalist system based on mechanisms that crystallize relationships of subordination between men" (Vicini) is contradictory to God's order.

The demand for social equality and justice finds its expression not only in treatises of activists, in slogans and protest camps, but also in fictionalized historiography and historical fiction.[17] A Thracian Sufi-rebel from the 14th/15th century, Şeyh Bedreddin, has inspired the creativity of authors from Turkey and other countries throughout the centuries. The most popular text is *The Epic of Sheik Bedreddin*, written by Nazım Hikmet in 1935. Şeyh Bedreddin, a historical figure with an outstanding biography, took part in the peasant rebellions which shook Anatolia and Thrace at the beginning of the 15th century. Today he is remembered for his alleged statement

[17] While Hayden White (1928–2018) would add that historiography uses the format of fiction genres anyway.

that in an ideal world people would share all property, production means, real estate, and harvest; only private relations, symbolized by the exemption of "women", or "the lover's cheek", as Nazım Hikmet formulated, would be excluded from common property. The role of the sheikh in the peasant rebellions is not clear. Was he a main instigator, or just an Ottoman scholar who for whatever reasons changed sides? Research indicates that the idea of common property was not promulgated by the sheikh but by Börklüce Mustafa, one of the rebels. The first historiographer to mention Börklüce was a Byzantine author. Regardless of how nebulous this story is, or what chroniclers transmitted, it was enough to create a hero who could be embraced by different ideological factions. In her paper "A Sufi Martyr and Harbinger of Anti-Capitalism. Şeyh Bedreddin as an Emblematic Figure in 'Progressive' Publications", Béatrice Hendrich discusses the position of the sheikh in publications of 'progressive' authors. The idea that shared property will stop wealth accumulation and in this way bring about social equality and justice, as well as the sheikh's execution, rendering him a martyr, motivated political historiographers and historical fiction writers of an anti-capitalist persuasion. The continuous public interest in Şeyh Bedreddin points to the significance of issues such as social equality, Islamic moral standards, and rebellion against oppression by the state for Turkey at present.

The last section of the volume, titled "Different Ways to Non-Capitalism", presents three papers which focus on rather individual ways to escape the moral pitfalls of capitalism, and emphasize that the rejection of capitalism does not necessarily lead to an inclination towards socialism. The notion of a distinctly Islamic economic system, brought forward by the aforementioned Islamist masterminds, was later interpreted as and developed into the Islamic Banking System or, as some call it, an Islamic financing industry. The financing industry attracted severe criticism from those Muslims who demanded a Sharia-based financial system, and not a system which only superficially implements rules of the Sharia. In addition to the critique based on religious considerations, the financial structure of the system as such has been disparaged as unstable. The way out of being trapped between global capitalist banking and an insufficient pseudo-Islamic system is often seen to be the creation of a fully metallic gold or gold-and-silver currency. Hans Visser provides in his paper "The Lure of Gold and Silver. Dinars and Dirhams for the 21st Century" the examples of individuals and movements that during the last decades have campaigned for a fully metallic currency: the Murabitun Movement, IMN-World Islamic Standard, the Islamic State, the British branch of *Ḥizb ut-Taḥrīr*, the Minaret of Freedom Institute and others. To an outsider, the Islamic State (IS) and its endeavor to create a genuine and independent financial system is better known than the other organizations. However, the Malaysian initiative proves that this is not a discussion limited to a few marginal figures: In 2006 the Malaysian state of Kelantan, governed by the Pan-Malaysian Islamic Party, introduced gold dinar coins in three denominations. Visser analyzes and compares in detail the practices of the different institutions and concludes that from an economic point of view there is more to lose than to win with the implementation of a fully metallic currency. What renders these systems attractive is that they are perceived to be elements of a distinct Muslim state identity: "It is first and foremost a drive to club together as Muslim countries" (Visser).

In his paper titled "Three Images of Anti-authoritarian Socialism within Islamic Contexts: Isabelle Eberhardt/Mahmoud Essadi, Muammar Qaddafi's Green Book, and Heba Raouf Ezzat", Anthony T. Fiscella repeats the question of how a Muslim or an Islamic community can lead a life independent of global and regional capitalisms. One way out seems to be the establishment of an anti-authoritarian, non-state based socialism; yet, the examples studied by Fiscella present quite contrasting images. What connects them is the conviction that faith has to be the fundament of every economic system. The concept of Ezzat, "a third path amongst third paths: acceptance of the state but emphasis upon smaller-scale forms of economic and political action" (Fiscella), could be discussed fruitfully together with polycentricity as it is outlined by Anas Malik in this volume. From Fiscella's point of view, Ezzat's concept, based on respect towards both humankind and nature, on solidarity, and on the subordination of capital to the state while people are subordinated only to God, seems to be the only concept which results neither in a dictatorship (Qaddafi) nor self-destruction (Isabelle Eberhardt).

The ambivalent attitude towards the West by Muslim thinkers and activists can be regarded as a main feature of their concepts, particularly when it comes to the description of proper economic relations. In Turkey, this ambivalence has been observable since the early 19th century. Although with the establishment of the Republic and the introduction of European-style institutions, this ambivalence should have dissipated, the opposite is true, not only recently with the assumption of power by an Islamically-oriented party but throughout Republican history. What in fact has happened is that the number of answers to this challenge has multiplied. Michelangelo Guida presents two proponents of Turkish Islamism, Nurettin Topçu (1909–1975) and Necmettin Erbakan (1926–2011), and discusses their differing approaches towards industrialization and national economy. Against the backdrop of critical Modernization Studies, Guida traces their common features which were informed by a European and Muslim/Sufi education. The author discusses "Turkish Islamists' Enthusiasm for Versace: Islamism between Rejection and Adoption of the West", concluding that while Necmettin Erbakan and his dream of an automobile 'made in Turkey' seems to be in the long run the victorious variant of Turkish Islamism, both men were arguing inside "the framework of Western epistemology". In this sense, Guida's final conclusion can be read as a general conclusion regarding the issues and conflicts dealt with in the chapters of this volume:

> These two important examples of Turkish Islamism verify the premises of 'multiple' and 'later modernities', which assume historical precedence, but also the fact that Western patterns of modernity are the basic and inescapable reference point. From our examples we may even say that Islamism has introduced a lexicon apparently traditional, but epistemologically inside the pattern of Western modernity.

*

In conclusion, a remark is necessary regarding the transcription of names from languages written in a non-Latin alphabet: Since the articles cover a wide geographical range, including several languages, not to mention Arabic dialects which can only insufficiently be transcribed anyway, we decided not to squeeze every language into the same scheme. Self-evidently, transcription has to be consistent throughout one article. All terms and familiar names which are listed in English dictionaries appear in their Anglicized form. In articles focusing on the Arabic and Persian speaking world, we adopted the transcription of the Library of Congress, while in articles related to Turkey, the Turkish or Turkified forms are used. Urdu and other languages are transcribed according to an internationally established standard which enables the reader to gain at least an idea of the original pronunciation of a word or a name.

The initial workshop in 2014 could not have been realized without the generous funding of the Fritz Thyssen Stiftung, Cologne, to which we are truly grateful.

Part One:
The Past and the Future

Primary Islamic Texts on Land, Water, and Capital Ownership

Mouez Khalfaoui

Is there an Islamic economic theory? What does it consist of? When and where was it born? What impact do religious texts have on it? And how original and authentic is it? These questions have been debated intensively in modern scholarship, for instance in the second half of the 20th century, when several Muslim scholars, especially in Iran and Pakistan, tried to provide evidence concerning the originality of an Islamic economic conception and presented it as an alternative to liberal and socialist economy.[1] In the last decades, the debate on Islamic economic thought has changed in many aspects. Instead of focusing on the originality and the exclusive characteristics of this economy, scholars–for instance in Western academia–concentrate rather on studying intensively the founding texts to understand the mechanisms of this thought. They try to debate the concepts of economy in the Islamic thought within the global framework of world economy and approach it through interdisciplinary methods. This is also the methodological instrument of this paper. It deals with the founding texts of Islamic economic thought in order to understand how economic subjects were debated in the past and the impact those texts had on subsequent literature on the subject. Before going ahead, it is worth mentioning that the term 'primary Islamic texts' used in the title of this paper needs to be specified. This term would normally refer to texts from the early Islamic period. The Islamic formative period is widely understood as the first three centuries of Islamic history (7–9th centuries AD). When referring to the period of time under consideration, the term 'text' encompasses both oral and written literature, without any distinction. By the end of the second or at the latest the beginning of the third Islamic century (9th century), literature was mostly still orally transmitted and there was an intensive effort towards the written fixation of this oral literature observable at the same time. Therefore, the term 'primary text' does not, in fact, refer to a written corpus only, but rather to founding texts both written and oral. This term, when used for

---

1 The book of Muḥammad Bāqir al-Ṣadr illustrates this tendency of establishing an Islamic economic theory on 'pure' Islamic sources. Muḥammad Bāqir al-Ṣadr, *Iqtiṣādunā: dirāsah mauḍūʿīyah tatanāwal bi-al-naqd wa-al-baḥth al-madhāhib al-iqtiṣādīyah lil-mārksīyah wa-al-raʾsmālīyah wa-al-islām fī ususihā al-fikrīyah wa-tafāṣīlihā* [*Our Economy: A Thematic Study on the Handling of Critiques and Investigations by the Economical Schools of Marxism, Capitalism and Islam and their Foundations of Thought and Their Details*], 16th edition, Beirut: Dār al-Taʿāruf lil-Maṭbūʿāt 1982.

dealing with such a complex subject as primitive economic thinking in early Islamic culture, always refers to all kinds of literature that touch on the general subject of economy. In view of the period under consideration in this article (7th–9th century) and with the objective of determining the first moment and the first genuine idea of economic thought in Islamic culture, one should consider all kinds of intellectual production that deal with the subject in order to identify specific features which would be considered as the genuine ideas of that thinking.

In this paper, I intend to shed light on the primary sources of Islamic economic thought by referring specifically to texts that deal with issues of land, water, capital and work. The latter (labor) has only seldom been the object of research in the literature on the subject of Islamic economy, although it represents one of the main features if not the most important one in Islamic economic thought. Therefore, I will not limit my research only to the subjects of water, land and money, but I will also present an overview of the literature on work and work ethics. This will help in outlining the general and specific framework in which this literature was written and the general religious, societal and philosophical trends that existed. In this regard, I would like to argue that the primary texts which focused on the subjects of land, water and capital in the Islamic culture bear witness to a genuine 'non-capitalist' and rather 'social-oriented'[2] economic line of thought that is embedded in something that we can consider as 'primitive' Islamic economic thought. By 'primitive', I refer to the ideas on economic subjects that were spread out across different religious texts and which–in the course of their amalgamation–would represent the fundamental pillars of an Islamic conception of economy.

Founding Religious Texts: Quran and Sunna

I would like to argue that the economic thinking of the very first Muslim state was based on a specific concept of sharing, which rested in turn on a macro-economic understanding. In this framework the Muslim state played the role of the distributor of the spoils of war between its needy Muslim subjects.[3] This act of helping the needy was not understood in the sense of the pre-Islamic conception of piety, which sees the receipt of alms as an act of submission of the poor to the rich, but rather it was regarded–according to Islamic doctrine–as an act of giving the needy their right (*ḥaqq*). The

2 The use of modern concepts in this paper is just meant to simplify the idea and make the statement clear.

3 Michael Bonner, "Poverty and Economics in the Qur'an", *Journal of Interdisciplinary History* 35: 3 (2005), 391–406.

same principle applies also to the taxes of zakat (*zakāh*), which were understood as the entitlement of the poor to participation in the richness of the wealthy; this represented a very new aspect regarding the relation of both parties, the rich and the poor.[4] This egalitarian and progressive Islamic conception concerning the redistribution of money as an instrument for societal compensation did not hold for a long time.

By the time the center of power of the Islamic state had shifted from Syria (the Umayyad dynasty) to Iraq with the establishment of the Abbasid dynasty in Baghdad (132 AH/750 CE), the economic ideology of the Muslim state had gradually changed. The non-capitalist macro-economic thought belonging to the first two centuries of Islamic economic conceptualization, shifted to an 'individualist' (and somehow 'capitalist') micro-economic ideology. Literature from the 8th century onward, such as the *Kitāb al-Iktisāb fī al-rizq al-mustaṭāb* by Muḥammad al-Shaybānī (d. 805), presents a detailed picture of the debate between the two competing concepts mentioned above (i.e. the new tendency and the old one).[5] The new economic tendency, as depicted in al-Shaybānī's book, stresses the importance of work and incites people to take the initiative; it sees individuals as responsible for themselves and their relatives and encourages them to give up waiting for help and gifts.[6]

It goes without saying that the first references to the economy in the Muslim culture were those of the Quran and the Sunna of the prophet Muḥammad. The Quran can therefore be considered as the very founding text of Islamic economic thought. It contains recommendations concerning land, money, payment, taxes, sharing and finance. Nevertheless, these recommendations cannot be considered to be a holistic conception; they are brief and general. The commandments of the Quran regarding the economy in this respect provide a general framework and the groundwork for articulating the main principles regarding the way to deal with wealth and exceptional situations.[7] As a case in point, the Quran regards tax payment as a religious duty of the wealthy vis-à-vis the poor and needy; this tax is therefore understood not as charity but as a right (*ḥaqq*), respectively a duty; there we read: "[70:25] And those in whose wealth there is a recognized right [70:26]

4 The previous conception which was dominant in the pre-Islamic era was that the wealthy help the poor and accordingly the poor become dependent on the rich; the relation of help and assistance ends often in a kind of belonging to the rich. This is not the case in Islamic faith, see Bonner, "Poverty and Economics", 403.

5 Bonner, "Poverty and Economics".

6 Mouez Khalfaoui, "The Debate about Work in Muslim Culture and the Birth of the Literary Genre of '*kasb*'", in: Sigal Nagar-Ron, ed., *Work in the Contemporary World. Contours of Work from Interdisciplinary Perspectives*, Oxford: Inter-Disciplinary Press 2015, 54–60.

7 Muḥammad ʿAmāra, ed., Abū ʿUbayd al-Qāsim ibn Sallām, *Kitāb al-Amwāl* [*The Book of Revenue*], Beirut: Dār al-Shurūq 1989, 6.

For one who asks *for help* and for one who does not."[8] These Quranic verses make the state responsible for the collection of taxes from the wealthy classes and their distribution among the deprived people. This principle was implemented by the very first Muslim states.[9] As far as the economic theory of Islam is concerned, it should be stressed that the Quran contains general commandments with regard to several economic subjects such as taxes, payment, inheritance, work, sharing, trade and partnership, but it must not be elevated to the extent that it is considered to be a book of the economy. If we mean by text a fixed written text with clear definitions, the Quran cannot be considered as such, but if we refer to the text as offering general guidance then we can agree that the Quranic text has induced the Muslim community to think deeply about wealth and finance, land and water in the general framework of the relation of the human being to nature, to other individuals and to himself. Thus, the importance of the Quranic text for the development of Islamic economic thought should not reduce the importance of other external influences on Islamic economic thought such as Greek economic philosophy and the Persian conception of state and administration.[10]

Returning to the genuine texts referring to the economy in Muslim culture, the teaching of the Prophet Muḥammad has been understood for decades as a reference for an Islamic way of dealing with economic affairs. The role of the Sunna in this regard has been understood as complementary to that of the Quranic texts. Nevertheless, the Sunna is a subject for itself. One of the first books on economy such as the book on work ethics attributed to Muḥammad al-Shaybānī[11] is mainly based on prophetic hadiths and applies them in order to develop a framework for thinking the values of work and wealth. This book will be subjected to a more detailed examination later on in the writings of subsequent authors.[12]

---

8 Maulvi Sher Ali, "The Holy Quran: Chapter 70: Al-Ma'arij", *Al Islam. The Official Website of the Ahmadiyya Muslim Community* (2018), www.alislam.org/quran/search2/showChapter.php?submitCh=Read+from+verse%3A&ch=70&verse=23 (last accessed: 23 Jan 2018).

9 It is worth noting that the first war declared by the Muslim state at the time was waged on economic grounds and aimed at establishing a balance between poor and rich: After Muḥammad's death, some Arab tribes refused to pay *zakāh* to the Muslim state. They argued that these taxes had been paid to Muḥammad and his death effectively removed the necessity of any further payment. Abū Bakr, the first caliph, responded that he will fight them even if they refuse to give him one piece of money less than they used to give to Muḥammad.

10 See on the influence of Greek Philosophy on the Muslim economic conception, Yassine Essid, *A Critique of the Origins of Islamic Economic Thought*, Leiden: Brill 1995.

11 Muḥammad Al-Shaybānī, *Kitāb al-Iktisāb fī al-rizq al-mustaṭāb* [*Book about the Acquisition of an Appreciable Subsistence*], Beirut: Dār al-Kutub al-ʿIlmiyah 1986.

12 Mouez Khalfaoui, "Erwerbsarbeit aus muslimischer Perspektive", in: *Eine Arbeitsgesellschaft – auch für Muslime: Interdisziplinäre und interreligiöse Beiträge zur Erwerbsarbeit,*

The Emergence of Profane Literature on Land, Taxes and Water

In contrast to the founding religious texts of the first era of the Islamic tradition, the texts from the 8th–10th centuries provide insight into the emergence of the first written profane texts on economic issues in Muslim culture. Contrary to Quranic texts which consistently describe economical subjects in a rather more general manner, the texts from the 9th and 10th centuries contain detailed information on economic issues; they were either recommendations submitted by the Muslim state in order to find solutions for the recurring economic problems of that period,[13] or written by scholars who wanted to clarify and simplify complicated economic issues for laypeople. Unfortunately, several important texts written in this period were lost, and only a very few, but extremely valuable texts dealing with those economic issues are at our disposal.

Therefore, it is worth saying that the first texts on money, taxes, land, sharing etc. go back to the period during which the establishment of the two first Muslim dynasties (Umayyads and Abbasids) took place. I consider the Umayyads and the Abbasid dynasty to be the first Islamic states that had to deal with difficult economic issues such as taxes, poll taxes (*jizyah*), land taxes (*kharāj*), zakat etc. In the framework of the establishment of an effective and just administration within the empire the rulers were facing the pressing need to conceptualize the administration of economic institutions such as those responsible for assessing and collecting taxes. These issues were addressed mainly through the adoption of solutions that had been used by other former dynasties like the Roman, Byzantine and the Persian dynasties. On the other hand, the first books on these subjects bear witness of the reason why and how the authors were trying to introduce genuine religious principles into the conceptions of land taxes and division of territories.

In order to see what was going on during this period, it is worth providing a short list of the books at hand. The following list presents the most popular texts which deal with money, land, and taxes as well as other economic issues of high value, which are still in use today:

- Ḥafṣawayh[14] (d.?): *Kitāb al-Kharāj* (The book of land tax). This author was listed by Ibn al-Nadīm as the first author who wrote on the subject of *kharāj*.[15]

Mouez Khalfaoui, Matthias Möhring-Hesse, eds., Münster: Waxman-Verlag 2015, 233–246.

13 The book of Abū ʿUbayd on currency and the *Kitāb al-Kharāj* of Abū Yūsuf were written on the recommendation of the Abbasid caliphs.

14 There is no sure evidence about his right name, he is always referred to as "Ḥafṣawayh", in few books he is referred to as Abū Bakr Muḥammad ibn Ḥafṣawayh. His date of death is also not fixed.

- Al-Ḥasan ibn Ziyād al-Luʾluʾī (d. 809): *Kitāb al-Kharāj* and *Kitāb an-Nafaqāt* (The book of land tax and expenses)
- Abū Saʿīd ʿAbd al-Malik ibn Quraib al-Aṣmaʿī (831 AD): *Kitāb al-Kharāj* (The book on land taxes)
- Abū al-Ḥasan ʻAlī ibn ʻAbd Allāh ibn Jaʻfar al-Madīnī (849 AD): *Kitāb al-Amwāl* (The book of finances)
- Abdullah ibn al-Muqaffaʿ (762 AD): *Risālat al-ṣaḥābah* (The epistle on the companions of the Prophet)
- Yaḥyā ibn Ādam al-Qurashī (818 AD): *Kitāb al-Kharāj* (The book on land taxes)
- Abū ʻUbayd al-Qāsim ibn Sallām (838 AD): *Kitāb al-Amwāl* (The book on money and currency)
- Abū Aḥmad ibn Zanjawayh (865 AD): *Kitāb al-Amwāl* (The book of finances).[16]

The majority of the literature mentioned above dates back to the 8th and 9th century. This list demonstrates how important the writing on economic issues was during the first centuries of Islamic culture. To illustrate the content of this literature I will take the book of Abū ʿUbayd ibn Sallām (*Kitāb al-Amwāl*) as a case study.[17] The book on money and currency of Abū ʿUbayd contains significant details about how the first Muslim administrative machineries may have dealt with issues of monetary transactions; it describes the way in which Quranic and prophetic teachings/instructions on this matter had been interpreted and implemented.[18] The book under consideration consists of several chapters on different economic issues. The first chapters list the various sources of income that entered the Muslim state treasury: spoils of war, taxes on land (*kharāj*), and poll taxes (*jizyah*), as well as the usual taxes of zakat. One of these opening chapters is entitled: "Chapter on the categories of money that the imams should give to their subjects and the evidences regarding this from the Quran and the Sunna."[19]

15 For this reference, see A. Ben Shemesh, *Yaḥyā ben Ādam's Kitab al-Kharāj* [*Book on Taxation*], Brill: Leiden 1967, 4–5.

16 The list is available in A. Ben Shemesh, *Yaḥyā ben Ādam's Kitab al-Kharāj* mentioned above.

17 Doing so, I explicitly avoid refering back to the famous book of Abū Yūsuf on landtax (*Kitāb al-Kharāj*) which has been exlusively used for a long time, whenever the subject of taxes and finance in Islamic civilization is debated. Muḥammad ʿAbd al-Ḥafīẓ al-Manāṣir, ed., Abū Yūsuf Yaʿqūb ibn-Ibrāhīm al-Anṣārī, *Kitāb al-Kharāj*, Amman: Dār Kunūz al-Maʿrifah al-ʿIlmīyah lil-Nashr wa-al-Tauzī 2009, see also Ahmed A. F. El-Ashker and Rodney Wilson, *Islamic Economics: a Short History*, Leiden: Brill 2006.

18 Abū ʿUbayd, *Kitāb al-Amwāl*, Islāmābād: Islāmābād Idārah-ʾi Taḥqīqāt-i Islāmī 1968/69, 69.

19 Abū ʿUbayd, *Kitāb al-Amwāl*, 75–86.

As far as the sources of the *Kitāb al-Amwāl* are taken into account, the majority of the references in this book are hadiths of the prophet Muḥammad or references to narrations about his companions. Furthermore, the book has an apologetic character. It refers to religious texts to support the conception that Abū ʿUbayd presented for the first time a guideline for financial management in view of the various sources of revenue. Another section of *Kitāb al-Amwāl* deals with the various ways the state made use of the gathered money. The section on the division of the spoils of the war among the Muslim population starts with a hadith of the prophet Muḥammad who recommends that everyone should take only things that he does not have: "Who needs a slave, who needs a boat, who needs a wife, who needs a house ... should have that and do not exceed that."[20] The hadiths of the prophet are followed by narratives about the companions, for instance the four caliphs. Other chapters of *Kitāb al-Amwāl* have almost the same structure, so that the main principles of dividing state financial resources, as they are depicted in *Kitāb al-Amwāl*, were taken from the founding religious sources (Quran and Sunna). This illustrates also that the first writings on the subject were mainly based on the explanation of the religious recommendations and their practically orientated interpretation in view of their fruitful usage for administrative purposes. As far as the terminology used in the *Kitāb al-Amwāl* is concerned, the overall character of this literature consists of a terminology of dividing and sharing. This is also reflected in the issue of the categories of people concerned by the book. The first category consists of those who were supposed to pay. Those who were obliged to pay were mainly divided into three categories: Landlords, who own fertile territories, non-Muslims, whose territories had been conquered, and the Muslim affluent classes. When speaking of these categories, the common term is that of taking (arab. *akhadha*), which refers to the governor, who takes taxes and goods from those groups. This term is in opposition to the term "give" (arab. *aʿṭā*). This section confirms the assumption that the issue of gathering money was not defined as an issue of benevolent giving; it was not understood as a gesture of charity. Rather the issue is that it is the Muslim state's responsibility, represented by the Muslim governor, to take money or force people to pay taxes and to find arguments to explain this undertaking. When it comes to those who are supposed to benefit from the wealth and the money gathered through zakat, the list of those who benefit from state aid encompasses almost all classes of society.

In conclusion, the *Kitāb al-Amwāl* of Abū ʿUbayd bears witness to the economic situation of the first Muslim state–an economic situation in a very specific period of Islamic history. The main issue here is that of the

---

20 Abū ʿUbayd, *Kitāb al-Amwāl*, 357.

controversial role played by the Muslim state, which collected taxes from the wealthy non-Muslims and landowners in order to divide them among those in need, but also used this function as a legitimization for its existence. Does the economic conception, as presented in *Kitāb al-Amwāl*, represent the entirety of Muslim economic conceptions at that time? Did other economic issues exist which were neglected? The reading of *Kitāb al-Amwāl* of Abū ʿUbayd in the light of the economic literature of that time reveals a one-dimensional view of the economy. It is true that this economic course of action is of a non-capitalist nature and is based on the concept of sharing. Nevertheless, the reality of this first era was more complicated.

Indeed, other literature of that time attests a struggle between two opposing economic concepts. On the one hand the concept of accumulation which emphasizes the role of the individual and his responsibility for prosperity of himself and the group. On the other hand there exists the conception of sharing, which aims at the limitation of the economy in order to face the urgent problems of poverty through a compensatory respectively equalizing principle. This conception evolves the intervention of the state in controlling the economic situation of the society.

In this regard, it is worth mentioning that an important economic aspect is missing in the book of Abū ʿUbayd, namely, the subject of work. The neglect of the subject of work can be explained by the state of the economic debate in the era of Abū ʿUbayd. His book was rather a listing of the sources and the categories of subjects from whom the state could take and of the rules for the subsequent distribution of the levied taxes and gathered money. The Arabic term "*amwāl*" is used in this regard as a concept for the gathering of incomes. Thus the missing debate on work in *Kitāb al-Amwāl* should not be seen as a general character of the literature on economy of that period, since other literature does emphasize work and debate it.

Muḥammad al-Shaybānī: Kitāb al-Iktisāb fī al-rizq al-mustaṭāb and the Debate on Work

In 1984, the *Kitāb al-Iktisāb fī al-rizq al-mustaṭāb*, attributed to the leading Hanafi scholar Muḥammad al-Shaybānī (d. 805), was published for the very first time.[21] The book is one of the first writings that dealt with the subject of work in the formative period of Islamic economic thinking. Here, al-

21 Until that time it was unknown. After being published there is still an ongoing debate about the authenticity of the book and its attribution to Muḥammad al-Shaybānī. See Michael Bonner, "The Kitāb al-Kasb Attributed to al-Shaybani: Poverty, Surplus, and the Circulation of Wealth", *Journal of the American Oriental Society* 121: 3 (2001), 410–427.

Shaybānī depicts the debate on work and work ethics in the first centuries of the Islamic era. In this text, there are two theological conceptualizations in conflict with one another. The first concept is that of the Sufis (Muslim mystics) and many other people, who argue that the highest duty of human beings is to pray to God. They base their opinion on Quranic verses in which God guarantees human beings help if they just pray. The advocates of this ideology interpret praying as the ultimate obligation of human beings, who should devote themselves exclusively to it. In contrast to this ideology there is another concept which highlights the idea that people are individually responsible for their own lives. According to this notion, work could be seen as a form of worship. Thus, in the *Kitāb al-Iktisāb*, al-Shaybānī depicts the debate held between the two mainstream schools of thought in this period. In the economic history of the Muslim world, this book verifies the shift that took place in the third Islamic century (9th century AC) from the macro-economic level (based on gathering money and dividing it among those in need) to the new micro economic ideology that attempted to encourage people to work. This change was mainly due to the fact that by the 8th century the Muslim Dynasties of the Umayyads and Abbasids had increased their influence and power across larger and larger territories in Asia, Africa and elsewhere. Accordingly, the trade relations with India, China and Europe had increased and there was a rising demand and urgent need for workers and traders. This transformation in economic activities, in turn, led to a theological debate about work. *Kitāb al-Iktisāb* of al-Shaybānī, with regard to this issue, bears witness to this stage of development.

Summing up, as far as primary texts on economic issues are concerned, the *Kitāb al-Iktisāb* of al-Shaybānī and *Kitāb al-Amwāl* of Abū ᶜUbayd give a clear picture of that period. While Abū ᶜUbayd portrays the stage of primitive economic ideology as being based on the heritage of the Quran and its traditions, the book of al-Shaybānī bears witness to the moment of change from the old ideology to the new. Both texts have one major point in common: they are both strongly related to theology. They testify to the relationship between economy and theology, while the first book of Abū ᶜUbayd reveals that theology had the upper hand over economy, and that the macroeconomic ideology, in this instance, had its origin in theology. The second book (of al-Shaybānī) indicates the moment when the economy became paramount and shows how political-economic thought was trying to use theology to justify the change in economic ideology.

Beyond State and Market: Institutional Diversity and Polycentricity in Islamic Contexts

Anas Malik

In discussing capitalism in Islamic contexts, and in societies generally, many will focus on the role of the market in relation to the state. My main thesis is that the emphasis on ideal types of market and state are inadequate and misleading, particularly when considering development issues. Instead, understandings of property, authority, and governance generally require more sensitivity to institutional diversity. Changing the starting point to an appreciation of institutional diversity greatly improves analyses and understandings of potentials. A society's cultural endowment, including religious tradition, can be understood as a set of institutions responding to collective action problems in society.

While much of the literature on political economy in Islamic contexts has emphasized diversity in ideas, interests, and attitudes, institutions have largely been treated as derivative or epiphenomenal. In contrast with monolithic depictions of 'Sharia' or 'Islamic Law', the Islamic tradition presents a rich heritage of institutional diversity, and the means to accommodate institutional diversity. Combined with a political economic approach that emphasizes institutional diversity and polycentric order, this heritage suggests underappreciated development potentials in contemporary Islamic contexts. Considering these potentials requires going beyond the market-state dichotomy.

The New Institutionalism and Polycentricity

The basic political question can be defined as who gets what, when, and how, in the famous formulation of Harold Lasswell. This definition overlaps substantively with the notion of economics as the study of the allocation of scarce goods. The rules of the game in society shape political economic outcomes, and the rules themselves are a major focus of social contestation. The New Institutionalist Economics emphasizes the role of rules–formal and informal, official and unofficial–in constraining and shaping social interactions. The prior focus on institutions in political economy had emphasized formal legal structures of government. Pioneering figures such as Douglass North and Vincent Ostrom and Elinor Ostrom have received extensive recognition for their work on institutions. Understanding the cultural foundations for institutional change matters for assessing the adaptive potentials of societies, and is of critical significance in many Islamic contexts today.

Roughly speaking, institutions can be understood as a set of instructions that specify who is forbidden, permitted, or obliged to do what in what context and to face what sanction for noncompliance. A fuller way to map the "grammar of institutions" has been developed by Sue Crawford and Elinor Ostrom.[1] The critical aspect of institutional diversity is that the number of possible combinations is simply too great to come up with an understanding of the optimal rule set. Rather, tradition is an important embodiment of many institutional responses that have shaped interactions in a community, often addressing some collective action problems while creating new ones. Broadly speaking, a society's culture can be defined as "the cumulative structure of rules and norms (and beliefs) that we inherit from the past that shape our present and influence our future"[2].

Polycentricity is the notion that governance in a society takes place at many locations rather than at a single center. In a polycentric system, there are "(1) many autonomous units formally independent of one another, (2) choosing to act in ways that take account of others, (3) through processes of cooperation, competition, conflict, and conflict resolution"[3]. Well-functioning polycentric order rests on habits of self-governance and civic artisanship that promote institutional adaptation by individuals in association with each other. These civic virtues originate in an outlook that, while not denying self-interest, moves individuals to seriously consider the interests and perspectives of others; they also result from the practical and lifelong experience of local governance at the municipal level and in other associational forms. Unlike the tendency to define 'democracy' by the act of voting or participating in large assemblies (which easily succumb to oligarchy and are practically limited by scarce attention time to each participant), the polycentric perspective emphasizes civic artisanship through the whole breadth of human affairs. This crosses the public-private distinction that is so central to the standard liberal theory of politics, and replaces that with the notion of institutions which can be found in all spheres of human interaction.

Polycentric arrangements are vulnerable to strategies of dominance, from external and internal sources. Polycentric arrangements also have the poten-

1 See E. S. Crawford and Elinor Ostrom, "A Grammar of Institutions", *American Political Science Review* 89: 3 (1995), 582–600.

2 Douglass North, *Understanding the Process of Economic Change*, Princeton: Princeton Univ. Press 2005, 6.

3 Vincent Ostrom, *The Meaning of American Federalism: Constituting a Self-governing Society*, Institute for Contemporary Studies Press: San Francisco 1994, 225.

tial for resilience and adaptive efficiency that arise, paradoxically, from redundancies, and from policy learning among different associations. Competitive markets, scientific communities, and federal orders are all possible examples of polycentric orders. As elaborated below, it seems to me that the Islamic tradition has also functioned in some notably polycentric ways and represents a cultural endowment generally conducive to polycentricity, although there are serious challenges and vulnerabilities in contemporary contexts.

The State-Market Dichotomy

Particularly in neoliberal formulations, the market is typically understood as the arena of voluntary transactions by rational economic agents pursuing their self-interest. The neoliberal version of capitalism usually emphasizes restrictions on state interventions in the market, except for those state actions concerned with securing property rights. In traditional courses on microeconomics, a widely used model is the perfectly competitive market in which agents have perfect information, no buyer or seller can set the market price, and there are no barriers to entry and exit from markets. Under monopolies, the seller can influence the market price, and extract rents from consumers, producing a socially inferior outcome to the perfect competition model.

The ideal type of the unitary state and the theory of sovereign rule are associated with the philosophy of Thomas Hobbes. Hobbes emphasized the need for coercive capacity on the part of the central state authority, famously asserting that "covenants, without the sword, are but words and of no strength to secure a man at all".[4] In this view, the sovereign authority makes the law but cannot itself be held accountable to the law. Reasonable people submit to such an arrangement because life under the alternative, anarchy, is "nasty, brutish, and short". The modern norm of state sovereignty, traceable to the Treaty of Westphalia, presumes that the state represents the ultimate authority over a fixed territory and population, answerable to no higher power.

Neither model captures reality well. Property rights, far from the simple or obvious legal definitions, are in fact complex bundles of claims, entitlements, and exclusions resting on both formal and informal understandings. The particular manifestation of property rights also draws on often unwritten or implicit social views of propriety, referring to that which is socially

4 Thomas Hobbes, *Leviathan or the Matter, Forme and Power of a Commonwealth Ecclesiasticall and Civil*, Adelaide: Ebooks@adelaide 2016 [1651], https://ebooks.adelaide.edu.au/h/hobbes/thomas/h68l/chapter17.html (last access Feb 24 2018).

proper or appropriate (and unsurprisingly, there is a linguistic link between the terms property and propriety). The use of 'the market' overgeneralizes and oversimplifies what are complex and context-specific sets of institutional understandings specific to particular action arenas.

The 'state' is usually presented as the monocentric governance center, providing the rules by which society operates. The reality is that the rules that govern social interactions emerge from many agents and origins that may or may not be endorsed by, enforced by, or even permitted by the official 'state' apparatus. This is all the more apparent in post-colonial weak state contexts where a juridical state provides a thin legal claim over a messy empirical picture filled with instances of individual and collective choices only tenuously related to official writ. The reality, in other words, is polycentric, and polycentricity is productive and functional to different degrees depending on the context and the type of intersubjective understandings between individuals and between collective choice units about the integrity and autonomy of respective spheres.

The Tragedy of the Commons

Perhaps the most famous contribution of the Bloomington school to understanding governance has been in relation to the "tragedy of the commons". As described by Garrett Hardin in an influential article,[5] the tragedy of the commons refers to a situation where a 'commons', such as a pasture, is destroyed by overgrazing by shepherds pursuing their self-interest. The conventional view has held that preserving the commons requires either the command and control takeover by an external third party with coercive capacity (the 'state'), or by division into private property parcels that could be traded and sold (the 'market'). The Bloomington school research community demonstrated with rigorous empirical evidence that this was a false dichotomy. Instead, in many cases around the world, communities had managed to not succumb to the tragedy of the commons by devising and using shared understandings–institutions–for self-governance. These institutions overcame their collective action problems and managed the resource in ways that secured the commons sustainably.

Some further clarity in terms is useful here. The 'commons' can apply to several different kinds of goods. A more precise term is a common-pool resource (CPR). A CPR is a resource from which it is difficult to exclude users, but in which use of the resource by one user reduces the amount available to other users. CPRs are distinguished from private goods (highly

5 Garrett Hardin, "The Tragedy of the Commons", *Science* 162: 3859 (1968), 1243–1248.

excludable and subtractable), public goods (low in excludability and subtractability), and club goods (low in subtractability, and highly excludable). In the case of rechargeable CPRs (such as pastures, fisheries, forests, some aquifers), use of the resource beyond a certain threshold may undermine its ability to replenish itself in the future. Drawing on many cases from existing research, Elinor Ostrom and others in the Bloomington school argued that successful CPR governance shows certain shared characteristics of the community arrangements.[6] These shared characteristics have been summarized as eight "design principles" (a somewhat misleading label, as it implies that adopting these will necessarily produce sustainable governance, and that outside experts can impose designs on local contexts and expect intended outcomes to obtain, which are both fallacies).

These empirically grounded findings appreciably complicated the conventional picture of governance. One can try to describe the cases of community self-governance as a type of communal ownership, and the Hardin 'commons' as closer to an open-access situation with no local or external restrictions on use. But the important implication remains: the conventional state-market dichotomy is not sufficient for understanding potentials for sustainable development. Further, one of the critical suggestions for development is to value the local arrangements as representing institutional solutions to complex problems. However, the complexity is often so great as to preclude a decisive claim about the 'optimal' institutional response. From the language of property rights, such community arrangements rest on common property, with control shared by a community, but with restrictions on outsiders. In practice, this may not be a result of formal property rights enforcement, but rather a consequence of the transactions costs outsiders face in trying to appropriate the relevant resources.

Polycentricity in Islamic Context

Over much of Islamic history, particularly in the Sunni context, there have been numerous claimants to authority and sources of certification. These have been relatively open, given the lack of a central ordaining or certifying entity, and epistemic authority among religion-interpreters has been partly a function of reputation for scholarly prowess and personal piety. Some of the challenges faced in contemporary Islamic contexts can be traced to the push for monocentricity in a context better suited to polycentric govern-

6 Elinor Ostrom, *Governing the Commons: The Evolution of Institutions for Collective Action*, New York: Cambridge Univ. Press 1990. Elinor Ostrom, Roy Gardner and James Walker, *Rules, Games, and Common-Pool Resources*, Ann Arbor: University of Michigan Press 1994.

ance. Strikingly, the effort to centralize religious certification and codify a diverse, contextually-variant tradition often came with colonial authority, although not exclusively. When the post-colonial state claims exclusive religious authority, and passes official decrees that are purportedly 'the' Islamic position, alternative understandings risk becoming anathemized as not simply heterodox, but also treasonous. This potentially sets up the grounds for severe religious civil strife. Thus, a critical question for the success of polycentric order in contemporary Islamic contexts rests on the degree of acceptance of polycentric metanorms–foundational understanding of how self-governing agents are to relate to each other, in ways that protect the internal integrity and external autonomy of each collective choice arrangement.

De facto polycentricity, where governance comes from many units that may not have formal autonomy, exists in most post-colonial societies. While the juridical state entity and its office-holders are often depicted in a monocentric fashion, under which the central state apparatus is the exclusive rule-giver and enforcer over 'society', the reality–particularly in states with weak apparatuses of governance–is significant rule-making and enforcing capacity in the hands of other agents in the polity. If there are no productive shared understandings about how rule-devising entities are to interact (particularly when there are conflicts), such polycentricity can be the basis for destructive social strife. A crucial question, therefore, is the degree to which there are such shared foundational meta-constitutional understandings, what I have elsewhere called "polycentric metanorms"[7].

The presence and efficacy of such shared understandings as polycentric metanorms is ultimately an empirical matter. One of the major suggestions of Vincent and Elinor Ostrom of the Bloomington school, and of other well-known figures such as Douglass North, is that culture provides one source of such shared understandings. What I have explored in several recent and forthcoming publications is some of the potential sources for polycentric metanorms in Islamic contexts, drawing on both the religious tradition and on the contemporary national self-conception and political evolution of states.[8] All the while, it is important to emphasize that although there is some necessary simplification, the focus on meta-constitutional understandings should not be read as a crude essentialism that draws a monotonic tie between 'Islam' and particular social outcomes.

7 Anas Malik, *Polycentricity, Islam, and Development: Potentials and Challenges in Pakistan*, Lanham: Lexington Books 2018.

8 Anas Malik, "Minarchist Political Islam", in: *Islam, the State, and Political Authority: Medieval Issues and Modern Concerns*, Asma Afsaruddin, ed., New York: Palgrave Macmillan 2011; Anas Malik, "Challenging Dominance: Symbols, Institutions, and Vulnerabilities in Minarchist Political Islam", *The Muslim World* 98 (2008), 501–518.

A Note on the 'Islamic Context' and 'Islamic Tradition'

Using the term 'Islamic tradition' or the modifier 'Islamic' for a particular context can suggest a faith-based claim that the referent is truly in keeping with 'Islam' as in 'submitted to the Divine Will'. There have been attempts to come up with alternative labels, but they are not completely satisfactory. For example, changing the modifier to 'Muslim' could work because it suggests a context or tradition mediated by those who proclaim the identity 'Muslim'. However, the word Muslim also signifies one who submits to the Divine Will, which in turn again conflates the fallible claims of individual Muslims with the actual 'true' Muslim position. Marshall Hodgson, an influential American historian of Islam and author of the widely-cited work *The Venture of Islam*,[9] preferred the term 'Islamicate', which potentially gets around this analytic challenge. And while this is probably the most preferable solution, it works only if it becomes widely adopted, which it has not been, at least in the political economy literature with which I am familiar.

Thus, although not persuaded that my choice is the best strategy, I nevertheless will proceed as follows. I will use the term 'Islamic context' not to suggest a theological validation or legitimation of a particular social order or community arrangement as being truly 'Islamic' from the point of view of Divine Judgment. Rather, I use it loosely in an ethnographic sense as a label that actors in a particular situation themselves use. In other words, this is not a theological endorsement of any specific practice or claim. It does however draw on the fallibilist presumption of traditional approaches to *fiqh*, particularly the Sunni heritage. From this perspective, the true Divine Law, or Sharia, is considered to exist in the mind of God. Human efforts to use scripture and other traces in the religious heritage to try to understand what the Sharia might require in a particular context are the rulings from jurisprudence, or the *aḥkām al-fiqh*, which are open to contestation and carry the presumption of fallibility (the exception being a question on which there is consensus, which begs the second-order question of whose views count as part of the deliberative process). Indeed, the widespread norm for offering a religious opinion–a fatwa–was and is to end with "And God knows best" (*w-allāhu 'a'lam*), an acknowledgement that despite one's best efforts at interpretation and jurisprudential reasoning, one is fallible, as true understanding lies ultimately with God.

It is appealing for analytic purposes to try to offer a set of ingredients that define the 'Islamic tradition', and indeed to some degree this is inescapable. One expansive view is that whatever practitioners view as 'apt performance' in keeping with the tradition counts as being within the tradi-

[9] Marshall G. S. Hodgson, *The Venture of Islam*, Chicago: Univ. of Chicago Press 1974.

tion. Thus, the claim that 'capitalism' is in keeping with the Islamic tradition, is valid to the extent that proponents validate their claims in a way other practitioners see as apt performance. Of course, a counter-claim could also be regarded as apt performance. And this further affirms the fact that the decentralized nature of religious authority allows room for diversity in religious opinion. At the same time, the diversity under the 'Islamic' penumbra does not mean a lack of any coherence; rather, the religious tradition retains an 'itness' and supplies a master signifier by which the wide-ranging threads are connected.[10]

One critical question from the point of view of social harmony or productive relations is the degree to which practitioners in the tradition accept prescriptions and understandings different from their own. Traditionally, state authority in the Muslim tradition after the sacred history period has not been able to claim exclusive authority over religious legal interpretation. Much of Islamic law can be said to have developed in conscious opposition to state authority.[11] An exception, which may be considered a loose and pale parallel to an 'inquisition' in the Muslim context, occurred under the Abbasid dynasty, when Caliph al-Ma'mūn (813–833) tried to impose a Mutazilite doctrine as the universal authoritative Islamic one, and was resisted by prominent religious authorities. This episode can be understood as demonstrating the incompatibility of the Islamic tradition with centralized hierarchy of the type associated with Catholicism in Europe. The actual history is more complex than these archetypal claims; for example, in the Safavid dynasty of Iran, there was relative centralization of claimed religious authority. Moreover, the decentralization in the Sunni contexts did not mean an easily accessible open field of religious interpretation. Achieving the level of epistemic authority needed to speak authoritatively within the tradition required overcoming a high threshold of facility with sources and branches of knowledge.

With changes in communication technologies, the rise of literacy, and particularly the separation of texts from traditional teaching communities, there has been a substantial crowding of the field of voices claiming to offer religious legal interpretation in the Islamic context. This development over the last few centuries has been facilitated by a lowering of the barriers to religious legal interpretation. This normative shift was exemplified in such developments as the Salafiyya movement of the 19th century in Egypt. Combined with new social questions generated by modern political economic arrangements, and the pressing problems of colonialism experienced

10 Bobby S. Sayyid, *A Fundamental Fear: Eurocentrism and the Emergence of Islamism*, London: Zed 2003.

11 Sherman Jackson, "Jihad and the Modern World", *Journal of Islamic Law and Culture* 7: 1 (2002), 1–26.

in many Muslim communities around the world, a variety of intellectuals, activists, and political movements have advanced claims in religious terms. There are divergent contemporary positions about 'Islam' in relation to 'capitalism'.

Potential Support for Institutional Diversity and Polycentric Order

The Bloomington school provides tools for mapping institutional diversity, and emphasizes polycentricity, the productive co-existence and interrelation of diverse, self-governing centers of decision-making. In contemporary Islamic contexts such as post-colonial Muslim-majority states, political leaders and activists often present 'Islam' as a rigid rule-set to be administered by a monocentric, monolithic, monovalent state entity with hegemony over competing claims. Yet the religious tradition appears to encompass tremendous institutional diversity, as well as the norms of accepting and respecting diverse institutional arrangements and choices according to context, conscience, and reasoning.

In several other publications,[12] I have described rationales and supporting references from Islamic religious tradition and practice that support an embrace of institutional diversity and self-governance. Taken together, these suggest a substantial cultural endowment supporting polycentric governance in Islamic contexts. A key, underlying aspect of civic virtue is enlightened self-interest, or self-interest rightly understood, that takes the interests and perspectives of others into account. This provides a social orientation that helps support self-governance as individuals engage with others to problem-solve, identify complementarities, and devise arrangements for mutual benefit. A type of covenantal civic mindset is conducive to a norm of non-dominance and to identifying the complementarities that support productive social relations underlying a well-functioning polycentric order.

A central underpinning of the covenantal civic orientation is the Golden Rule grounded in a foundational understanding of human equality before the Divine. This is expressed in the well-known hadith "One of you does not believe until he loves for his neighbor what he loves for himself" (recorded in *Ṣaḥīḥ Muslim*, *Kitāb al-Imān*, 67–1, Hadith no. 45). This can potentially be understood as an injunction to take seriously the perspective and preferences of others in one's proximity. The notion of human equality and the Golden Rule are important in that they support an attitude of civic artisanship in which pietists engage with others in efforts to devise ways of addressing collective needs. This does not necessarily imply utterly self-

[12] Malik, *Polycentricity*; Malik, "Minarchist Political Islam"; Malik, "Challenging Dominance".

effacing, saintly altruism, but may also include self-interest rightly understood.

Well-established aspects of the jurisprudential tradition, such as considering social habits (*'ādāt*) and customs *('urf)*, suggest openness to rule-diversity. The context of application (*wāqi'a*) is critical for *fiqh*. There is the frequent if not ubiquitous possibility of multiple analogies applied to a given context. This results in an additional role for the ethical judgment of the jurist, namely, how to choose an appropriate analogy among competing plausible possibilities. Hashim Kamali suggests that this process, formally known as *istiḥsān*, and sometimes used without formal acknowledgment, is a recurrent element of juristic decision-making.[13] Further, there is the matter of understanding the context of application, the *wāqi'a*. In a world where no agent is omniscient, and where knowledge is dispersed, the fuller understanding of how a religious injunction is to operate in a particular context requires expertise in that context. That knowledge base usually resides at least partially with those who operate within the context of application.

Specific religious injunctions potentially promote associational activity by requiring some interaction and decision-making. These include but are not limited to the emphasis on mutual consultation (*shūrā*), the local requirements in such matters as moon-sighting to determine calendar time, the practical cooperation needed for construction of places of worship, the collection and distribution of zakat funds, and the requirements of identifying reputable persons to bear witness to contracts. The Islamic heritage also contains numerous historical practices and understandings that potentially can be interpreted as aspects of a self-governing order: the prevalence of guilds in pre-modern Muslim contexts, the role of Sufi brotherhoods, the millet structure in the Ottoman Empire; and the practice of endowing organizations (*waqf*). While different inferences about the implications of such injunctions and practices can be drawn, my recent work has sought to describe ways in which they represent potential rationales for self-governing arrangements in a polycentric order.[14]

What the above suggests for the relationship of Islamic contexts to 'capitalism' is that a greater sensitivity to the cultural endowment and religious tradition is needed regarding institutional diversity. A further implication is that the study of development in contemporary Islamic contexts needs to more seriously and rigorously consider the religio-cultural and historical roots of polycentric governance. My own scholarship has suggested possibilities and vulnerabilities. But these efforts are only some possible entry points to a scholarly engagement rather than an exhaustive evaluation.

---

13 M. Hashim Kamali, *Equity and Fairness in Islam*, Cambridge: The Islamic Texts Society 2005.

14 Malik, *Polycentricity*.

Ultimately a key motor to the success of a self-governing order rests with the mores of the populace. Social mores connected to civic entrepreneurship and self-interest rightly understood help parlay potentials into social artifacts. This approach has a strong affinity to Ibn Khaldun's[15] emphasis on the eco-social-generational culture of a community in driving its political well-being. A well-functioning polycentric order rests on a sophisticated type of solidarity–one that permits tremendous diversity while having a foundational shared understanding and respect for self-governance. This is difficult to sustain in practice, and Ibn Khaldun theorized a process of decline driven by the erosion of solidarity and virtue that provided the initial foundation for a complex political order. Tocqueville also stressed the central problem of the intergenerational transfer of habits of heart and mind required for self-governance. Ultimately these rest on education, understood not simply as formal schooling, but also as the broad range of civic education a person receives from the orientation and experience taught through religious community, to the practical experience of living in municipalities and trying to negotiate common problems and challenges, to the broader conception of community.

Monocentric Aspirations in Post-Colonial States

In a polycentric polity, what observers term 'the state' is better characterized as a central association, an association of associations alongside other associational forms. A major issue in associational forms relates to who can legitimately do what actions: the rules of participation in a particular context. In a religious context, the participation rule becomes in part a matter of determining the legitimate interpreters of tradition. In a context where traditional authority has been increasingly challenged, and where *takfir* (excommunication) has gained prominence, there can be severe difficulties in achieving a peaceable shared understanding on the participation question.

This raises a key challenge: the odd, atraditional marriage of central state authority and religious law. In some post-colonial Muslim states, the central state authority has become a main arbiter of orthodoxy. A monocentric metanorm now competes with the more polycentric metanorm prevalent in Islamic tradition. The emergence of monocentricity is problematic in that it suggests that the decisive role in determining religious orthodoxy is not argument, deliberation, or apt performance judgments by communities of

---

15 Muḥammad ibn Khaldūn al-Ḥaḍramī (1332–1406), Arab historiographer, best known for his *Muqaddima* (Introduction) where he focuses in an almost sociological manner on the concept of 'generation' and the dichotomy between sedentary and nomadic life in order to explain the forces behind 'history'.

believers, but the power of a central authority. Particularly where there are severe legitimacy problems for new or weak state authorities, there is a temptation to adopt the mantle of religion. And yet in the long term this undermines the authoritative character of religious opinion, making it closer to the authoritarian than the authoritative. Ideally, religious argument would be tied neither to the state authority nor the opinions of mass publics, but to the conscientious interpretative efforts of well-qualified specialists who also acknowledge their own fallibility and the validity of other interpretative efforts.

In many places, the quality of discourse has sunk to the level of crude sectarian religious nationalism–a substantial danger to public order. Particularly amid communal conflict and straitened economic circumstances, such divides seem to rapidly transform intra-religious differences into identity-group conflicts. This 'ethnification' of religious difference slides all-too-easily into an ethno-nationalist, us-them mentality. This then becomes an existential threat to pluralism in Islamic contexts. A key part of civic education and orientation in Muslim contexts should be the effort to inoculate people against the mentality of religious-identity based nationalism. There are numerous injunctions in the tradition, such as the Golden Rule, the obligations of *shūrā*, *naṣīḥa* (sincere advice), and *farḍ kifāya* (collective obligations), that may help promote such civic engagement.

Markets and Polycentric Order

The concentration of capital and its resultant increasing social inequality has far-reaching social consequences that raise important questions for the viability of self-governing polycentric orders in Islamic (and other) contexts. One such question is whether capital concentration allows capital-holders to dominate the economic landscape in an oppressive way that precludes meaningful alternative opportunities for capital-poor individuals, and effectively restricts the scope of practical choices for many individuals and collectivities. This may be the condition under monopolies or some robber-baron situations. The prospect of capital concentration also relates to questions of the Quranic condemnation of *ribā* (often translated as "usury"), and the matter of determining when transactions are considered to be forms of *ribā*, by whom, and subject to what sort of sanction. These considerations beg the question of who has the responsibility to intervene to ensure basic individual choice.

Another question is whether a polycentric order with established patterns of local self-governance is disrupted by the larger scale intervention of investors who bring in outside resources. These can clearly be disruptive to local arrangements. Consider how a lucrative offer might lead some to overexploit a resource. Such external changes can be threatening to carefully crafted community arrangements.

In Karl Polanyi's well-known description of the "great transformation", social relations become gradually subordinate to market exchange, rather than the market remaining firmly embedded within constraints based on community norms.[16] In this process, deeply held community associations and shared understandings can become marginalized. Human labor and natural resources are reduced to commodity inputs into production, and their worth is estimated only in contribution to the bottom line of economic returns. Over the social transformation, the fuller dignity of human beings as well as cultural and metaphysical connections to the natural world are diminished.

Understanding and appreciating this possibility probably means a more socially interventionist or active model of political economy than many neoliberals are likely to embrace. But the precise mix of possibilities cannot be specified in an acontextual, ex ante fashion. Part of the problem is information dispersal: no single entity has the comprehensive information needed to fully map policy choices and related outcomes. This relates to the 'objective' conditions (a problematic designation in that the very categories used to describe and measure are the result of choices related to the observer's epistemology and ontology) and also to 'subjective' preferences, meaning the actual values shaping agent behavior (which, in many cases, agents may be unable to articulate, or might not be known until the actual context and situation arises in which the choices are made). Further, the nature of human reflexivity and the paradox of predictability are such that when an informed prediction regarding behaviors is made, people–as thoughtful reflective agents–take this information into account in their strategic behavior. And taking that possibility into account simply introduces a further higher order possibility, and so on in a recursion ad infinitum.

There is a further issue: according to the conventional neoliberal theory of economic efficiency, market integration is a good thing. It eliminates waste through economies of scale and increased competition and benefits consumers by reducing arbitrage opportunities. And a polycentric order that has many jurisdiction-specific fiscal and regulatory powers could result in a segmented market. But this is not necessarily the case. Part of self-governance is that every society arrives at its own mix of central and local and other jurisdictional authority. Markets themselves are a form of polycentric order. Additionally, the institutional diversity characterizing particular rules of market operation is best specified more contextually through a

---

16 Karl Polanyi, *The Great Transformation: The Political and Economic Origins of Our Time*, Boston: Beacon Press 1944.

careful mapping rather than an abstract ideal-type. And it is worth noting that ideas of value and 'development', in a truly polycentric system, are ultimately determined by users and polity participants in their respective action arenas. In other words, the determination of what is of satisfactory value should privilege the local users of a resource, rather than outside 'experts' with abstract pronouncements. And yet there is a crucial role for outside expertise and information, particularly in the circumstances of ecological hazards such as toxins and public health threats, as local agents are often not equipped to generate specialized, scientific information. The polycentric approach should not be thought of as invariably privileging local authority, but as supporting a mix of collective choice units appropriate for the particular context and needs. In some cases, a bigger, more encompassing jurisdiction (for example, the 'central state jurisdiction') is the more appropriate scale for providing the needed service.

A Concluding Note

Given the diversity of social-ecological circumstances, a substantial degree of analytic and prescriptive humility is needed in assessing the institutional fit of 'capitalism' with 'Islam'. A key takeaway from an appreciation of institutional diversity is that there is no panacea, and no one-size-fits-all solution. There may be a role for open access (where any agent is free to appropriate a given resource) in some situations, or 'market' relations in others, outside party intervention in some, and for self-organized self-governing forms in yet others. Or some combination of central state bureaucracy, community organization, and 'market' forces might be well-suited for a particular social-ecological context. Institutional diversity means that identifying an optimal solution is computationally so complex as to be practically impossible. Additionally, the human capacity to adjust behavior in light of the best information available about patterns of behavior may introduce new, difficult-to-anticipate variability into choices and outcomes, making it impossible to produce a complete model of social behavior. From the perspective of political economic development, rather than offering a single answer, one must be open to many answers, and indeed many experiments. In well-functioning polycentric contexts, policy and choices can be seen as experiments for learning by different collective choice units in a polity. This offers a kind of empirically-grounded adaptive efficiency in a society; while the appearance may be somewhat chaotic, the polycentric approach can reduce the risk of grand failures that can result from a monocentric approach. Of course, polycentric orders can have their own vulnerabilities, including the potential for a well-organized faction to dominate others in the polity.

For well-functioning community self-governance and polycentric order, it helps if there is an expectation of long-term interactions and if the shadow of the future plays a significant role. Amid disruptions and migrations caused by war, ecological disasters such as drought and famine, and other economic challenges, instability and continuing uncertainty about the future can make it difficult to come up with viable arrangements for common purposes. And this present situation in many places does not bode well for self-governing community arrangements. Yet the reality of weak formal state apparatuses means that there is a strong need for broader thinking about sources of governance. I have sought to advance this conversation through my above mentioned book, *Polycentricity, Islam, and Development*, which considers related issues in general and also through a case examination of potentials and challenges in Pakistan.

States, markets, community arrangements, complex mixes of these, and 'tradition' can all be thought of as efforts to address collective action problems. Tradition signifies meanings at many levels and should not be reduced to only instrumental solutions to collective action problems. Yet the collective action implications provide an analytic thread of value to political economists looking at how uncertainty is reduced and how human interactions are made less costly. In Islamic contexts, traditional modes of accommodating institutional diversity may support development possibilities outside the state-market dichotomy commonly deployed by political economists.

Part Two: Marxism, Anti-Capitalism, Islam

The Tempestuous Affair between Marxism and Islam: Attraction, Hostility, and Accommodation since 1917

Manfred Sing

The relation between Marxism and religion has been complicated and ambivalent, theoretically as well as practically, ever since Karl Marx stated in 1844 that "the *criticism of religion* has been essentially completed, and the criticism of religion is the prerequisite of all criticism."[1] Although Marxists have a long record of being atheistic and anti-religious, it is striking that academic discussions in particular often deal with Marxism as something religious or rather similar to it and even use categories from the studies of religions.[2] Marxism has been described as a "political religion"[3] staging "quasi-religious rituals,"[4] as a "messianic religion" seeking for inner-worldly salvation,[5] as a "political creed"[6] offering "opium for the intellectuals,"[7] or as a kind of dogmatic "fundamentalism."[8]

---

1 Karl Marx, "Zur Kritik der Hegelschen Rechtsphilosophie. Einleitung" (1844), *Karl Marx/Friedrich Engels, Werke I*, Berlin: Dietz Verlag 1981, 378–391, 378; for the English version see: www.marxists.org/archive/marx/works/1843/critique-hpr/intro.htm (31.03.2017).

2 Anja Kirsch, *Weltanschauung als Erzählkultur. Zur Konstruktion von Religion und Sozialismus in Staatsbürgerkundeschulbüchern der DDR*, Göttingen: Vandenhoeck & Ruprecht 2016, 36f.

3 Eric Voegelin, *Die politischen Religionen*, Stockholm: Bermann-Fischer 1939.

4 For the rituals in socialist countries see for example the 1983 focus edition of the *Anthropological Quarterly* and David A. Kideckel, "Introduction: Political Rituals and Symbolism in Socialist Eastern Europe," *Anthropological Quarterly* 56: 2 (1983), 52–54; also Camelia Lelesan, "The Power of the Ritual–the System of Rites as a Form of Legitimacy in the Soviet Union," in: *History of Communism in Europe* V, The Institute for the Investigation of Communist Crimes and the Memory of the Romanian Exile (Bucharest), ed., Bucharest: Zeta-Books 2014, 193–206.

5 See for example Leszek Kolakowski, *Main Currents of Marxism: The Founders, the Golden Age, the Breakdown*, New York etc.: Norton 2008 [[1]1978]; Murray N. Rothbard, "Karl Marx as Religious Eschatologist," *MisesInstitute* (10/09/2009), https://mises.org/library/karl-marx-religious-eschatologist (25.04.2017).

6 Robert C. Tucker, "Marxism–Is it Religion?," *Ethics* 68: 2 (1958), 125–130.

7 Raymon Aron, *L'opium des intellectuels*, Paris: Gallimard 1955; Michail Ryklin, *Kommunismus als Religion. Die Intellektuellen und die Oktoberrevolution*, Frankfurt am Main: Suhrkamp 2008; Gerd Koenen, *Was war der Kommunismus?*, Göttingen: Vandenhoek & Ruprecht 2010.

8 Horst Heimann, "Marxismus als Fundamentalismus?," in: *Fundamentalismus in der modernen Welt. Die Internationale der Unvernunft*, Thomas Meyer, ed., Frankfurt am Main: Suhrkamp 1989, 213–230.

Especially in political studies after the demise of the Soviet Union, the usage of a religious vocabulary for the description of Marxist theories and politics has become a common practice, yet it remains vague and an analogy at best.[9] Thus, when Marxism is depicted as a surrogate religion and a quasi-religious ideology or worldview, the notion of a "true" or "real" religion, ideology, or worldview swirls through the air and is difficult to grasp. What the terminology reveals is that "religion" is not a neutral term, especially not in this context; rather, it serves different means and ends when used by anti-communists, Marxists, and religious practitioners: On the one hand, the notion of Marxism as religion helped to debunk Marxism-Leninism as "pseudo-religious" and thus, inter-alia also as pseudo-scientific. Conservative as well as leftist critics of communism traced its failure back to a quasi-religious veneration of the October revolution, a veneration that signals a relapse to a romantic infatuation for a doctrine, rather than a sober analysis of reality.[10] On the other hand, a reference to faith could help to explain that Marxists have endured hardship and ordeals in their endless struggle for justice because of an inner conviction one could call faith, "the strongest form of ideology;" yet, Marxist "faith" could be differentiated from other acts of faith as it has never lost its link to rationality in the way religious faith has.[11] Finally, relating the Marxist critique of exploitation to the Christian "option for the poor"[12] could also point at a common responsibility to build a better world and support a dialogue between religious believers, theologians, and Marxists, from Eastern Europe to Latin America.

Actually, references to religion can already be found in the early reception of the Bolshevist revolution. The partially-known facts paled against the meaning that was given to "the world-historical event" by critics, supporters, and sceptics. Thus, for different reasons, the reception of the revolution not only reflected a teleological understanding of history, but often bore religious or eschatological overtones. Christian opposition to socialism and communism not only long predated 1917 and saw them as a "deadly

9 Kirsch, *Weltanschauung*, 36–55.

10 See Aron, *L'opium*, Ryklin, *Kommunismus*, and Koenen, *Was war der Kommunismus?*

11 See a book written by the former politician of the SED, the PDS and The Left, Uwe-Jens Heuer (1927–2011), *Marxismus und Glaube*, Hamburg: VSA 2006, 289; also idem, "Marxismus und Glaube," *Sitzungsberichte der Leibniz-Sozietät* 87 (2006), 87–108, http://leibnizsozietaet.de/wp-content/uploads/2012/11/06_heuer1.pdf (25.04.2017). For a critique see the article by theologian and GDR politician Günther Wirth (1929–2009), "Marxismus, Glauben, Religion. Notwendige Bemerkungen zu einem Buch von Uwe-Jens Heuer," *Utopie kreativ* 201/202 (2007), 724–739.

12 On the Catholic side, the principle was articulated in the Second Vatican Council (in *Gaudium et spes*, 1965), the Latin American liberation theology since the 1960s, the encyclical *Centesimus annus* (1991) and the exhortation *Evangelii gaudium* (2013). On the Protestant side, it was for example used in the *Darmstädter Wort* (1947) by the Confessing Church (Bekennende Kirche) in Germany.

plague;"[13] for Catholics and Protestants alike, the Bolshevist regime formed the apotheosis of secularism, materialism, and a godless threat to the Christian social and moral order.[14] When the World War II alliance between the USA and the USSR broke up, Pope Pius XII (papacy 1939–1958) endorsed President Harry S. Truman's (in office 1945–1953) anti-Soviet foreign policy, "claiming its battle against communism was an extension of the church's two thousand-year conflict against evil."[15] The pro-Soviet camp, in contrast, saw the revolution as an existential moment of truth, a kairós,[16] sometimes even as the aim and end of history. A famous example of this view is the German philosopher Ernst Bloch's (1885–1977) remark "ubi Lenin, ibi Jerusalem."[17] It was not only meant as a direct criticism of the Zionist answer to the "Jewish question," but indicated that Bloch mixed Jewish messianism with his understanding of Christian heretical movements, chiliasm, and communist utopianism and saw the "Bolshevist implementation of Marxism" as a return of "the age-old fight for God ... of the radical Anabaptists."[18] The British philosopher Bertrand Russell used another, more unfavourable religious analogy by comparing Bolshevists to Muslims: "Bolshevism combines the characteristics of the French Revolution with those of the rise of Islam. ... Marx has taught that Communism is fatally predestined to come about; this fits in with the oriental traits in the Russian character, and produces a state of mind not unlike that of the early successors of Mahomet."[19] Defining Bolshevism as a religion,[20] Russell confessed:

---

13 See Dianne Kirby, "Christian anti-communism," *Twentieth Century Communism* 7 (2014), 126–152, 127, and the encyclical *Quod apostolici muneris* (1878) of Pope Leo XIII, which opposed socialism, communism, and nihilism. Further encyclicals, which condemned communism and socialism and declared them incompatible with the teachings of the Catholic Church were: *Quanta cura* (1864), which mainly opposed the separation of church and state; *Rerum novarum* (1891), *Quadragesimo anno* (1931), *Divini redemptoris* (1937), and *Centesimus annus* (1991).

14 Paul Hanbrink, "European Protestants Between Anti-Communism and Anti-Totalitarianism: The Other Interwar Kulturkampf?", *Journal of Contemporary History* 53: 3 (2018), 622–643.

15 Kirby, "Christian anti-communism," 135.

16 On kairós see for example Roland Boer, *In the Vale of Tears. On Marxism and Theology V*, Leiden: Brill 2014, 207–244.

17 Ernst Bloch, *Das Prinzip Hoffnung*, Gesamtausgabe Band 5/1, Frankfurt am Main: Suhrkamp 1959, 711. The *Principle of Hope* was written between 1938 and 1947 in American exile and published in the GDR from 1954 to 1959.

18 Ernst Bloch, *Thomas Münzer als Theologe der Revolution* (1921), Gesamtausgabe Band 2, Frankfurt am Main: Suhrkamp 1959, 128: „So kehrt doch gerade auch im bolschewistischen Vollzug des Marxismus der alte gotteskämpferische, der taboritisch-kommunistisch-joachimitische Typus des radikalen Täufertums erkennbar wieder."

19 Bertrand Russel, *The Practice and Theory of Bolshevism*, London: George Allen & Unwin 1920, 5 and 29; https://archive.org/details/bolshevism00russuoft (13.04.2017).

> One who believes, as I do, that the free intellect is the chief engine of human progress, cannot but be fundamentally opposed to Bolshevism, as much as to the Church of Rome. Among religions, Bolshevism is to be reckoned with Mohammedanism rather than with Christianity and Buddhism. Christianity and Buddhism are primarily personal religions, with mystical doctrines and a love of contemplation. Mohammedanism and Bolshevism are practical, social, unspiritual, concerned to win the empire of this world.[21]

Suffice it to mention that Russell's Orientalist stereotypes about Russians and Muslims had close to nothing to do with the situation of Muslims in the USSR or the reception of Bolshevism in Muslim countries, as will be shown further below.

With these examples that speak of a contradiction or an overlap between religion and Marxism, we are in the midst of socio-political struggles over meaning that cannot help us to determine what religion or the religious in Marxism "really" is; they rather show us that, at the very heart of the whole issue, lies a structural ambivalence of the relation between religion and Marxism.

In recent years, academic scholars as well as Marxists have tried to come to grips with the intersections between Marxism, religion, spirituality, atheism, and revolution.[22] Some authors are motivated to contribute to a rapprochement between Christianity and Marxism,[23] while others critically re-

---

20 Ibid, 113f: "[A] set of beliefs held as dogmas, dominating the conduct of life, going beyond or contrary to evidence, and inculcated by methods which are emotional or authoritarian, not intellectual."

21 Ibid, 114.

22 See the special issue "Marxism and Spirituality" of *Rethinking Marxism* 28 (2016) and the volume dedicated to the work of David McLellan: David Bates et al., eds., *Marxism, Religion, and Ideology. Themes from David McLellan*, New York, London: Routledge 2016. Also see Roland Boer, "Between Old and New: On Socialism and Revolutionary Religion," *International Journal of Žižek Studies* 10: 2 (2016), 1–22, http://zizekstudies.org/index.php/IJZS/article/view/956/949 (11.09.2017); Anindy Bhattacharyya, "Marx and Religion," *Socialist Worker* 1990 (2006), https://socialistworker.co.uk/art/8187/Marx+and+religion (25.04.2017); Dave Crouch, "The Bolsheviks and Islam," *International Socialism* 110 (2006); www.marxists.org/history/etol/newspape/isj2/2006/isj2-110/crouch.html (25.04.2017); John Molyneux, "More than Opium: Marxism and Religion," *International Socialism* 119 (2008), www.marxists.org/history/etol/writers/molyneux/2008/xx/religion.html (25.04.2017); Roland Boer, "The Full Story: On Marxism and Religion," *International Socialism* 123 (2009), http://isj.org.uk/the-full-story-on-marxism-and-religion (25.04.2017); Philip Gasper, "Marxism and Religion," *International Social Review* 63 (2009), http://isreview.org/issue/63/marxism-and-religion (25.04.2017); Alan Woods, "Marxism and Religion," *In Defense of Marxism* (2001), www.marxist.com/marxism-religion-liberation-theology220701.htm (25.04.2017).

23 See Andrew Collier, *Christianity and Marxism: A Philosophical Contribution to Their Reconciliation*, London etc.: Routledge 2001; for a critical review see James Daley, "Salvation According to Luther and Althusser," *Journal of Critical Realism* 5: 1 (2002), 71–79. Organized religious socialists can also be visited at https://ilrs.org, the website of the International League of Religious Socialists, founded in the 1920s. "Tradi-

read a new philosophical valorisation of Christianity's and Marxism's universalism.[24] Roland Boer, author of a five-volume series on "Marxism and theology," characterized their relation as "a difficult and tempestuous love affair,"[25] when he recently finished his project. By discussing the works of Marx, Engels, and two dozen other Marxist intellectuals, Boer shows that their works bear witness to an intensive engagement with religious motives and narratives that go beyond scattered references.[26] Taking up an observation by Ernst Bloch, Boer argues that Marx and Engels developed central theoretical elements–"historical materialism," "alienation," "false consciousness," and "fetishism"–in relation and in opposition to what they saw as religion.[27]

Islam and Muslims are largely absent in these new debates on Marxism and religion, although political Islam forms a major driving force in the background of the scholarly re-thinking of the relations between politics, ideology, and religion in the 21st century. One reason for this neglect, apart from a lack of knowledge,[28] is that Marx and Engels did not discuss Islam or Muslim societies in any systematic manner. Their scattered remarks encompass some sentences on Islamic history, the "Asiatic mode of production," "Oriental despotism," and developments in colonial Algeria, Egypt, and India.[29] When Friedrich Engels, for example, wrote in 1894 that "the history of early Christianity has notable points of resemblance with the

---

tions of Catholicism and Communism" are listed at www.angelfire.com/md/Toby Terrar/index.html (both 25.04.2017).

24 For a critique of ideas held by the philosophers Slavoj Žižek and Alain Badiou see Nathan Coombs, "Christian Communists, Islamic Anarchists?–Part 1," *International Journal of Žižek Studies* 3: 1 (2009), 1–19, and idem, "Christian Communists, Islamic Anarchists?–Part 2," *International Zizek Studies Journal* 3: 3 (2009), 1–24, http://zizek studies.org/index.php/IJZS/article/view/128/128 and http://zizekstudies.org/index.php/IJZS/article/view/194/194 (both 11.09.2017).

25 Roland Boer, *In the Vale of Tears. On Marxism and Theology V*, Leiden: Brill 2014, xi.

26 Roland Boer, *Criticism of Heaven. On Marxism and Theology*, Leiden: Brill 2007; idem, *Criticism of Religion: On Marxism and Theology II*, Leiden: Brill 2009; idem, *Criticism of Theology: On Marxism and Theology III*, Leiden: Brill 2011, idem: *Criticism of Earth. On Marx, Engels and Theology*, Leiden: Brill 2012; idem, *In the Vale of Tears*, 2014.

27 Boer, "The full story." Bloch writes „Niemals zu vergessen hierbei, daß ohne vorangegangene Beschäftigung mit der Religion und der sich anschließenden Religionskritik die Entfremdungslehre und Warenkritik Marxens kaum entstanden wäre," see idem, *Atheismus im Christentum. Zur Religion des Exodus und des Reichs*, Gesamtausgabe Band 14, Frankfurt am Main: Suhrkamp 1968, 349.

28 For sure, scholars try to fill the gaps, see for example the study on Muslims in the USSR after 1941 by Yaacov Ro'i, *Islam in the Soviet Union: From the Second World War to Gorbachev*, London: Hurst 2000.

29 For an overview of these scattered remarks see Wolfgang G. Schwanitz, "Arabischer Sozialismus," in: *Historisch-Kritisches Wörterbuch des Marxismus*, Wolfgang Fritz Haug, ed., Hamburg: Argument Verlag 2004, vol. I: 392–401, www.trafoberlin.de/pdf-dateien/ArabischerSozialismusHKWM.pdf (30.05.2017).

modern working-class movement,"[30] his remark that Islam forms a strange opposition is only a short footnote; Engels noted periodically recurring religious uprisings in Islamic history, presumably drawing on Ibn Khaldun's thesis about a permanent transition of power from effeminate, sedentary tribes in the cities to the puritan Bedouin.[31]

Another reason is that post-colonial critics since the 1970s have attacked Marxism as an inept Westernizing force, by exposing racist stereotypes in Marx's and Engels' remarks on Islam and the Middle East.[32] These attacks have been so forceful that even Marxists admit that Marx's and Engels' remarks have "proved something of an ideological embarrassment for Marxists, since their observations have often been interpreted as a justification for colonialism."[33] Some Marxists also concede that Marx's and Engels' treatment of the Middle East and Islam "regressed behind their ancestors in the tradition of European reflection on Asia."[34]

The 9/11 attacks in 2001 as well as the Arab uprisings in 2011, however, have put the relation between the left and Islam back on the agenda.[35] The question, which is differently answered by different factions of militant leftists and Muslims, is whether anti-capitalism and anti-imperialism form a sufficient basis for theoretical intersection and practical action.[36] In a simi-

30 Friedrich Engels, "Zur Geschichte des Urchristentums," Karl Marx/Friedrich Engels, Werke XXII, 447–473, 447. Here, Engels also drew the comparison that, after 300 years of persecution, Christianity–which "first appeared as the religion of slaves and emancipated slaves, of poor people deprived of all rights, of peoples subjugated or dispersed by Rome"–became the "recognized state religion in the Roman World Empire, and in barely sixty years socialism has won itself a position which makes its victory absolutely certain."

31 Ibid, footnote 1. Ibn Khaldun is not mentioned.

32 Andrej Kreutz, "Marx and the Middle East," *Arab Studies Quarterly* 5: 2 (1983), 156–171.

33 Bryan S. Turner, *Marx and the End of Orientalism*, London: George Allen & Unwin 1978, 3.

34 Perry Anderson, *Lineages of the Absolutist State*, London: New Left Books 1974, 492, quoted by Kreutz, "Marx and the Middle East," 168.

35 See for example Coombs, "Christian Communists, Islamic Anarchists," and Joseph Daher, "Marxism, the Arab Spring, and Islamic Fundamentalism," *International Social Review* 106 (2017), http://isreview.org/issue/106/marxism-arab-spring-and-islamic-fundamentalism (11.09.2017). For an overview of new Marxist literature of the relation to Muslims and Islam in past and present see the links collected on the website *modkraft*, http://spip.modkraft.dk/biblioteket/undersider/article/socialists-on-religion-on-islam and http://spip.modkraft.dk/biblioteket/undersider/article/socialists-on-religion-appendix-on (both 11.08.2017).

36 Fred Halliday, "The Left and the Jihad," *openDemocracy* 2006, www.opendemocracy.net/globalization/left_jihad_3886.jsp (30.05.2017). This question mainly worries pundits of the security sector: Hendrik Hansen and Peter Kainz, "Radical Islamism and Totalitarian Ideology: a Comparison of Sayyid Qutb's Islamism with Marxism and National Socialism," *Totalitarian Movements and Political Religions* 8: 1 (2007), 55–76; Emmanuel Karagiannis and Clark McCauley, "The Emerging Red-Green Alli-

lar vein, political Islam has triggered not only the "new atheism" movement, but also a new wave of re-reading the Marxist critique of religion, since several Marxists have taken issue with "new atheism."[37] A main point raised against the "new atheists" is that they pontificate about the incredibility, irrationality, and stupidity of religious ideas without seeing them as products of social and historical conditions, not even as fruits of intellectual endeavour. Curiously enough, one of the most articulate proponents of "new atheism" was the Anglo-American self-proclaimed "anti-theist" Christopher Hitchens (1949–2011), a former Trotskyist anti-imperialist who became an advocate of George W. Bush's "war on terror." In the title of his major work *God is Not Great* (2007), Hitchens mocked the Islamic creed and pleaded for an interventionist policy in the Middle East, arguing that it had to fight "fascism with an Islamic face."[38]

Against this multi-facetted background, the following chapter aims at de-provincializing the study of Marxism and religion in several respects. Firstly, I will argue that under the umbrella term of "religion" Islam is often neglected, although its relation to Marxism is important and somewhat different from Christianity's. Secondly, a focus on the relations between Marxists and Muslims contributes to our understanding of Marxism as a global movement and sheds light on understudied parts of European, Russian, Chinese, Asian, African, and Arab histories. Thirdly, against the prejudice that issues pertaining to Islam should mainly be explained by Islam itself, this chapter brings to the forefront the impact of socialist ideas on the Middle East and discusses the hybrid forms of Arab socialism and Islamic socialism as political rivals of communism. Fourthly, against a post-colonial critique that depicts Marx–and his followers–as Westernizers importing a foreign ideology, a historical overview sketches the different forms of adoption and adaptation of Marxist ideas by different Middle Eastern groups since the late 19th century, many of whom looked–and are still looking–for a "third way" beyond capitalism and communism.

The following analysis is based on a functionalist–not a theological–understanding of religion and a relational view on what is termed religion and what constitutes its relation to various forms of Marx-inspired politics. The terms "religion," "Islam," "Marxism," and "capitalism" do not bear

ance: Where Political Islam Meets the Radical Left," *Terrorism and Political Violence* 25 (2013), 167–182.

37 The "four horsemen" of "new atheism" are Richard Dawkins, Christopher Hitchens, Sam Harris, and Daniel Dennett. For a Marxist critique see for example Molyneux, "More than Opium," and Boer, "The Full Story." For the argument that the "newness" in "new atheism" is its condemnation of Islam, which "is consistently depicted as irrational, immoral, and, in its purest form, violent," see William W. Emilsen, "The New Atheism and Islam," *The Expository Times* 123: 11 (2012), 521–528, 524.

38 Molyneux, "More than Opium."

eternally fixed meanings, but refer to each other in complex ways. This allows for a wide-ranging ambiguity, internal to each of these four conceptions, as well as for changing relations between them. Drawing on these concepts, different actors could lend support to opposing political interests, as will be shown. For practitioners on both sides of the religious/materialist divide–no matter whether they tried to delineate incompatibility, difference, congruency, or overlap between religion and Marxism–, the supposed opposition between religion and Marxism appeared to be meaningful, and they used it to carve out their own position in a cultural and at times deadly war.

In the first part of this contribution, I start with some general remarks on the ambivalent relation between Marxism and religion and move on to the status of Islam in different phases of Soviet history. Then I briefly outline the proliferation of Marxist ideas and communist parties in Muslim countries and the Middle East, before looking at the role of atheism in communist practices in some European, Asian, African, and Arab countries. In the second part, which focuses on Nasserist Egypt, I show that Muslims mainly took offence at communism because of its atheism and materialism, which is exemplified by some *fatāwā* (legal opinions) against communism issued by Sunni scholars at the Azhar. In spite of their condemnation of communism, religious scholars, however, supported Arab or Islamic socialism, a socialism without class struggle and atheism. To this end they used opposing historical reconstructions. While they traced Arab and Islamic socialism back to early Islam, they identified the roots of communism in pre-Islamic and anti-Arab religious heresies that aimed to destroy Islam and Arabism. In the short third part, I sketch different forms of interactions between the Marxist left and Islamists in the post-Nasserist and post-Soviet era. Finally, I will briefly discuss the Muslims' contribution to the emergence of capitalism, thus arguing against the notion that Marxism has basically failed in Muslim societies, a notion which is often based on the view that Islam is essentially anti-capitalist because Muslim societies have remained outside capitalist development for a long time.

The over-all aim of this chapter is to give an overview of the multifacetted relations between Marxism and Islam that ranged from attraction over co-optation to outright hostility. These relations were open for renegotiations according to political circumstances. And since the issues of religion and social justice played an important role during the Cold War, both Marxists and representatives of religions laid claim to fundamental principles like solidarity, justice, and equality and accused their opponents of a religious or materialist takeover. Drawing on the multiple examples of interactions between (orthodox and undogmatic) Marxists and Muslims, I argue that Marxism, in spite of the demise of the USSR, formed and still forms a powerful political imaginary (about liberation, justice, equality, and political struggle) that has even inspired its political rivals and opponents.

From Marx over the Bolshevist Revolution to the Middle East

Marx and Religion

What was new about Karl Marx's analysis of capitalism was that he was critical of religious elements in capitalism as well as in socialism, meaning that he strictly avoided treating non-religious things as religious. His socialist predecessors had instead directly drawn on biblical terms–the spirit of charity–to ground their demands. Yet, in spite of Marx's approach, socialist parties and workers' movements found themselves in opposition to representatives of state and religion, who accused them of atheism, mainly because of the close relations between crown and church in Europe. This structure started to change at the beginning of the 20th century and especially after the Great War, when the alliances between throne and altar were shaken. New organizations and networks emerged that championed religious forms of socialism and tried to bridge the gap between socialism and religion. Even a number of theologians started to embrace socio-critical ideas, and socialist intellectuals of different religious background tried to combine their worldview with arguments taken from religious history.[39]

As Marx's main subject was society, his critique was not directed against religion *per se*, but at the social conditions that formed it. Marx depicted religion as an ambivalent worldview with ambivalent effects. "*Religious* suffering is, at one and the same time, the *expression* of real suffering and a *protest* against real suffering," according to Marx's famous proclamation about religion as the people's opium, "Religion is the sigh of the oppressed creature, the heart of a heartless world, and the soul of soulless conditions."[40] Marx conceded that religion is, on the one hand, "the general theory of this world, its encyclopaedic compendium, its logic in popular form, its spiritual *point d'honneur*, its enthusiasm, its moral sanction, its solemn complement, and its universal basis of consolation and justification."[41] Yet, on the other hand, it is "an *inverted consciousness of the world*" because it is directly connected with state and society, which form "an *inverted world*."[42] Therefore, Marx concluded that the struggle against religion is "indirectly the

39 For the intellectual history of Marxist thought in Germany see Christoph Henning, *Philosophy after Marx: 100 Years of Misreadings and the Normative Turn in Political Philosophy*, Leiden: Brill 2014.
40 Marx, "Zur Kritik der Hegelschen Rechtsphilosophie," 378.
41 Ibid.
42 Ibid.

struggle *against that world* whose spiritual *aroma* is religion."[43] Marx explained that the criticism of religion "ends with the teaching that *man is the highest essence for man*–hence, with the *categorical imperative to overthrow all relations* in which man is a debased, enslaved, abandoned, despicable essence, relations which cannot be better described than by the cry of a Frenchman when it was planned to introduce a tax on dogs: Poor dogs! They want to treat you as human beings!"[44]

These sentences show that for Marx the main struggle is a political and social one, not a struggle against religion. Religion can even be part of the struggle against exploitation and its religious legitimation. This is why Marx and Engels sided with the reformation against the Catholic Church, but also with Thomas Müntzer against Luther[45], with Feuerbach against theology, and with their own materialist theory against Feuerbach and transcendence philosophy. From a Marxist point of view, the same religio-political position, though partially contributing to liberation, can be judged differently when compared with other positions. Religious views and their Marxist interpretation are not absolutes, but rather stand on relational terms. Put differently: Like religion, Marxism can theoretically be understood as both an expression of and a protest against real suffering; and like religion, it practically functioned as an ideology of both revolution and domination after 1917.

That the suppression of religious freedom would most certainly amount to political failure was already discussed by Marx and Engels. In his comments to the Gotha Program of the German Social Democrats (1875), Marx rejected state intervention in religious freedom,[46] although he also underlined that the workers' party should not only have expressed its toleration of "all possible kinds of religious freedom of conscience," but should also have made clear that it wanted to strive to liberate consciousness from "the witchery of religion."[47] Similarly, Engels derided the Blanquist act to prohibit religion by decree, arguing that "persecution is the best way of strengthening undesirable convictions" and that "the only service that can still be rendered to God today is to make atheism a compulsory dogma."[48]

---

43 Ibid.

44 Ibid, 385.

45 For a detailed analysis see Hartmut Lehmann, "Das marxistische Lutherbild von Engels bis Honecker," in: idem, *Luthergedächtnis 1817 bis 2017*, Göttingen: Vandenhoeck & Ruprecht 2012, 257–270.

46 "Jeder muß seine religiöse wie seine leibliche Notdurft verrichten können, ohne daß die Polizei ihre Nase hineinsteckt," see Marx, "Kritik des Gothaer Programms," *Karl Marx/Friedrich Engels, Werke XIX*, 13–32, 31.

47 Ibid.

48 Friedrich Engels, "Flüchtlingsliteratur," *Karl Marx/Friedrich Engels, Werke XVIII*, 519–567, 532.

Lenin followed this line of reasoning prior to the Bolshevist revolution in articles written in 1905 and 1909 respectively, arguing for the religious freedom of the party members and against including atheism in the party program, which was, by itself, avowedly atheist.[49] Although he regarded the Russian Orthodox Church as a tool of class exploitation, he held that the anti-religious struggle should always be subordinated to the party's interests (the seizure of power) because otherwise the party's enemies would seize the opportunity to divide the proletariat along religious lines.[50]

Bolshevism and Islam

Once in power, Lenin and the Soviet State dealt with the Russian Orthodox Church as a bastion of the ancien regime and persecuted its representatives relentlessly; the other small Christian churches, especially Protestant free churches, flourished during the first decade of Bolshevist rule and the Vatican signalled its willingness to agree to a concordat up to 1927.[51] As the constitution of 1918 guaranteed the freedom of "religious and anti-religious propaganda," this meant, practically, the separation of state and education from the Russian Orthodox Church (1918) and resulted in the confiscation of church property (1921), the closure of seminaries, and the persecution and killing of priests.[52] In spite of anti-religious measures that reduced the number of Russian Orthodox parishes to 500, or one percent of the prerevolutionary number, secret religious activities continued, even before the repression softened after 1941. Although the Soviet Union should have been an atheist state by 1937 according to Stalin's plans, census material from 1937 was classified and became accessible only in 1991, because it revealed that the number of believers in the illiterate Orthodox population

49 Vladimir Lenin, "Socialism and Religion" (1905), in: *Lenin Collected Works 10*, Moscow: Progress Publishers 1965, 83–87; idem, "The Attitude of the Workers' Party to Religion" (1909), in: *Collected Works 15*, Moscow: Progress Publishers 1973, 402–413. Both articles are available at www.marxists.org/archive/lenin/works/cw (10.04.2017). Compare Crouch, "The Bolsheviks and Islam."

50 Wolfgang Heller, "Die Russisch-Orthodoxe Kirche 1917–1941," in: *Politik und Religion in der Sowjetunion 1917–1941*, Christoph Gassenschmidt and Ralph Tuchtenhagen, eds., Wiesbaden: Harrassowitz 2001, 13–46, 22.

51 See for example Gassenschmidt and Tuchtenhagen, *Politik und Religion*; Dimitry V. Pospielovsky, *A History of Soviet Atheism in Theory, and Practice, and the Believer*, 2 volumes, New York: St Martin's Press 1987/88; Crouch, "The Bolsheviks and Islam;" Kirby, "Christian anti-communism," 127; Winfried Becker, "Diplomats and Missionaries: The Role Played by the German Embassies in Moscow and Rome in the Relations between Russia and the Vatican from 1921 to 1929," *Catholic Historical Review* 92 (2006), 25–45, 32.

52 For a short overview see Glenn E. Curtis, ed., *Russia: A Country Study*, Washington: GPO for the Library of Congress 1996 on http://countrystudies.us/russia/38.htm (31.03.2017).

made up 67.9 percent, "while among the literate, the number was 79.2 percent."[53] The problem with these figures was not only that the Stalinist party program of the 1930s had declared education an important element for overcoming religion as well as for achieving the transition from socialism to communism, but that education seemed to have had the opposite effect since the percentage of believers among the literate was even higher.

The Bolshevist approach to Islam, the second religion in the Russian Empire in 1917 (16 million followers, ten percent of the population), was at first different from their treatment of the Orthodoxy because the Bolshevists regarded Muslims as colonized peoples and promised them national, religious, and cultural autonomy in order to win them over. In their appeal to the "toiling and disinherited Muslims in Russia and the East", Lenin and Stalin urged them to support "the revolution and plenipotentiary government":

> Moslems of Russia, Tartars of the Volga and the Crimea, Kirghiz, and Sarts of Siberia and Turkestan, Turks and Tartars of Transcaucasia, Chechens and Mountaineers of the Caucasus–all those whose mosques and chapels have been destroyed, whose beliefs and customs have been trampled upon by the tsars and oppressors of Russia! Henceforth your beliefs and customs, your national and cultural institutions, are free and inviolable. Build your national life freely and unhindered. You have a right to do so. (…) Not at the hands of Russia and her revolutionary government does slavery await you, but at the hands of the marauders of European imperialism, of those who converted our fatherland into their ravished and plundered "colony."[54]

In September, 1920, the Communist International organized the "Congress of the Peoples of the East" with 1891 delegates in Baku, issuing a call for a "holy war" (*jihād*) against British imperialism.[55] Upon his stay in Moscow in 1923, the Indonesian communist Tan Malaka (1897–1947), who was convinced of the compatibility of religion and communism, could not only publish books in Russian, but was also appointed the Comintern representative for Southeast Asia.[56]

53 Kira V. Tsekhanskaia, "Russia: Trends in Orthodox Religiosity in the Twentieth Century (Statistics and Realty)," in: *Religion and Politics in Russia: A Reader*, Marjorie Mandelstam Balzer, ed., New York: Routledge 2010, 3–17, 7.

54 Council of People's Commissars "Appeal to the Moslems of Russia and the East," *Izvestija* (7 December 1917), http://soviethistory.msu.edu/1921-2/the-muslim-east/the-muslim-east-texts/appeal-to-the-moslems-of-russia-and-the-east (11.04.2017) (Slightly revised translation).

55 Brian Pearce (trans.), *Congress of the Peoples of the East, Baku, September 1920. Stenographic Report, translated and annotated by Brian Pearce*, New York: New Park Publications 1977. www.marxists.org/history/international/comintern/baku/cpe-baku-pearce.pdf (29.05.2017).

56 On this see Stephen Suleyman Schwartz, *Islam and Communism in the 20th Century. An Historical Survey*, London: Center for Islamic Pluralism 2009, 1–30, 3. www.islamicpluralism.org/documents/islam-communism.pdf (30.05.2017). See also Maka-

In the early years after the revolution, the Soviets had neither a clear idea of Islam nor a clear strategy on how to deal with it.[57] Although they confiscated the assets and lands of religious endowments (*awqāf*) in Central Asia and tried to eliminate religious influence from state, law, and schools, they temporarily backpedalled in 1922, giving up the confiscated assets for free and allowing parallel Sharia courts (for family affairs and smaller crimes) as well as parallel Islamic schools.[58] They not only lacked sufficient means to establish a region-wide secular school system, but still struggled to gain full control over Central Asian territories. From 1917 to 1926, the so-called "Muslim clergy" was allowed to convene congresses, elect the *muftī* and his *qāḍīs* in the reformed Muslim Spiritual Administration, and voice its demands; the *muftī* could also travel abroad to praise Soviet anti-colonial policy.[59]

In the "relatively pluralistic period"[60] until 1927, Soviet academic scholars offered different answers to the question of the class character of Islam and Muslim societies. While some argued that Islam was trade-capitalist by nature, since it emerged from the trading community of Mecca, others held that Islam reflected the interest of peasants and the Bedouin, and found pristine communist elements in Islam. In this context, Bandalī Jawzī (1871–1942), who descended from a Christian family in Jerusalem and had taught Arabic Literature in Kazan and Baku since the end of the 19th century, wrote a study on socio-revolutionary movements in early Islam, published in Arabic in Jerusalem.[61] Drawing on the Persian and Zoroastrian Babak's (d. 838) revolt against the Arab caliphate, he argued that remnants of this movement were assimilated by various revolutionary Shiite groups like the Ismailites and Qarmatians, which followed similar social and "internationalist" goals and in-

la's speech at the Comintern in 1922, in which he equated Pan-Islamism with "the practical liberation struggle" of "all the oppressed Muslim peoples," Tan Makala, "Communism and Pan-Islamism," www.whatnextjournal.org.uk/Pages/Back/Wnext21/Panislam.html (11.08.2017).

57 Michael Kemper, "The Soviet Discourse on the Origin and Class Character of Islam, 1923–1933," *Die Welt des Islams* 49 (2009), 1–48; idem, "Red Orientalism: Mikhail Pavlovich and Marxist Oriental Studies in Early Soviet Russia," *Die Welt des Islams* 50 (2010), 435–476; Greg Castillo, "Soviet Orientalism: Socialist Realism and Built Tradition," *Traditional Dwellings and Settlements Review* 8: 2 (1997), 33–47.

58 Frank Nesemann, "Der Sowjetstaat und der Islam 1917–1941," in: Gassenschmidt and Tuchtenhagen, *Politik und Religion*, 207–234, 214–216.

59 See Michael Kemper, "From 1917 to 1937: The Muftī, the Turkologist, and Stalin's Terror", *Die Welt des Islams* 57 (2017), 162–191, 169, 171 and 172f.

60 Kemper, "The Soviet Discourse," 1.

61 Bandalī Jawzī, *Min tārīkh al-ḥarakāt al-fikriyya fī l-Islām*, Jerusalem 1928; Tamara Sonn, *Interpreting Islam. Bandali Jawzi's Islamic Intellectual History*, New York: Oxford Univ. Press 1996.

fluenced many Muslim philosophers and Sufis.[62] Similar views were also expressed by the Volga Tatar Zinatullah Navshirvanov and his (anonymous) wife in 1923, who detected several forms of (primitive) communism from the times of Muḥammad up to heterodox and Sufi movements, in the revolts against the feudal systems of ʿAbbasid, Selcuk, and Ottoman dynasties; the climax of this "Sufi communist movement" was Shaykh Bedreddin of Simavna, executed by the Ottomans in 1416, whose disciples set up the "first revolutionary government of Anatolia."[63]

Under Stalin, after the Bolshevists had won the Civil War, the approach to religion in general and to Islam in particular changed fundamentally. Not only was the League of the Godless (1925) and the subsequent League of the Militant Godless (1929) established, a new law for religious communities prohibited "religious propaganda" (1929). By the end of the 1920s, the view had crystallized that Islam was "feudal" in character and had not emerged as a progressive protest movement. This theory was taught to students of colonial countries from outside the USSR via the Communist University of the Toilers of the East (CUT)[64] between 1921 and the late 1930s and after that via different universities in the Soviet Union. The scholar Liutsian Klimovich (1907–1989), member of the League of the Militant Godless in his hometown Kazan, even argued in 1930 that the Quran and Muḥammad were mere inventions.[65] Such views underpinned the increasing pressure on Islamic institutions and Muslims.[66]

By then, the Communist Party had already initiated the so-called *hücum* ("attack") in Uzbekistan, Tajikistan, Turkmenistan and Transcaucasia, an unveiling campaign which started on International Women's Day, 8 March, 1927, and sought to eradicate the practice of wearing the *burqa*-like *paranja* within six months, just in time to celebrate the tenth anniversary of the revolution.[67] The Party's Women's Department (Zhenotdel), mostly com-

---

62 Tamara Sonn, "Bandali al-Jawzi's Intellectual History of Islam: an Original Interpretation from Azerbaijan," *Islamic Studies* 33 (1994), 203–226, 214–216.

63 Kemper, "The Soviet Discourse," 6–8, 7.

64 Students included, among others, the Syrian Secretary-General Khālid Bakdāsh (1912–1995), the Iraqi First Secretary Yūsuf Salmān Yūsuf (1901–1949), and the Turkish poet Nâzım Hikmet (1902–1963).

65 On Klimovich see Kemper, "The Soviet Discourse," 28–34; on the lecture "Did Muḥammad Exist?" ibid., 32f.

66 See Kemper, "The Soviet Discourse," and idem, "From 1917 to 1937."

67 Douglas Northrop, *Veiled Empire: Gender and Power in Stalinist Central Asia*, Ithaca: Cornell Univ. Press 2004; idem, "Hujum: unveiling campaigns and local responses in Uzbekistan, 1927," in: *Provincial Landscapes: Local Dimensions of Soviet Power, 1917–1953*, Donald J. Raleigh, ed., Pittsburgh: Univ. of Pittsburgh Press 2001, 125–145; Adrienne Edgar, "Bolshevism, patriarchy, and the nation: the Soviet 'emancipation' of Muslim women in pan-Islamic perspective,"*Slavic Review* 65: 2 (2006), 252–272.

posed of Russian and other Slavic members, believed that the status of Muslim women could be elevated by this campaign.

> As late as August 1925–only slightly more than one year before the *hujum* started–the main speaker at an all-Uzbek Zhenotdel meeting portrayed unveiling as positively un-Bolshevik, arguing that ensuring the "economic and material security of women is the fundamental path for the solution of the 'woman question'" … .[68]

The campaign met with different forms of opposition and resistance and turned the *paranja* into an identity marker. It further increased the social pressures on unveiled women and led to different forms of harassment, "in which thousands of Uzbek women were attacked, raped, even murdered and mutilated", so that special laws were passed "deeming such acts 'counter-revolutionary' state crimes, and 'terrorist acts' meriting the death penalty."[69]

These reactions to the *hücum* campaign provided the pretext and set the stage for the following crackdown on the so-called "anti-progressive" Islamic institutions and their representatives. New legislative and administrative measures–like the decree for the obligatory registration of religious communities (1929)–provided the Bolshevists with the opportunity to outlaw most Islamic communities, nationalize the religious endowments, and prohibit alms-giving (*zakāh*).[70] The number of mosques decreased to 1,300 (from more than 26,000), the number of religious scholars (*ʿulamāʾ*) to about 8,800 (from several ten thousands) until 1941.[71] The Gulag system had a category of prisoners called "Arabists," whose ability to read Islamic texts in Arabic was deemed "hostile to the state;" many of the Marxist writers of Islam as well as Muslim communists perished in Stalin's terror.[72] Apart from these measures, the nationality and language policy aimed at artificially separating Muslims from each other. On the one hand, different dialects were treated as "languages," which helped to separate Turkestan into five Soviet republics in the mid-1920s.[73] On the other hand, alphabets based on Latin script–"the international script of the coming world revolution"–were imposed in the Muslim regions at the end of the 1920s, but replaced by the Cyrillic script between 1937 and 1940. Thus, Muslims were

---

68 Northrop, *Veiled Empire,* 81. That "Bolshevik women were encouraged to wear the hijab to enter the villages to help educate young Muslim women" before Stalin's campaign against the veil, is mentioned by Chris Bambery, "The Moon and the Stars: Bolshevism and Islam," *Counterfire* (15.02.2017), www.counterfire.org/articles/history/18769-the-moon-and-stars-bolshevism-and-islam (11.08.2017).

69 Douglas Northrop, "Subaltern dialogues: subversion and resistance in Soviet Uzbek family law," *Slavic Review* 60: 1 (2001), 115–139, 119.

70 Nesemann, "Der Sowjetstaat und der Islam," 219f.

71 Ibid, 221.

72 Ibid, 222; also Kemper, "The Soviet Discourse," and Ben Fowkes and Bülent Gökay, "Unholy Alliance: Muslims and Communists–An Introduction," *Journal of Communist Studies and Transition Politics* 25: 1 (2009), 1–31, 14f.

73 Nesemann, "Der Sowjetstaat und der Islam," 218.

not only separated from their cultural heritage written in Arabic script, but also from the Republic of Turkey, which started to use Latin script after the language reform in 1928.[74] A growing Russification in the school system, from the 1930s onwards, additionally widened the artificial gulf to include Uyghurs and Kazakhs in China, Tajiks and Uzbeks in Afghanistan, and Azeri-Turks in Iran.

The number of Muslims inside communist party organizations in the predominantly Muslim parts of the USSR had steadily grown until the end of the 1920s. Because many shared pan-Turk and pan-Islamic ambitions, they met with growing suspicion and, as the highest ranks were reserved for Russians, they were also more likely to fall victim to the Great Purge like, for example, the Volga-Tatar Mirsaid Sultan-Galiev (1880–1940) and his supporters.[75] Sultan-Galiev, who became a Communist Party member prior to the October revolution, was active in organizing the defence against the Whites in Kazan in 1918 and 1919 and became the highest ranking Muslim in the Bolshevist party apparatus in Moscow, working together with Stalin in the People's Commissariat of Nationalities (Narkomnats), where he spoke for the Tatar Autonomous Soviet Socialist Republic (TASSR), created in 1920 with Kazan as its capital. Arguing that the revolution also meant a liberation of non-Russians from their Russian masters, he worked to form an autonomous republic for Turk peoples which might also include non-Turk Muslims. In 1923 he was arrested and expelled from the party on the charges of nationalist, pan-Islamic, and pan-Turk deviations. When freed the following year, he intensified his plans to form an "International of colonized peoples," believing that "Islam was the key to throwing off the yoke of imperialism in its domain" and tried to form a "union of colonized peoples against the metropolitans."[76] He was arrested again, convicted of the same charges, and finally executed.

The German assault on the Soviet Union in 1941 instigated a religio-political course correction. After the crackdown on religious institutions in Russia and Central Asia in the 1930s, Stalin now sought a *modus vivendi* with the Russian Orthodox Church and the other religions in order to enhance the Soviet peoples' resilience in the face of the assault. For Muslims, the war had two contrary effects. Under the pretext of collaboration with the German occupiers of Crimea, the Crimean Tatars and other pre-dominantly

74 Ibid, 222f.

75 On Galiev see Maxime Rodinson, "A Forgotten Precursor," in: idem, *Marxism and the Muslim World*, London: Zed Books 2015, 133–141; Fowkes and Gökay "Unholy Alliance," 4f. On the background of the growing tensions between Stalin and Galiev see also Alfred J. Rieber, *Stalin and the Struggle for Supremacy in Eurasia*, Cambridge: Cambridge Univ. Press 2015, 72–80.

76 Sonn, "Intellectual History," 210.

Muslim "nationalities" from the Caucasus were deported in 1943 and 1944 to Siberia and Central Asia. At the same time, four spiritual administrations for Muslims in the USSR were created, headed by muftis, all of whom had been in exile, prison, or banishment before.[77]

With the final consolidation of Soviet rule after the war, the Bolsheviks accepted loyal religious activities within narrow limits. In Bukhara and Tashkent–towns which once were famous for having over a hundred schools for Islamic teaching (*madrasas*)–two schools of higher education became the only legally accessible Islamic universities in the Soviet Union: The Mir-i-Arab Madrasa in Bukhara, founded in 1540, shut down in the 1920s and re-established in 1945, and the Baraq-Khan Madrasa in Tashkent (1956–1961), which was turned into the Tashkent Islamic Institute of Imam Bukhari in 1971.[78] Official religious scholars aimed to reconcile Islam with science, presented it as a bulwark of progress and peace, and portrayed Muḥammad as a reformer, revolutionary, and socialist.[79] For this purpose, the official monthly "Muslims of the Soviet East" was published in Tashkent from 1968.

As the Soviets sought to transform Central Asia into a "display window,"[80] the relationship between Islam and the Soviet Union has been described as "a growing process of give and take,"[81] since Central Asia "became the most technologically advanced region in the Islamic world"[82] since the 1950s. In spite of a similarly devastating crackdown on its religious institutions and education system, Islam, as a religion and an identity, was less competitive with communism than Christianity;[83] Communist Party members throughout Central Asia could publicly appear as self-proclaimed Muslims, although atheist ones, since Muslim identity was treated as part of an ethnic or national marker.[84]

The Reception of Marxist and Bolshevist Ideas in the Middle East

The adoption and reworking of Marxist ideas in the Ottoman Empire, the Middle East, North Africa, and Muslim-majority countries happened in

77 Nesemann, "Der Sowjetstaat und der Islam," 226.

78 Ashirbek Muminov, Uygun Gafurov, and Rinat Shigabdinov, "Islamic Education in Soviet and post-Soviet Uzbekistan", in: *Islamic Education in the Soviet Union and Its Successor States*, Michael Kemper, Raoul Motika and Stefan Reichmuth, eds., London: Routledge 2010, 223–279, 250f.

79 Seyfettin Erşahin, "The Interpretation of Islam under the Soviet Regime," *Journal für Religionskultur* 77 (2005), 1–19.

80 Schwartz, *Islam and Communism*, 13.

81 Paul Froese, "'I am an Atheist and a Muslim': Islam, Communism, and Ideological Competition," *Journal of Church and State* 47: 3 (2005), 473–501, 487.

82 Ibid.

83 Ibid, 498.

84 Ibid, 497.

several stages that can be divided into the period before World War I, the interwar period, the Cold War, and the period after the demise of the USSR. As the Eastern Mediterranean formed an internationalized labour market since the mid-19th century, workers and worker movement activists were formative in spreading Marxism and Anarchism at the turn of the century, often inspired by their European co-workers and European–mainly British, French, Italian or Greek–anti-imperialists.[85] The interwar period saw the formation of communist parties in most Arab countries or countries with a Muslim-majority population. The 1960s and 1970s were characterized by the formation of a new left and the Sino-Russian conflict, both of which also left their imprint on the Middle East. In the 1990s, Marxists tried to revise their policies, while the formation of a "new new left" has taken shape in recent years.[86]

The first socialist and Marxist organizations in the late Ottoman period were founded as underground groups by members of non-Muslim minorities.[87] After the Young Turk Revolution in 1908, Avraam Benaroya, a Sephardic Jew from Bulgaria and member of the Bulgarian Social Democratic Workers' Party, formed the most powerful workers' movement, the Socialist Workers' Federation, in Salonika, which included all ethnic and nationalist

85 Ilham Khuri-Makdisi, *The Eastern Mediterranean and the Making of Global Radicalism, 1860–1914*, Berkeley: Univ. of California Press 2010; Joel Beinin and Zachary Lockman, *Workers on the Nile: Nationalism, Communism, Islam and the Egyptian Working Class, 1882–1954*, Princeton: Princeton Univ. Press 1987; Joel Beinin, *Workers and Peasants in the Modern Middle East,* Cambridge: Cambridge Univ. Press 2001.

86 See Jacques Couland, Ziba Moshaver and William Hale, "Shuyuʿiyya," *Encyclopedia of Islam*[2] IX, Leiden: Brill 1997, 517–524; Anne Alexander, "Communism in the Islamic World," in: *The Oxford Handbook of the History of Communism*, Stephen A. Smith, ed., Oxford: Oxford Univ. Press 2014, 268–284; Sami A. Hanna and George H. Gardner, eds., *Arab Socialism. A Documentary Survey*, Leiden: Brill 1969; Tareq Y. Ismael, *The Communist Movement in the Arab World*, London: Routledge 2005; Orit Bashkin, *The Other Iraq. Pluralism and Culture in Hashemite Iraq*, Stanford: Stanford Univ. Press 2009; Roel Meijer, *Quest for Modernity. Secular Liberal and Left-Wing Political Thought in Egypt 1945–1958*, London: Routledge 2002; Hanna Batatu, *The Old Social Classes and the Revolutionary Movements of Iraq: A Study of Iraq's Old Landed and Commercial Classes and of its Communists, Baʿthists, and Free Officers*, Princeton: Princeton Univ. Press 1978; Faleh A. Jabar, "The Arab Communist Parties in Search of an Identity," in: *Post-Marxism and the Middle East*, idem, ed., London: Saqi Books 1997; Sune Haugbolle, "Bassem Chit and Revolutionary Socialism in Lebanon," *Middle East Topics and Arguments* 6 (2016), 65–74.

87 These groups were the Hunchak (1887), founded by Armenian Marxists, the Dashnak, founded by Armenian Socialists and Nationalists, the Bulgarian Social Democratic Workers' Party (1891) and the Internal Macedonian Revolutionary Organization (1892), see Yavuz Köse, "'Ich bin Sozialist, gib mir die Hälfte deines Vermögens.' Rezeption des Sozialismus und Kommunismus in spätosmanischer Zeit (1870–1914)," in: *Judaism, Christianity, and Islam in the Course of History: Exchange and Conflicts*, Lothar Gall and Dietmar Willoweit, eds., München: Oldenbourg 2011, 105–122, 111; also see George S. Harris, *The Origins of Communism in Turkey*, Stanford, Calif.: Hoover Inst. on War, Revolution and Peace 1967.

groups;[88] he later also played a key role in the foundation of the Communist Party in Greece in 1918. In Egypt, the drive for equality and full citizenship made Syrian Christians–Faraḥ Anṭūn, Shiblī Shumayyil, and Niqūlā Ḥaddād–and the Coptic intellectual Salāma Mūsā the foremost advocates of socialism in the Arab world in the opening decades of the 20th century.[89] Generally speaking, the members of religious and ethnic minority groups (Jews, Berbers, Armenians, Kurds, Alawites, Druze, and Shiites), who suffered discrimination from the state or the social majority, were often over-represented in socialist and communist parties in North Africa and the Middle East since they were inclined to openly downplay religious or ethnic identities in politics and rather underlined the communalities of all human beings or internationalism.

While communist groups that came into being from Morocco to Indonesia after the Bolshevist revolution remained relatively small in membership in the 1920s, they began to attract broader support in the emerging middle class (students, lawyers, journalists, and teachers) since the 1940s.[90] Migrant workers, teachers, and students also spread leftist ideas in the Gulf region since the 1940s.[91] After strikes in the Saudi oil industry in 1953 in 1956 and a harsh crackdown, they were forced underground or into exile, but managed to maintain transnational networks. As the situation in every Arab country was different, and the conditions for Marxist activities changed over time, phases of toleration and co-optation followed phases of persecution, which made the Marxists adopt parliamentarian, authoritarian, clandestine, and armed tactics.[92]

Mostly, the communist party of the colonial power was a key link between the local groups and Moscow.[93] That the Soviet, French, and British communist parties were ideologically dogmatic, but politically pragmatic often created difficulties for Marxists in colonial countries. This became visible in their hesitant support for the national independence movement in Algeria and Palestine and, more generally, in their backing-down on their own interests for the sake of geo-political deliberations by their Soviet or European counterparts. For example, the largest Egyptian communist organization, *al-Ḥaraka al-Dimuqrāṭiyya li-l-Taḥarrur al-Waṭanī* (HADITU,

88 Köse, "'Ich bin Sozialist'," 113.

89 Donald M. Reid, "The Syrian Christians and Early Socialism in the Arab World," *International Journal of Middle East Studies* 5 (1974), 177–193.

90 Alexander, "Communism," 273.

91 Toby Matthiesen, "Migration, Minorities, and Radical Networks: Labour Movements and Opposition Groups in Saudi-Arabia, 1950–1975," *International Review of Social History* 59: 3 (2014), 473–504.

92 For the trajectories of some of the major Arab communist parties see Ismael, *The Communist Movement*.

93 Alexander, "Communism," 273.

Democratic Movement for National Liberation), had to face "stern criticism by leading figures in the British and French communist parties for its initial support for the Free Officers, partly because Soviet leaders were concerned that the Free Officers might be pro-American."[94] The British CP proposed a common front between HADITU and the Muslim Brotherhood, "which it had previously characterized as fascist."[95] With the nationalization of the Suez Canal and the Tripartite Aggression in 1956, the Soviet Union changed its assessment and declared ʿAbd al-Nāṣir (1918–1970) the leader of a "victorious national revolution."[96]

That the 20th Party Congress of the CPSU in 1956 adopted a new strategy, supporting "national independence movements" and "non-capitalist development" in post-colonial countries, made Soviet foreign policy more flexible in its search for allies, even in cases like in Egypt, where a regime which aligned itself with the Soviets, persecuted, imprisoned and tortured local communists. The new strategy also helped local communists to take the role of junior partners in authoritarian regimes that pledged themselves to state-led modernization. However, when the hopes for economic and political modernization were shaken by the 1970s, "the communist movement itself fragmented, as dissident groups critical of the alliances with nationalist regimes emerged."[97]

South Yemen was the only Arab country and–besides Albania (1944–1991), Somalia (1969–1977), and Afghanistan (1978–1992)–one of the few Muslim-majority countries under Marxist-Leninist rule (1969–1990). With Soviet blessings and at South Yemen's request, East Germany implemented what can be termed "a socialist state- and nation-building policy close to neo-colonialist aspirations."[98] Since East Berlin was tasked by the Soviet Union to develop the fields of law, governance, economy, education, media, and the security apparatus, it tried to model the People's Democratic Republic of Yemen according to its own version of a socialist state; Soviet support for its close Yemeni ally was mainly restricted to military and ideological concerns.

---

94 Ibid, 276.

95 Ibid.

96 Ibid.

97 Ibid, 277f. A telling example is the fragmentation of Syrian communists and Marxists since 1970.

98 Miriam M. Müller, *A Spectre is Haunting Arabia. How the Germans Brought Their Communism to Yemen*, Bielefeld: Transcript 2015, 376.

The Role of Atheism in Communist State-Building

Although militant atheism was a determining element of Soviet politics, it was not a central element of its ideology.[99] This subtlety–that atheism is only a side effect of a materialistic worldview–explains not only Lenin's flexibility, but becomes more obvious, when the Soviet practices are compared to the practices of other socialist regimes or communist parties in Muslim-majority countries. The establishment of communist regimes after World War II generally went hand in hand with the suppression of independent religious organizations, the abolition of religious courts and schools, and the cooptation of those religious scholars who survived persecution. Yet, the anti-religious rationale locally played out in different trajectories and different phases of persecution and accommodation.

In Yugoslavia, after the liberation from German occupation, the communists under Josip Broz Tito (1892–1980) subdued aspirations for autonomy among Muslims in Bosnia by means which also included massacres and expulsions in 1948.[100] Muslims were forced to choose between a Croatian or Serbian identity, and the central mosque in Zagreb was torn down. This policy of assimilation was gradually loosened beginning in 1955, and in 1968 Bosnians were recognized as a "Muslim nationality" alongside four other nationalities, while their fellow Muslims in Kosovo and Macedonia were still treated separately and counted among the respective Albanian and Macedonian nationalities. Former restrictions on religious life–like restrictions on performing the *hajj* to Mecca–were removed, Sufism was permitted to revive, the building of mosques and the opening of madrasas for religious instruction were allowed again, and children could receive religious education.[101] Sarajevo thus became a center for state-visits by politicians and religious representatives from all over the Muslim world.

In neighboring Albania, in a kind of reverse process, the first decades of communist rule were characterized by cooptation, "with the appointment of official heads of both the Sunni community and the Bektashi Sufis, who had the job of pretending to the outside world that Muslims were both well-

---

99 The three defining elements of Marxism-Leninism, as formulated by Stalin in 1938, were dialectical and historical materialism (as the historical and epistemological basis), political economy (as the sociological understanding of the relations of productions), and scientific communism (as the doctrine of class struggle and revolution). These elements constituted Marxism-Leninism as a "scientific worldview," which was opposed to superstition and religion and, because of its philosophical and practical consequences, "immanently atheistic."

100 On Yugoslavia see Durán Khalid, "Der Islam in der Diaspora: Europa und Amerika," in: *Der Islam in der Gegenwart*, Werner Ende and Udo Steinbach, eds., München: Beck [3]1991, 440–469, 440–448.

101 Fowkes and Gökay, "Unholy Alliance," 18.

treated and entirely supportive of the communist government."[102] After the break with Yugoslavia in 1948 and the USSR in 1961, Enver Hoxha (1908–1985) started to rely massively on Chinese support (until 1978) and followed Mao's example of a Great Proletarian Cultural Revolution (1966–1976), declaring Albania "the first atheist state on earth," whereby all places of worship were closed, all religious communities dissolved, and religious names forbidden.[103] The Chinese Red Guards, at the same time, also mounted attacks on, among others, Muslim believers in Xinjiang (East Turkestan), destroying mosques and cultural assets, and prohibiting the study of the Quran.[104] Prior to these attacks, pressure on Muslims in Xinjiang had steadily increased after the Soviets, who had indirectly controlled the regional players since the 1930s, helped to bring the multi-ethnic region under Chinese communist rule.[105] After the takeover, the Chinese communists created the state-controlled Islamic Association of China (1953), curbed traditional Muslim activities, and facilitated the settlement of Han Chinese in Xinjiang, which earned them the charge of a "Sinicization" of the region, levelled at them by Uyghur activists and the Soviets after the Sino-Soviet split (since 1960).

The German Democratic Republic has never defined itself as an atheistic state; atheism was rather the "unloved stepchild"[106] of GDR philosophy, and the term as such was used sparsely.[107] Although the historian of philosophy Hermann Ley (1911–1990) wrote a multi-volume history of atheism, an academic research focus on atheism comparable to the USSR could not be established, and the only professorship for "scientific atheism" was a short-lived institution in the 1960s.[108] The subject as such was an import from the USSR and the bulk of publications on atheism appeared at the end of the 1950s and in the early 1960s, at the height of the Cold War.[109] Beginning in 1973, however, the state and the "churches in socialism" aimed at an arrangement, after different incidents of confrontation and attempts at rapprochement.[110] After the self-immolation of Pastor Oskar

102 Ibid.

103 Ibid.

104 Thomas Heberer, "Volksrepublik China," in: *Der Islam in der Gegenwart*, Werner Ende and Udo Steinbach, eds., München: Beck ^{5}2005, 306–318, 313.

105 On this see for example Eva-Maria Stolberg, *Stalin und die chinesischen Kommunisten 1945–1953. Eine Studie zur Entstehungsgeschichte der sowjetisch-chinesischen Allianz vor dem Hintergrund des Kalten Krieges*, Stuttgart: Fritz Steiner 1997.

106 Manfred Lauermann, "Der Atheismus – das ungeliebte Stiefkind der DDR-Philosophie," in: *Atheismus: Ideologie, Philosophie oder Mentalität?*, Richard Faber and Susanne Lanwerd, eds., Würzburg: Königshausen & Neumann 2006, 121–147.

107 Horst Groschopp, "Atheismus und Realsozialismus in der DDR," *humanismus aktuell* 20 (2007), 62–83.

108 Kirsch, *Weltanschauung*, 374f. For the USSR see Konstantin Antonov, "Der 'wissenschaftliche Atheismus' in der UdSSR," *una sancta* 67: 2 (2012), 115–124.

109 Lauermann, "Der Atheismus," Kirsch, *Weltanschauung*, 375.

110 Lauermann, "Der Atheismus," 134; Wirth, "Marxismus, Glauben, Religion ," 734f.

Brüsewitz (1929–1976), who protested against the repression of religion, denigrating reports about him and his action appeared in the state media. In order to control the damage caused by these reports, the state changed direction and the head of the State Council, Erich Honecker (1912–1994), agreed to his only-ever reception of high church representatives in 1978. Finally, a common commemorative year for Marx and Luther, who was formerly also dubbed "the gravedigger of revolution," was held in 1983.[111]

With these examples in mind, it is therefore not surprising that–in the broader context of anti-colonial struggles and post-World War II nation-building–communist organizations in Muslim-majority countries, which did not hold political power, were instructed by Moscow not to engage in anti-religious propaganda, but to forge alliances with "progressive" bourgeois forces.[112] They adopted a rather lenient approach on religion and Islam, which appeared inconsistent or outright opportunistic. The fact, for example, that the Iraqi Communist Party had mounted an anti-religious campaign in 1929–in order to "liberate the Arab woman from the fetters of degradation and ignorance"–was already in 1935 seen as a serious tactical error.[113] In contrast, the communists in Indonesia not only tried to reconcile Marxism with Islam, but openly adopted, in 1960, President Sukarno's (1901–1970) *pancasila* (Five Principles), the first of which stipulated "belief in one God," hoping that this would appeal to Muslims or at least help "to avoid rejection out of hand as a party of atheists."[114] This did not, however, prevent top army leaders and the main Muslim organizations from calling for the annihilation of the Communist Party after an alleged attempted coup, shortly after Sukarno had declared in 1965 that Indonesia had to enter the second stage of its revolution, namely socialism; thousands of

111 For the background of this shift see Hartmut Lehmann, "The Rehabilitation of Martin Luther in the GDR; or, Why Thomas Müntzer Failed to Stabilise the Moorings of Socialist Ideology," in: *Religion and the Cold War*, Dianne Kirby, ed., Basingstoke: Palgrave Macmillan 2003, 200–210; idem, "Die 15 Thesen der SED über Martin Luther" and "Zur Entstehung der 15 Thesen über Martin Luther für die Luther-Ehrung der DDR im Jahre 1983", in: idem, *Luthergedächtnis 1817 bis 2017*, 213–231 and 232–256. Also see *Der Spiegel*, "Mit Herrn Luther ist alles in Butter" (07.03.1983), www.spiegel.de/spiegel/print/d-14018281.html (12.04.2017); Axel Noack, "Das Jahr, in dem Luther zum Nationalhelden wurde" (06.03.2017), www.mitteldeutsche-kirchenzeitungen.de/2017/03/06/das-jahr-in-dem-luther-zum-nationalhelden-der-ddr-wurde (12.04.2017); Webpage *Luther2017*, "Altbischof Leich: Honecker feierte das Lutherjahr 1983 'mit einer Träne im Knopfloch'," https://www.luther2017.de/de/wiki/jubilaeum/altbischof-leich-honecker-feierte-das-lutherjahr-1983-mit-einer-traene-im-knopfloch (12.04.2017).

112 Fowkes and Gökay, "Unholy Alliance," 18.

113 Ibid, 15 and footnote 66.

114 Ibid, 21.

communists were massacred without any resistance and the army moved to depose Sukarno.[115]

Another example of a pro-Islamic stance is provided by the Indian communists prior to the partition of India. When the allied powers helped the USSR to fight the German assault after 1941, the communists took sides with Britain and also preferred the All-India Muslim League to the Indian National Congress, because the latter started a "Quit India" campaign against the colonial power just at that time. While the Congress leadership was imprisoned, the communists were allowed to act freely and supported Muhammad Ali Jinnah's (1876–1948) two-nation-theory, which claimed that India was inhabited by two nations, Muslims and Hindus. On the basis of Stalin's nationality theory, the communists listed 16 Indian "nations," based on language and religion, in a resolution in 1942. They thus collaborated with the Muslim League in its aim of partition, on the grounds that Jinnah, later the first president of Pakistan, stood for secular and even anti-religious politics.[116] Accordingly, the communists also partitioned–and weakened–their own party organization by sending Muslim members to East and West Pakistan to help form communist organizations there in early 1948.

In South Yemen, the East German constitution of 1968 served as the blueprint for the Yemeni constitution of 1970; nevertheless the GDR advisers obviously saw no problem in justifying political measures by referring to religious sources. Even the inclusion of Islam as the state religion in article 47 seems to go back to the East German advice that the national front government should "harness Islam for its cause," as "Islam could be adapted to the regime's ideology in what was called 'liberation theology'."[117] The GDR and USSR cadres in South Yemen did identify clan structures and tribalism, not Islam, as the major obstacle to socialist nation-building, and although they mounted "radical measures to abolish tribalism and tradition," they came to realize that even radical leaders could not escape their collective identities and "mostly drew their political power from tribal ties."[118]

In socialist Somalia, Muḥammad Ziyād Barre (1910–1995) likewise declared the compatibility of "scientific socialism" with Islam, because both demanded the realization of justice; meanwhile, he filled all important posts with members of his own clan. Islam remained the state religion and

---

115 The events and their background still remain largely in the dark.

116 See Donald Eugene Smith, *India as a Secular State*, London/Bombay: Oxford Univ. Press ^{2}1967, 142f.; for the background: Sobhanlal Datta Gupta, *Komintern und Kommunismus in Indien 1919–1943*, Berlin: Dietz 2013. After the partition, the communists changed direction several times.

117 See Müller, *A Spectre*, 261.

118 Ibid, 389f.

Islamic law was preferred to customary law, but the codification of family and inheritance laws in 1975, according to the South Yemeni example, strengthened the position of women, which led to protests among Islamic scholars, some of whom were executed.[119] The lost war over the Somali-inhabited Ogaden region (1977/78) prompted the break with the Soviet Union because it backed the socialist opponent Ethiopia together with the GDR and Cuba. This break, however, also secured new support from Western as well as Islamic financial sources for Somalia, among others from the USA, Italy, West Germany and the Arab Gulf.[120] In neighboring Ethiopia, the socialist regime (1974–1991) under Mengistu Haile Mariam (b. 1937) had meanwhile declared religious equality and freedom, yet not only pushed religion in general out of the public sphere, but also continued to politically marginalize Ethiopian Muslims.[121] The "Red Terror" (1976–78), mainly targeting rivaling Marxist-Leninist organizations, also prompted many Ethiopian Muslims to flee the country.

In the notorious case of Afghanistan, the communists' religious policy was divided into two contrasting phases: before and after the Soviet invasion. Although the People's Democratic Party of Afghanistan (PDPA) declared its respect for the principles of Islam following its seizure of power in April 1978, it also aimed "to cleanse Islam in Afghanistan of the ballast and dirt of bad traditions, superstition and erroneous belief" and to "have progressive, modern and pure Islam,"[122] in the words of President Nūr Muḥammad Tarakī (1929–1979). In practice, the regime in Kabul arrested Muslim religious leaders immediately after the coup and launched another concerted purge in January 1979.[123] It closed down religious colleges, abolished the Sufi orders, implemented confiscatory land policies, tried to reorganize the court system and failed to prevent party militants from attacking veiled women in rural areas. However, it not only alienated traditional

119 Hans Müller, "Horn von Afrika," in: *Der Islam in der Gegenwart*, Werner Ende and Udo Steinbach, eds., München: Beck ⁵2005, 455–468, 457f. Another reason for Islamic protests was that when Somali was declared the official language in 1972, its script was changed from Arabic to Latin.

120 For the background see Harry Ododa, "Somalia's Domestic Politics and Foreign Relations since the Ogaden War 1977–78," *Middle Eastern Studies* 21: 3 (1985), 285–297. West Germany paid 100 Million Marks in economic aid, after Somalia allowed the West German anti-terror group GSG 9 to end the hijacking of Lufthansa Flight 181 by a Palestinian commando, which had demanded the release of Red Army Faction prisoners in Germany, in Mogadishu Airport in 1977.

121 Müller, "Horn von Afrika," 463; Patrick Desplat and Terje Østepø, "Muslim Ethiopia: The Christian Legacy, Identity Politics, and Islamic Reformism," in: *Muslim Ethiopia: The Christian Legacy, Identity Politics, and Islamic Reformism*, idem, eds., New York: Palgrave Macmillan 2013, 1–20, 6f.

122 John Anderson, "Islam and the Afghan Regime," *Religion in Communist Lands* 14: 2 (1986), 172–179, 174.

123 Ibid, 175.

society, but failed to bring effective control over growing parts of the country. The Soviet invasion in late December 1979 had the immediate aim to depose Ḥāfiẓullāh Amīn[124] (1929–1979) and end internecine fighting, but also tried to soften the anti-Islamic image of the Afghan government. The newly-appointed President Babrak Kārmal (1929–1996) promised "respect for the sacred principles of Islam" in his first speech, and Islam was officially recognized as the state religion; Kārmal further decreed an amnesty for religious activists, agreed to the renovation of many mosques, subsidized pilgrimages to Mecca, and allowed the broadcasting of Quranic readings on state radio and the re-opening of many madrasas without the formal requirement that the colleges had to accept female students.[125] In this phase, the PDPA government followed the Soviet practice "to use an Islam that it could not ignore"[126] and created a Supreme Council of ʿUlamāʾ, made up mostly of young and unknown Muslim scholars, who defended its policies. Reacting to the worldwide Islamic critique of the Soviet invasion, the Soviet muftiate, responsible for the five Central Asian republics, not only formed the model for the Afghan course correction, but also became deeply involved in propaganda and diplomacy for the Afghan case.[127] On their regular visits to Kabul, Soviet Muslim leaders justified the Soviet presence in the name of Muslim solidarity, while delegations of Afghan mullahs in Tashkent praised the religious freedom of Muslims in the Soviet Union. From the mid-1980s, Afghan communists not only wished to appear respectful of Islam, but started to consider themselves true Muslims–as opposed to the *mujahidin*, whom they called bandits, criminals, counterrevolutionaries, and agents of imperialism, thus denying them any Islamic motivation.[128] In 1987, Kārmal's successor Muḥammad Najībullāh (1947–1996), the much-feared former chief of the Afghan secret service, went even further when he announced a new phase of the revolution, "the phase of national reconciliation," and recognized the *mujahidin* as "opposition forces."[129] In the course of the Soviet withdrawal, Najībullāh had all remaining references to Marxism and communism removed, and the 1990 constitu-

---

124 He was held responsible for the death of his long-time comrade Tarakī in October 1979 and was killed on the first day of the invasion.

125 Anderson, "Islam and the Afghan Regime," 176. Also compare Chantal Lobato, "Islam in Kabul: The Religious Politics of Babrak Karmal", *Central Asian Survey* 4: 4 (1985), 111–120; idem, "Kabul 1978–1988: Communists and Islam," *Religion in Communist Lands* 16: 4 (1988), 345–351.

126 Lobato, "Kabul 1978–1988," 345. See also Olivier Roy, "The Sovietization of Afghanistan," in: *Afghanistan and the Soviet Union: Collision and Transformation,* M. Hauner and R.L. Canfield, eds., Boulder: Westview Press 1989, 48–60.

127 See Eren Tasar, "The Central Asian Muftiate in Occupied Afghanistan, 1979-87," *Central Asian Survey* 30: 2 (2011), 213–226.

128 Lobato, "Kabul 1978–1988," 350f.; Tasar, "The Central Asian Muftiate," 218.

129 Lobato, "Kabul 1978–1988," 346.

tion declared Afghanistan an Islamic state. All these efforts to garner popular support and gain control of the country with an increasingly Islamic rhetoric failed and did not even save the regime's leaders like Najībullāh, whom the Taliban cruelly murdered on the grounds that he was against Islam, when they took Kabul.

The examples from different countries show that the accusation of atheism stuck to the communists in spite of phases of conciliatory policies and pro-Islamic rhetoric.

On the intellectual level, Soviet "scientific atheism" did not represent a monolithic approach to religion; it was rather compatible not only with differing practices but also with other historical and philosophical views. For example, it left some imprints on Arab and Muslim intellectuals that GDR historian Hermann Ley shared with Ernst Bloch not only an interest in early materialist and atheist tendencies in Christian Europe, but also in Ibn Sīnā (Avicenna) and Arab-Muslim philosophers. In his ceremonial address for the 1,000th anniversary of Ibn Sīnā's (980–1037 AD/370–428 AH) birthday according to the hijri calender, Bloch coined the term of the Aristotelian left.[130] Syrian philosopher Ṭayyib Tīzīnī (b. 1934), who had studied in Berlin and written his master's and doctoral thesis under the supervision of Ley in the 1960s, adapted Ley's methodological approach to the Islamic history of philosophy. Tīzīnī's approach is summarized in his book titles *Mashrūᶜ ru'ya jadīda li-l-fikr al-ᶜarabī fī l-ᶜaṣr al-wasīṭ* (*Project of a New View on Arabic Thought in the Middle Ages*, 1971) and *Min al-turāth ilā l-thawra* (*From Heritage to Revolution*, 1976). Tīzīnīs work coincided with a similar two-part work by the Lebanese Communist Ḥusayn Muruwwa (1910–1987) about *al-Nazaᶜāt al-maddiyya fī l-falsafa al-ᶜarabiyya al-islāmiyya* (*The Materialist Trends in Arab-Islamic Philosophy*, 1978).[131] For Tīzīnī and Muruwwa, it was clear that early Muslim philosophers had influenced thinkers in Europe and laid the basis for both a philosophical-scientific worldview and the dialectical-materialist theory.[132]

What these works express, however, is that a serious engagement with the history of early Islam was largely absent among Marxist Arab intellectuals

130 Ernst Bloch, *Avicenna und die aristotelische Linke*, Berlin: Rütten und Loening 1952. Avicenna was also commemorated in the USSR and by the World Peace Council in 1952; the "Deutsche Post" of the GDR printed a stamp in his honour, yet giving his birth date as 952, by mistaking Hijri for Gregorian years, see https://de.wikipedia.org/wiki/Datei:GDR-stamp_Avicenna_1952_Mi._314.JPG (04.09.2017).

131 Also compare the work: Maḥmūd Amīn al-ᶜĀlim, Ḥusayn Muruwwa, Muḥammad Dakrūb, and Samīr Saᶜd, *Dirāsāt fī l-Islām*, Jerusalem: Manshūrāt Ṣalāḥ al-Dīn 1980.

132 On Tīzīnī and Muruwwa see Anke von Kügelgen, *Averroes und die arabische Moderne. Ansätze zu einer Neubegründung des Rationalismus im Islam*, Leiden: Brill 1994, 237–260; Thomas Hildebrandt, *Neo-Mu'tazilismus? Intention und Kontext im modernen arabischen Umgang mit dem rationalistischen Erbe des Islam*, Leiden: Brill 2007, 252–265.

up to the 1970s. Bandalī Jawzī's work did not fall on fertile ground after its publication in 1928,[133] although it was later deemed to be an early precursor of writing Arab-Islamic history from a Marxist viewpoint.[134] The most prominent book on the history of atheism in Islam was not written by a Marxist, but by the Egyptian existentialist philosopher ʿAbd al-Raḥmān Badawī (1917–2002) in 1945.[135] Marxist analyses either dealt with the current problems of Arab societies and issues of contemporary history[136] or tried to apply the frame of an "Asian mode of production" to Arab history.[137] The search for another take on the history of early Islam in the 1970s primarily seems to have been a reaction to the ease with which Arab socialists, who had their heyday in Nasserist Egypt in the 1960s, blended socialism and Islam and spoke of Muḥammad and some of his companions as early socialists (see below). Muruwwa, for example, criticized representatives of Arab nationalism and Islamic socialism because of their "idealist" dealing with the heritage, by simply picking its positive sides and exaggerating them. What was needed, according to Muruwwa, was a revolutionary reinterpretation of the past, not the tendency to "modernize the heritage" (*taḥdīth al-turāth*), because lumping together modern theories and history trivialized both modern theories and historical thought.[138] Influenced by Soviet and GDR historians or works like French Marxist Maxime Rodinson's biography of Muḥammad,[139] Tīzīnī and Muruwwa tried to highlight the structural and materialist contexts of Arab-Islamic thought in history and argued–while the Islamic revolution in Iran was under way–that their interest in the past was part of the ideological struggles with bourgeois and conservative opponents.[140] Yet, their approaches did not remain unchal-

133 See Werner Ende, *Arabische Nation und islamische Geschichte. Die Umayyaden im Urteil arabischer Autoren des 20. Jahrhunderts*, Beirut: Steiner 1977, 89f.

134 See Ḥusayn Muruwwa, "Hākadhā naqraʾ Bandalī Jawzī," in: *Silsilat muʾallafāt Ḥusayn Muruwwa*, Muḥammad Dakrūb, ed., Beirut: Dār al-Fārābī 1993, 156–162.

135 ʿAbd al-Raḥmān Badawī, *Min tārīkh al-ilḥād fī l-Islām*, Cairo: Maktabat al-Nahḍa al-Miṣriyya 1945.

136 See for example the works by Anwar ʿAbd al-Malik, *Egypt: Military Society: The Army Regime, the Left, and Social Change under Nasser*, 1964, in English 1968, Mahmoud Hussein, *La lutte des classes en Égypte de 1945 à 1968*, Paris 1969, and Samīr Amīn, *La nation arabe: nationalisme et lutes des classes*, Paris 1976.

137 See Aḥmad Ṣādiq Saʿd, *Fī ḍaw al-namat al-āsyawī li-l-intāj: Tārīkh Miṣr al-ijtimāʿī al-iqtiṣādī*, Beirut: Dār Ibn Khaldūn 1979; Maḥmūd al-Kurdī, *Al-Takhalluf wa-mushkilat al-mujtamaʿ al-miṣrī*, Cairo: Dār al-Maʿārif 1979; on both of them see Wolfgang Schwanitz, "Karl A. Wittfogel, das Fünf-Stufen-Dogma und die Ägypter Ṣādiq Saʿad und Maḥmūd al-Kurdī," *asien, afrika, lateinamerika* 20 (1992), 29–41.

138 See Ḥusayn Muruwwa, *Al-Nazaʿāt al-maddiyya fī l-falsafa al-ʿarabiyya al-islāmiyya*, vol. I, Beirut: Dār Farābī 1978, 10–12; see, also for a critical reading, Hildebrandt, *Neo-Muʿtazilismus?*, 254–256.

139 Maxime Rodinson, *Mahomet*, Paris: Éditions du Seuil 1961.

140 See the interview with Muḥammad Dakrūb and Iliyās Shākir, "Marḥala jadīda fī dirāsat al-turāth," *al-Ṭarīq* 1 (1979), 21–79, 65–69.

lenged by the Marxist-Leninist orthodoxy. Tawfiq Sallūm, a scientist residing in Moscow, worked his way through Tīzīnī's and Muruwwa's books, highlighting inconsistencies and terminological weaknesses in the use of central terms like "materialism" and "materialist trends."[141]

After the downfall of the Soviet Union, the author Ibrahim Mahmoud of the pan-Arab Marxist-Leninist journal *al-Nahj* lamented that there had never existed a systematic Arab Marxist theory of religion or any real interest in Islam as a historical, social, or political phenomenon.[142] He argued that the treatment of Islam among Arab Marxists had either been informed (1) by the ideologically pre-conceived view that religion was irrational, (2) by Soviet Orientalism[143] or (3) by a mechanical application of Marxist terminology, for which he also faulted Tīzīnī and Muruwwa. By ignoring Islam to a large degree, Arab Marxists had failed to fulfil their own aim to change the world, which they had not even been able to understand in spite of their adoration of objective knowledge.[144]

Even in the face of the growing Islamic movement since the 1980s, the Marxist left was unable to find a common viewpoint on political Islam; leftist intellectuals could not decide whether it was a culturally appropriate or retrograde answer to neo-imperialism, whether it was reactionary or revolutionary, whether it disrupted or united Muslim-majority societies, and whether it represented the authentic will of the masses or the seduction of the mob.[145] Such discussions inside the Arab left foreshadowed similar discussions in the European left on Islam, Islamophobia, and terrorism after 9/11.

The Islamic Critique of Communism

Fatāwā *against Communism*

Islamic religious authorities have opposed Bolshevism, communism, and socialism on different occasions. In 1919, after the Soviets had revealed the se-

---

141 Tawfiq Sallūm, "Al-Māddiyya wa-tajalliyyātihā fi l-ʿaṣr al-wasīṭ," *al-Ṭarīq* 3 (1979), 181–194; idem, "'Al-Tārīkhiyya' fi dirāsat al-turāth al-falsafi," *al-Ṭarīq* 4 (1979), 193–210; idem, "Ḥizbiyyat al-falsafa," *al-Ṭarīq* 6 (1979), 131–145.

142 Ibrāhīm Maḥmūd, "Mafhūm al-dīn fi l-khiṭāb alʿarabī al-mārksī," *al-Nahj* 30 (1990), 181–202.

143 For Soviet Orientalism see Michael Kemper and Stephan Conermann, eds., *The Heritage of Soviet Oriental Studies*, London: Routledge 2011.

144 The author quotes Maḥmūd Amīn al-ʿĀlim, "The central point in Marxism lies not in the critique of heaven, but of earth. Marxism is not an institution to spread atheism, but a theory of the struggle to change and renew life. From this standpoint, Marxism treats religious movements and phenomena in an objective manner."

145 See for example Alexander Flores, *Säkularismus und Islam in Ägypten. Die Debatte der 1980er Jahre*, Berlin: LIT-Verlag 2012, 159–163.

cret Sykes-Picot-Sazonov agreements, the British authorities were concerned about anti-British agitation and the activities of a nascent socialist party in Egypt and asked the Grand Mufti, Shaykh Muḥammad Bakhīt (1854–1935), to issue a legal opinion (*fatwā*), which they also wanted to distribute in other parts of the British Empire to fight Bolshevism.[146] In the *fatwā*, Bakhīt described Bolshevism as a "teaching," "school" or "way" (*ṭarīqa*), destroying all Divine laws, especially those of Islam, and legalizing bloodshed, treachery, lies, and rape, thus "causing anarchy to spread among the people with regard to all their social affairs, finances, women, children, and heritages until they become at last worse than beasts."[147] Bakhīt also held that Bolshevism roused "the lower classes against every system based upon reason, moral, and virtue"[148] and aimed at destroying human societies, the order of the world, and religion. "Accordingly, every true Muslim ought to beware of them, stay far away from their errors (*ḍalālātuhum*), corrupt doctrines (*ʿaqāʾiduhum al-fāsida*), and badly selling deeds (*aʿmāluhum al-kāsida*) because they are without the slightest doubt infidels (*kuffār*), who do not believe in any of the Divine laws and revealed religions nor do they recognize any order."[149]

The British efforts to discredit Bolshevism backfired because the public and media interest provided socialists and Marxists with the opportunity to explain their cause. Several writers–among them even Muslim reformer Muḥammad Rashīd Riḍā (1865–1935)[150]–challenged the image of an anarchic, irreligious, and immoral Bolshevism, claiming that it was not contrary to Islam or any other religion, but consistent with the religion's stance against poverty and oppression and for freedom.[151] A Marxist leaflet even argued that Bolshevism was "a power which God has sent upon earth … in order to restore to Islam its old form and its famous justice."[152] Others, like the socialist writer Niqūlā Ḥaddād (1878–1954) with a Christian back-

[146] For the political background see Tareq Y. Ismael and Rifaʿat El-Saʿid, *The Communist Movement in Egypt 1920–1988*, New York: Syracuse Univ. Press 1990, 22–25; for a partial and free English translation ibid., 163–167; for the original text: Muḥammad Bakhīt, "Al-Madhhab al-bāshifi [sic!]" (02.07.1919), *Fatāwā Dār al-Iftāʾ al-Miṣriyya* http://shamela.ws/browse.php/book-432/page-2568 (13.04.2017). That the *fatwā* was released in response to a question in *The Times* is mentioned in Couland, Moshaver and Hale, "Shuyuʿiyya," 517.

[147] Bakhīt, "Al-Madhhab al-bāshifi;" revised translation following Ismael and El-Saʿid, *The Communist Movement*, 166.

[148] Ibid., 167.

[149] Ibid.

[150] See Couland, Moshaver and Hale, "Shuyuʿiyya," 517. He added that Muslims must hope for the success of communism, although it was not in conformity with Islamic law, but neither were the activities of European governments against Islam, see Albert Hourani, *Arabic Thought in the Liberal Age, 1798–1939*, London: Oxford Univ. Press 1962, 304.

[151] See Ismael and El-Saʿid, *The Communist Movement*, 24f.

[152] Ibid, 24.

ground, argued that socialism was a social, not a religious doctrine and "had nothing to do with religion."[153]

Azhar's opposition to communism was, however, unwavering. State Muftis like Ḥasanayn Muḥammad Makhlūf (1890–1990)[154] and Shuyūkh al-Azhar like Muḥammad Shaltūt (1893–1963) and ʿAbd al-Ḥalīm Maḥmūd (1910–1978) declared from the mid-1940s to the mid-1970s that communism was irreconcilable with Islamic principles; as the main points of difference, they named its social doctrine of class struggle, its materialistic philosophy, its anti-religious stance, and its prohibition of private property.

In 1948, the Fatwā Commission of the Azhar acted on a request by the Egyptian interior ministry to take a stand on a book that presented one of Muḥammad's companions, Abū Dharr al-Ghifārī (d. 652/3), as an early communist.[155] The commission voted against the further distribution of the book, stating that there was "no communism in Islam"[156] in the general sense that the author had claimed. In its ruling, the commission clarified that Abū Dharr held a singular opinion in believing that a Muslim should not accumulate wealth beyond his own needs, an opinion which had been widely debated and found wrong during his lifetime.

Reading between the lines, one sees that the Azhar ruling was about the question of who had the right to claim Abū Dharr. The ruling opposed left-leaning nationalists, who understood Abū Dharr as a revolutionary fighting the ruling Umayyads in his time. For conservative Muslims, he simply represented an ascetic preacher and an example of Muslims' early engagement for social justice. In the 1890s, pan-Islamic intellectual Jamāl al-Dīn al-Afghānī (1838–1897) had spoken of a different, Islamic form of socialism, drawing on the principle of solidarity (*taḍāmun*) and the example of Abū Dharr.[157] Beyond isolated remarks by different authors, the work *Abū Dharr al-Ghifārī al-ishtirākī al-zāhid* (*Abū Dharr al-Ghifārī, the Ascetic Socialist*) by the Sunni author ʿAbd al-Ḥamīd Jūda al-Saḥḥār (1913–1974) marked a major breakthrough in re-claiming an Islamic version of socialism; the book, published in 1943 with a foreword by the founder of the Egyptian Muslim

153 Ibid, 25.

154 Ḥasanayn Muḥammad Makhlūf, "Ḥukm al-Islām fī mabādiʾ al-shuyūʿiyya" (31.08.1953), in: *Fatāwā Dār al-Iftāʾ al-Miṣriyya*, http://shamela.ws/browse.php/book-432/page-2568#page-2570 (11.09.2017).

155 Ende, *Arabische Nation*, 213; M. N., "Oriente in Generale. Fetwa di el-Azhar sul Comunismo," *Oriente Moderno* 28: 4–6 (1948), 80–81, the *fatwā* is partially reprinted in: Muḥammad al-Ghazzālī, *Al-Islām al-muftarā ʿalayhi bayn al-shuyūʿiyīn wa-l-raʾsmālīyīn*, Cairo: Nahḍat Miṣr [6]2005 [[3]1953], 102–104.

156 M. N., "Oriente in Generale," 81.

157 Hanna and Gardner, *Arab Socialism*, 266–274. As Afghānī's essays were only published in 1931, the Lebanese Shiite Aḥmad Riḍā seems to be the first author who positively mentioned Abū Dharr's "socialist views" in passing in 1910, see Ende, *Arabische Nation*, 211.

Brothers, Ḥasan al-Bannā (1906–1949), was later translated into Persian with a foreword by ʿAlī Shariʿatī (1933–1977), a prominent precursor of the revolution in Iran (1978/79).[158]

In August 1965, the renamed Fatwā Board at the Azhar issued a ruling stating that a communist was not allowed to marry a Muslim women, thus categorizing communism as an anti-religious religion.[159] In the *fatwā*, the scholars argued, based on quotes taken from Marx, Lenin and Stalin, that communism, while refuting any religion and Islam, was itself a "cohesive ideology" (*madhhab mutarābiṭ*) that could not be separated into "its practical order" (*niẓāmuhu l-ʿamalī*) and "its dogmatic and philosophical basis" (*asāsuhu l-ʿaqāʾidī wa-l-falsafī*).

> While Islam did not permit a Muslim woman to marry someone from among the People of the Book (*ahl al-kitāb*)–Christians and Jews–although they believe in God, His books, His prophets, and the Last Day in general, then why would it allow a Muslima to marry someone who does neither believe in divinity, nor prophecy, nor resurrection and judgement?[160]

This ruling meant, as State Mufti ʿAbd al-Ḥalīm Maḥmūd explained in another *fatwā*,[161] (1) that a Muslim man is also not allowed to marry a communist woman, (2) that, if a communist dies, he or she cannot be buried in a cemetery for Muslims, and (3) that a communist can neither be heir to Muslim relatives nor bequeath them anything.[162]

In 1976, during the anti-leftist campaign under president Sadat, Maḥmūd also sent a letter to leaders of Arab states and asked them to contribute financially to the expansion of al-Azhar, arguing that it had always fought "'deviant' (*munḥarifa*) tenets such as socialism, which represented 'a danger for Muslim countries.'"[163] Like his predecessor Muḥammad Fahhām, who had declared student demonstrators "unbelievers" in 1972, Maḥmūd wrote that "communism is impiety (*kufr*) and those who support it have no faith."[164] He also argued that every communist who pretended to be a Muslim should be considered a "hypocrite" (*munāfiq*).[165] That "they take the book of Marx for their Qurʿān, Marx for their prophet, and communism

---

[158] On this work see Ende, *Arabische Nation*, 212. The Persian version was published as ʿAbd al-Ḥāmid Jūda al-Saḥḥār and ʿAlī Shariʿatī, *Mardī az rubẕah: Abū Ẕarr Ghifārī*, Tehran: Shabdīz 1977.

[159] ʿAbd al-Ḥalīm Maḥmūd, *Fatāwā ʿan al-shuyūʿiyya*, Cairo: Dār al-Maʿārif [4]1990, 70–72, 87–88.

[160] Maḥmūd, *Fatāwā*, 72.

[161] Ibid, 91–94 (undated).

[162] Ibid, 93f.

[163] Malika Zeghal, "Religion and Politics in Egypt: The Ulema of Al-Azhar, Radical Islam, and the State (1952–94)," *International Journal of Middle East Studies* 31 (1999), 371–399, 378.

[164] Ibid, 381; Maḥmūd, *Fatāwā*, 9.

[165] Ibid.

for a religion (*dīn*),"[166] proves that "atheism is a part of communism that cannot be taken away from it."[167]

It's worth mentioning that the 1965 *fatwā* was issued just months before thousands of communists were massacred in Indonesia and the second largest Muslim organization in Indonesia, the Muhammadiyah, spread a ruling declaring that the extermination of communists ought to be considered a religious duty.[168]

The Islamic Support for Arab Socialism

Curiously enough, these *fatāwā* against communism were valid or even issued during ʿAbd al-Nāṣir's turn to Arab socialism (1961–1970), which made the Soviet Union Egypt's most important international partner. This political reorientation towards socialism and the Soviet Union was not an Egyptian exception, but went hand in hand with the practical and ideological implementation of Arab socialism in other Arab states in the 1960s.[169] What was exceptional, however, was that the turn to socialism also went hand in hand with the nationalization of al-Azhar through Law no. 103 in 1961. While the Azhar scholars had already had to consent to the expropriation of *waqf* land and the abolition of Sharia courts in the 1950s, they now had to accept state control of their most important institution and were summoned to support an explicitly leftist socio-political agenda.

The astonishing rapprochement between the *shuyūkh* and ʿAbd al-Nāṣir was possible because both sides moved towards each other and legitimatized each other's ambitions, yet without pursuing congruent aims. Before the revolution of 1952, al-Azhar's antagonism to both the British and the Egyptian parliament turned it into a royalist bastion.[170] The parliament's attempt to gain control of the Azhar budget in 1927 was thwarted by the opposition of the king and the *shuyūkh*; parliament in return discriminated against

---

166 Ibid, 11.

167 Ibid, 9.

168 Fowkes and Gökay, "Unholy Alliance," 22; Bernard Johan Boland, *The Struggle of Islam in Modern Indonesia*, The Hague: Marinus Nijhoff 1982, 145f. The Vatican had already in 1949 excommunicated communists and their aides, see Kirby, "Christian anti-communism," 142.

169 The following states pledged themselves to Arab Socialism: Syria (1963–), Iraq (1963–2003), Algeria (1963–1988), South Yemen (1967–1970), Libya (1969–2011), Sudan (1969–1981), and Tunisia (during the 1960s). For an overview see Schwanitz, "Arabischer Sozialismus," and Ingrid El Masry, "Arabische Sozialismen im Vergleich. Praxis, Scheitern und Spätfolgen in Ägypten, Syrien und Irak," in: *Sozialismen. Entwicklungsmodelle von Lenin bis Nyere*, Joachim Becker and Rudy Weissenbacher, eds., Wien: Promedia 2009, 160–174.

170 Daniel Crecelius, "Al-Azhar in the Revolution," *Middle East Journal* 20: 1 (1966), 31–49, 32.

Azhar graduates when they applied for government positions and held up appropriations for the Azhar budget so that the king had to subsidize al-Azhar from his private treasury.[171] With the 1961 law, ʿAbd al-Nāṣir's government not only managed to radically re-organize the Azhar and its university, but it also tried to gain control over the religious field as such and an ever-increasing number of thousands of mosques affiliated with the Azhar.[172] State control of Islamic institutions and the Azhar's consent thereto were achieved because the government increased the Azhar's budget more than four times from 1952 to 1966 alone, which allowed the Azhar to double its student enrolment, increase the salaries of its scholars, offer scholarships, and increase the number of foreign missions sevenfold.[173] At the same time, the number of faculty not only dropped from 298 to 170 between 1959 and 1968, but its composition was radically transformed, replacing older staff reluctant to accept the changes by younger reform-oriented graduates.[174] These measures were accompanied by a press campaign criticizing traditional religiosity by stating that "from the beginning, Islam was a profession of work. The prophet used to work like everybody else. Islam was never a profession."[175] Even the Shaykh al-Azhar, Maḥmūd Shaltūt, publicly admitted that the *ʿulamāʾ* had to live "for the sake of Islam and not by means of it."[176] The demand, taken up by the Azhar's journal and its various spokespersons, was that the *ʿulamāʾ* should inculcate the new revolutionary thought and teach Islamic Socialism to the masses.[177]

The ideological meeting point between the Azhar and Arab Socialism can be described as both an area of intersection and a grey area. Much to the dismay of the Soviets, who tried to lecture ʿAbd al-Nāṣir on socialism and convince him to release imprisoned Egyptian communists,[178] Arab socialism was defined as "pre-eminently pragmatic"[179] and thus in contradistinction to the "immutable and rigid doctrine"[180] that the Soviets derived from their Marxist-Leninist philosophy and applied to their society. Propo-

---

171 Ibid, 33.

172 Tamir Moustafa, "Conflict and Cooperation between the State and Religious Institutions in Contemporary Egypt," *International Journal of Middle East Studies* 32 (2000), 3–22.

173 Ibid, 6.

174 Ibid, 5f.

175 Quoted by Zeghal, "Al-Azhar," 375. Also compare Crecelius, "Al-Azhar," 40.

176 Ibid, 42.

177 Ibid, 43f.

178 Rami Ginat, "Nasser and the Soviets. A Reassessment," in: *Rethinking Nasserism: Revolution and Historical Memory in Modern Egypt*, Elie Podeh and Onn Winckler, eds., Gainesville: Univ. Press of Florida 2004, 230–250.

179 Sami A. Hanna and George H. Gardner, "The Scribe on Ishtirākiyyah, 1961: Arab Socialism and Communism," in: *Arab Socialism*, idem, eds., 335–343, 335.

180 Ibid.

nents of Arab Socialism not only ruled class struggle out and expressed their respect for individual freedom and private ownership, but also stated that "one of the basic differences between Arab socialism and Communism resides in the faith, in spiritual values and in God."[181] On different occasions, ʿAbd al-Nāṣir explained that the prophet Muḥammad had established "the first socialist nation" because Islam was not only a religion, but also stood for social justice. Although he laid claim to a "scientific socialism," this was neither a "materialist" nor a "Marxist" socialism: "We did not say that we departed from religion ... but we said that our religion is a socialist religion and that Islam in the Middle Ages fulfilled the first socialist experiment in the world."[182]

Loyal intellectuals followed this understanding that Islam and socialism basically meant the same. For example, the writer Maḥmūd Shalabī produced a book series on socialism as practised by Muḥammad, his wife Khadija, the aforementioned Abū Dharr, as well as by the caliphs Abū Bakr, ʿUmar, and ʿUthmān, thus demonstrating that "we have an independent socialism, springing from our history, our beliefs and our nature."[183] The playwright ʿAbd al-Raḥmān Sharqāwī (1921–1987) depicted Ḥusayn b. ʿAlī (d. 680) as a revolutionary and Muḥammad as "the prophet of freedom." Similarly, the writer Aḥmad ʿAbbās Ṣāliḥ (1930–2006), editor of the Nasserist journal *al-Kātib*, described the struggle between the right and the left and the struggle for social justice as a continuous trend since early Islam.[184]

Under these premises, some Azharīs were ready to condone an Islamic version of socialism. Since the late 19th century, conservative religious scholars and Islamic intellectuals following al-Afghānī had argued that Islam possessed its own different kind of socialist teachings, which they called "mutual social responsibility" (*al-takāful al-ijtimāʿī*) and "social justice" (*al-ʿadāla al-ijtimāʿiyya*)[185] in order to distinguish them from modern social-

[181] Ibid, 339.

[182] See Yvonne Yazbeck Haddad, *Contemporary Islam and the Challenge of History*, Albany: State Univ. of New York Press 1982, 231 (note 50).

[183] Maḥmūd Shalabī, *Ishtirākiyyat Muḥammad*, Cairo: Maktabat al-Qāhira al-Ḥaditha 1962, 72, quoted after Charles Tripp, *Islam and the Moral Economy. The Challenge of Capitalism*, Cambridge: Cambridge Univ. Press 2006, 99 (footnote 67); also compare Menahem Merhavy, "Arab Socialism and Ecumenical Tendencies in Egypt 1962–1970," *British Journal of Middle Eastern Studies* 43: 4 (2016), 472–485, 477–479. For the other works see Shalabī, *Ishtirākiyyat Abī Bakr*, Cairo: Maktabat al-Qāhira al-Ḥaditha 1963; idem, *Ishtirākiyyat ʿUmar*, Cairo: Maktabat al-Qāhira al-Ḥaditha 1964/65; idem, *Ishtirākiyyat ʿUthmān*, Cairo: Maktabat al-Qāhira al-Ḥaditha 1968; idem, *Ishtirākiyyat Abī Dharr*, Beirut: Dar Jil 1974.

[184] Aḥmad ʿAbbās Ṣāliḥ, *Al-Yamīn wa-l-yasār fī l-Islām*, Beirut: Al-Muʾassasa al-ʿArabiyya li-l-Dirāsāt wa-l-Nashr 1972.

[185] See Sayyid Quṭb's eponymous work *Al-ʿAdāla al-ijtimāʿiyya fī l-Islām*, Cairo 1949.

ism.[186] The dean of the Sharia Faculty in Damascus, Syrian Muslim Brother and founder of the "Islamic Socialist Front" in 1949, Muṣṭafā Sibāʿī (1915–1964), went so far as to speak of *Ishtirākiyyat al-Islām* (The Socialism of Islam) in 1959. Yet, he made it immediately clear that Islamic socialism must not be confused with other socialist or communist ideas, since it broadened the concept of socialism to include "all material and moral aspects of life."[187] Sibāʿī enumerated ten types of *takāful* in Islam and 29 laws that regulate their application.[188]

Taking up and developing the term *takāful*, prominent Egyptian Azharīs, starting with the reform-oriented Shaltūt down to the anti-progressive Muḥammad al-Bahī (1905–1982),[189] depicted Islam as "the religion of socialism."[190] What these *shuyūkh* argued was that the state is allowed to become a command system worthy of obedience insofar as those in command are rightly guided,[191] or as long as property "is guarded by all for the benefit of all,"[192] as Shaltūt remarked. With their secular counterparts, these religious scholars shared "an optimism, but also a naiveté"[193] about both the benefits of state power and administrative efficiency that should restore harmony to a society riven by differences. Although the *shuyūkh* presented Islam as a "third way"–in the words of Muḥammad al-Ghazālī (1917–1996): "communism is the enemy at the gates and capitalism is the enemy within"[194]–, they legitimized, with utilitarian arguments, a state invested with wide and absolute authority. Inadvertently, they succumbed to state socialism, although they had argued against the danger of materialist philosophies, communist or capitalist, by invoking the socialism of Islam.[195]

Therefore, the claim of Islamic scholars and secular intellectuals that Islamic or Arab socialism represented a "third way" beyond capitalism and

---

186 See for example Hamid Enayat, "Islam and Socialism in Egypt," *Middle Eastern Studies* 4: 2 (1968), 141–172; Sami A. Hanna, "Al-Takāful al-ijtimāʿī and Islamic Socialism", *The Muslim World* (1969), 275–286; Hanna and Gardner, *Arab Socialism*, 49–79; Merhavy, "Arab Socialism."

187 See Hanna and Gardner, *Arab Socialism*, 150, also 67f. On Sibāʿī see Youssef M. Choueiri, *Islamic Fundamentalism. The Story of Islamist Movements*, London: Continuum 2010, 75–79; Ruth Roded, "Lessons by a Syrian Islamist from the Life of the Prophet Muhammad," *Middle Eastern Studies* 42: 6 (2006), 855–872.

188 Hanna and Gardner, *Arab Socialism*, 150–169.

189 On his changing positions see Enayat, "Islam and Socialism," 155f.

190 See for example Aḥmad Sharabāṣī and Aḥmad Farrāj, *Al-Islām dīn al-ištirākiyya: min mukhtārāt al-idhāʿa wa-l-tilīfizyūn*, Cairo: Dār al-Qawmiyya 1961; Maḥmūd Shaltūt, *Al-Islām wa-l-takāful al-ijtimāʿī*, Cairo 1960.

191 Tripp, *Islam and the Moral Economy*, 81.

192 Shaltūt, *Al-Islām wa-l-takāful*, 20f., quoted after Tripp, *Islam and the Moral Economy*, 87.

193 Tripp, *Islam and the Moral Economy*, 90.

194 Ghazzālī, *Al-Islām al-muftarā*, 14, quoted after Tripp, *Islam and the Moral Economy*, 97.

195 See ibid.

communism did not find the unanimous support of religious scholars. A critic of the Nasserist state like Sayyid Quṭb (1906–1966), imprisoned by the regime and finally executed, argued that such a justification of state activities with reference to the public interest and Islamic values merely represented "a modern form of 'idolatry'."[196] In Pakistan, 113 religious scholars even signed a *fatwā* against "Islamic socialism" in 1970 and declared Zulfikar ʿAli Bhutto (1928–1979) an unbeliever.[197] Accordingly, when the socialist regimes from Algeria to Iraq had degenerated into authoritative regimes by the end of the 1960s, Muslim intellectuals everywhere looked to redefine the idea of an Islamic society founded on Islamic values, for the most part demanding a clear break with state socialism and advocating the virtues of private entrepreneurial activities guided by Sharia norms.[198] They started to opt for a more Islamically "third way," which was "neither East nor West," in the diction of intellectuals like Sayyid Quṭb and ʿAlī Sharīʿatī or Āyatullāhs like Bāqir al-Ṣadr (1935–1980) and Rūhollāh Khomeini (1902–1989). The authoritarian character of Arab socialist regimes not only divided Islamic intellectuals, but also Marxists, and both groups came to revise their support.

Communism as Heresy

The incompatibility of communism with Islam was not the only argument on which Sunni religious scholars and Muslim intellectuals drew to ground their rejection of communism. Other–nationalist and religious–aspects also played a role in their arguments against communism and for Arab or Islamic socialism. Firstly, communism strongly appealed to religious and ethnic minorities, who longed for radical social change; this made it possible in turn to discredit communism as an anti-Arab movement. Secondly, while Sunni scholars or intellectuals claimed that Islam possessed authentic socialist ideals, which were much older and better than modern socialism,

[196] Ibid, 92.

[197] The People's Party slogan was "Islam is our religion, democracy our ideology, and socialism our economy." Bhutto's party won the Pakistani elections after the breakaway of Bangladesh in 1972; after protests by the Muslim League and a military putsch he was sentenced to death and hanged. See Munir D. Ahmad, "Pakistan: The Dream of an Islamic State," in: Carlo Caldarola, ed., *Religion and Society. Asia and the Middle East*, Berlin: De Gruyter 1982, 261–288, 268; Nasim Ahmad Jawed, *Islam's Political Culture: Religion and Politics in Predivided Pakistan*, Austin: Univ. of Texas Press 1999, 115; Syed Mujawar Hussain Shah, *Bhutto, Zia, and Islam*, Larkana: Shaheed Z. A. Bhutto Publications 2014, 89f, 247–249, http://bhutto.org/Acrobat/Bhutto_Zia_and_Islam.pdf (24.04.2017).

[198] Tripp, *Islam and the Moral Economy*, 97 and 100.

they traced communism back to a fifth century Zoroastrian heresy, thus claiming that it was a pre-Islamic as well as non-Muslim doctrine.

ʿAbd al-Nāṣir's turn to Arab socialism had a nationalist downside that accompanied and partly overshadowed the socialist one. The engagement for Arab unity, rooted in pan-Arab nationalism, had already found its expression in the Egyptian constitution of 1956. The preamble stated that the Egyptian people–realizing that it forms "an organic part of a greater Arab entity"–was aware of its "obligations toward a common Arab struggle for the glory and honor of the Arab nation;" the first three articles proclaimed that Egypt was an independent Arab state, Islam its state religion, Arabic the official language, and the Egyptian people "an integral part of the Arab nation."[199] These principles were reaffirmed by the proclamation of the constitution of the United Arab Republic, issued in 1964.[200] The interior and exterior dimensions of Arab nationalism displeased the Soviets as well as the communists in Egypt and Syria. Several years of ideological and political disagreement culminated with Khrushchev's only lengthy visit to Egypt in May 1964.[201] Khrushchev argued with ʿAbd al-Nāṣir that it was impossible to reconcile Arab nationalism and socialism and that workers and peasants should unite across borders, not with Arab "feudal lords and capitalists."[202] ʿAbd al-Nāṣir defended his position by stating that the division between the Arab peoples had been only recently imposed by imperialism and that Arabs were already united by a common history, consciousness, and language so that "all the factors and bases for unity are in fact existing."[203]

As Hanna and Gardner have pointed out, some Arab nationalists even saw communism as a modern form of *shuʿūbiyya*, a movement among non-Arab Muslims, which refused to recognize the privileged position of the Arabs during the time of the ʿAbbāsid Empire.[204] As communists in Arab

199 Middle East Institute, "The New Egyptian Constitution," *Middle East Journal* 10: 3 (1956), 300–306, 300. The constitution of 1923 neither mentioned the Arab character of the Egyptian state nor of its people and only mentioned Islam as state religion and Arabic as official language in Article 149, see Dustūr Miṣr 1923 on https://ar.wikisource.org/wiki/%D8%AF%D8%B3%D8%AA%D9%88%D8%B1_%D9%85%D8%B5%D8%B1_1923 (21.04.2017).

200 For the 1964 constitution see Hanna and Gardner, *Arab Socialism*, 386–408, 387f.

201 During his visit to the USSR in 1955, ʿAbd al-Nāṣir frankly announced "our anti-communist principles," explaining that communism was atheist and controlled by Moscow. The Soviets articulated their ideological and practical criticism on several occasions. During the formation of the Egyptian-Syrian unity (1958–1961), Khālid Bakdāsh, the leader of the Syrian CP, fled to Eastern bloc countries and published an article criticizing ʿAbd al-Nāṣir's policy, see Ginat, "Nasser and the Soviets," 238–241.

202 See Sami A. Hanna and George H. Gardner, "Al-Shuʿūbiyyah Up-Dated", in: *Arab Socialism*, idem, eds., 80–97, 93. Also compare Ginat, "Nasser and the Soviets," 242f.

203 Hanna and Gardner, "Al-Shuʿūbiyyah Up-dated", 94.

204 Ibid, 80–97.

countries recruited an over-proportional number of their members from ethnic and religious minorities, the dichotomy was not only between an internationalist worldview, pejoratively labelled as *shuʿūbiyya*, and a pan-Arab nationalism, positively called *ʿurūba*.[205] A difference also existed between the Arab-Sunni majority, who merged socialism with Arab nationalism and Islam, and the ethnic and religious minorities, who had a problem with either the nationalist or religious component of this merger. Thus, the criticism of communism revived an old Sunni belief, going back 500 years, that there was a close relationship between non-Arabs and heretical Islamic groups.[206] This idea also gave rise to a Sunni form of red-baiting that tried to relegate communism to the field of religious heresies.

Especially from the mid-20th century onwards, the expression *shīʿī-shuyūʿī* ("Shiite–Communist") was used in the Arab world "to discredit political, economic, and social demands of Shiite communities"[207] who began to strive for emancipation in Iraq and Lebanon. In his 1919 *fatwā*, Shaykh Bakhīt had traced Bolshevism back to Mazdakism, a gnostic movement in the fifth century, which stood for antinomianism and a just distribution of women and wealth.[208] Bakhīt mainly drew on sources hostile to Mazdakism, of which quite a few had survived in Arabic. His interest in the movement was neither singular nor new: "The rise of communism and socialism in Europe has spurred special interest in the movement, and Mazdakism has received considerable attention."[209] The first systematic academic study of Mazdakism as an early kind of Oriental socialism was provided by the German Orientalist scholar Theodor Nöldeke (1836–1930) in 1879.[210] Yet, the Ottoman press, reporting about the Paris Commune in 1871, was already drawing parallels to Mazdakism and to the Assassins.[211] The pan-Islamist al-Afghānī also traced the ideas of socialists, communists, and nihilists back to Mazdak in his treatise on the "refutation of the mate-

205 Ibid, 94.

206 Ende, *Arabische Nation*, 233–241, 235f.

207 Siliva Naef, "*Shīʿī - Shuyūʿī* or: How to Become a Communist in a Holy City," in: *The Twelver Shia in Modern Times: Religious Culture and Political History*, Rainer Brunner and Werner Ende, eds., Leiden: Brill 2001, 255–267, 255.

208 On Mazdakism see Ehsan Yershater, "Mazdakism," in: *Cambridge History of Iran: The Seleucid, Parthian and Sasanian periods*, vol. III, 2, idem, ed., Cambridge: Cambridge Univ. Press 1983, 991–1024; idem, "Mazdakism," in: *Encyclopedia of Religion*, vol. 9, Lindsay Jones, ed., New York: Thomson Gale ²2005, 5800–5802.

209 Yershater, "Mazdakism," 991.

210 Theodor Nöldeke, "Orientalischer Socialismus," *Deutsche Rundschau* 18 (1879), 284–291, https://archive.org/stream/DeutscheRundschau0181879#page/n287/mode/2up/search/Socialismus (21.04.2017).

211 Christoph K. Neumann, "Mazdak, nicht Marx: Frühe osmanische Wahrnehmungen von Kommunismus und Sozialismus," in: *Türkische Wirtschafts- und Sozialgeschichte von 1071 bis 1920*, Hans Georg Majer and Raoul Motika, eds., Wiesbaden: Harrassowitz 1995, 211–225.

rialists,"[212] written in Persian in 1881 and later translated into Arabic and Turkish; in it, he tried to prove that materialists were responsible for the ruin of several extinct civilizations. Even in recent literature on communism, the reference to Mazdak is still mentioned.[213] Quite similarly, but with a positive undertone, the above-mentioned Palestinian Marxist Bandalī Jawzī from Baku constructed a line from Mazdak over Babak to Shiite revolutionary movements.[214]

The liberal Egyptian writer Aḥmad Amīn (1886–1954), an Azhar graduate, took a more intricate–and for Shiite communities more insulting–approach in his works on the beginnings of Islam, *Fajr al-Islām* (1928) and *Ḍuḥā l-Islām* (1933–36), by connecting Abū Dharr's views not only with Mazdak's socialism, but also with the allegedly Jewish convert Ibn Sabaʾ.[215] Thus, he repeated the age-old Sunni prejudice that the Shia was a refuge for everyone who wanted to subvert Islam with Jewish, Christian, Zoroastrian, or Indian doctrines. This exposition not only connected Abū Dharr, a hero of Shiite historiography, with communism, but fed also the idea that both the Shia and communism were Jewish conspiracies. That communism was an offspring of Zionism and both were born out of Judaism, is a common anti-Semitic trope, which was also a "foundational element in Christian anti-communism"[216] and produced "one of the twentieth century's most consequential myths."[217] Its Muslim propagators, like the Egyptian liberal-conservative ʿAbbās Maḥmūd ʿAqqād (1889–1964), tried to prove it by referring to the vast numbers of important Jewish leading figures among Russian socialists and communists.[218] With such re-constructions–in the context of the Arab struggle against Zionism and the USSR recognition of the state of Israel–, the mark stuck with Arab communist parties, which had to tow the Soviet line, that they were national traitors.[219]

---

212 See Nikki R. Keddie, *An Islamic Response to Imperialism. Political and Religious Writings of Sayyid Jamāl al-Dīn "al-Afghānī". Including a Translation of the "Refutation of the Materialists" from the original Persian by Nikki R. Keddie and Hamid Algar*, Berkeley: Univ. of California Press 1968, 160.

213 See Muḥammad b. Ibrāhīm al-Ḥamad, *Al-Shuyūʿiyya*, Riyadh: Dār Ibn Khuzayma 2002, 13.

214 Sonn, "Intellectual History," 215.

215 Ende, *Arabische Nation*, 126–128, 212 and 221.

216 Kirby, "Christian anti-communism," 127.

217 Ibid, 128.

218 ʿAbbās Maḥmūd ʿAqqād and Aḥmad ʿAbd al-Ghafūr al-ʿAṭṭār, *Al-Shuyūʿiyya wa-l-Islām*, Beirut: Dār al-Andalus 1972, 134–158 (chapter "Al-Shuyūʿiyya walīdat al-Ṣuhyūniyya").

219 For the Soviet politics regarding Palestine in this period of time see Ismael, *The Communist Movement in the Arab World*, 57–70.

Post-Nasserist and Post-Soviet Interaction between Marxists and Islamists

Paradoxically, ʿAbd al-Nāṣir's defeat in the Six-Day War of 1967 brought the issues of Palestine and Arab nationalism more forcefully back to the agenda of Arab communists than ever before. With Palestinian guerrilla groups, most of which understood themselves as radical Marxists, springing up, the Arab CPs made it clear to Moscow, in slightly different formulations, that they conceived the Palestinian struggle as an important common Arab cause because Israel had turned into an imperialist and occupying force.[220] Although the Soviets tried to moderate this positioning, they could prevent neither the fragmentation of the Syrian CP in the 1970s nor the formation of an Arab militant "new left" that supported the guerrilla tactics independently of the USSR. Even worse, Communist, Left, New-Left, and Palestinian organizations formed an alliance to fight their cause with arms in the so-called Civil War in Lebanon (1975–1990), in which they finally turned out the political losers.

With the failure of Arab socialism in Egypt (1970), the Islamic revolution in Iran (1978/79), the military defeat in Lebanon, and the end of the Cold War, the political field fundamentally changed and several new forms of leftist-Islamist interaction came into being:

(a) The Egyptian philosopher Ḥasan Ḥanafi (b. 1935) tried to resuscitate the idea of an "Islamic left" (*al-yasār al-islāmī*) in 1981, reiterating that Islam was the religion of socialism and the Prophet Muḥammad "the leader of the socialists" (*imām al-ishtirākīyīn*).[221] While he expressed his uneasiness about the use of the term "Islamic socialism" by the autocratic Nasserist state, he still yearned for another form of application, half criticizing the regime, half rehabilitating its principles.[222]

(b) The pre-revolutionary Iranian intellectual ʿAlī Sharīʿatī attempted to expose the fallacies of Marxist philosophy, but interpreted Shiite Islamic principles in a rather Marxist or Third-Worldist way.[223] Yet, he maintained that he had laid bare the authentic truth about "red" revolutionary Islam as opposed to its traditional "black" counterpart. This kind of resistance theology was also to be found among the Iranian Mujahidīn-e Khalq (People's Mujahideen), who at first fought the Shah and then the Khomeini regime.

220 Usāma Ghazzī, "Azmat al-Ḥizb al-Shuyūʿī l-Sūrī wa-l-qaḍāyā l-filasṭīniyya: Dirāsa muqārana maʿa baʿḍ al-aḥzāb al-shuyūʿiyya," *Shuʾūn Filasṭīniyya* 12 (1972), 127–137.

221 Tripp, *Islam and the Moral Economy*, 100.

222 Ibid, 100f.

223 Assef Bayat, "Shariati and Marx: A Critique of an 'Islamic' Critique of Marxism," *Alif* 10 (1990), 19–41.

(c) In the wake of the Islamic revolution in Iran, some groups and individuals shifted from a leftist to an Islamist ideology, without changing much of their basic political orientation, like, for example, their engagement in armed struggle against Israel.[224]

(d) While all liberal and leftist opposition groups were disbanded, the Iranian Communist Party, Tudeh, supported the Khomeini regime to the verge of self-denial as "the last non-clerical group;" its Secretary-general, Nūr al-Dīn Kianūrī (1915–1999), continued to praise the achievements of the Islamic republic right up to the time of his arrest in 1983.[225] In a televised show trial, he was forced to confess on state TV that he had spied for the Soviet Union. The official Soviet reaction to his arrest and the execution of many Tudeh members was restrained and low-key (similar to the Egyptian case in the 1960s).

(e) In his New Year's message to Gorbachev 1988/89, Khomeini advised the Soviet leader to embrace Islam rather than capitalism after the impending downfall of communism.[226] Khomeini wrote that Gorbachev should understand that the cardinal mistake of communism was its disrespect for God and religion. By suggesting to the Soviet leader the authority of Muslim Sufis and philosophers like Suhrawardī, Ibn al-ʿArabī, Molla Sadra and Ibn Sīnā, Khomeini revealed his unorthodox mystical and philosophical inclinations, which infuriated some clerics in Qom, who sent him a letter of protest. Khomeini, also annoyed about the "stupid reactionary mullahs," wrote in turn: "When theology meant no interference in politics, stupidity became a virtue."[227]

(f) Some Arab communists interpreted Khomeini's letter to Gorbachev as an invitation to "a dialogue between ideologies,"[228] especially after the end

---

224 Manfred Sing, "Brothers in Arms. How Palestinian Maoists Turned Jihadists," *Die Welt des Islams* 51: 1 (2011), 1–44.

225 Farhang Jahanpour, "The Rise and Fall of the Tudeh Party," *The World Today* 40: 4 (1984), 152–159, 154.

226 Imām Khomeinī, "A Call To Divine Unity (1989). Letter from Imām Khomeinī to Mikhail Gorbachev," Teheran 1993 [The Institute for Compilation and Publication of Imām Khomeinī's Works], www.imamreza.net/eng/imamreza.php?id=430 (08.08.2017). On the background: Marcin Rzepka, "Religion, diplomacy and identity. Some remarks on the Ayatollah Khomeini's letter to Garbachev," *Orientalia Christiana Cracoviensia 5* (2013), 79–86.

227 Quoted after Michael Axworthy, *Revolutionary Iran. A History of the Islamic Republic*, London: Penguin Books 2014, 301. Adam Lewis, "Reconceptualizing Khomeini. The Islamic Republic of Iran and U.S. Democratization Policies in the Middle East," 51–63, http://triceratops.brynmawr.edu/dspace/bitstream/handle/10066/5454/2010LewisA.pdf (24.04.2017).

228 Karīm Muruwwa, "Ḥiwār maʿa risālat al-Khumaynī ilā Jurbātshūf," *Qaḍāyā Fikriyya* 13/14 (1993), 149–157, 152; Karīm Muruwwa, ed., *Ḥiwārāt. Mufakkirūn ʿarab*

of the Cold War. While their initiative fizzled out at first, several dialogue forums were actually organized between individuals and groups from a broad Islamist and leftist spectre.[229] These dialogue initiatives partly resulted in political co-operation against repressive states and their divide-and-rule politics, for example between the Revolutionary Socialists and the younger generation of the Muslim Brothers in Egypt in the run-up to the uprising in 2011. Following British Trotskyist Chris Harman's (1942–2011) slogan "sometimes with the Islamists, never with the state,"[230] Marxists started in the 1990s to explore the conditions and limits of alliances with Islamists.

(g) In their immediate reaction to the terror attacks of 9/11, communist parties in the Arab countries condemned terrorism–"wherever it came from or [for] whatever reason or pretext it [was] declared"–because of its consequences, since it "serves only the most reactionary, brutal and racist forces in the imperialist camp. Terrorism, at the end of the road, hinders the natural development of the national liberation struggle."[231]Thus, their statement made clear that the US administration "has always backed the Israeli terrorism and supported the terrorist organizations worldwide," while it now "has effectively utilized the 11 September events to realize the complete domination of the world and to continue with plundering the wealth of nations."[232] The statement did not dwell on–nor even mention–the Arab-Islamic background of the attacks, but criticized Arab governments working together with the US administration and called for internal (Arab and Palestinian) unity and for international "cooperation, collaboration, and solidarity"[233] in confrontation with the one-pole world, capitalist globalization, the war against Afghanistan, and the "genocide by the hands of Zionist gangs" in Palestine as well as in support of democracy in Arab countries, the intifada in Palestine, and the establishment of an independent Palestinian state. Such a critique of the incipient US-led "war on terror" as the utmost danger for the world precipitated the accommodation between parts

yunāqishūn Karīm Muruwwa fī l-qawmiyya wa-l-ishtirākiyya wa-l-dīmuqrāṭiyya wa-l-dīn wa-l-thawra, Beirut: Dār al-Fārābī 1990.

229 Michaelle L. Browers, *Political Ideology in the Arab World. Accommodation and Transformation*, Cambridge: Cambridge Univ. Press 2009.

230 From the treatise "The Prophet and the Proletariat" (1994), which was translated into Arabic in 1997 and distributed by the Revolutionary Socialists in Egypt, a group, which was later to play a significant role in the uprising against the Mubarak regime in 2011. Harman's treatise is available on www.marxists.org/archive/harman/1994/xx/islam.htm (22.05.2017).

231 "A Statement [by] The Communist and Workers Parties in the Arab Countries", *SolidNet.org* (12.01.2002), www.solidnet.org/old/cgi-bin/lprf818.html?parties/0480=jordan,_jordanian_communist_party/995jordan 6f02.doc (01.08.2017).

232 Ibid.

233 Ibid.

of the global left, Islamic groups, leftist leaders of South America, and representatives of Islamic states.[234]

(h) In the wake of the Arab upheavals in 2011, the Egyptian socialist scientist Sameh Naguib (Sāmiḥ Najīb) saw a chance to capitalize on the inherent social contradictions of Islamism and win "collections of young Islamists" to the left,[235] "if we are creative enough"[236] which meant that Marxists should finally leave behind "Stalinist Marxism," atheism, and "silly materialism."[237] Following Haman's analysis that the Islamists were neither natural allies nor enemies, Naguib had, since the late 1990s, criticized the dominant trend among Egyptian communists of seeing Islamists as political rivals.[238] Similarly, but with an initiative from the Islamic side, the Turkish group which calls itself Antikapitalist Müslümanlar (Anti-capitalist Muslims), publicly joined left-wing activists in the May Day celebrations in 2011 as well as during the Gezi Park protests in 2013, condemning capitalism as an "enemy of God and humanity."[239] Their indictment was not only directed against the world economy, but also against the ruling Justice and Development Party (*Adalet ve Kalkınma Partisi*, AKP) in Turkey, which they faulted "not only for its moral conservatism ..., but also its 'neo-liberalism'."[240] Their speaker, the theologian İhsan Eliaçık, bases his socialist inclinations not only on the Quran, but also on predecessors like ʿAlī Sharīʿatī and is considered by some "the first proponent of an 'Islamic socialism' in Turkey."[241]

Conclusion: Islam, Anti-Communism, and Anti-Capitalism

Although Marxism is not a religion and religions are not ideologies, they can fulfil similar social functions. Historically, both Marxism and religions

234 See Halliday, "The Left and the Jihad." For a Muslim voice from the Stop the War Coalition see Salma Yaqoob, "Islam and the left" (25.10.2005), www.international viewpoint.org/spip.php?article892 and idem, "Stop the War Coalition 15 Years On" (08.10.2016), www.youtube.com/watch?v=QCekHxM4uug (11.08.2017).

235 "The Prophet and the Proletariat" (2011, 1:17:25 h, uploaded by John Molyneux, 13.08.2012), www.youtube.com/watch?v=juvepJnRCgQ (01.08.2017), at 30 min, 20 sec.

236 Ibid, 34:17.

237 Ibid, 34:25.

238 See Browers, *Political Ideology*, 125f. and Sāmiḥ Najīb, *Al-Ikhwān al-muslimūn: ru'ya ishtirākiyya*, Giza: Markaz al-Dirāsāt al-Ishtirākiyya 2006.

239 Mustafa Akyol, "Why Turkey has 'Anti-Capitalist Muslims'", *Al-Monitor* (17.07.2013), www.al-monitor.com/pulse/originals/2013/07/turkey-anti-capitalist-muslims-gezi-social-justice-activism.html (01.08.2017).

240 Ibid.

241 Ceyda Nurtsch, "The Koran and social justice. Interview with Turkish theologian Ihsan Eliacik", *Qantara* (15.01.2014), https://en.qantara.de/content/interview-with-turkish-theologian-ihsan-eliacik-the-koran-and-social-justice (01.08.2017).

have served as tools legitimating revolt as well as oppression, liberation as well as exploitation, and armed resistance as well as genocidal violence. As ambivalent systems of thought, they are open to divergent interpretations that can converge, partially intersect, and fundamentally clash with each other. Although Marxism and religion are based on different forms of political, social, and cultural capital and their adherents follow different interests, their relation is not wholly determined by what represents their inner core or their adherents' interests; their relation depends instead on the interpretations of actors and their ability to read, understand, and influence the social and political circumstances.

As the previous pages have shown, the relations between Marxism and Islam can not only be characterized by permanent ups and downs, but also by different views of what characterizes Marxism, Islam, or religion. The relations between Marxism and Islam appear different in the logic of state policies, religious authorities, and party organizations. They are differently analysed by politicians, religious scholars, and intellectuals, dependent on their own power position, their view of the state apparatus, and their attitude towards the Marxist critique of the role of religion in society. These views further involve different interpretations of the history of early Islam and also touch on the history and status of religious and ethnic minorities in Muslim-majority societies. Anti-communist *fatāwā* that portrayed communism as a dogmatically anti-religious religion took neither the practical flexibility of many individual Marxists and communist organizations into account nor the different phases of conflict and accommodation; they also cast a veil of silence on the support that several religious scholars lent to Arab or Islamic socialism.

While communism was deemed un-Islamic by many Muslim scholars, Marx-inspired socialist thought could still combine with nationalism and political Islam, as it did, for example, in Nasserism, during the Iranian revolution, or in parts of the Arab uprisings in 2011. In these moments, it inspired the masses and adopted religious overtones beyond a narrow Islamic sense, rather representing utopia in the making, for, according to Ernst Bloch, "where there is hope, there is religion."[242]

In light of the previous pages, two questions finally deserve attention. The first question is about the extent to which the complex, at times even contradictory web of relations between Marxism and religion can be incorporated into a reasonably coherent narrative, encompassing the periods before, during, and after the Cold War. The second question is whether the difficulties of communism in Muslim-majority countries can be explained by Islam, either because Muslim societies proved ill-suited to Marxism or

242 Bloch, *Atheismus im Christentum*, 23.

because Marxism proved ill-suited to Muslim societies. In other words: Does Islam lack an original capitalist development and therefore represent a better, authentic form of anti-capitalism?

(1) The historical trajectory: Although Marx and Engels were against the suppression of religious freedom, Marxists and socialists, in practice, found themselves in their struggle against bourgeois and capitalist society in opposition to religious institutions. As the Great War shattered the alliance of throne and altar, a greater number of religious scholars and intellectuals of different religious background turned to socialism–in spite of the outright anti-religious Soviet policy. During the early years of the Bolshevist Revolution, communists capitalized on anti-colonialist sentiments among "peoples of the East," and many Muslims responded by joining their ranks inside and outside the Soviet Union.

During the Cold War, both the US-Americans and the Soviets competed with each other to win the hearts and minds of Muslims. The Soviets continued their anti-colonial efforts and sent ambassadors from Central Asia, until their strategy to "help" Muslims suffered shipwreck with the intervention in Afghanistan. The US administrations since Truman forged an anti-communist alliance with the Vatican and, with their growing global role, tried to expand anti-communism, that was underpinned by Christian "values", into a global religious movement against the Soviets and their allies. These efforts contributed to "a significant religious dimension to the Cold War."[243] In the attempt to contain Soviet influence, US foreign policy also relied on Islamic anti-communism, for which anti-communist *fatāwā* are a telling example. The US policy failure, exemplified by the Iranian revolution and al-Qāʿida's turn on the West, has resulted in an atmosphere of cultural struggle against Islam in Western societies that, at least partly, recalls the early Soviet cultural struggle against religion.

Apart from this, both capitalist and socialist countries with their respective academic cultures saw Islam as detrimental and a hindrance to development; for different reasons, they believed that, with the march of progress, Islam would finally retrench. Although Western scholars generally pledged themselves to uphold religious freedom vis-à-vis Soviet atheism, they were mostly convinced that consumer culture would also subvert the status of religions in modern societies, while Soviet scholars knew that

243 Gavin Bowd et al., "A century of anti-communisms: a roundtable discussion," *Twentieth Century Communism* 6 (2014), 22–58, 42f. More generally on this see Dianne Kirby, ed., *Religion and the Cold War*, Basingstoke: Palgrave Macmillan 2003; Luc van Dongen et al., eds., *Transnational Anti-Communism and the Cold War. Agents, Activities, and Networks*, Basingstoke: Palgrave Macmillan 2014.

"remnants" of religious cultures had survived in spite of an atheist education system.[244]

Communist and Marxist actors in Arab and Muslim societies had a tough act to follow, in their societies as well as in relation to inimical and friendly foreign powers. Therefore, the post-colonial political left often looked for a "third option" as a way-out in order to balance its own aspirations with internal and external pressures. In the inter-war period, a choice for communism could be understood as a "third way" beyond the colonial system and nation-state system. Against the background of the Cold War, Arab socialism, merging socialism with Islam and nationalism, posed as a non-aligned "third way" beyond the capitalist and the communist bloc. With the crisis of Arab socialism in the 1970s, the Iranian revolution, and the Soviet intervention in Afghanistan, the "third way" underwent an Islamic rebirth as a kind of Islamic antithesis to both the materialist West and the atheist East.

In spite of the shifting political grounds, Marxists and non-Marxists have always been keen to politically stand on the "right" side. In this respect, the difference between "atheism" and "religion" also functioned as a marker for pro- and anti-communism. Dissidents like Bloch and Third Worldists called into question such a stereotypical boundary-drawing in the inter-war, respective Cold War period. With the end of the Cold War, the markers of "atheism" and "religion" lost their politically defining meaning to a considerable degree, which is visible in the recent confrontation between Marxists and "new atheists" and in forms of interaction between leftists and Muslims. At the same time, it has not become easier to decide where the "right" side for the left lies.[245] This is visible in nearly every controversial issue connected with Islam, from headscarf to political violence, which divides different groups on the left.[246] The only form of consensus, on which the left is able to agree, is that rightist populist movements want to capitalize on Islamophobia. Therefore, a united "global left" with a "common lan-

---

244 Jacques Waardenburg, "The Study of Religion during the Cold War: Views of Islam," in: *The Academic Study of Religion during the Cold War. East and West*, Iva Doležalová, Luther H. Martin, and Dalibor Papoušek, eds., New York: Peter Lang 2001, 291–311. Compare also Michael Kemper and Artemy M. Kalinovsky, *Reassessing Orientalisms. Interlocking Orientologies during the Cold War*, London: Routledge 2015.

245 The statement by British Trotskyist John Molyneux at the end of his essay on Islam may serve as an example here: "To put the matter as starkly as possible: from the standpoint of Marxism and international socialism an illiterate, conservative, superstitious Muslim Palestinian peasant who supports Hamas is more progressive than an educated liberal atheist Israeli who supports Zionism (even critically);" see Molyneux, "More than Opium."

246 For parts of the European left see Gilbert Achcar, "Marxists and Religion – yesterday and today" (Marxismes et religions, hier et aujourd'hui, 2004), *International Viewpoint* (16.03.2005), www.internationalviewpoint.org/spip.php?article622 (07.06.2017).

guage" is not in the making,[247] nor does the moral condemnation of exploitation that is today often shared by religious institutions–from the Pope to the Azhar–express a utopian leftist-religious consensus. From a Marxian viewpoint, moral condemnation–as opposed to structural analysis and class struggle–leaves everything untouched and affirms the *status quo,* since it is based on the same norms and laws that have helped, or at least not prevented, the production of capitalist conditions, which are nevertheless "morally" condemned; moral condemnation in secular or religious guise is part of the "inverted world" that Marx wanted to be overthrown.[248]

Having said this, the Marxists' discord in their search for global unity–their "plurality in unity"–should not be seen as a major weakness, but as an inevitable outcome of their aspirations, something all too familiar for theologians. "The best thing about religion is that it makes for heretics,"[249] Ernst Bloch wrote in his *Atheismus im Christentum* (1968), after his forced retirement in 1957 and after having left the GDR in 1961. Not just Bloch's own experience suggests that his saying also holds good for Marxism and its heretics.[250] Marx had complained about the rivalries between anarchist and socialist groups in France and declared that because of them he no longer considered himself a "Marxist."[251] Thus, the inevitable tendency to heresy reflects the potential richness and overload of a tradition which aims to analyse and overthrow all social conditions and relations.

(2) *Islam vis-a-vis anti-communism and anti-capitalism*: With the demise of the Soviet Union, Marxist and non-Marxist intellectuals took stock of Marxism-Leninism, and especially with Marxism in the Arab world. While some pointed out general theoretical deficits in Marxist theories (the neglect of cultural diversity or gender, ecological, and emotional issues), others examined practical and tactical failures–the half-hearted support of liberation

247 See Susan Buck-Morss, "Can there be a Global left?," in: *Thinking Past Terror. Islamism and Critical Theory on the Left,* idem, London: Verso 2003, 92–112. The US-American philosopher delineates how a global left should aim to speak across cultural rifts and idioms to find a "common language" beyond Euro- and Islamocentrism, which would allow it to form a political opposition against the ravages of global capitalism and the "clash of civilizations" (Huntington).

248 This is one of the main arguments in Henning's criticism of the normative misreading of Marxist thought, see Henning, *Philosophy after Marx.* For a recent criticism of the rights discourse by the "loose left" see Luciana Bohne, "The Terrorism of Moral Indignation," *Counterpunch* (11 August 2017), www.counterpunch.org/2017/08/11/the-terrorism-of-moral-indignation (07.09.2017).

249 Bloch, *Atheismus im Christentum*, 23: „Das Beste an der Religion ist, daß sie Ketzer schafft."

250 Lauermann, "Der Atheismus," 133.

251 See Rudolf Walther, art. "Marxismus," *Geschichtliche Grundbegriffe. Historisches Lexikon zur politisch-sozialen Sprache in Deutschland,* Otto Brunner, Werner Conze and Reinhart Koselleck, eds., Stuttgart: Klett-Cotta 2004, Vol. 3, 937–976, 950.

struggles from Algeria to Palestine, the adherence to Moscow's rigid dogmatism, false political alliances or petty bourgeois politics.[252] If we add that self-proclaimed Marxist groups, which were not always acknowledged by Moscow as truly Marxist, hailed political violence, defended terrorist tactics, and sponsored suicide bombing in the Middle East, then it seems that close to nothing is right with Marxism in Arab or Muslim-majority countries. In other words: it appears to be more detached from reality than any "religion" could ever be.

Basically, two opposing explanations have been offered for this alleged failure: either Muslim societies were not suitable for Marxism or Marxism was not suitable for Islam.

The first form of explanation is represented by post-colonial critics, who located the problem rather inside Marxism than inside Muslim societies, claiming that Marxism was based on racist stereotypes and Orientalist premises.[253] In *Orientalism* (1978), Edward Said attacked Arab Marxism as both a Westernizing and self-Orientalising force.[254] He also asked "why many forward-looking Muslims still regard Marxism as alien to much in their lives" and why "Marxists in the Muslim world have never successfully translated Marxism from nineteenth-century European categories into modern Middle Eastern ones."[255] For critics following Said, both the "Asiatic mode of production" and "Oriental despotism" were categories that obviously manifest the main contradiction between Marxists' universalism and their particular criticism of non-European countries.

As an example of the second explanation, Max Weber noted in the introduction to the *Protestant Ethic*: "Just because the world has known no rational organization of labor outside the modern Occident, it has known no rational socialism."[256] The various historical socialistic and communistic experiments in the world, he wrote, had little to do with the modern conflict of the large-scale industrial entrepreneur and free-wage workers: "Thus there could be no such problems as those of socialism."[257] Max Weber's statement can be interpreted as a way of saying that the Middle East was

---

[252] See, for example, Wolfgang Schwanitz, "Zehn Schwächen im marxistischen Denken. Ein Angebot zum Nachdenken," *asien, afrika, lateinamerika* 18 (1990), 932–933; Ismael, *The Communist Movement*, 102–123.

[253] See for example Kreutz, "Marx and the Middle East."

[254] Edward Said, *Orientalism*, New York: Pantheon 1978, 325. For a re-evaluation see Manfred Sing and Miriam Younes, "The Specters of Marx in Edward Said's *Orientalism*," *Die Welt des Islams* 53: 2 (2013), 149–191.

[255] Edward W. Said, "*Europe and the Middle East* by Albert Hourani, *Marxism and the Muslim World* by Maxime Rodinson, *What is Islam?* by W. Montgomery Watt", *Arab Studies Quarterly* 4 (1980), 386–393, 389f.

[256] Max Weber, *The Protestant Ethic and the Spirit of Capitalism*, New York: Charles Scribner's Sons 1958, 23, quoted by Hanna and Gardner, *Arab Socialism*, 21.

[257] Ibid.

not conducive for the application of Marxism. The Syrian dissident Marxist Yāsīn Ḥāfiẓ (1930–1978),[258] maybe involuntarily, reflected Weber's take by arguing that all Arab countries were stuck in the middle of the road between tradition and modernity. He coined the composite terms *taʾakhkhurākiyya* ("backwardialism" from backwardness and socialism) and *taʾakhkhurāliyya* ("backwarditalism" from backwardness and capitalism) for socialist and capitalist Arab states, meaning in the first case that socialist regimes had merely adopted socialist slogans to cover their traditionalism, and in the second case that capitalist transformations in the oil monarchies had merely scratched the surface of a traditional society.[259]

What speaks against both the "Saidian" and "Weberian" explanations is not only the near-complete spread of communist and socialist groups in Muslim-majority countries since the end of the 19th century; the number of workers' strikes, the death tolls and personal tragedies also bear witness to a political imaginary, provided by Marxism and Bolshevism, that has even been adopted and re-worked by nationalists and Islamists. Whether the reference to socialism was used to call for anti-colonialism, to legitimate state power or to invoke the spectre of social disorder–it was a central prism for political struggles for several decades.

Thus, both the post-colonial critique of Marxism's Eurocentrism and Weber's focus on industrial capitalism in Europe can nurture the (mis-) understanding that they attest either a European or Islamic exceptionalism. Islam might then appear to be not only a non-Western, but also an anti-capitalist force. Yet, neither Euro-centric nor Islamo-centric perspectives that separate Islamic history from the Western European capitalist development are correct. The idea that (industrial) capitalism is an exceptional formation in socio-economic history, and that it only developed in Europe, is a claim that downplays external influences, predecessors in long-distance trade, and the importance of Euro-African-Asian trade connections under Muslim control from Late Antiquity to the 18th century. "Not only did the Muslim world know a capitalistic sector," as French Marxist historian Maxime Rodinson has argued, "but this sector was apparently the most extensive and highly developed in history before the establishment of the world market created by the Western European bourgeoisie."[260] Muslim societies were neither lacking capitalism nor untouched by the dynamic develop-

---

258 Ḥāfiẓ broke with the Syrian Baath Party after 1967 and formed the Revolutionary Socialist Workers Party (*Ḥizb al-ʿUmmāl al-Thawrī al-Ishtirākī*) with members of the Marxist wing of the Baath Party. He was arrested because of his political views and upon his release in 1968 moved to Beirut.

259 Yāsīn al-Ḥāfiẓ, "Ittijāhāt al-taṭawwur al-ʿarabī al-muqbil," in: *Al-Hazīma wa-l-idiyūlūjiya l-mahzūma, al-Aʿmāl al-kāmila 4*, idem, Damascus: Dār al-Ḥaṣād ²1997 [1976], 151–193, 174.

260 Maxime Rodinson, *Islam and Capitalism*, New York: Pantheon Books 1973, 56.

ment that has been described as characteristic for European cities. Muslims provided mathematical, commercial, and financial instruments which formed part and parcel of trade and capitalism in Europe. Italian trading cities did not invent capitalism, but adopted many instruments from other, often Muslim, Mamluk or Ottoman, merchants who had already made "big money."[261]

Claiming the birth of ("true") capitalism for Western Europe or the birth of ("true") anti-capitalism for Soviet Russia is neither a natural nor a neutral act. It lays claim to originality, authority, rationality, modernity, class consciousness, and liberation. Re-claiming parts of capitalist history for Muslims means demonstrating that Islamic commerce and European capitalism were genealogically inter-connected. In the same vein, European, Arab, Marxist, Christian, or Islamic forms of anti-colonial resistance, with all their errors and successes, were also genealogically interwoven with the rise of European imperialism and the demise of Muslim empires.

In this sense, this chapter should have made clear that the features of Muslim-majority societies made their members neither particularly susceptible to anti-capitalism and anti-communism nor immune to them. Rather, Marxist and Muslim actors dealt differently with each other according to the changing local, regional and global conditions and the means at their disposal. Thus, episodes of persecution and hostility coexisted with phases of accommodation and alliance, depending on whether the actors prioritized their differences or communalities and whether they legitimized the struggle against each other or against a common enemy.

---

261 For this discussion see John M. Hobson, *The Eastern Origins of Western Civilisation*, Cambridge: Cambridge Univ. Press 2004; idem, "Islamic Commerce and Finance in the Rise of the West," in: *The Role of the Arab-Islamic World in the Rise of the West. Implications for Contemporary Trans-Cultural Relations*, Nayef R. F. Al-Rodhan, ed., New York: Palgrave MacMillan 2012, 84–115; Jairus Banaji, "Islam, the Mediterranean and the Rise of Capitalism," *Historical Materialism* 15 (2007), 47–74; Nelly Hanna, *Making Big Money in 1600. The Life and Times of Ismaʿil Abu Taqiyya, Egyptian Merchant*, Syracuse: Syracuse Univ. Press 1998; Kerem Nisancioglu, "The Ottoman Origins of Capitalism: Uneven and Combined Development and Eurocentrism," *Review of International Studies* 40 (2014), 325–347; Murat Çizakça, *Islamic Capitalism and Finance: Origins, Evolution, and the Future*, Cheltenham: Elgar 2011.

Left-Wing Perspectives on Political Islam: A Mapping Attempt

Leandros Fischer

Introduction

The emergence of contemporary political Islam, or 'Islamism',[1] from the late 1970s onwards, has confronted the Left with an enormous challenge. While standing in opposition to secularism and women's rights, Islamist movements in the Middle East have coopted standard left-wing causes, such as resistance to the state and foreign intervention. In doing so, contemporary Islamism has gained the allegiance of vast swathes of the population in Muslim-majority countries, whose socioeconomic position would, under other circumstances, dictate a left-wing orientation. This paradox has given birth to two interrelated questions: Is there something unique about 'Islamic culture' that hinders Marxist ideas from gaining a mass following in the Arab and Muslim world? Conversely, is Marxism 'Eurocentric'? These questions have preoccupied the Left within and outside the Arab and Muslim world, as it struggles to grapple with the phenomenon of political Islam.

This article aims at presenting an overview of the approaches to political Islam prevalent within the Left. It focuses largely on Marxist discussions on Islamist movements active in the region stretching from the Atlantic to the Hindukush. However, debates concerning the Left's general attitude towards Islam within the Western context of Islamophobia, secularism and integration are also considered, given the overlapping character of both discussions.

---

1 The characterizations 'Islamism' and 'political Islam' are also a matter of contention, and are used here solely for lack of a better term. Gilbert Achcar, referring to the school of post-1979 French Orientalists, rejects the term (as well as the terms 'political Islam' and 'militant Islam'), arguing that it represents a concession "to the pretension of the so-called 'Islamists' to hold exclusive rights to the militant interpretation of Islam". Achcar uses the term 'Islamic fundamentalism' instead. However, as Ervand Abrahamian points out, the term 'fundamentalism' offers an inadequate description of contemporary Islamism, since the term denotes a literal interpretation of religious texts, as well as an overall rejection of modernity, elements that do not apply to the Khomeinist movement in Iran. The terms 'political Islam' and 'Islamism' are used here in opposition to 'Islamic', to denote a position in the sphere of the political rather than the religious. See Gilbert Achcar, *Marxism, Orientalism, Cosmopolitanism*, Chicago: Haymarket Books 2013, Kindle-Position 401; Ervand Abrahamian, *Khomeinism: Essays on the Islamic Republic*, Berkeley: University of California Press 1993, 13ff.

To illuminate the various responses, a brief introduction to the attitudes of Karl Marx and Friedrich Engels towards religion is provided, as is an overview of the policies of the early Bolsheviks towards the Muslim populations of the former Russian Empire. The article argues that the Left's attitude towards political Islam is not so much guided by an adherence to Marxist atheism but should rather be placed in the context of the concrete political strategies pursued by various left-wing actors over the course of the 20th and early 21st century.

Who Is the 'Left'? Which 'Political Islam'?

Any discussion on the Left's attitude towards Islamism must begin with a definition of the two political currents. The Left as a self-referenced force originates in the seating arrangement of the Estates General during the French Revolution. Its political program was initially associated with political equality, citizenship rights, and anticlericalism. With the growth of industrial capitalism during the 19th century, the Left's character expanded to include socioeconomic demands of wealth redistribution through the revolutionary overthrow of capitalism and its replacement by a socialist mode of production. This anti-capitalist perspective and the ideology of proletarian internationalism, which is inextricably linked with the life and work of Karl Marx, forms the key, defining feature of the Left today. A third element entered the fore around the time of the Russian revolutions of 1905 and 1917. A critique of imperialism as "the highest state of capitalism"[2] and the corresponding support for the right of oppressed nations to self-determination, were added to the Left's ideology and practice. The term Left as defined here, pertains to those political currents that subscribe to these three principles. It also includes anarchist and autonomist currents that share the Marxist Left's universalist and anti-capitalist outlook. Accordingly, what is not included in this working definition of the Left is mainstream social democracy, not only because of its abandonment of anti-capitalism and its embrace of neoliberalism, but also because of its collusion with colonialism and imperialism. In the Arab and Muslim context, the definition of the Left excludes all movements subscribing to the inherently particularistic ideologies of 'Arab' or 'Islamic socialism'.

The concept of a 'return to Islam' as a political program predates the advent of Islamism as a hegemonic oppositionist current in the late 1970s. During most of the 20th century, secular nationalism, and to a lesser extent communism, became the main avenues through which discontent with the

2 Vladimir Lenin, *Der Imperialismus als höchstes Stadium des Kapitalismus*, Berlin: Dietz Verlag 1979.

colonial and neocolonial status quo was articulated in the Arab and Muslim world. In the postwar period, Islamism was broadly seen as a conservative social force, either supported by traditionalist states such as Saudi Arabia, or used by secular states as a weapon against the Left.[3] However, a combination of factors, condensed in simultaneously occurring events such as the Iranian revolution and the Soviet invasion of Afghanistan, contributed to a significant political radicalization of preexisting Islamist currents. The Islamist movements of interest to this article are those that manifest themselves as radical oppositionist forces with a mass following among the working class and the poor, such as the Egyptian Muslim Brotherhood, the Tunisian An-Nahda, the Palestinian Hamas, and others. Nominally 'Islamic states' like Saudi Arabia, where the ruling ideology of Wahhabism is essentially used to legitimize the capitalist transformation of a tribal elite, are not considered in this article, but the Islamic Republic in Iran is, due to its fusion of clerical authority with participatory republican elements, as well as the regime's revolutionary self-perception.

Marxism and Religion, Marxism and Islam

That Marx and Engels considered religion "the opium of the people" has been cited widely, both by followers and detractors, to underline Marxism's unrelenting hostility to religion. However, a closer examination of the relevant passage from Marx's 1844 *Contribution to the Critique of Hegel's Philosophy of Right* is needed, to better understand Marx and Engels' attitude towards religious beliefs:

> Religion is the general theory of this world, its encyclopaedic [sic] compendium, its logic in popular form, its spiritual point d'honneur, its enthusiasm, its moral sanction, its solemn complement, and its universal basis of consolation and justification. It is the fantastic realization of the human essence since the human essence has not acquired any true reality. The struggle against religion is, therefore, indirectly the struggle against that world whose spiritual aroma is religion. Religious suffering is, at one and the same time, the expression of real suffering and a protest against real suffering. Religion is the sigh of the oppressed creature, the heart of a heartless world, and the soul of soulless conditions. It is the opium of the people.

Marx's reference to religion as a narcotic has been wrongly attributed to a crude understanding of religion as a tool used by capitalists to divert the attention of the toiling masses away from economic exploitation. While it is certainly true that as a product of the Enlightenment tradition, Marxism

3 This was the case with Egypt's neoliberal turn under Anwar Sadat, who invited the previously persecuted Muslim Brotherhood to return from exile in the face of growing left-wing opposition to his economic policies.

precludes any ideological convergence with the realm of the otherworldly, it must also be emphasized, that the same materialist worldview that informed the rejection of religious ideas by Marx and Engels, also structured their understanding of religion as a social phenomenon. By viewing religious suffering as "the expression of real suffering", Marx regarded religious ideas as a source of comfort against the alienation endured by individuals under capitalism, as well as an element of protest against the same alienation. As religious beliefs were the product of material circumstances, they could only wither away through a revolutionary overthrow of those circumstances. Marx and Engels sought to analyze the contradictory class interests often given expression by the same religious beliefs. Hence their attitude towards certain movements inspired by religion, such as the one led by Thomas Müntzer during the German Peasant Wars, was determined by their class content, not their religious coloration.

If Marx and Engels dealt systematically with the question of religion from a philosophical point of view, their references to Islam remained overwhelmingly circumstantial.[4] Undoubtedly, their understanding of the Muslim world could not be anything but limited. The most systematic Marxist endeavor in analyzing the socioeconomic dynamics of Muslim societies would come from the French Marxist Maxime Rodinson, whose pioneering 1966 work *Islam and Capitalism* debunked widespread assumptions in the West about Islam as an unchangeable element hindering modernization, while tracing the root causes of their underdevelopment to sociological factors common to other societies. Rodinson not only demonstrated the absence of

4 For example, Friedrich Engels: "Islam is a religion adapted to Orientals, especially Arabs, i.e., on one hand to townsmen engaged in trade and industry, on the other to nomadic Bedouins. Therein lies, however, the embryo of a periodically recurring collision. The townspeople grow rich, luxurious, and lax in the observation of the 'law.' The Bedouins, poor and hence of strict morals, contemplate with envy and covetousness these riches and pleasures. Then they unite under a prophet, a Mahdi, to chastise the apostates and restore the observation of the ritual and the true faith and to appropriate in recompense the treasures of the renegades. In a hundred years, they are naturally in the same position as the renegades were: a new purge of the faith is required, a new Mahdi arises and the game starts again from the beginning. That is what happened from the conquest campaigns of the African Almoravids and Almohads in Spain to the last Mahdi of Khartoum who so successfully thwarted the English. It happened in the same way or similarly with the risings in Persia and other Mohammedan countries. All these movements are clothed in religion but they have their source in economic causes; and yet, even when they are victorious, they allow the old economic conditions to persist untouched. So, the old situation remains unchanged and the collision recurs periodically. In the popular risings of the Christian West, on the contrary, the religious disguise is only a flag and a mask for attacks on an economic order which is becoming antiquated. This is finally overthrown, a new one arises and the world progresses", "On the History of Early Christianity", first published in: *Die Neue Zeit* 1894–1895, available at *Works of Frederick Engels 1894*, www.marxists.org/archive/marx/works/1894/early-christianity/ (status: 12 June 2017).

any incompatibility between Islamic societies and capitalism, but also recognized the potential of left-wing ideas to gain influence among them.

His assumptions were backed by the historical experience of powerful communist parties in the Middle East in the 1940s, especially in Iran and Iraq, as well as the Marxist-oriented New Left within the Palestinian movement in the late 1960s. However, the question of compatibility between Marxist ideas and the Muslim context would resurface in the late 1970s due to several overlapping factors. On the political level, the period was characterized by the decline of secular nationalism and the Left, and the parallel ascendancy of Islamism. On the intellectual level, Edward Said's *Orientalism* had ignited a debate on Marx, whom Said portrayed as trapped within an Orientalist mindset due to his writings on British colonial rule in India.[5] Marxists from within the Muslim world vigorously contested his postulate, such as the Lebanese Mahdi Amel, the Indian Aijaz Ahmad, and the Syrian Sadik Jalal al-'Azm,[6] who felt that Said effectively legitimized the onslaught conducted at the time by the Islamists against the Left. However, the Said controversy would help cement the idea of a Muslim exceptionalism, in which Marxist ideas seemed irrelevant due to their inherently European character.

The Bolshevik Experience and the Long Shadow of Stalinism

On the level of practical politics, however, the oldest example of Marxist policies towards Islam can be traced to a time predating the Said controversy and the parallel decline of the Left in the Arab and Muslim world. Common assumptions, both friendly and hostile towards the Russian revolution, have sought to portray the Bolsheviks' treatment of Islam in the early period of the Soviet state as one of downright hostility. However, studies have cast doubt on this premise. According to them, the privileges of the Orthodox Church were severely curtailed, whereas previously persecuted religious communities, such as non-Orthodox Christian denominations, were granted new freedoms. Concerning the tsarist empire's formerly oppressed Muslims, the revolutionary period witnessed not only attempts at syncretizing Islam with socialism, such as in the case of the Tatar revolutionary Mirsaid Sultan-Galiev, but also benevolent Bolshevik policies towards Is-

5 Karl Marx, "The British Rule in India", *New York Daily Tribune* dated 25 June 1853, www.marxists.org/archive/marx/works/1853/06/25.htm (status: 12 June 2017).

6 Achcar, *Marxism, Orientalism, Cosmopolitanism*, Kindle-Position 1359. Al-'Azm coined the term "Orientalism in reverse" in criticizing Said. By that he described a tendency among thinkers like Said, to reproduce the key tenets of Orientalism by essentializing the Occident and its thinkers, especially Karl Marx. See Sadik Jalal al-'Azm, "Orientalism and Orientalism in Reverse", in: *Khamsin* 8 (1980), 5–26.

lam, such as the establishment of a parallel Sharia court system in the Caucasus and Central Asia. It is possible to interpret these policies as a tactical measure designed to gain the allegiance of the Muslim population in the face of foreign intervention and civil war. However, as Dave Crouch insists,[7] far from being an aberration from Marxist principles, Bolshevik policy towards Islam was guided by a materialist understanding of religion and was aimed on the one hand at rectifying past religious oppression, and on the other at accelerating the process of class differentiation within the Muslim population. The policy was not without controversy, as it had to contend with residues of nationalism among the ethnic Russian Bolsheviks in Central Asia, as well as with ultra-leftist tendencies within the Bolshevik party, which viewed any talk of self-determination for previously oppressed minorities as a concession to separatism.[8]

The real break in Bolshevik-Muslim relations, however, came during the consolidation of Stalin's rule in the late 1920s, which witnessed campaigns to forcibly unveil women and a clampdown on Islamic institutions, measures that provoked enormous resentment among Soviet Muslims. Just as the attitude of the early Bolsheviks towards Islam was guided by predominantly political considerations, so too was Stalin's assault on Islam. Specifically, this change of policy must be situated within the context of the general rolling back of social rights, which also included the penalization of homosexuality and abortion, as well as policies of effective Russification in the Soviet Union's non-Russian republics. The main reason underlying all these measures was the goal of rapidly industrializing the Soviet Union in the spirit of Stalin's slogan of "socialism in one country", following the abandonment of world revolution. It was an effort that required the partial rehabilitation of Russian nationalism, to the detriment of gains made by oppressed ethnic and religious minorities in the early phases of the revolution. Far from being an outgrowth of ideological atheism, the attack on Islam was part of a policy of Russification, which also strived to forcibly integrate Muslim women into the workforce. Nevertheless, its legitimization on modernizing and progressive grounds would help cement the idea of an unbridgeable gap between Marxism and Islam, due to ideological atheism.

Instances of Left-Wing Uncritical Support for Islamism

Marxist attempts to theoretically substantiate an accommodating attitude towards Islamism as a progressive force have remained limited to non-

7 David Crouch, "The Bolsheviks and Islam", *International Socialism* (6 April 2006), http://isj.org.uk/the-bolsheviks-and-islam/ (status: 12 June 2017).

8 Ibid.

existent. Maxime Rodinson alluded to a trend within Arab communism in the 1940s and 1950s to mix appeals for social justice with references to the Muslim tradition.[9] However, this was before the advent of present-day Islamism, during the time when the communists' main rivals in the Arab world were secular nationalists, who regarded Islam as an integral part of Arab national identity. Another attempt at fusing progressive ideas with a religious outlook appeared during the Lebanese Civil War. Maoist intellectuals Fawwaz Traboulsi and Mohsen Ibrahim had coined the theory of "community class", by which the Christians of Lebanon were identified with the bourgeoisie, whereas the struggle of the Muslims, particularly the Shia, was identified as a form of class struggle.[10] Yet this theory mostly constituted an ideological concession to Lebanese communalism, rather than an ideological acceptance of Islam as a political end in itself.

In almost all the instances where left-wing forces have supported Islamist actors uncritically (to the detriment of their defence of social rights), this was not so much the result of a progressive reading of Islamism but rather the outgrowth of the primacy of anti-imperialist struggle in the Middle East. This holds true for much of the Iranian Marxist Left in the early phases of the Iranian revolution, as well as for certain Palestinian factions. Such support was usually justified 'dialectically' with references to the 'primary contradiction' of fighting imperialism, as opposed to the 'secondary contradiction' (anti-capitalism, women's, and minority rights and so forth). It is worth noting that neither Marx nor Lenin ever advanced this line of thought. On the contrary, it was developed by Mao Zedong in the 1930s[11] and it is therefore not surprising that such a policy of uncritical support emanated mostly from organizations adhering to Maoist paradigms of guerilla warfare, such as the Iranian People's Fedayeen.[12]

Among Western thinkers, it was Michel Foucault who initially greeted the rise of Islamism. Despite not being a Marxist, Foucault's thinking has had an enduring influence on radical autonomist and anarchist thought. The philosopher had been a correspondent for the Italian *Corriere Della Serra* covering events leading to Khomeini's return from exile. Foucault's praise of the Ayatollah resulted from his fascination with Shia martyrdom and political spirituality, but it was also congruent with the philosopher's

9 Maxime Rodinson, *Marxism and the Muslim World*, London: Zed Books 2015, 51–52.

10 See Joseph Daher, *The Political Economy of Hezbollah*, London: Pluto Press 2016, Kindle-Position 468–473.

11 Mao Tse-Tung, Mao, "Über den Widerspruch" (1937), in: *Fünf philosophische Monographien*, Peking: Verlag für fremdsprachige Literatur, 27–87, available at www.marxists.org/deutsch/referenz/mao/1937/wider/ (status: 12 June 2017).

12 Cf. Ervand Abrahamian, *Iran Between Two Revolutions*, Princeton: Princeton University Press 1982, 483–489.

general critique of modernity, which also included a rejection of Marxism.[13] His writings provoked a storm of criticism in France, including from feminists and Marxists like Rodinson,[14] whose concerns Foucault never properly addressed. His fascination with Islamism also characterized certain tendencies in French academic Orientalism;[15] however, this remained a limited and short-lived phenomenon. The 1980s in Iran witnessed a bloodbath of dramatic proportions, directed not only against the Marxist, but also against the Islamic Left of the People's Mujahedin. Around the same time, secular regimes in Egypt and Turkey adopted an instrumentalist approach towards political Islam against the Left, during their turn away from state-directed policies and towards neoliberalism. Combined with the war waged by the Islamists against the Left from Algeria to Lebanon in the 1980s and 1990s, all these events precluded any subsequent reading of mainstream political Islam as a natural ally of the Left. Overall, the idea of a 'leftist-Islamist' alliance currently displays far more substance as a concept in neo-conservative polemics against the radical Left in the West, rather than an actual self-referenced political project.

Political Islam as 'Fascist' and/or 'Pro-Imperialist'

The experience of the Iranian revolution proved crucial for the ensuing debate. Fred Halliday articulated a feeling widespread at the time, namely that the Iranian Left's biggest mistake during the revolution was its inability to find common cause with non-leftist "moderate democratic forces" against Khomeini's regime, which he described as "fascism with an Islamic face".[16] In the West, the related term 'Islamo-fascism' was used extensively by formerly left-wing intellectuals like Christopher Hitchens and thinkers associated with the German *Antideutsch* current.[17] However, these positions have been consistent with a general drift of their exponents to the right, and should therefore not be dealt with further here as typical left-wing approaches.

On the other hand, the implications of the analogy with fascism for left-wing forces in several Muslim-majority countries was to support the secular

13 Janet Afary & Kevin B. Anderson, *Foucault and the Iranian Revolution. Gender and the Seductions of Islamism*, Chicago: Chicago University Press 2005, Kindle-Position 204.

14 Ibid., Kindle-Position 975ff.

15 See Achcar, *Marxism, Orientalism, Cosmopolitanism*, Kindle-Position 759.

16 Fred Halliday, "The Iranian Revolution and its Implications", *New Left Review* (November-December 1987), https://newleftreview.org/I/166/fred-halliday-the-iranian-revolution-and-its-implications.

17 Writers associated with the *Antideutsch* in Germany have popularized the historically inaccurate notions, that German Nazism was crucial in the ideological formation of Arab nationalism and contemporary political Islam.

state as the 'lesser evil'. This had been the position of the Egyptian Tagammu party, formerly part of the 'loyal opposition' to the Mubarak regime, against the Muslim Brotherhood. A similar view is currently adopted vis-à-vis the Syrian uprising by the Assad-supporting Syrian Communist Party, as well as by the influential anti-Mubarak Nasserist Left, during and after the overthrow of Mohammad Morsi by the Egyptian military.[18] Indeed, for great parts of the Left in the Muslim world, the negative characterization of Islamism is often the immediate derivative of an idealized conception of the secular state.

For elements of the Left stemming from 'orthodox' (i.e. pro-Soviet) communist traditions, this harmonizes completely with the general view of secular regimes as essentially historically progressive entities forming the 'national democratic stage' of a two-stage revolution, as opposed to the regressive Islamists.[19]

It must be stressed, however, that this type of ideological rejection of political Islam by the 'old Left' has been highly inconsistent. As nationalism forms the dominant frame of reference of established communist parties in the region today,[20] the characterization of Islamists as fascists has often acted as a cover for the main motive of their rejection: their perceived alliance with imperialism due to their links with the US-allied states of the Gulf. Conversely, these parties generally do not take issue with the backing of the 'secular' Assad regime by the Islamic Republic of Iran and sectarian Shia Islamist militias like the Lebanese Hezbollah. Furthermore, and similar to the left-wing discourses advocating an alliance with the Islamists because of their 'anti-imperialist' character, the rejection of the Islamists as 'fascist' has been lacking in theorization. However, it can be observed that both views are guided by the objective weakness of the Left in the Middle East and the subsequent predisposition to form 'popular fronts'[21] with non-leftist actors deemed to be playing an historically progressive role, be it the liberal bourgeoisie or 'anti-imperialist' regimes and certain Islamist movements.

---

18 Gilbert Achcar, *Morbid Symptoms: Relapse in the Arab Spring*, London: Saqi Books 2016, Kindle-Position 1680ff.

19 Ironically, the characterization of Khomeini as representative of the 'national democratic stage' of the Iranian revolution, was a hallmark of the communist Tudeh party before its eventual purge by the Islamist regime.

20 Bassem Chit, "Nationalism, resistance and revolution", *International Socialism* (5 January 2015), http://isj.org.uk/nationalism-resistance-and-revolution/ (status: 12 June 2017).

21 The Popular Front strategy was adopted by the Comintern in the 1930s as a response to Hitler's rise to power. The policy prescribed strategic electoral alliances between communist parties on the one hand, and social democratic and liberal forces on the other to stem the rise of fascism. It should not be confused with the Comintern policy of the United Front in the 1920s, whose foundation was a class-based alliance of communist and social democratic workers around specific issues.

The Marxist critique of political Islam articulated by the dependency theorist Samir Amin[22] is more sophisticated, because it represents a more consistent criticism of Islamist notions of state and society. Unlike Halliday, Amin does not advocate a coalition with pro-Western liberalism against Islamism. Instead, Amin rejects the notion of political Islam as anti-imperialist, claiming that Islamism is a natural ally of "dependent capitalism", while also warning against alliances between the Left and Islamist organizations. Historical precedent supports Amin's thesis; in the 1950s and 1960s, the West did indeed actively support Islamist opposition to secular Arab regimes, whereas the predecessors of Hamas in the 1980s were tolerated by the Israeli authorities as a counterweight to the leftist and nationalist PLO organizations.[23] In the case of Iran, Amin attributes Western hostility towards the regime to Iranian nationalism, rather than a fundamental conflict between political Islam and imperialism. However, like the orthodox communist parties, Amin's rejection of Islamism is linked to a comparatively lenient position towards the secular postcolonial states in the Middle East.

Marxist Perspectives of Islamism as a Class-Based Movement

Completely outside the perspectives mentioned above on political Islam, stands the Trotskyist tradition. Due to its critique of 'Third-Worldism', prevalent in the 1960s as well as its insistence on the classical Marxist notion of the working class as the historical agent of social change, Trotskyist analysis was less constrained by a positive perception of the secular developmental states established by military circles in Egypt, Iraq, Syria and elsewhere, viewing these as class-based entities with inherent limitations. The main feature differentiating Trotskyist perspectives from other Marxist approaches to Islamism has therefore been its focus on the analysis of contemporary political Islam as a middle-class movement. Trotskyism has been notoriously fragmented, however, two perspectives on political Islam emanating from its ranks will be considered here. The first comes from Gilbert Achcar, a prominent scholar on the Middle East affiliated with the 'reunified' Fourth International led by Ernest Mandel after World War II. The other was formulated by the British Marxist Chris Harman, affiliated with the London-based International Socialist Tendency.

---

22 Samir Amin, "Political Islam in the Service of Imperialism", *Monthly Review. An Independent Socialist Review* 2007, https://monthlyreview.org/2007/12/01/political-islam-in-the-service-of-imperialism/ (status: 2 November 2018).

23 Helga Baumgarten, *Hamas. Der Politische Islam in Palästina*, Munich: Diederichs 2006, 32, 73f.

Achcar had published a number of theses in 1981,[24] where he used the term "Islamic fundamentalism" to describe the newly emergent Islamist forces in Iran and beyond. With terminology borrowed from the *Communist Manifesto*, Achcar identifies political Islam as an essentially petty bourgeois movement of the traditional middle classes, striving for the implementation of a reactionary utopia. The emergence of Islamism is not attributed to the workings of imperialism, but to the triple outcome of economic stagnation and crisis in the Middle East, the limits of bourgeois nationalist leaderships, as well as the betrayal of the Stalinist communist parties, whose passive acceptance of bourgeois nationalism has rendered them unable to form an independent pole of attraction of the working class, capable of absorbing the discontent felt by the middle classes. At the same time, Achcar warns about confusing the fight against Islamic fundamentalism with the fight against religion, as many of its followers could be "pulled out of its orbit and won to the workers' cause".

Chris Harman on the other hand was the author of the 1994 political brochure *The Prophet and the Proletariat*, where he sought to develop left-wing strategies of relating to oppositionist Islamist movements. Harman makes a distinction, classifying Islamism along four strands: the "Islamism of the old exploiters" (e.g. feudal landlords); the "Islamism of the new exploiters", by which he meant emerging private capital in countries such as Egypt and Turkey; the "Islamism of the poor" adhered to by the formerly rural population proletarianized by socioeconomic transformation; and the "Islamism of the new middle classes", which characterizes the cadre of oppositionist Islamist movements on which Harman's analysis mainly focuses. Harman draws similar conclusions to Achcar regarding the middle-class composition of Islamism; however, in emphasizing the key role played by a modern but downwardly mobile intelligentsia in various Islamist movements, Harman regards the latter as essentially modern phenomena rather than an effort to return to a pre-modern past. Given its middle-class composition, Harman sees political Islam as torn between violent, yet futile resistance to the status quo on the one hand, and eventual accommodation with it on the other through "reformism". Accordingly, he advocates a position of "with the Islamists sometimes, with the state never", to legitimize tactical alliances of the Left with the Islamists on certain issues such as the struggle against the authoritarian state and opposition to imperialism, while maintaining the Left's organizational independence and criticism of Islamist ideology.

Evidently, Harman's perception of political Islam borrows heavily from Ervand Abrahamian's perspective on the Khomeini movement in Iran. Like

---

24 Gilbert Achcar, "Eleven Theses on the Resurgence of Islamic Fundamentalism", *International Viewpoint* 1981, www.internationalviewpoint.org/spip.php?article1132 (status: 2 November 2018).

Harman, Abrahamian rejects the term 'fundamentalism', as this implies dogmatic rigidity and an outright rejection of the modern world, something not valid in the case of the Islamic Republic. Instead, by drawing a comparison to the Peronist movement in Argentina, Abrahamian describes Khomeinism as a middle-class populist movement combining radical rhetoric against imperialism with a commitment to safeguarding private property, and using "charismatic figures as well as symbols, imagery and language that have potent value in ... popular culture".[25] Moreover, he is careful to distinguish this definition of populism from other historical movements commonly associated with the term, including European fascism. This is because, according to Abrahamian, fascism depoliticized the masses whereas populism invites the masses into the political scene.

In the aftermath of the 'Arab Spring', organizations in the Middle East that adhere to these interpretations of political Islam have been noticeable in their unconditional support of struggles against the *ancien régime*, something contrasting with the occasionally hostile attitude of the 'old Left'. From a sociological perspective, groups like the Egyptian Revolutionary Socialists or the Revolutionary Left Current in Syria, differ from the traditional communist parties and the nationalist Left in two ways. On the one hand, their membership profile is much younger, compared to the aging membership of communist parties. On the other, their members have been socialized in civil society spaces formed in the 1990s and 2000s in opposition to increasingly neoliberal authoritarian states, often finding themselves compelled to engage with Islamist actors in the process. Thus, elements of the Egyptian radical Left formed an alliance with some Islamist forces in the October 2011 parliamentary elections, whereas the Revolutionary Socialists supported the Muslim Brotherhood candidate in the runoff to the 2012 presidential elections, to block the election of a candidate associated with the Mubarak regime.[26] In Syria and Lebanon, Trotskyist-oriented groups have found themselves isolated from an established Left, which threw its weight behind the Assad regime as an alleged bulwark of 'resistance' against Gulf-funded 'takfiris'.

ISIS and the Debate on Fascism

Actors subscribing to the Trotskyist tradition have also sought to further develop Harman's understanding of political Islam as a class-based movement, especially as regards the rise of ISIS from 2013 onwards. Jamie Allin-

25 Abrahamian, *Khomeinism*, 17.

26 Mostafa Ali, "A Reply on Egypt's Elections", *Socialist Worker* (3 June 2012), http://socialistworker.org/2012/06/03/reply-on-egypts-elections (status: 24 April 2017).

son undertakes a partial revision, questioning Harman's description of groups like the Muslim Brotherhood as 'reformist' which, according to him, falsely denotes a resemblance to European social democracy. Allinson points instead to the lack of organic links between Islamists and the working class, as well as their clientelist rather than integrative relation to the subaltern classes.[27] He then situates the rise of ISIS, among others, in the context of mainstream Islamism's failure to win over the existing state and the majority of the population in the aftermath of the 'Arab Spring'.

ISIS has also been the focal point of a debate around the Marxist definition of fascism. The Syrian Marxist Ghayath Naisse proposes in *International Socialism* a view of "Daeshism" through the prism of Leon Trotsky's description of European fascism. According to him, not only is ISIS constituted by what Trotsky described as "human dust", the atomized layers of the petit bourgeoisie, but also by its propensity to genocidal violence, and its declared aim of crushing all popular mobilization resulting from the 2011 Syrian uprising.[28] In the pages of the same journal, Anne Alexander retorts that while ISIS shares features common to classical fascism, the absence of any desire to structure itself along the lines of a social movement precludes a description of ISIS as "fascist".[29] On the other hand, Allinson points to the impossibility of applying a precise definition of fascism, arguing for posing the question in terms of "how much fascism" ISIS contains instead.[30]

Debates on Islam among the European Left

The left-wing debate around political Islam in the West presents a substantially different structure. Here, the attitude towards political Islam is often an epiphenomenon of the wider discussion on Islam as a religion, itself embedded within the wider problematics of racism and secularism and played out in a context of Islamophobia and rising social polarization. People of Muslim immigrant backgrounds are over-proportionally represented in the lower socioeconomic strata of many European societies, and the question of how the Left should relate to them has been particularly

27 Jamie Allinson, "Disaster Islamism", *Salvage* 4 (2017), http://salvage.zone/in-print/disaster-islamism/ (status: 24 April 2017).

28 Ghayath Naisse, "The 'Islamic State' and the counter-revolution", *International Socialism* 147 (2015), http://isj.org.uk/the-islamic-state-and-the-counter-revolution/ (status: 24 April 2017).

29 Anne Alexander "Fascism and Isis", *International Socialism* 148 (2015), http://isj.org.uk/fascism-and-isis/ (status: 24 April 2017).

30 Allinson, ibid.

contested. The issue has been condensed in debates around the hijab, the niqab and the burka.

France especially was the scene of intense debates on the subject within the Left. Some Trotskyist organizations like Lutte Ouvrière, as well as more mainstream organizations like the French Communist Party, have taken positions in support of banning the hijab in public schools, either justified on the grounds that this constitutes a symbol of women's oppression, or as a defence of republican laicité. The Trotskyist Nouveau Parti Anticapitaliste suffered a split on the issue when it decided to run a hijab-wearing candidate in the 2010 regional elections.[31] It can be argued that different national discourses structure the Left's attitude towards Islam. In the case of France, a majority of the Left adheres to a specifically French brand of secularism deemed as inherently progressive, an assumption which, however, has been contested.[32] Conversely, the British Left, acting in a context devoid of a similar national ideology of secularism, has displayed less aversion to building grassroots coalitions with Muslim organizations centered on opposition to war and racism. The debate is structured somewhat differently within the German Left. Central to it has been the strong impact of events in Turkey and northern Syria, given Germany's large Turkish and Kurdish populations. The strong Kurdish and Turkish presence within Die Linke, the most visible party on the left, has translated into vocal opposition towards Turkey's Islamist-rooted AKP party. However, this opposition has sometimes been extended to Muslim organizations such as the Turkish-Islamic Union for Religious Affairs, which operates several mosques and has close relations to the AKP, indicating that in the context of a Western country, the borders between criticism of political Islam on the one hand, and Islam as a religion on the other, are highly fluid in practice.

At the heart of these debates lies the question whether Islam as a religion is open to progressive political interpretations similar to Latin American 'liberation theology'. Gilbert Achcar, while opposing the ban on the hijab, rejects the possibility of such an interpretation, by pointing to Islam's origins as a political religion of merchants, in contrast to Christianity's origins as the religion of an oppressed community.[33] This premise is contested by organizations adhering to the tradition of "socialism from below".[34] The

---

31 Members opposed to the candidacy of Ilham Moussaid eventually left the party, whereas she decided to leave the party afterwards (Felix Boggio, personal correspondence).

32 Ian Birchall, "The Wrong Kind of Secularism", *Jacobin Magazine* (19 November 2015), www.jacobinmag.com/2015/11/charlie-hebdo-france-secular-paris-attacks-lacite/ (status: 24 April 2017).

33 Achcar, *Marxism, Orientalism, Cosmopolitanism*, Kindle-Position 401.

34 The term was first coined by the American Marxist Hal Draper in the 1960s in his essay *The Two Souls of Socialism*, in which he contrasted the Marxian axiom that "the

emphasis here is placed on the sociological capacity of religion as a set of ideas defined primarily by the social context of their adherents, rather than their historical origin.[35] Indeed, the rise of the Black Lives Matter movement has witnessed a renaissance of debates around the connections between class and race. In Europe, this has gone in tandem with a growing politicization among so-called 'people of color', which is conditioned by socioeconomic factors and opposition to institutional racism. This trend has already found organizational expression in the French Indigènes de la République party, formed as a response to the adherence of the majority of the French Left to republicanism, as well as the phenomenon of mostly young individuals describing themselves as both Muslim and left-wing.

Conclusion

There hasn't been just one, but rather a multitude of left-wing perspectives on political Islam, as well as Islam itself. As a product of the Enlightenment tradition, Marxism is inherently opposed to any political project whose declared aim is the construction of a social order based on religion. At the same time, Karl Marx and Friedrich Engels advanced a materialist understanding of religion as a social phenomenon, capable of giving expression to a variety of class interests. In concrete practical terms, this means that Marxism's attitude to religious ideas cannot be viewed in isolation from material phenomena, such as the state, imperialism, national oppression, and racism. This is exemplified by the Bolshevik policy towards religion after 1917. Religious communities oppressed by the tsarist regime were given more rights, including the Muslim communities of the Caucasus and Central Asia. This policy was later reversed under Joseph Stalin through a campaign of forced unveiling, a policy accompanied by an implicit rehabilitation of Russian nationalism. Accommodation and hostility towards Islam in the Soviet Union were not rooted in dogma, but in the material conditions of a workers' revolution and its subsequent degeneration under Stalinism.

On the philosophical level, the idea of an ontological opposition between Marxism and Islamic culture was strengthened by the advent of poststructuralism as a theoretical current in the late 1970s. Whereas Marxists

emancipation of the working classes must be conquered by the working classes themselves", with bringing "socialism from above", a practice he associated with social democracy and Stalinism. Groups following Draper's ideas have also adopted a theory of the Soviet Union as 'state capitalist', differentiating themselves from 'orthodox' Trotskyism which viewed the regimes of the Eastern Bloc as 'degenerated workers' states'.

35 John Molyneux, "More than Opium. Marxism and Religion", *International Socialism* 119 (2008), http://isj.org.uk/more-than-opium-marxism-and-religion/ (status: 24 April 2017).

such as Maxime Rodinson had previously sought to dismiss Orientalist assumptions on Islam as an element hindering modernization, postcolonial thinkers such as Edward Said classified Marx in the category of Western thinkers trapped in an Orientalist mindset. Echoing this critique of the Enlightenment and modernity, Michel Foucault briefly embraced the Islamism of the Iranian revolution. This perception of incompatibility between Marx and the Muslim world was arguably reinforced by the general decline of anti-capitalist critique and the parallel ascendancy of Cultural Studies in academia. However, it was also rooted in political developments.

In the postwar period, the communist Left in the Middle East and North Africa followed a policy of strategically supporting the secular postcolonial state that emerged in several countries of the region, as a progressive entity. Accordingly, the Left also tended to support the state in its struggle against a reinvigorated Islamism from the late 1970s onwards. Political Islam was either denounced as 'fascist' or as an agent of imperialism. For the surviving remnants of the communist Left in the Middle East, the authoritarian secular state is currently the 'lesser evil' in the struggle against the various strands of Islamism, something shown in the aftermath of the 'Arab Spring'. This hostility towards Islamists, however, is selective; political Islam is equated with fascism, but this characterization is rarely applied to 'resistance' regimes and actors, such as the Iranian Islamic Republic or the Lebanese Hezbollah. This reflects the primacy of anti-imperialist nationalism among wide parts of the 'old Left', as well as a certain nostalgia for the secular state before its neoliberal turn.

It is therefore not surprising that a more systematic analysis of political Islam was undertaken by Trotskyism, the theoretical tradition whose aim was to save Marxism from Stalinist distortions. Trotskyist thinkers recognized the Islamist currents appearing in the 1970s as autonomous movements anchored in the middle classes, whose emergence constituted a direct response to the failures of the secular nationalists and the communists in the struggle for social equality and democratic rights. However, Trotskyist currents differ in their practical attitudes towards the Islamists. While some have labeled political Islam 'fundamentalist', effectively ruling out any tactical understanding, others have taken a more accommodating attitude towards temporary alliances with Islamist actors around specific issues. Leftist currents in the Middle East influenced by Trotskyism currently distinguish themselves by a more consistent opposition to all existing regimes, both religious and secular. Furthermore, thinkers adhering to the same tradition have sought to modify its analysis of Islamism by incorporating recent phenomena into it, such as the emergence of ISIS.

For the left-wing debate in the West, the question of Islamism is simultaneously one concerning the compatibility of Islam as a religion with progressive politics. This question becomes even more acute for the Left, given the rise of Islamophobia amidst growing social polarization. It can be observed that specific national contexts structure the Left's attitude towards Islam. In France, a significant part of the Left has attempted to claim the state ideology of laicité for itself, thereby alienating many people of Muslim background. Conversely, the absence of such an ideology in Britain (or the United States) has enabled common fronts between left-wing and Muslim organizations around various issues. The historic absence of a 'melting pot' ideology in Germany means that debates within the Left on Islam there are played out much more intensely in the background of outside events, specifically in Turkey and Syria, than in other Western countries.

The global protracted crisis of capitalism, combined with the recent advent of movements that seek to illuminate the connections between race and class, signals a potential change in the way the Left's relation to Islam is being discussed, thus challenging binary perceptions of an incompatibility between both. A symptom of this is the growing signs of self-organization among immigrant communities in the West, as well as the emergence of left-leaning Muslims as the active subjects, rather than the passive objects of various social struggles. All this suggests that the debate on the Left and Islam might be entering a new era.

Iranian Godfathers of Islamic Socialism – "It Is the Marxists Who Have Learned It from Islam"

Katajun Amirpur

The so-called first proponent of an Islamic Socialism in Turkey, İhsan Eliaçık, whose books criticise the neoliberal politics of the AKP and call for a Socialist reading of the Quran, refers to the Iranian ʿAlī Sharīʿatī as an early exponent of his ideas. He even calls Sharīʿatī "one of our chief influences".[1] In this article, I will introduce Sharīʿatī and I will also take a closer look at the man who is considered the founder of Iranian anti-imperialism, Jalāl Āl-i Aḥmad. Besides that, I will examine the distinctions between Sharīʿatī and his much younger exegete Eliaçık.

Iranian socialism has its roots in anti-imperialism and this is the background of Jalāl Āl-i Aḥmad, one of the main protagonists of Iranian discourse on religion in the modern world of the 1960s. As a matter of fact the discourse on religion and politics among Iranian intellectuals of the 1960s was not dominated by clerics, but by two lay thinkers: ʿAlī Sharīʿatī (1933–1977) and Jalāl Āl-i Aḥmad (1923–1969).[2] These two men returned religion to a previously secular and mostly Marxist debate where it had only featured as a negative quality of the old society, if at all.[3]

It is well known that the dominant subject of public debate in 1960s Iran was engagement with the West, its culture, and Western culture's effects on Iran. Secular intellectuals of the decade were inspired by the West as much as they were critical of it. Hiroshima, Vietnam, Algeria, the Cold War, and Soviet expansionism had come to discredit the ideas of both liberalism and socialism, and many Iranian thinkers joined in the criticism that Western intellectuals such as Albert Camus (1913–1960), Erich Fromm (1900–1980),

---

1 Ceyda Nurtsch, "The Koran and Social Justice", Interview with Ihsan Eliacik, *Qantara*, (15 January 2014), https://en.qantara.de/content/interview-with-turkish-theologian-ihsan-eliacik-the-koran-and-social-justice, accessed 08 August 2018.

2 On Āl-i Aḥmad see Mehrzad Boroujerdi, *Iranian Intellectuals and the West. The Tormented Triumph of Nativism*, New York: Syracuse Univ. Press 1996, 65–74; Ali Gheissari, *Iranian Intellectuals in the 20th Century*, Austin: Univ. of Texas Press 1998, 88–92; Hamid Dabashi, *Theology of Discontent. The Ideological Foundation of the Islamic Revolution in Iran*, New York: New York Univ. Press 1993, 2006, 39–101.

3 On the intellectual climate of those years see Negin Nabavi, "The Changing Concept of 'Intellectual' in Iran of the 1960s", *Iranian Studies* 32 (1999), 333–350; on intellectuals in the 1940s and 1950s see Gheissari, *Iranian Intellectuals in the 20th Century*, 40–60.

Herbert Marcuse (1898–1979), Jean-Paul Sartre (1905–1980), George Bernard Shaw (1856–1979), Arnold Toynbee (1889–1975), and before them the pioneers Oswald Spengler (1880–1936), and Henri Bergson (1859–1941) had expressed. Āl-i Aḥmad in particular embraced this critical stance and translated several works by the abovementioned writers into Farsi.[4]

The path that led him to develop his view of religion was complex. Born to a family that included many clergymen, he was a member of the Communist Tudeh Party (pers.: *Tūdih*) for many years.[5] After breaking with Communism, he founded the Third Power Party *(Nīrū-yi Sivvum)* in 1952 together with Khalīl Mālikī (1903–1969), a leading political activist of the time.[6] In 1964, he made a pilgrimage to Mecca.[7] There, he experienced a religious revelation that made him aware of the potential power of religion as part of an Iranian identity.[8]

In 1962, he published his famous book *Gharbzadigī*, literally: Struck by the West. Struck here should be understood both in the sense of an obsession and a violent assault. The title is difficult to translate: R. Campbell rendered it as Occidentosis.[9] Another common translation into English is "Westoxication".[10]

> I say *Gharbzadigī*, infected by the West, just like *vabā zadigī* – infected by cholera, or, if that is not appealing, then like sun stroke *(garmā zadigī)* or frost bite *(sarmā zadigī)*. Or – no. It is at least as bad as an infection of parasites *(sin zadigī)*. Have you seen how they spoil the wheat? From the inside. The wheat stands with an unbroken husk, but that is only on the outside. It is like the shell that the butterfly leaves behind on the tree. In any case, we are talking about a sickness.[11]

---

4 See Boroujerdi, *Iranian Intellectuals and the West*, 75.

5 On the Tudeh Party and its importance to Iranian intellectuals in the 1950s and 1960s see Maziar Behrooz, *Rebels with a Cause. The Failure of the Left in Iran*, London: I. B. Tauris 1999; Sepehr Zabih, *The Communist Movement in Iran*, Berkeley: Univ. of California Press 1966.

6 On Mālikī see Homa Katouzian, "Khalil Maleki: The Odd Intellectual Out", in: *Intellectual Trends in Twentieth Century Iran*, Negin Nabavi, ed., Gainsville: Univ. Press of Florida 2003, 24–53.

7 He describes his experiences in Jalal Al-e Ahmad, *Lost in the Crowd* [*Khaṣī dar mīqāt*], Washington: Three Continent Press 1985.

8 On authenticity in Iranian discourse during this time see Negin Nabavi, "The Discourse of 'Authentic Culture' in Iran in the 1960s and 1970s", in: Nabavi, *Intellectual Trends*, 91–110; Farzin Vahdat, "Return to which Self? Jalal Al-e Ahmad and the Discourse of Modernity", *Journal of Iranian Research and Analysis* 16 (2000), 55–71.

9 Jalal Al-i Ahmad, *Occidentosis, a plague from the West.* Annot. and introd. by Hamid Algar [*Gharbzadigī*, Westoxication], Berkeley: Mizan 1984.

10 The book itself is discussed in Boroujerdi, *Iranian Intellectuals and the West*, 65–74; Gheissari, *Iranian Intellectuals in the 20th Century*, 88–92; Vahdat, "Return to which Self?", 55–71; Ali Mirsepassi, *Intellectual Discourse and the Politics of Modernization. Negotiating Modernity in Iran*, Cambridge: Cambridge Univ. Press 2000, 98–114.

11 Jalāl Āl-i Aḥmad, *Gharbzadigī* [Westoxication], Tehran: Amīr Kabīr 1977, 21. Unless otherwise indicated, the translations of Persian quotes are mine.

Gharbzadigī made Āl-i Aḥmad the most influential writer in the shaping of modern Iranian identity through the 1960s. It stands as one of Iran's most influential works of the twentieth century alongside Mīrzā Muḥammad Ḥusayn Nā'īnī's (1860–1936) *Tanbīh al-ummah wa-tanzīh al-millah* (*The Awakening of the Community and Refinement of the Nation*) published in 1909[12] and Rūḥullāh Khumeinī's (1902–1989) *Ḥukūmat-i Islāmī* (Islamic Government).[13] Its most distinguishing characteristic was its very critical view of the West and its imperialist policies. This made *Gharbzadigī* the reference work *par excellence* for all intellectuals of the decade. Hamid Dabashi even claims that if there was one single important text in Iran's modern history, it was this one,[14] and Mehrzad Boroujerdi calls it the "holy book" of several generations.[15] For more than two decades, this essay supplied Iran's social critics with a vocabulary and shaped the essence of the anti-Western disposition that dominated the anti-Western Islamic discourse. Āl-i Aḥmad's ideas had a huge impact on most intellectuals of the 1960s, and it is likely true that, as Iranian journalist Morad Saqafi stated, in 1978, just before the revolution, you could not have found an Iranian intellectual who questioned Āl-i Aḥmad's analysis of Iranian society.[16]

Jalāl Āl-i Aḥmad analysed the unquestioning adoption of Western customs and goods, called it Iran's sickness and in doing so gave poignant expression to his coevals' feelings. He stated that his generation–unlike earlier ones that had blindly copied the West as when moderniser Ḥasan Taqīzādah had called on Iran to become European from head to toe–took a much more sober view of the West because of its imperialism and colonialism, and strongly desired authenticity. Having rediscovered Islam as the sole authentic culture, he pledged himself to the religion's potential strength and declared the clergy an important part of Iran's authentic identity[17] as they were the only group that had withdrawn from the West. He credited Islam with saving Iran from being Christianised, colonised, and

12 The most comprehensive study of Nā'īnī is provided in Abdul-Hadi Hairi, *Shi'ism and Constitutionalism in Iran. A Study of the Role Played by the Persian Residents of Iraq in Iranian Politics*, Leiden: Brill 1977, 109–151; for *Tanbīh al-ummah wa-tanzīh al-millah*, ibid., 154–164; Fereshteh Nouraie, "The Constitutional Ideas of a Shi'ite Mujtahid: Muhammad Husayn Nai'ni", *Iranian Studies* 8 (1975), 234–247.

13 On this work see also Hamid Dabashi, "By what Authority? The Formation of Khomeini's Revolutionary Discourse 1964–1977", *Social Compass* 36 (1989), 511–538.

14 Dabashi, *Theology of Discontent*, 73–74.

15 Boroujerdi, *Iranian Intellectuals and the West*, 67.

16 Morad Saqafi, "Crossing the Desert: Iranian Intellectuals after the Islamic Revolution", in: Nabavi, *Intellectual Trends*, 111–135, 115.

17 Further information on the subject of 'authenticity' in the Iranian discourse of that decade can be found in Nabavi, "The Discourse of 'Authentic Culture' ", 91–110.

exploited by the West and imperialism.[18] In Huntingtonian fashion, he writes: "The twelve centuries of conflict between West and East must be understood as a struggle between Islam and Christianity."[19]
As the clergy had been Iran's last line of defence against the West in its history, they now ought to be fighting the unjust, Western-supported rule of the Shah. Āl-i Aḥmad cites the tobacco protest[20] and Faḍl Allāh Nūrī (1842–1909),[21] whom he regards as a martyr of this fight, as positive examples of the clerics' facing off against the West. He does not view Nūrī as an outright opponent of the constitution of 1906–*mashrūṭah*–but claims that his criticism of it was solely due to the fact that it was not based on the Sharia and thus was not *mashrūʿ*–legal in terms of the Sharia–because it was based on the ideas of "the Christian, Mālkūm Khān[22] and the Social Democrat Ṭālibūf"[23]–which brings Āl-i Aḥmad back to his subject of 'Westernisation' and Social Democracy, Western style.

Rehabilitating the cleric Nūrī is an unexpected move by Āl-i Aḥmad, especially when we consider Nūrī's reactionary criticism of the constitution which focused–among other subjects–on women's right to vote. Still, Āl-i Aḥmad has nothing but harsh criticism for Nūrī's opponents, mainly for the secular intellectuals, Social Democrats like Ṭālibūf, whom he blames for the failure of the constitutional project and subsequent events, i.e., the dictatorship of Riẓā Shāh and of his son which, in his eyes, were a consequence of this failure. For him, the cause of both dictatorships–which were accompanied by a massive Westernisation of Iran–were the disproportionate expectations of the constitutional movement's intellectuals whose sole

18 Āl-i Aḥmad, *Gharbzadigī*, 33.

19 Ibid.

20 On this subject, see Ann Lambton, "The Tobacco Regie: Prelude to Revolution", *Studia Islamica* 22 (1965), 119–157; Nikki Keddie, *Religion and Rebellion in Iran. The Tobacco Protest of 1891–92*, London: Cass 1966.

21 On this subject, see Vanessa Martin, "Nūrī, Shaykh Faḍl Allāh", in: *Encyclopaedia of Islam, Second Edition*, Peri Bearman, Thierry Bianquis, Clifford E. Bosworth, Emeri van Donzel, and Wolfhart P. Heinrichs, eds., Leiden: Brill 2010, http://dx.doi.org/10.1163/1573-3912_islam_SIM_5996, accessed 17 February 2017; Abdul Hadi Hairi, "Shaykh Fazl Allah Nuri's Refutation of the Idea of Constitutionalism", *Middle Eastern Studies* 13 (1979), 327–339; Vanessa Martin, "The Anti-Constitutionalist Arguments of Shaikh Fazlallah Nuri", *Middle Eastern Studies* 22 (1986), 181–196.

22 A study of Mālkūm Khān's life and work can be found in Hamid Algar, *Mirzā Malkum Khān. A Study in the History of Iranian Modernism*, Berkeley: Univ. of California Press 1973; see also Mangol Bayat, *Mysticism and Dissent. Socioreligious Thought in Qajar Iran*, Syracuse: Syracuse Univ. Press 1982, 137–140; and Farzin Vahdat, *God and Juggernaut. Iran's Intellectual Encounter with Modernity*, Syracuse: Syracuse Univ. Press 2002, 30–36.

23 Āl-i Aḥmad, *Gharbzadigī*, 78. For information on Mīrzā 'Abd al-Rahīm Ṭālibūf, see Bayat, *Mysticism and Dissent*, 140, 163, 164, 174; Vahdat, *God and Juggernaut*, 48–54.

orientation was towards the West and who did not take Iran's Islam into consideration.[24]

At the time, no one could escape this discourse. For most Iranians, *Gharbzadigī* was the starting point of their thought. In fact, it was this book that gave a great many people the idea that Islam should have a role in politics, and that it had a solution to offer to all the challenges Iran was facing, growing economic inequality being among them.

Let us now turn to the shaper of Iranian Islamist ideology: ʿAlī Sharīʿatī. Āyatullāh Maḥmūd Ṭāliqānī (1914–1979), another important figure in the revolution, stated that it was thanks to Sharīʿatī that the youth became part of the revolutionary movement, and Āyatullāh Muḥammad Bihishtī (1928–1981) claimed that while Khumeinī's books did not speak to the young generation, Sharīʿatī's were essential to the revolution, especially *Ummat wa-Imāmat* (*Islamic Community and Imamate*), a text based on his lectures at *Ḥusaynīyah-i Irshād,* a religious centre in Tehran founded to bring Islam to young people in modern language and with immediate relevance to questions of modern life,[25] and first published in Iran in 1972.[26] Āl-i Aḥmad had recognised the potential of Islam, but it was ʿAlī Sharīʿatī who used it to shape a modern ideology.

Born in Mashhad, ʿAlī Sharīʿatī came from a family of renowned scholars.[27] Though he was not a *mulā*, his father Muḥammad Taqī Sharīʿatī authored standard works on Quranic studies.[28] He was also the founder of a short-lived movement of God-worshipping Socialists in which his son was a member and through which he received his first critical Islamic education.[29]

After graduating from secondary school and teacher training college, Sharīʿatī initially worked as a village teacher and began writing books on Islam. In 1956, he enrolled at the literary faculty of Mashhad University to

24 Āl-i Aḥmad, *Gharbzadigī*, 78.

25 On this issue, see Shahrough Akhavi, *Religion and Politics in Contemporary Iran: Clergy-State Relations in the Pahlavi Period*, Albany: State University of New York Press 1980, 145; Ali Rahnema, *An Islamic Utopian. A Political Biography of Ali Shariʿati*, London: I.B. Tauris 1998, 226.

26 Ervand Abrahamian, *Radical Islam: The Iranian Mojahedin,* London: I.B. Tauris 1989, 105.

27 Detailed information on his life and work can be found in Rahnema, *An Islamic Utopian*; Ervand Abrahamian, "ʿAli Shariʿati: Ideologue of the Iranian Revolution", in: *Islam, Politics and Social Movement*, Edmund Burke and Ira Lapidus, eds., Berkeley: University of California Press 1988; Boroujerdi, *Iranian Intellectuals and the West*; Abdulaziz Sachedina, "Ali Shariati: Ideologue of the Iranian Revolution", in: John L. Esposito, ed., *Voices of Resurgent Islam*, New York: Oxford Univ. Press 1983, 191–214; Dabashi, *Theology of Discontent*, 102–146.

28 The book *Waḥī wa-nubūwwat* [*Revelation and Prophecy*], Tehran, no year, was especially widely read.

29 Assef Bayat, "Shariati and Marx: A Critique of an 'Islamic' Critique of Marxism", in: *Alif* 10 (1990), 19–41, 20.

study history and the philosophy of history. He was arrested together with his father over their political activities in 1957, but freed again six months later.[30] In 1959, he passed his university exam as one of the top-ranking graduates which earned him a scholarship to study abroad. He chose to go to Paris, capital of a leading colonial power. This move proved to be a watershed in Sharīʿatī's political activities and intellectual development, as this period coincided with intense anti-colonial struggle throughout the world. He met with Frantz Fanon (1925–1961), famous proponent of decolonisation, and translated his *Les Damnés de la Terre*, a key document of anti-colonial resistance to this day, into Farsi. He was also influenced by Jean-Paul Sartre, sympathised with the Algerian independence movement, and published a journal titled *Īrān-i Āzād* (*Free Iran*).[31]

Returning to Iran in 1965, Sharīʿatī was arrested at the border and charged with political agitation against the Shah. After his release several months later, he began teaching at a village school again, but quickly moved on to upper secondary school and then to a professorship of Islamic History at Mashhad University. Another arrest followed. After his release in 1969, Sharīʿatī was active at *Ḥusaynīyah-i Irshād.* His meteoric rise as an ideological leader began here. His lectures were taped or published in print in several dozen volumes, the most important of which is the multi-volume *Islām-shināsī* (usually translated as Islamology, although I would prefer Islamic Studies). They were widely circulated among Muslim youth.

The main thesis he advocated in his lectures quickly gained notoriety among both students and clerics: that an originally revolutionary Shia had been turned into a religion of contrite penitents, with its thought stagnating. Sharīʿatī distinguishes 'red' and 'black' Shia, with black being reactionary and cooperating with the rulers, while the red was the true, revolutionary Shia of Imam ʿAlī. Red Shia represented an Islam of warriors and martyrs, black Shia the religion of mourners. Today, he claimed, believers were reduced to wailing and moaning, only remembering their faith on religious holidays. Sharīʿatī blames the clergy: The *mulā*s had repressed Islam's revolutionary potential to protect their own privileges.[32] He criticises both that the clergy placed themselves between the faithful and God by claiming the monopoly of interpreting the will of God, and that they dissuaded the people from reading and understanding the Quran themselves. Sharīʿatī writes:

---

30 Yann Richard, *Der verborgene Imam. Geschichte des Schiismus in Iran*, Berlin: Wagenbach 1983, 113.

31 On the journal, see ibid., 111–112.

32 Sharīʿatī's chastisement of the clergy is discussed in Mangol Bayat-Philipp, "Shiʿism in Contemporary Iranian Politics: The Case of ʿAli Shariʿati'", in: *Towards a Modern Iran. Studies in Thought, Politics and Society*, Elie Kedourie and Sylvia Haim, eds., London: Cass 1980, 155–168, 157–158.

> A Quran that is neither read nor understood is a book like any other, an unwritten sheet. That is why so much effort is put into keeping us from reading, understanding and discussing it. They claim that we would not understand it, that it is too complicated. A rational interpretation of the Quran is banned.[33]

That is, Sharīʿatī proposes an Islam without *mulās* *(Islām minhā-yi Rūḥānīyat)*. Interpreted correctly–by people other than the corrupt clerics who stood in the way of its necessary revolutionising and ideologising–Islam would be an ideology that could answer all political, social, and economic questions. This ideologised Islam he called for would then take over secular government.[34]

His incendiary rhetoric led to Sharīʿatī being arrested again in 1973.[35] This time, he was not released until 1975, when the Algerian government interceded on his behalf. In May 1977, he was given permission to travel to London where he died three weeks later, on 19 June 1977, of unknown causes. His death, contrary to the hopes of those who disliked him, increased his popularity "... and made Shariati a virtual legend among his supporters".[36]

Ironically, it was Sharīʿatī who contributed notably to the victory of the clergy over the other revolutionary factions. Mahdī Bāzargān (1907–1995), one of the most important revolutionary leaders, contends that the emergence of a religious leadership was mainly due to Sharīʿatī's efforts. Only through his book *Ummat wa-Imāmat* had the figure of the Imam taken on a positive significance to the wider public.[37]

Sharīʿatī thought that Āl-i Aḥmad had correctly identified the problem, but failed to develop a solution. He intended to offer one. Unlike Āl-i Aḥmad, Sharīʿatī was able to write about the West from long personal experience; his argument was influenced by thinkers such as Georges Gurvitch (1894–1965), Carl Gustav Jung (1875–1961), Claude Lévi-Strauss (1908–2009), André Malraux (1901–1976), and Jean-Paul Sartre, and through their works, he was familiar with Western self-doubt. Sharīʿatī saw the solution to putting Iran's culture and identity beyond Western reach in a "return to it-

---

33 ʿAlī Sharīʿatī, "Fāṭimah, Fāṭimah ast" [Fatima is Fatima], *Zan* [*Woman*], Tehran 1991, 40.

34 On his criticism of the clergy, see also Bayat-Philipp, "Shiʿism in Contemporary Iranian Politics", 157–158.

35 A complete list of Sharīʿatī's work is found in Nikki Keddie, *Roots of Revolution. An interpretative history of modern Iran*, New Haven: Yale Univ. Press 1981, 51. English translations exist: *On the Sociology of Islam*, Berkeley: Mizan Press 1979, and *Marxism and Other Western Fallacies,* Berkeley: Mizan Press 1980, both edited by Hamid Algar. Other works were translated under the auspices of the *Ḥusaynīyah-i Irshād*. Several of his most important works were also translated into German as part of the "Islamische Renaissance" series issued by the Iranian embassy in Bonn.

36 Assef Bayat, "Shariati and Marx", 22.

37 Mahdī Bāzargān, "Duktūr Sharīʿatī wa-rūḥānīyat" [Doctor Shariati and the clergy], in: Jaʿfar Saʿīdī, *Shakhṣīyat wa-andīšah-i duktūr-i ʿAlī Sharīʿatī* [*Person and Thoughts of Doctor ʿAlī Sharīʿatī*], Tehran 1993, 19; further on the clergy's response to Sharīʿatī, Rahnema, *An Islamic Utopian*, 266–267.

self" (*bāzgasht bih khvīshtan*).[38] Here, he took his cue from Frantz Fanon, who had talked of the return of the suppressed.

While Sharīʿatī's ideas gained him many enemies in the clerical establishment, the younger generation's clerics as well as religious lay people became his followers: the charismatic, inspiring orator Sharīʿatī, who left everything that did not fit his ideology out of his lectures, had an enormous impact which not even the considerable incongruities in his speeches could diminish. The most far-reaching consequences developed out of his criticism of imperialism and thus of the West: according to Sharīʿatī, the West claimed that the form of government that most respected human rights was democracy, but that it wanted those human rights only for itself.[39]

> When the humanists' call for democracy, liberalism, individual freedom and human rights arose in Europe, the fever of humanism rose and produced the most beautiful creations of the word, such wondrous and brilliant poems, masterpieces of music, theatre, literature and painting; when paeans to liberty and liberalism excited the homeless intellectuals and the honourable, naive humanists, the democratically elected government of France, chosen by the majority of the electorate following the Great French Revolution, declared in a proclamation: Ladies and gentlemen, citizens of France: Whoever wishes to view the bombardment of Algiers up close may show up on day X at place Y which the French army has provided for spectators wishing to observe military operations closely. Yes, the liberal government elected through democratic vote proclaimed the bombardment of a major city and the mass murder of its people whose sole offense it was to be weak. This democratic and liberal government, heir to the achievements of the Great French Revolution, has 45,000 people killed in Madagascar on a single day. These crimes did not take place at the time of Louis, lord of Versailles. Colonialism and the mass murder of peoples, the destruction of the cultures, wealth, stories and civilisations of non-European peoples that came with it are owed to governments that were elected democratically, governments that believed in liberalism. These crimes were not committed by priests, inquisitors and caesars, but in the name of democracy and western liberalism. When? In the 19th and 20th centuries–that is to say, in the years when Europeans proclaimed liberalism, democracy, brotherhood and humanism to the world; when art, literature, poetry, culture and philosophy were swept away on this new wave, and when intellectuals from the plundered countries of the third world, themselves helpless and ignorant victims of these tempting words, burned with excitement for it.[40]

But Sharīʿatī's criticism did not end with Western governments; he also–even more poignantly–criticised the Western nations' intellectuals: in his

38 Further information on this can be found in Gheissari, *Iranian Intellectuals in the 20th Century*, 97–106.

39 About Sharīʿatī's ideas on democracy, see also Forough Jahanbakhsh, *Islam, Democracy and Religious Modernism in Iran (1953–2000). From Bazargan to Soroush*, Leiden: Brill 2001, 119–126.

40 ʿAlī Sharīʿatī, *Ummat wa-Imāmat* [*Islamic Community and Imamate*], Tehran 1980, 163–164.

eyes, they had not put up any resistance against, had voiced no criticism of their governments' actions, but rather had taken their side, and only campaigned for Westerners' human rights, and they had not opposed imperialism. A prominent point of criticism is the West's ubiquitous application of double standards, which, to him, completely discredited both the governments and the intellectuals.[41]

> What thinker, humanist, Socialist or Communist in Europe ever raised his voice to object when colonialism and capitalism–legitimised by democracy and masked by liberalism–started this fire around the world? When millions of helpless Muslims, Indians, black and yellow peoples were robbed and destroyed? I cannot forgive Marx, Engels, Proudhon and the other Socialists and revolutionaries that they only stood for the just distribution in the West of what was stolen in the East–a distribution among capitalists and workers. They called this the right of the workers to the goods they produced. Marx called Western goods concentrated labour. I as an Oriental bear witness that they are concentrated crime, concentrated robbery.[42]

Thus, Sharīʿatī had demarcated his position by adding his criticism of Western Socialism and Communism to that of liberal democracy. In 1977, a pamphlet attributed to him was published with the title *Insān, Islām wa-mārksīsm* (Man, Islam and Marxism) which systematically addresses Marxist principles.[43] From this point, Sharīʿatī progressed directly to his third way, Islamic Socialism. For him, Islam has two dimensions: justice *(ʿidālat)* and right guidance *(hidāyat)*. Guidance refers to contact between God and man, a purely personal relationship between the faithful and the Creator. This needed to be revived by putting the *mulā*s back in their place.

To this undertaking, Sharīʿatī added the aspect of justice, the social dimension of Islam. He sought to revive these dimensions of religion on the assumption that, if religion were to be turned into a unified ideological mode of thought, it could be both *ʿidālat* and *hidāyat* to the people. The name he gave this programme was *niẓām-i tawḥīd,* the system of oneness (God's oneness). He understood it as a system of values, i.e. a set of commandments and prohibitions. A religion had to be able to offer answers to all questions, but above all, it had been revealed in order to have social and political impact. The Prophets were sent to fight oppression. Muḥammad had sought not only to establish a religious community, but a society forever striving towards progress and greater social justice. This order would unite humanity through one set of principles: virtue, joint struggle for jus-

---

41 Ibid., 165.

42 Ibid., 165.

43 Assef Bayat sees this critique as a fundamental misunderstanding of Marx. Assef Bayat, "Shariati and Marx", 26. Bayat also points out that the text or parts of it may be the work of someone other than Sharīʿatī. However, its importance is independent of its putative authorship.

tice, equality, brotherhood, joint ownership of the means of production, and above all, the desire to create a classless society on earth. In Shariᶜati's reading, Islam had been historically appropriated by the Muslim petit-bourgeoisie and thus the ascetic revolutionary spirit congenial to the cause of the downtrodden was sacrificed.[44] Revolutionary asceticism is not something modern Muslims have learned from Marxists: "It is the Marxists who have just learned it from Islam."[45] We should not forget that the threat of losing the young generation to Marxism–a Western ideology–for want of a clear explanatory model felt particularly acute to him. In the 1960s and 1970s, Marxism was extremely attractive for young people. The Tudeh party, a Communist party, was so popular that the words intellectual and *Tūdih'ī*–follower of the Tudeh party–were almost synonymous. So, in opposition to Western ideologies, Sharīᶜati sought to develop a competitive Islamic answer to current problems.

From Muḥammad's intent to create such a society with a unitary mode of thinking, Sharīᶜatī postulated that each Muslim had a direct political responsibility to further it. He regarded the loss of such a unitary set of principles as the root of all problems the Islamic world was confronting in the 1970s. To solve them, the young generation had to be offered a new, unique identity based on the principle of *tawḥīd*, the oneness of God. Only this genuinely Islamic identity would make Muslims independent from the West.

In pointing at the anti-capitalist outlook of Islam, Sharīᶜatī's main point of reference was Abū Ẕarr, a companion of the Prophet Muḥammad. Little is known of Abū Ẕarr's life before his conversion to Islam. He is said to have been a serious young man and a monotheist even before converting. He is considered one of the greatest and most loyal companions, *ṣaḥābah*, and he is especially important in Shiite Islam where he is regarded as one of the most loyal followers of Imām ᶜAlī.

It is not only Sharīᶜatī who credits Abū Ẕarr al-Ghifārī as a principal antecedent of Islamic socialism because of his protest against the accumulation of wealth by the ruling class during ᶜUthmān's caliphate and support for an equitable redistribution of wealth. Other Muslim thinkers, too, rediscovered Abū Ẕarr in the first half of the twentieth century, among them the Lebanese Shiite Aḥmad Riḍā (d. 1953) who published an article in 1910 calling Abū Ẕarr an *ishtirākī*, a socialist.[46] In the 1940s, this idea gained fol-

44 ʿAlī Sharīʿatī, *Jahatgīrī-i ṭabaqātī-i Islām* [*Class Orientation in Islam*], no year, no place, 5, http://ketabnak.com/book/53711/جهت-گیری-طبقاتی-اسلام?dlid=53711&page=all or https://drive.google.com/open?id=0B6Y4eT-aEgUXT19ONWloX0ZDa3RoOW5UY24tbjNBSm1fZ1M4, accessed 17 February 2017.

45 Sharīʿatī, *Jahatgīrī-i ṭabaqā tī-i Islām*, 6.

46 Abū Ẕarr's interpretation of Surah 9:34 was seen as a prediction of socialist ideas. With reference to this verse, he had argued that in Islam no one should have more

lowers among Egyptian intellectuals, and in 1945 the Egyptian ʿAbd al-Ḥamīd-Jūdah al-Saḥḥar (1913–1974) wrote a book calling Abū Ẕarr an ascetic socialist and a model for socialism in Islam.

Sharīʿatī translated this book into Farsi between 1951 and 1953 and commented on it. It was published in 1955 as *Abū Ẕarr, God's Socialist Servant* (*Abū Ẕarr-i Ghifārī: Khudāparast-i sūsyālīst)*. Here, Sharīʿatī presented Abū Ẕarr as the perfect model of a devout socialist and as a model for the Iranian People's Party just founded one year earlier. Abū Ẕarr was seen as a hero of the poor and with them, of authentic Islam. This authentic Islam represented the exact opposite of what the third caliph of Islam, ʿUthmān, introduced.

> Umar also left and 'Uthman, this incompetent, pseudo-religious old man, took over the reins of rulership, and the instability which had come into being in the foundation of Islamic rule became so strong that the infrastructure of Muhammad (PBUH) was immediately destroyed. During 'Uthman's rule, the Caliphate was changed into a monarchy and the mud homes of the Islamic rulers were changed into king's palaces; simplicity changed into the splendid ceremony of the court of Mu'awiyah and the extravagant organization of 'Uthman. Abu Dhar [sic!], who was the fourth or fifth person who joined Islam, and whose sword had been most effective in assisting the progress of the Islamic movement, saw this deviation. 'Ali, the image of piety and truth, became isolated and the enemies of Islam had found their way into the Caliphate organization and, like termites, they were eating away at Islam.[47]

Sharīʿatī continues to explain in exhaustive detail what deviation took place under the caliphate of ʿUthmān and how Abū Ẕarr tried to rescue true Islam by opposing him:

> Abu Dhar was watching these shameful scenes and because he could no longer bear it, could no longer remain silent, he rebelled, a manly and wonderful rebellion; an uprising which caused rebellion in all the Islamic lands against 'Uthman; an uprising from which the waves of enthusiasm can still be felt until the present day in the situations of human societies. Abu Dhar was trying to develop the economic and political unity of Islam and the regime of 'Uthman was reviving aristocracy. Abu Dhar believed Islam to be the refuge of the helpless, the oppressed and the humiliated people and 'Uthman, the tool of capitalism, was the bastion to preserve the interests of the usurers, the wealthy and the aristocrats.
>
> This struggle between Abu Dhar and 'Uthman began, and Abu Dhar, in the end, lost his life upon this path. Abu Dhar would cry out, 'This capital, wealth, gold and silver which you have hoarded must be equally divided among all Muslims. Everyone must share in the others' benefits in the economic and ethical system of Islam, in all blessings of life.' But 'Uthman saw Islam in ceremonies, external show

goods than were needed to satisfy his basic needs. Islam meant that no one should accumulate wealth.

47 Ali Shariati, *And Once Again Abu Dharr*, Raleigh: Lulu Press Inc. 2014, 3, www.playandlearn.org/reader.asp?Type=Books&fn=102, Persian: https://drive.google.com/open?id=0B6Y4eT-aEgUXcXByZ2pudXN1cVU, accessed 17 February 2017.

> and the pretence of piety and sanctity. He did not believe that religion should interfere with the poverty of the majority and the opulence of the minority. Abu Dhar, who had begun the struggle for the development of Islamic equality, would not be pacified and would not let the enemy be pacified, either...[48]

Sharīʿatī felt so close to Abū Ẕarr that he even described himself as Abū Ẕarr‘s reincarnation at one point. After his death, his followers referred to Sharīʿatī as the Abū Ẕarr of his time.

As mentioned earlier, İhsan Eliaçık, Turkey's main proponent of Islamic Socialism, sees himself as very close to the teachings of Sharīʿatī. However, he also claims to have learned from Sharīʿatī's experience to always refer to the Quran when arguing that something is genuinely Islamic, since in his opinion, Sharīʿatī's arguments were weak because Sharīʿatī was educated at the Sorbonne and did not speak Arabic.[49] The second claim is demonstrably untrue as Sharīʿatī was educated in Islamic Studies by his father Taqī Sharīʿatī. He knew his Quran. Nonetheless İhsan Eliaçık might be right that Sharīʿatī's Western education was a dangerous argument in the hands of his opponents. Yet I would argue against Eliaçık and emphasise that Sharīʿatī succeeded in firmly rooting his argument for non-capitalist Islam in the teachings of Islam despite choosing a Shia role model and basing his argument much more on this role model than on the Quran itself. It seems likely that Sharīʿatī was not looking for a universal Islamic ecumenical idea, but rather for a Shia approach. All the more interesting, then, that an approach that is very critical of Sunni Islam and strongly biased when it comes to the companions of the Prophet can have such a large impact in today's Turkey, or at least for a modern Turkish intellectual.

This takes me to Sharīʿatī's influence in his homeland Iran today. After the revolution, two parties had important messages regarding economics: The Leftists and the so-called Moderates. Victory ultimately went to the so-called Moderates with their capitalist agenda. Akbar Rafsanjānī, who became president in 1989 for the first time, followed a completely different strategy from his predecessor Mīrḥusayn Mūsawī, who was much more influenced by ideas of a planned economy and solved Iran's economic problems during the Iran-Iraq war through these approaches. When Rafsanjānī came to power, he changed the agenda. Having become one of Iran's richest men even before the revolution through trading pistachios, he opened the market and went back to capitalist policies. Foreign investment was allowed, state companies sold, and state subsidies reduced. Since the late 1990s, Islamic capitalism has been the prevailing economic vision. No voices proposing to revive Sharīʿatī's ideas are heard now.

48 Shariati, *And Once Again Abu Dharr*, 5–6.
49 Nurtsch, "The Koran and Social Justice", Interview with Ihsan Eliacik.

Quite the contrary: In contemporary Iranian discourse which, following Assef Bayat, I would classify as mainly post-Islamic,[50] the ideas of Sharīʿati and Āl-i Aḥmad are typically addressed and some, such as his criticism of the clergy whom the majority of the people followed in unreflected imitation,[51] are seeing a renaissance. However, Sharīʿati and Āl-i Aḥmad are forcefully criticised by modern Iranian intellectuals for their radical and unconstructive criticism of the West and of imperialism and "... for leading Iran's intellectuals tradition astray at a critical juncture in the country's history."[52] The author shares Assef Bayat's view that these people are the first post-colonial intellectuals of note in the Islamic world.[53] Bayat writes:

> Post-colonial intellectuals discarded 'orientalism in reverse', refusing to view either the Muslim world or the West as an undifferentiated, unitary, and unchangeable entity, or in binary opposition. Rather, they discarded differentiation, change, and hybridity within these worlds, and flow and dialogue between them.[54]

In this sense, ʿAbd al-Karīm Surūsh turns against the concept of "return to ourselves" *(bāzgasht bih khvīsh)* that Sharīʿatī coined, saying: "Whatever our heart and mind are willing to accept belongs to us."[55] If in the past the Iranian people had not acted according to this principle, Iran would have had to reject Islam. Western influence, Surūsh said, is nothing new. Claiming that western progress does not fit into Iranian culture is wrong; after all, Iranian culture has always been a melting-pot of three cultural influences: the Arabic, the indigenous Iranian, and the Western.

Surūsh rejects the radical condemnation of the West expressed in Āl-i Aḥmad's slogan "Westoxication"; what he wants is rather to make choices

---

50 The idea that the Iranian intellectuals who led the Revolution are the first to be rightly considered post-Islamic is argued in Asef Bayat, *Making Islam Democratic. Social Movements and the Post-Islamist Turn*, Stanford: Stanford University Press 2007.

51 As professor Hāshim Āqājirī took up these accusations in one of his lectures and levelled them at the Islamic Republic, he was sentenced to death in May 2003. The judgement caused public consternation and was quickly revised due to the outcry. This was one reason why the theses of Āqājirīs and thus of Sharīʿatī became widely known. Āqājirī's defense was published in book form, and remains in print in Iran as Puryā Hāʾzāde, Hāshim Āqājirī, *Matn-i kāmil-i hamadān, lāyah-hā-yi defāʿiyih* [*The Complete Text of Hamadan, the Defense*], Tehran 2003. The book contains the lecture by Āqājirī, his court defense, and statements by several people of great prominence on the case, among them then president Muḥammad Khātamī, Āyatullāh Miṣbāḥ Yazdī, and the editor of the ultraconservative daily paper *Kayhān*, Ḥusayn Sharīʿatmadārī.

52 Mehran Kamrava, *Iran's Intellectual Revolution*, Cambridge: Cambridge Univ. Press 2008, 52.

53 Bayat, *Making Islam Democratic*, 88.

54 Ibid.

55 ʿAbd al-Karīm Surūsh, "Sih farhang" [Three Cultures], in: idem, *Rāzdānī wa-Rūshanfikrī wa-Dīndārī* [*Knowledge of Secrets: Intellectualism and Religiosity*], Tehran 1993, 105–130, 121.

informed by a critical mindset which differentiates between things worth adopting and those that must be rejected. He wants to plant the best of other cultures inside his own culture's mind, just as Greek philosophy was developed further by Muslims. According to him, this first encounter with the West through the translation of Greek philosophers into Arabic was beneficial for both Islam and Iran. Future exchanges between the two cultures could be just as beneficial. Surūsh thus also categorically rejects Āl-i Aḥmad's thesis that the West infected Iran like a disease. On the contrary: "If the West had not come in, we would not have developed; we would have died."[56] He does not see *Gharbzadigī* as a disease, but a historical fact. Surūsh no longer looks for the origins of Iran's problems in Western imperialist policies, but in the despotism that has dominated Iranian political culture for many centuries.

Iranian philosopher Rāmīn Jahānbiglū has posited that, historically, there have been four distinct generations of Iranian intellectuals since their emergence as a recognisable social class in the second half of the 19th century. Each of these generations corresponded to a phase in the recent history of Iran. The first is the generation that formulated the goals of the constitutional revolution. The second is that of the Pahlavi era. The third generation held sway in the 1960s and 1970s and produced the slogans of the Islamic Revolution. Jalāl Āl-i Aḥmad and ʿAlī Sharīʿatī are representatives of this revolutionary cohort. Now, there is a fourth generation of intellectuals whose emergence Jahānbiglū dates to the decade following the Revolution, when changed political dynamics allowed renewed activism.[57] The thesis that the fourth generation of Iranian intellectuals have mostly freed themselves from the thought patterns of anti-imperialist, anti-colonial discourses proposed by Jahānbiglū and also by Bayat in his *Making Islam Democratic. Social Movements and the Post-Islamist Turn* seems largely correct, and it is all the more interesting that these ideas are not dead in Turkey today.

56 Ibid., 112.

57 The thesis is developed in his book: Rāmīn Jahānbiglū, *Mūj-i Chahārum* [*The Fourth Wave*], Tehran: Nashr wa Pizhūhish-i Farzān Rūz 2002.

The Emergence of Anti-Capitalist Muslims in Turkey: "God, Bread, Freedom"*

Bayram Koca

This study aims to analyze the reasons behind the emergence of Anti-capitalist Muslims in Turkey. In this context, it will focus on aspects of AKPs compatibility with Islam and capitalism and then highlight the objections of Anti-capitalist Muslims to relevant AKP policies. Finally, actions and discourses of Anti-capitalist Muslims will be analyzed. This study covers the period from 2012 to 2015; at the end of this period the movement underwent a re-structuring under different names.

After the 1980 Military Coup

With the declaration of the Republic in 1923, Islam was banished from both the political and institutional arena in Turkey. The separation between Islam and political power continued even during the reign of right-wing parties up until the 1980 military coup.

Under the leadership of Turgut Özal[1], Turkey implemented neoliberal policies during the 1980s, a practice which was widespread outside Turkey. The goals of these policies were improvement of the balance of payments in the short term, reduction of inflation, assurance of economic stability and creation of an export-oriented, market-based economy in the long term.[2] Market economy, also, increased the value of the 'present'.[3] The concept of time in politics changed in parallel with the market economy. Politics, especially left politics, which targeted revolution until the 1970s, focused on solving the current problems of politics during the 1980s. In sum, the liberalization and globalization processes wiped away revolutionary struggles and began to be focused on the 'present' instead of the 'future' in Turkey. Turkey went through this transition under an oppressive post-military coup-regime. As the market economy became dominant, the ideo-

* Data used in this study is based on the findings of the master thesis of the author submitted in 2013. For this thesis participant-observer and in-depth interview methods were used. For this article findings have been revised about developments on Anti-capitalist Muslims since 2013.

1 Halil Turgut Özal (1927–1993), Prime Minister (1983–1989) and President of Turkey (1989–1993).

2 Şevket Pamuk, *Türkiye'nin 200 Yıllık İktisadi Tarihi,* Istanbul: Türkiye İş Bankası Kültür Yayınları 2014, 265.

3 Nilüfer Göle, *Melez Desenler. İslam ve Modernlik Üzerine,* Istanbul: Metis 2011, 7.

logical conflict between the state and Islam ended during the 1980s. The Turkish state had been performing a distanced stance towards expressions of Islam in the public sphere as well as the dissemination of Islamic knowledge and values by state institutions before the 1980 Military Coup took place on September 12th. This event paved the way for collaboration between Islamic reasoning and capitalist market activities with the aim of preventing the rise of socialism. A new paradigm was finally set up with *political* Islam. Menderes Çınar explains the situation as follows: "The September 12th coup put great pressure on the radical left and right and thus created a gap in the political space. This gap was largely filled by political Islam."[4] Prime Minister Turgut Özal was the one who established a link between the free market and Islamic morality. According to this logic, if the free market was regulated by Islam, it would not be as brutal as in Western countries.[5] With this reasoning, Özal paved the way for an urbanized and middle-class conservative social base, which he consolidated with market and neoliberal values.[6] Out of this formation an Islamic capitalist business group came about. This group supported Necmettin Erbakan,[7] the leader of the Welfare Party (*Refah Partisi*, RP), in the 1990s, and Recep Tayyip Erdoğan in the 2000s. The Welfare Party, which represented political Islamism in Turkey, adapted to neoliberalism with its new program Just Order *(Adil Düzen)*. With *Adil Düzen*, the RP accepted neoliberalism and adapted to it, thinking that when it came to power, inequalities originating from neoliberalism would be reduced to some extent with social justice policies. With regard to structural changes in the Muslim world, Patrick Haenni called this new economic practice "Market Islam"[8]–a practice that emerged in Turkey with this distinct background and led to the emergence of Anti-capitalist Muslims.

As far as economic practice and market norms and values are concerned, Turkey has been witnessing the emergence of two different approaches to Islam throughout the last decades. The first approach, Market Islam, current-

4 Mederes Çınar, "Yükselen Değerlerin İşadamı Cephesi: MÜSİAD", *Birikim* 9 (1997), 52–66, 64–65.

5 Yüksel Taşkın, *Anti-Komünizmden Küreselleşme Karşıtlığına Milliyetçi Muhafazakâr Entelijansiya*, Istanbul: İletişim 2007, 302.

6 Taşkın, *Anti-Komünizmden Küreselleşme Karşıtlığına*, 295.

7 Necmettin Erbakan (1926–2011) was the founder of the National Vision Movement (*Milli Görüş Hareketi*). This movement represents mainstream political Islamism in Turkey whereas the Welfare Party was this movement's political arm. For more information see Ruşen Çakır, "Milli Görüş Hareketi", in: *Modern Türkiye'de Siyasi Düşünce: İslamcılık*, Yasin Aktay, Murat Gültekingil, Tanıl Bora, eds., Istanbul: İletişim 2005, 544–575.

8 Patrick Haenni, *L'islam de marché: l'autre révolution conservatrice*, Paris: Seuil 2005. Transl. into Turkish by Levent Ünsaldı, *Piyasa İslamı. İslam Suretinde Neoliberalizm*, Istanbul: Özgür Üniversite 2011.

ly represented by the Justice and Development Party (*Adalet ve Kalkınma Partisi*, AKP), came to be the dominant one, whereas the Anti-capitalist Muslims movement can be considered a minority formation. The former became associated with neoliberalism and the right wing, and the latter with socialism and the left wing. Reality, however, is a little more complex. Business people with an explicitly Islamic/Islamist position established their association under the name of the Independent Industrialists' and Businessmen's Association (*Müstakil Sanayici ve İşadamları Derneği*, MÜSİAD) in 1990, and continued to rise during the 1990s, during which a moderation of the radical Islamic movement also began. The basic objective of political Islamists was "the development of economic opportunity spaces."[9] In particular, with the Welfare Party winning some municipalities in local elections, political Islamists began to receive state tenders. The services that the party provided through municipal policies enabled it to expand, thereby opening the way for the rise of political Islamists. In order to understand the logic of the political Islamists, the founding president of MÜSİAD Erol Yarar's words in 2009 are useful: "Thank God (*elhamdülillah*) I am the leader; we Muslims are no longer content with just 'a cardigan and a bite' (just enough to keep the body and soul together). We want 'a thousand cardigans and a thousand bites.'"[10] Anti-capitalist Muslims are trying to turn this slogan (a thousand cardigans–a thousand bites) around and go for 'a cardigan and a bite' motto. Nevertheless, division in the Islamic community did not fully develop during the 1990s and early 2000s, as there was considerable pressure on political Islamists due to the events of February 28th.[11] The events of February 28th forced political Islamists out of power in the short term; however, in the long term, it acted as a catalyst for political Islamists to take power. Therefore, political Islamists who had the same origins held together until the early 2000s. It was only during the implementation of AKP policies that political Islamists began to separate into two camps: Market Islam and Left-Islam (Anti-capitalist Muslims).

---

9 M. Hakan Yavuz, *Secularism and Muslim Democracy in Turkey*, Cambridge: Cambridge University 2009, 51.

10 Ahmet Arslan, "Erol Yarar Üzerine Tezler", *Hürriyet* (26 July 2009), www.hurriyet.com.tr/yazarlar/12148221.asp (status: 29 September 2015), translation is mine. Some MÜSİAD members live in luxury and they even fulfill Islamic obligations in luxurious fashion. For example, they arrange fast breaking in five-star hotels or *umrah* in five-star hotels in Mecca or Madinah, see "20 days 5-Star Luxury Umrah", *Müsiad*, www.emusiad.com/products/gaziturizm/20-gunluk-5-yildizli-luks-umre (status: 18 July 2017).

11 The events of 28th February process refer to a postmodern military coup on 28th February 1997. Prime Minister Erbakan, who was president of the RP, was forced out of government; see Ali Bayramoğlu, *28 Şubat. Bir Müdahalenin Güncesi*, Istanbul: İletişim 2013.

The AKP Period

After the November 3rd 2002 general elections, the Justice and Development Party came to power and has since implemented neoliberal politics. The economic crisis occurring in the 1990s was perceived to be connected to the lack of neoliberal regulations. Once in power, the AKP attempted to overcome the structural shortcomings of neoliberalism. In other words, political Islam began to rise with neoliberal politics. But it must be underlined, as Buğra and Savaşkan have indicated, that "the rise of political Islam constitutes a process shaped not by the system of beliefs or institutions intrinsic to Islam, but rather by political actors who followed, adapted to and used the opportunities presented by changing circumstances."[12] During the AKP period, religion was used as a "network resource" for building trust in relations between government and economic actors.[13] The AKP uses religion as a network resource with the purpose of creating their own party base and paving the way for economic growth for some pro-AKP groups. The ruling party has done this especially through the Public Procurement Law and Public Procurement Agency. Public Procurement Law regulates public construction projects involving bridges, ports, roads, or railways, and determines the legal framework for relations between government and business actors. The AKP administration changed the procurement law 29 times, making over 100 amendments to its scope from 2003 to 2013.[14] In this way, the AKP has opened the way for tenders to some specific pro-AKP groups. The government employed similar methods for the privatization of mining areas, energy, and used religion as a network resource as well. The AKP has used the numerous investments in the Housing Development Administration of Turkey (*Toplu Konut İdaresi Başkanlığı*, TOKİ) in the same way. In addition, while the government applies tax immunity for some groups who are close to them,[15] it imposes tax penalties on others who are dissident.[16] Perhaps the best example of the rise of Islamic capital is the growth of the previously mentioned Islam-oriented business association

12 Ayşe Buğra and Osman Savaşkan, *New Capitalism in Turkey: The Relationship between Politics, Religion and Business*, Cheltenham: Edward Elgar 2014, 14.

13 Ibid., 53.

14 Ibid., 79.

15 For example, as a result of diamond sales being exempted from value-added tax by the government, the Atasay Precious Metals Company which is pro-AKP was established: "KDV kalktı, 36 Gün Sonra Şirket Kuruldu", *Milliyet* (14 February 2009), www.milliyet.com.tr/kdv-kalkti-----gun-sonra-sirket-kuruldu/siyaset/siyasetdetay/14.02.2009/1059616/default.htm (status: 18 September 2016).

16 For example, a tax penalty was imposed on Doğan Holding, which is an opponent of AKP, see *Euroactiv*, "Turkey court adds to media group predicament", www.euractiv.com/section/enlargement/news/turkey-court-adds-to-media-group-predicament/ (status: 18 September 2016).

MÜSİAD. Shortly after the AKP had come to power, MÜSİAD chairman Ali Bayramoğlu declared in an interview on November 17th 2002 that they had 2100 members.[17] Today, they have more than 10 thousand members.[18] Therefore, the AKP administration provides the transition to political Islamists (Passive Revolution[19]) in a passive way and makes them compatible with the capitalist system by using religion as a network resource. In other words, these activities led to the rise of Islamic capital in Turkey. The conversion of political Islamists, which can be defined as a transition from radical Islamism to moderate Islamism and the rise of Islamic capital, resulted in what Anti-capitalist Muslims referred to as "yesterday's mujahideen being today's contractors" (*dünün mücahitleri bugünün müteahhitleri*).[20] However, it should be noted here, as Deniz Yıldırım underlined, that, "as the system was plunged into organic crisis and severed representation ties between the rulers and the ruled, the AKP emerged as a hegemonic project".[21] Therefore, the aim of AKP's coming to power was to make neoliberalism, which was in crisis, hegemonic again. The AKP makes neoliberalism and Islam suited to each other in two ways: On the one hand, the AKP manipulates Islamic politics to provide for the decentralization of neoliberalism, and on the other, it liberalizes Islamic politics.[22] Thus, in the AKP period, large Islamic/conservative groups have been integrated into Turkish neoliberalism.

To sum up, political Islamism has risen since the 1980 coup and has come to power with the AKP in the 2000s. The pressure on political Islamists brought about by the events of February 28th, was lifted with AKP's coming to power, and political Islamists became increasingly more liberated. This liberation also brought disagreements within the Islamic commu-

17 "İstihbarat Rapor Verdi 800 Üye Tasfiye Edildi", *Milliyet* (17 November 2002), www.milliyet.com.tr/istihbarat-rapor-verdi-----uye-tasfiye-edildi/ekonomi/haberdetayarsiv/17.11.2002/65563/default.htm (status: 16 September 2016).

18 "Meet with MÜSİAD", Müsiad, www.musiad.org.tr/tr-tr/musiadla-tanisin (status: 16 September 2016).

19 Political Islamism, especially after the millennium, has been "integrated to the system" by AKP policies, which are pro-EU and follow a neoliberal economic-political line which means that extremist political Islamists have gradually been integrated into the capitalist system and converted to moderate political Islamists; see Cihan Tuğal, *Passive Revolution: Absorbing the Islamic Challenge to Capitalism*, Stanford: Stanford University 2009. Tuğal defined "the integration" concept by using the passive revolution concept of Antonio Gramsci.

20 The basic reasons for economic growth in the AKP period are infrastructure and construction investments. That is why many political Islamists are now contractors, see Buğra and Savaşkan, *New Capitalism*.

21 Deniz Yıldırım, *2001 Krizi Sonrasında Bir Hegemonya Projesi Olarak AKP'nin Doğuşu*, Ankara University: unpubl. PhD Thesis 2010, 209.

22 Simten Coşar and Gamze Yücesan-Özdemir, "Sonuç", in: *İktidarın Şiddeti. AKP'li Yıllar, Neoliberalizm ve İslamcı Politikalar*, idem, eds., Istanbul: Metis 2014, 249–256, 255.

nity. While the AKP or Market Islam places emphasis on 'capital', anti-capitalist Muslims or Left-Islam places emphasis on 'labor'; and while the former associated itself with capitalism and the right wing and the latter with socialism and the left wing, both approaches claimed to be the 'true Islam'. However, the basic reason for Islamic stratification is the rise of Islamic capital.

Anti-Capitalist Muslims

Anti-capitalist Muslims is one of the first groups in the Islamic community in Turkey to object to Market Islam. At this point it needs to be clarified that various Islamic-leftist authors have coined different terms for what this author and others call Market Islam. Examples of such divergent terms can be found in the works of the following authors: Sayyid Quṭb's *Social Justice*,[23] Muṣṭafā al-Sibā'ī's *Socialism of Islam*,[24] Hasan Hanafi's *Islam in the Modern World*,[25] Roger Garaudy,[26] and in Turkey, İhsan Eliaçık's *Social Islam*,[27] have all discussed their approaches using distinctive concepts.

Anti-capitalist Muslims announced their name for the first time on May 1st 2012, on Labor Day, and began organizing all around Turkey.[28] This group's official name was The Association for Fighting Capitalism (*Kapitalizmle Mücadele Derneği*, KAMUDER). The reason for using the title KAMUDER was to express an antagonism towards the expression "The Association for Fighting Communism," which reflected the state-supported consensus during the Cold War.[29] In addition, at the time, Islamic groups supported the action and discourse of The Association for Fighting Communism in Turkey. There is still antagonism between Islamic groups and communist/socialist groups,

23 Sayyid Quṭb, *al-ᶜAdāla al-Ijtimā'īyyah fī al-Islām*, Cairo 1949. Translated as *Social Justice in Islam* by John B. Hardie, New York: Islamic Publications International 2000.

24 Muṣṭafā al-Sibā'ī, *Ištirākīyat al-Islām*, Damascus: Mu'assasat al-Maṭbū'āt al-'Arabīya 1959.

25 Hasan Hanafi, *Islam in the Modern World*, Cairo: Anglo-Egyptian Bookshop 1995; see Kazuo Shimogaki, *Between Modernity and Post-Modernity: The Islamic Left and Dr. H. Hanafi's Thought: A Critical Reading*, Yamato: Institute of Middle Eastern Studies, International University of Japan 1988.

26 Roger Garaudy and Faik Bercavi, *İslamiyet ve Sosyalizm*, Istanbul: Rebeze Kitaplığı 2012.

27 R. İhsan Eliaçık, *Sosyal İslam & Dinin Direği Paylaşımdır*, Istanbul: Destek 2011.

28 Bayram Koca, *Türkiye'de İslam ve Sosyalizm İlişkisi Bağlamında Emek ve Adalet Platformu ve Antikapitalist Müslümanlar*, Hacettepe Univesity: unpubl. Master Thesis 2013.

29 Nationalists, political Islamists and conservatives came and moved together against leftists/socialists in the Association for Fighting Communism during the 1960-1980 period. At this time communists were the common enemy; see Aylin Özman and Aslı Yazıcı-Yakın, "The Symbolic Construction of Communism in Turkish Anti-Communist Propaganda during the Cold War", *Journal of Language and Politics* 11:4 (2012), 583–605.

and therefore, Anti-capitalist Muslims are a very interesting association as they are the first Islamic group in Turkey to have good relations with the left/socialists. İhsan Eliaçık, the theoretical contributor to Anti-capitalist Muslims, says the following: "We reject the heritage of the Association for Fighting Communism and hold out an olive branch to the leftists."[30] The ironic name of KAMUDER was thus selected to express the objection to this heritage. Anti-capitalist Muslims are an Istanbul-based organization but they have organized in other big cities such as Ankara, İzmir, and Adana. They are horizontally organized and have no leader or president.[31] Every six months, the movement chooses a new spokesperson. Although İhsan Eliaçık is perceived as the president of Anti-capitalist Muslims, his support for them is more on a theoretical level, and the movement has been constituted by activists who came together around him. Especially Eliaçık's exegesis *Living Quran* (2007)[32] has acted as a catalyst for the organizational drive of Anti-capitalist Muslims.

The movement was inspired by *The Communist Manifesto* and their basic text "The Anti-capitalist Muslims' Manifesto" ("*Antikapitalist Müslümanlar Manifestosu*") took its name from that document. In their objection to capitalism, they declare in the "Manifesto" that humanity is in a state of frustration, the world is rolling into an abyss and capitalism is the enemy of God, humanity, nature, the poor, and the hungry. They underline historical aspects of their anti-capitalism: "Our stand against capitalism has a historical emphasis. The dominant system of our age is capitalism. Every prophetic message has stood against the dominant system of its time. That is why we are emphasizing anti-capitalism."[33] The movement defines the stance of prophets who rose up against the status quo of their own time as 'revolutionary', and so, being anti-capitalist means at the same time being revolutionary. The Islamic concept of *tevhit* (arab. *tawḥīd*), the oneness and singularity of God, has to be added to the movement's basic tenets. The Islamic credo "*Lailaheillallah*" (arab. *Lā ilāha illā ʾllāh*) means "There is no deity but God", and to fulfill this credo, they struggle against any other deity or authority. Since property and capitalism have turned into the deities of the neo-liberal world, this economic system contradicts the key element of

30 Eyüp Serbest, "Antikapitalist Müslüman Gençler 1 Mayıs'ta", *Hürriyet* (1 May 2012), www.hurriyet.com.tr/gundem/20458489.asp (status: 10 September 2016).

31 Koca, *Türkiye'de İslam*, 114.

32 R. İhsan Eliaçık, *Yaşayan Kur'an. Nüzul Sırasına Göre Türkçe Meal-Tefsir*, Istanbul: İnşa 2007.

33 "Antikapitalist Müslümanlar Manifestosu" 2012, n.p., n. d.: "Kapitalizme karşı oluşumuz ise tarihsel bir vurgudur. Çünkü çağımıza egemen olan sistemin adıdır Kapitalizm. Her peygamberî mesaj kendi zamanının egemen sistemine karşı durmuştur. Bunun için 'Antikapitalist' vurgusu yapıyoruz." The translations from the "Manifesto" are mine.

Muslim belief. The use of Quranic verses which express God's oneness adds sanctity to the movement's "cause": "Say, [O Muhammad], 'O mankind, indeed I am the Messenger of Allah to you all, [from Him] to whom belongs the dominion of the heavens and the earth. There is no deity except Him...' (A'raf: 158)."[34] Struggling against any deity other than God provides them with an anti-authoritarian position. The movement declares in its manifesto that there is a class structure in society because of the acquisition of property; in addition to capitalism, they struggle against a class based society.[35] The critique of both capitalism and class is one of the distinctive features of the Anti-capitalist Muslims. Serdar Şengül states that this is a new phenomenon in the progress of political Islamism in Turkey, in that an Islamic group is criticizing an Islamic ruling party based on class and economics.[36] The movement, which has a leftist discourse, acts together with left-wing groups: "We see all anti-capitalist output and rhetoric as our natural allies regardless of faith, race, language, color, or ideology. We want them to share the platforms or environments that we struggle in."[37] Moving together with groups on the left is an unusual situation for Islamic movements in Turkey. After anti-capitalism, this is the second unique feature of the movement. Anti-capitalist Muslims also promote an anti-imperialist position: "...Anti-capitalist Muslims are also anti-imperialists. It is unacceptable that capitalism kills, rapes or exiles millions of people, in order to find new raw materials and new markets."[38] The movement is against capitalism and imperialism, and it emphasizes 'labor' instead of 'capital': "According to Anti-capitalist Muslims, only labor produces value while capital doesn't. 'And there is nothing for man but to work' (Necm: 39)." Their manifesto emphasizes that race, religion, language, gender, or sect differences do not change the value of labor itself and it establishes an antagonism between oppressors and oppressed, instead of believers and non-believers. With this in mind, they express their purpose with the following Quranic verse in the manifesto: "We wished to favour those who

---

34 All Quranic verses quoted in this study are used in "Anti-capitalist Muslims' Manifesto".

35 See for the relationship between Islam and class: Şennur Özdemir, *İslam ve Sınıf*, Ankara: Nika 2014.

36 Serdar Şengül, "Teoloji ile Antropoloji arasında Antikapitalist Müslümanlar", *Toplum ve Bilim* 129 (2014), 195–222, 196.

37 "Antikapitalist Müslümanlar Manifestosu": "Antikapitalist her çıkış ve söylemi dini inancının veya inançsızlığının, ırkının, dilinin, renginin, ideolojisinin ne olduğuna bakmaksızın doğal müttefikimiz olarak görüyoruz. Onlarla aynı platform ve mücadele ortamlarını paylaşmak istiyoruz."

38 Ibid.: "...Antikapitalist Müslümanlar aynı zamanda anti-emperyalist bir kimliğe sahiptir. Kapitalizmin yeni hammaddeler bulması ve yeni pazarlar oluşturması adına, milyonlarca insanın öldürülmesi, tecavüze uğraması, yerlerinden ve yurtlarından sürülmesi kabul edilemez."

were weak in the land and make them leaders and heirs (Kasas: 5)." In their text, they call for a revolution to make leaders out of the oppressed: "Anti-capitalist Muslims call all people to a revolutionary struggle for a life devoid of luxurious consumption, which is very simple, humble, and sharing; and to a struggle against injustice shared by all prophets, to achieve a virtuous society and virtuous people."[39] The Anti-capitalist Muslims movement was founded for "a world order based on justice" respecting all differences. That is why they refer to "God, bread, freedom" (*Allah, ekmek, özgürlük*) and, in Turkified Arabic "*Lehu'l Mülk*" (property belongs to God) as their motto.

Anti-capitalist Muslims have built their discourse on the theories of ʿAlī Sharīʿatī and İhsan Eliaçık. They have utilized Sharīʿatī for creating their philosophy of history; and Eliaçık, for creating methods of exegesis.[40] In order to better understand Anti-capitalist Muslims, a basic framework involving both thinkers will be outlined.

The Iranian thinker ʿAlī Sharīʿatī analyzed history critically. Throughout history, religion has always been placed against another religion; not against atheism. He divides religion into two categories:[41] The first one is–in its Persian wording–the *Dīn-i Shirk* which serves the interests of the rulers and numbs the public.[42] He asserts that the second type is the *Dīn-i Tawḥīd*, which he positions against the *Dīn-i Shirk* that mostly affects ignorant societies. He defines *Dīn-i Tawḥīd* as something which engenders awareness and love, and provides access to salvation.[43] Sharīʿatī argues that this duality has existed since Cain and Abel. He discusses the struggle between Cain and Abel as one between two different economic systems. In Abel's time, there was no means of production and thus, no division of labor.[44] A means of production began to rise in Cain's time, along with a social order.[45] In the struggle between these two contrasting economic orders, the killing of Abel by Cain caused the transition to social classes from a natural order.[46] History was now in the hands of the ruling class and *Dīn-i Shirk* be-

39 Ibid.: "Antikapitalist Müslümanlar; bütün peygamberler, erdemli toplumlar ve insanlar gibi kendi gönüllüleri başta olmak üzere tüm insanları, lüks tüketimden, israftan, gösterişten uzak, gayet sade, mütevazı, zühde dayalı paylaşımcı bir hayat sürmeye ve haksızlığa karşı adaletin tesisi için devrimci bir mücadeleye çağırır."

40 Serdar Şengül, "Türkiye'de İslam'a ve İslamcılığa yaklaşımlar", *Birikim* 303–304 (2014), 27–35, 33.

41 Ali Şeriati, *Dine Karşı Din,* transl. by Doğan Özlük, Ankara: Fecr 2012.

42 ʿAlī Sharīʿatī bases his specific concepts on the Islamic tenets of *tawḥīd* (see above) and *shirk*, associationism or polytheism.

43 Şeriati, *Dine Karşı Din*, 36.

44 Ali Şeriati, *Marksizm,* transl. by Yakup Arslan, Kenan Çamurcu, Istanbul: Dünya 2004, 83.

45 Ibid., 85.

46 Ibid., 81.

gan to reign. This situation continued until the birth of Islam, and with Islam *Dīn-i Tawḥīd* would again reign over the earth. But Sharīʿatī says that it did not last long and the *Dīn-i Shirk* came to be dominant once again under Caliph Uthmān ibn ʿAffān (r. 644-656), the third of the four Rightly Guided Caliphs. Sharīʿatī asserts, as Abu Dhar al-Ghifari notes, that the riot of the hungry people will destroy *Dīn-i Shirk*.[47] Anti-capitalist Muslims have embarked on Sharīʿatī's antagonistic reading of history; accordingly, they struggle to make *Dīn-i Tawḥīd* dominant again on earth.

The next person, whom Anti-capitalist Muslims based their views on, is the Turkish activist and book author İhsan Eliaçık, born in 1961. Eliaçık is perceived by the public to be the leader of Anti-capitalist Muslims, though he is not. Eliaçık is an activist thinker, once involved in the *Akıncılar* group (Raiders) which was the youth branch of the Islamic *Millî Görüş Hareketi* (National Outlook Movement) in the period before 1980. He was imprisoned for a year after the September 12th coup. He states that his imprisonment was a milestone for him. In prison, he met with leftists and discussed many issues with them–a process which affected his current approach.[48] He also takes ʿAlī Sharīʿatī as an example. He wrote such books as *Revolutionary Islam* (1995), *State of Justice* (2003), *The Writings of the Property* (2009), and *Social Islam* (2011)[49] with his own distinctive approach. He states that there is no Quranic verse dictating getting rich or praising capital accumulation. The Quran advises people to share, and in this way Islamic political economy is close to socialism: The motto "*Lehu'l Mülk*" references communal property.[50] He calls this system "Social Islam". Eliaçık indicates that the main task of the state is to provide for justice and public benefit (*maslahat*), to stand for the common good (*maruf*) and to be against evil (*münker*).[51] According to him, religion was ritualized by power holders; true worship lies in resisting injustice and sharing in life, not in attending the mosque or the *cemevi*, the Alevi place of worship.[52] Not only his ideas, but also his Quran exegesis has inspired Anti-capitalist Muslims. In the preface of his *Living Quran* exegesis, he states that the Quran was revealed in the context of 23 years of fighting against "the gangs of Kaaba" who ruled Mecca;

47 Ali Şeriati, *Ebuzer*, transl. by Abdullah Yeğin, Ankara: Fecr 2012, 59.

48 Bayram Koca, "İhsan Eliaçık ile İslam ve Sol Üzerine Söyleşi", in: *Türkiye'de İslam ve Sol*, Bayram Koca, ed., Istanbul: Vivo 2014, 436–440, 436.

49 *Devrimci İslam*, Istanbul: Bengisu 1995; *Adalet Devleti: Ortak İyinin İktidarı*, Istanbul: Bakış Kitaplığı 2003; *Mülk Yazıları*, Istanbul: İnşa Yayınları 2009; *Sosyal İslam*.

50 Eliaçık, *Sosyal İslam*, 154.

51 R. İhsan Eliaçık, *Adalet Devleti*, Istanbul: İnşa, 2011, 11.

52 "İslam ve devrimcilik: Enver Aysever sordu, İhsan Eliacik yanıtladı–Aykırı Sorular", *Cnnturk*, www.cnnturk.com/video/2012/10/08/programlar/aykiri-sorular/aykiri-sorular/2012-10-08T2045/index.html (status: 10 February 2017).

therefore, it depicts an actually experienced struggle.[53] Referring to the religious practice of the Turkish secular elite of limiting Quran reading to the funeral rites, the author insists on perceiving the Holy Book as a constant part of life. For this reason, he describes the Quran as a book that aims to mobilize conscience and compassion.[54] In contrast to other exegeses, Eliaçık's Quran exegesis is based on action.[55] Aside from his intellectual contributions to Anti-capitalist Muslims' thinking, Eliaçık also allocated a meeting place for them between 2013 and 2015 and joined their meetings and conferences. In this context, Eliaçık's impact on Anti-capitalist Muslims is indisputable, especially during the foundation phase. However, over time a distance between Eliaçık and Anti-capitalist Muslims developed. After the foundation of Anti-capitalist Muslims, Eliaçık was perceived as a leader of the group and became more popular; as a result, his books started to sell more and he began to appear regularly in the TV program *Bana Dinden Bahset* (Tell Me About Religion) every Friday in KRT channel (*Kültür Radyo ve Televizyon*, Culture Radio and Television). For this reason, Anti-capitalist Muslims became irritated and withdrew from Eliaçık.[56] They left the place which Eliaçık had allocated and moved to a different place. A member of the Anti-capitalist Muslims stresses that "Eliaçık inspired us, but now we have surpassed him and come to a different point."[57]

Anti-capitalist Muslims, whose thoughts have been shaped under the influence of these two thinkers, struggle in the field to fight capitalism and encourage revolution. They might be the most prolific protest movement within the Islamic community. Many times they have exhibited their protest potential at rallies. The rationale for participating in protests is their conviction that the best form of worship is to resist oppression. The name of the Anti-capitalist Muslims was heard for the first time when they joined the 2012 protests of May 1st as a small group of people, who identified themselves as political Islamists. KAMUDER was officially founded and the Anti-capitalist Muslims' Manifesto appeared a few months later. Therefore, the movement's very foundation originated in action. This was a

53 Eliaçık, *Yaşayan Kur'an*, 5.

54 Ibid., 7.

55 The exegeses of pro-Left-Islamists Edip Yüksel and Yaşar Nuri Öztürk–who have been a source of benefit for Left-Islam– can be seen as resembling Eliaçık's exegesis.

56 Alpkan Birelma, "Antikapitalist Müslümanlar Grubu Üyeleriyle Söyleşi: 'Bizim Yapmak İstediğimiz, Mahalleler Arasında Geçişkenliği Sağlamak'", *Birikim* 293 (2014), 61–76, 66.

57 Bayram Koca, "İslamcılığın 'Sol' ile İmtihanı: Sol-İslamcılık", in: *Türkiye'de Yeni Siyasal Akımlar (1980 Sonrası)*, Evren Haspolat and Deniz Yıldırım, eds., Ankara: Siyasal 2016, 485–538, 516.

significant moment for Left-Islam,[58] because their thinking was broadly articulated in public for the first time. As noted above, Anti-capitalist Muslims emphasize that they advocate fighting against persecution of all the oppressed, without discrimination on the basis of language, religion or sect. Accordingly, they have joined in the May 1st protests every year with leftists, to oppose persecution by those in political power. They express their motive in joining the May 1st protests of 2013 in the following way: "To rulers who say 'Muslims have power, so what more do you want' … we reply: 'We wished to favor those who were weak in the land and make them leaders and heirs' (Kasas, 5). We meet at the Fatih Mosque on May 1st, at 9:30."[59] This message of the movement was a call disseminated on the internet to join the rally. Also in this way, they verbalized their wish for union between secular and Islamic neighborhoods.[60] The purposes of Anti-capitalist Muslims could be interpreted as an indication that the paradigm has changed. There has been a transition from a situation where leftists and political Islamists lived in their own separate ghettos without dialogue (or even fighting sometimes as on Bloody Sunday[61] or in the Sivas massacre), to a situation where leftists and political Islamists struggle together against injustice. Anti-capitalist Muslims have attempted to achieve rapprochement between leftists and political Islamists, and in doing so, reject the heritage of political Islamists who attacked leftists in the past. They have condemned political Islamists who threw rocks at leftists protesting against the 6th Fleet of the US Navy, and the political Islamists who caused the death of 37 participants in an Alevi Culture Festival in Sivas in 1993.[62] Moreover, they participated in the commemoration of the Sivas Massacre in 2013 and expressed the reason for their participation by saying the following: "All to-

---

58 Bayram Koca, "Türkiye'de İslam ve Sosyalizm İlişkisi Bağlamında Emek ve Adalet Platformu ve Antikapitalist Müslümanlar", in: *Türkiye'de İslam ve Sol*, Bayram Koca, ed., Istanbul: Vivo 2014, 287–336, 317.

59 "Antikapitalist Müslümanlardan Duyuru", *Antikapitalistmüslümanlar*, http://antikapitalistmuslumanlar.org/ (status: 12 September 2016). The translations are mine.

60 Birelma, "Antikapitalist Müslümanlar Grubu", 71.

61 The 6th Fleet is the United States Navy's operational fleet. It was established in 1950 and used in world affairs around the Mediterranean. The 6th Fleet came to Turkey a few times in response to Soviet threats during the Cold War, see U.S. Navy, *U.S. Naval Forces Europe-Africa / U.S. 6th Fleet*, www.c6f.navy.mil/ (status: 18 July 2017). On 16th February 1969 different leftist groups met together in order to protest against the American 6th Fleet at the Bosporus. But as the protests began, some political Islamists and nationalists attacked the leftists with sticks and knives. In the attack two people were killed and more than 100 people injured. One of the organizers of the attack was The Association for Fighting Communism (*Komünizmle Mücadele Derneği*); see Artun Ünsal, *Umuttan Yalnızlığa Türkiye İşçi Partisi*, Istanbul: Tarih Vakfı 2002, 377.

62 Elise Massicard, *The Alevis in Turkey and Europe: Identity and Managing Territorial Diversity*, London: Routledge 2013, 44–48.

gether for the unification with our slain Alevi brothers, for struggling for their demands, and for the prevention of sectarian wars!"[63]

Anti-capitalist Muslims, as expected, supported the 2013 Gezi Park protests from beginning to end. The Gezi Park protests were a set of nationwide uprisings, which began when police disproportionately intervened in the protests against the destruction of Gezi Park and the planned construction of a shopping mall in its place in Istanbul. As the protests continued, the AKP government tried to depict these protests as anti-religious, attempting to marginalize them in order to eliminate the unrest. The claims that all who joined the Gezi Park protests were anti-religious, were brought forward by the then-Prime Minister Erdoğan himself. Erdoğan claimed that "they entered the mosque with shoes on", "they consumed alcohol in the mosque" and "they attacked our veiled daughter and dragged her on the ground."[64] Neither did the Muezzin of the mosque,[65] about which Erdoğan made these allegations, confirm them, nor could the video recording that Erdoğan claimed to show the attack on the veiled women be found.[66] Moreover, *Takvim* newspaper wrote that two women were raped in Gezi Park.[67]

However, unlike the Prime Minister's statement, according to their own statements veiled activists joined the protest from the beginning to its end without ever getting harassed or attacked.[68] Another activist from Anti-capitalist Muslims shared the following post on Facebook during the Gezi Park protests in Ankara: "Azan is being recited, I should go to protest."[69] This post shows us that the movement regards fighting against persecution as the main prayer. Therefore, Anti-capitalist Muslims joining Gezi Park

63 "Antikapitalist Müslümanlar olarak 2 Temmuz Sivas Katliamının 20. yılında 23 Haziran'da Kadıköy'deyiz", www.facebook.com/events/653281948017816/?ref=22 (status: 11 February 2017).

64 "Yarın boşalttınız boşalttınız, yoksa polis girecek!", *Sözcü* (15 June 2013), www.sozcu.'com.tr/2013/gundem/gezidekiler-ihanet-sebekesiymis-315780/ (status: 11 February 2017).

65 The Muezzin states: "Firstly they took off their shoes and then entered" and "While I was working, I didn't see anything which did not meet the nation's values or any immoral things", *Cumhuriyet* (15 November 2014), www.cumhuriyet.com.tr/haber/turkiye/141679/Camii_gorevlisi__Once_ayakkabilarini_cikarip_girdiler.html (status: 18 February 2017).

66 Pro-government 'journalist' Cem Küçük regretted that the story of "a veiled daughter's assault and dragging on the ground" was a ridiculous fiction. Cem Küçük, *Star* (13 July 2015), http://haber.star.com.tr/yazar/cevap-bulmasi-gereken-sorular-var/haber-1043376 (status: 18 September 2016).

67 "Çapulcular", *Takvim* (8 June 2013), www.gazeteler.org/takvim-gazetesi/2013-haziran-08/ (status: 11 February 2017).

68 "Cuma Namazını 2. Kez Taksim'de Kıldılar", *Odatv*, www.odatv.com/n.php?n=gezi-parkinda-2.-cuma-namazi-kilindi-1406131200 (status: 11 February 2017).

69 Bülent Durukan, *facebook*, www.facebook.com/BulentDurukan?fref=ts (status: 11 February 2017).

protests, was consistent with their discourse and prevented them from taking a "religious–anti-religious" position.

By joining the Gezi Park protests, the movement of the Anti-capitalist Muslims attracted the attention of the AKP government. Whereas before, the government had not made any statements about Anti-capitalist Muslims, with Gezi Park the public targeting began. Firstly, pro-government newspapers accused İhsan Eliaçık of being a provocateur.[70] After that, Erdoğan called out to Anti-capitalist Muslims, saying that "We are the true anti-capitalists because we have downgraded interest rates, which constitute the greatest exploitation of capitalism."[71] *Yeni Şafak* newspaper tried to discredit them, claiming that alcoholic beverages were served during the *Yeryüzü Sofraları* (tables of earth), the Anti-capitalist Muslims' public breaking of the Ramadan fast.[72] Islamic magazines like *Haksöz* and *İktibas* condemned Anti-capitalist Muslims and Eliaçık for being on the same side with Kemalists and nationalists.[73] This is how the Gezi Protests rendered a stratification or even deep split inside the Muslim community of Turkey quite visible; a split between those Muslims in support of the AKP government, and those in opposition to it.

Anti-capitalist Muslims regard the Gezi Park Protests, where different social groups lived together for 19 days, as a small copy of heaven and indicate that this period is a small example of the life that they conceive for the aftermath of the revolution. They themselves took their place in Gezi Park with a small tent with the mottos "*Lehu'l Mülk*" and "Capital, Get Out! " written on it. In his essay entitled "Gezi: 19 days in the Utopian Park", Eliaçık claims that there was no police or hierarchy in Gezi Park; eating, drinking, library, and sickroom services were free of charge; people were given more than their needs; and the flags represented the pluralism.[74] During the Friday sermon, he stated: "People who have different beliefs and lifestyles are struggling together in unity and brotherhood in Gezi Park, where money is invalid, and

70 "İhsan Eliaçık'tan Skandal Başörtü Twiti!", *Yeni Şafak* (13 June 2013), www.yenisafak.com.tr/gundem/ihsan-eliaciktan-skandal-basortu-twiti-531510 (status: 11 February 2017).

71 "Başbakan Erdoğan'dan Gezi Parkı Mesajları", *Akşam* (11 June 2013), www.aksam.com.tr/siyaset/basbakan-erdogandan-gezi-parki-mesajlari/haber-214624 (status: 11 February 2017).

72 "Antikapitalist Müslümanlar'ın İftarında Bira İçildi", *Yeni Şafak* (13 July 2013), www.yenisafak.com.tr/gundem/antikapitalist-muslumanlarin-iftarinda-bira-icildi-542144 (status: 11 February 2015).

73 Özlem Avcı, "İslami söylem Gezi Parkı eylemlerinin neresinde?", *Birikim* 303–304 (2014), 141–158, 146–152.

74 İhsan Eliaçık, "Gezi: Ütopik Parkta 19 Gün", in: *Gezi Direnişi Üzerine Düşünceler*, Özay Göztepe, ed., Ankara: Notabene 2013, 195–198, 195–197.

no one is hungry."[75] In the immediate aftermath of the Gezi Park protests, they brought together believers and non-believers, fasting and non fasting, rich and poor, woman and man by means of the before mentioned *Yeryüzü Sofraları*. *Yeryüzü Sofraları* are defined as bringing together people from different strata of society, with no sponsors, no hierarchy, and no flags. Anarchist writer Gün Zileli emphasized that *Yeryüzü Sofraları* will not be forgotten in the revolutionary history of Turkey.[76]

Anti-capitalist Muslims also use social media like Facebook and Twitter to criticize the government. They usually base their critiques on Quranic verses or hadith to legitimize their arguments. In addition, they organize film screenings, reading groups on exegesis or world history, and they distribute soup one day per week to homeless people. Sometimes they organize public conferences to promote their group to people and find new activists for the movement. They have published a magazine named *Ehâd* (meaning "sole" and one of the names of Allah as well) since April 2014. By all these means, Anti-capitalist Muslims are trying to strengthen their discourse. Therefore, Anti-capitalist Muslims are active both in action and discourse.

Conclusion

Political Islamism has a long history as a political movement in Turkey. It has been transformed into Market Islam since the AKP came to power in 2002; and that is why a stratification in Islam has developed for the first time. Market Islam places emphasis on capital, whereas Left-Islam places emphasis on labor. Therefore, in the 2000s, Turkey witnessed two different approaches to Islam. The first approach represented by the AKP held the majority, while the Anti-capitalist Muslims represented the minority. The former was associated with capitalism and the right wing, and the latter with socialism and the left wing, with both approaches claiming to be the 'true Islam'.

The intellectual resources of Left-Islam were derived from Sayyid Quṭb, ʿAlī Sharīʿatī, and Abū l-Aʿlā al-Mawdūdī (1903–1979). However, the development of Left-Islam in Turkey began in 1980. The pioneer of Left-Islam in Turkey is İhsan Eliaçık, who follows the line of Sharīʿatī. Left-Islam has appeared as a reaction to the Islamic community who has relations with capital. For this reason, Left-Islam is a reactive movement. Left-Islam determined its political line and discourse on the basis of Islamic sources.

75 "Gezi Parkında 2. Direniş Cuması", *Adil Medya* (14 June 2013), www.adilmedya.com/gezi-parkinda-2-direnis-cumasi/ (status: 12 February 2017).

76 Gün Zileli, "Birleşik Haziran Hareketi" (30 December 2014), www.gunzileli.com/2014/12/30/birlesik-haziran-hareketi/ (status: 13 February 2017).

Left-Islam has links to the left on a personal level (with figures like Zeki Kılıçarslan, Cem Somel, Ertuğrul Günay who were protagonists of Left-Islam) or on a conceptual level (labor, revolution, class); a fact which once more demonstrates the essential importance of Islam and its tenets for the movement. It could be said that Left-Islam has two aspects:[77] Firstly, they criticize class and capitalism and have an anti-authoritarian attitude. Secondly, contrary to traditional Islamists, they can easily come together with leftists both in discourse and in action. When considered from this perspective, Left-Islam, especially Anti-capitalist Muslims, prepares the ground for a paradigm shift by defining a different 'true Islam'. The political field can expand with political Islamists and leftists moving together for the same purpose. It could be said that Anti-capitalist Muslims have played a crucial role in breaking down the Turkish left's prejudices about the Islamic community, especially by participating in the Gezi Park protests. Contrary to AKP's revengeful religious beliefs, Anti-capitalist Muslims have projected a different understanding of 'true Islam'. Furthermore, opposing AKP's efforts to attribute to them a 'religious–anti-religious' position in the Gezi Park protests, Anti-capitalist Muslims prevented this duality by participating in the Gezi Park protests both in action and word. Within this framework, Anti-capitalist Muslims were a unique part of the Gezi Park protests.

Turkish public opinion has paid attention to Anti-capitalist Muslims. However, they are not a mass movement. After May 1st and the Gezi Park protests, their popularity increased, but now they are losing popularity and numbers. The Turkish public has also got accustomed to them; that is why they no longer dominate the agenda. It could be said that Anti-capitalist Muslims were not able to turn into a mass movement, because they addressed the radical left with leftist discourse and seemed to neglect the outer forms of Islam and visible rituals in the eyes of the Muslim majority. Moreover, there is a perception in the Islamic community that Anti-capitalist Muslims is a radical left organization. If Anti-capitalist Muslims can address Islamic ground, it might become a mass movement. Contrary to AKP's corruption and wastage, Anti-capitalist Muslims' true Islam is modest, sharing, egalitarian, and may be supported by other Islamic groups. In other words, as the relationship between Islam and capitalism becomes more problematic, the relationship between Islam and the Left/socialism may become the main agenda.

In conclusion, if Anti-capitalist Muslims continue to address an Islamic ground without severing its relationship with the Left, they may organize a Left-Islam instead of Market Islam and thereby may extend their politics to more people.

---

77 Koca, "İslamcılığın 'Sol' ile İmtihanı", 528.

Ubaidullah Sindhi as a Revolutionary: A Study of Socialist Activism in Deobandi Islam

Tahir Kamran

Renowned historian Aziz Ahmed credits Pan-Islamist Ubaidullah Sindhi as "the only political thinker of any considerable calibre to come directly in contact with Russian communism at an early stage".[1] Ubaidullah Sindhi epitomised the pluralistic character of the Ghadar Movement, of which he became a member in 1926. Therefore, he represents an antithetical viewpoint, which is in clear juxtaposition to the exclusionary and sectarian tendencies that are the general focus of the current study. In this chapter, the focus will be squarely on his political activism that emanated from his Pan-Islamist vision, which had a tangible socialist slant. Moreover, unlike other Deobandi scholars and activists, Ubaidullah Sindhi's political ideology as well as his interpretation of religious text(s) was inclusive, pluralistic and egalitarian. That was what differentiated Ubaidullah Sindhi from the rest of the Ulema.

Ubaidullah Sindhi was born on 10th March 1872, as a posthumous child at Chianwali, to a Sikh household in Daska Tehsil of Sialkot, British India. His parents were Ram Singh and Prem Kaur. His family had traditionally been associated with the profession of goldsmith. Some of them later joined government service, and others became moneylenders. He was known to be related to Mulraj, the famous Diwan of Multan who put up valiant resistance against the British.[2] According to M. Hajjan Shaikh, Ubaidullah's father Ram Singh had converted from Hinduism to Sikhism, and Ubaidullah was born a Sikh named Buta Singh, who revolted against

---

1 Aziz Ahmed, *Islamic Modernism in Indian and Pakistan, 1857–1964*, London: Oxford Univ. Press 1967, 195.

2 Diwan Mulraj Chopra was the leader of the Sikh rebellion against the British from Multan. He was the son of Diwan Sawan Mal Chopra, a governor of the city of Multan under the Sikh ruler Maharaja Ranjit Singh (1799–1839). His territory included the Southern Punjab region of Jhang. After the annexation of Lahore palace by the British, the Sikh Army fought valiantly in the two Anglo-Sikh wars. Diwan Mulraj was part of the last Sikh stand against the British and was supported by Sikh Saint Bhai Maharaj Singh, Sikh Sardars from West Punjab, and Punjabi Muslims. After the British captured Multan, they imprisoned Diwan Mulraj and later on he died in a jail near Calcutta, India. See for further details, Raj Mohan Gandhi, Punjab: *A History from Aurangzeb to Mountbatten*, Delhi: Aleph Book Company 2013, 183–186. A Diwan is "(in Islamic societies) a central finance department, chief administrative office, or regional governing body. A Diwan is a chief treasury official, finance minister, or prime minister in some Indian states" (*English Oxford Living Dictionary*, "diwan", https://en.oxforddictionaries.com/definition/diwan [accessed on 09/08/2017]).

his family religion and embraced Islam in 1887.[3] It is significant that at this time the trend in India was to convert to Christianity. Ubaidullah's conversion to Islam was therefore an important ideological step. He attended school at Jampur in the Dera Ghazi Khan district in the Punjab, where his maternal uncle lived. It is said that books like *Tuhfatul Hind*, *Taqwiyatul Iman*[4] and *Ahwaalul Aakhira* instilled in him an interest in Islam, leading eventually to his conversion. In fact, he changed his name to Ubaidullah because that was the name of the author of *Tuhfatul Hind*. (*Ahwaalul Aakhira* by Maulvi Muhammad Lakhoki was a Punjabi book that Sindhi claims had inspired him, but no specific reference to the book can be found in the available literature.)[5] However, this claim can be disputed because it is unlikely that Sindhi, at such a tender age, could have comprehended or been influenced by such pithy narratives.

In the same year he went to Sindh where, as Sara Ansari notes, the "pirs in Sind became more conscious of the Pan-Islamic sentiment which had been stoked by the decline of the Ottoman Empire as an important world power."[6] Thus, a number of Sindhi pirs forged close links with Pan-Islamists in other parts of India, most notably with Deobandi Ulema. This newly-forged connection between Ulema and Sufis provided the context for Ubaidullah Sindhi's flitting between Sindh (land with Sufi culture) and Deoband, a seminary according primacy to religious 'text'.

It is important to underline that the last quarter of the 19th century, the time Ubaidullah Sindhi was coming of age, was the high noon of British colonialism. Within India, religious reform movements were re-defining the prevailing socio-religious ethos by emphasising the primacy of the 'texts' rather than the lived religious experience.

In essence, these reform movements were puritanical. Thus, the Deobandi movement was the puritanical response to the Colonial dispensation. Two reformist scholars, Muhammad Qasim Nanautvi (1833–1877) and Rashid Ahmed Gangohi (1829–1905), founded a seminary in Saharanpur in the United Provinces–which in due course became the fountainhead of Islamic puritanism[7]–the Darul Ulum Deoband, an institution of religious higher

3 Shahid Perwez, *The Deobandi Movement till 1920: The Ideological and Institutional Dimensions*, PhD Thesis, Aligarh Muslim University: India 1999, 164–165. Also see Muhammad Sarwar, *Maulana Ubaidullah Sindhi: Halat-i-Zindagi, Talimaat aur Siasi Afkar*, Lahore: Sind Sagar Academy 1943, 17–18.

4 Ismael Shaheed, *Taqwiyat al-Iman*, Lahore: Bait al Koran 1825–1826.

5 Abu Salman Shahjahanpuri, *Imam-i-Inqilab: Maulana Ubaidullah Sindhi, Hayat o Khidmaat*, Lahore: Darul Kitab 2007, 35.

6 Sara Ansari, *Sufi Pirs and State Power: The Pirs of Sind, 1843–1947*, Cambridge: Cambridge Univ. Press 1992, 78.

7 Barbara Metcalf, *Islamic Revival in British India: Deoband, 1860–1900*, New Jersey: Princeton Univ. Press 1982.

education. It drew inspiration from the thoughts of Shah Waliullah Delhvi (1704–1762) and the campaign of Syed Ahmed from Rai Bareilly, which proved to be a continuous source of motivation for Deobandi scholars. The Deobandi denomination also acquired prominence as an anti-British movement with Mehmudul Hasan and Ubaidullah Sindhi as its stalwarts.

Internationally Pan-Islamism was gaining importance, with Jamalud Din Afghani (1839–1897)[8] as its chief proponent. A term of European origin, *pan-Islamism* denotes the intellectual and institutional trends toward Islamic unity that emerged among Muslim peoples, starting in the mid-nineteenth century and continuing throughout the twentieth century. The need for a unified Islamic identity was a product of the challenges posed by Western intervention in, and domination of, Muslim societies during the colonial period.[9] Both of these developments profoundly influenced Ubaidullah Sindhi. It should be borne in mind that for him Deoband acted as a conduit in linking him up with a Pan-Islamist ideology. At this point, it seems pertinent that Ubaidullah Sindhi's initiation into religious instruction is brought into focus with the aim of putting his life and the anti-British campaign in historical context.

Sindhi in Deoband

His biographical account reveals that Sindhi went to Deoband for the first time in 1889. At Deoband, it seems he exerted as much influence on his teachers and colleagues as they did on him. The Rowlatt Committee[10] characterized him as having "infected some of the staff and students with his own militant and anti-British ideas." It was here that he came under the influence of Mehmudul Hasan, his mentor and guide, who was galvanizing Sindhi on the path "to war with Britain,"[11] since he was the principal

8 For a detailed account, see Nikki R. Keddie, *Sayyid Jamal al-Din 'al-Afghani': A Political Biography*, Berkeley: University of California Press 1972.

9 Jacob M. Landau, *The Politics of Pan-Islam: Ideology and Organization*, Oxford: Clarendon Press 1990.

10 "The Rowlatt committee was a Sedition Committee appointed in 1917 by the British Indian Government with Justice Rowlatt, an English judge, as its president. The purpose of the committee was to evaluate political terrorism in India, especially Bengal and Punjab, its impact, and the links with the German government and the Bolsheviks in Russia. It was instituted towards the end of World War I when the Indian Revolutionary movement had been especially active and had achieved considerable success, potency and momentum and massive assistance was received from Germany which planned to destabilise British India" (*Revolvy*, "Rowlatt Committee", www.revolvy.com/main/index.php?s=Rowlatt%20Committee [accessed on 09 August 2017]).

11 S. A. T. [Sidney Arthur Taylor] Rowlatt, *Report Sedition Committee 1918*, Calcutta: Superintendent Government Printing 1919. Quoted in Muhammad Qasim Zaman,

source of inspiration for Ubaidullah Sindhi. Mehmudul Hasan exposed Sindhi to the political vision that he tried all his life to realise.

Born in Bareilly to Maulana Zulfiqar Ali, who was inspector of schools there, Mehmudul Hasan acquired his early education from his uncle Maulana Mehtab Ali, a student of Arabic College Delhi and an alim. Mehtab Ali taught him Arabic and Persian. At the age of fifteen, Mehmudul Hasan was sent to Darul Ulum Deoband, where he received instruction from Mulla Mahmud and Muhammad Qasim Nanautvi. It was here that he developed unequivocal devotion to Shah Waliullah and Syed Ahmed of Rai Bareilly, both of whom he tried to emulate all his life. When Mehmudul Hasan completed his education in 1873, he became a member of the staff at Darul Ulum. He taught there for forty years and was the "dominating influence in its (Darul Ulum's) teaching and administration."[12]

Known for his exuberance and energy, Mehmudul Hasan used to teach "ten lessons each day". His loyalty to the Darul Ulum was beyond any doubt and he "resisted all [significant] invitations to leave it."[13] Teaching hadith was his *forte* and in the course of his protracted career he instructed "over a thousand students from such distant places as Kabul, Qandahar, Balkh, Bukhara, Mecca, Medina, and Yemen".[14] Scholars of the calibre of Anwar Shah Kashmiri, Shabbir Ahmed Usmani, and Hafiz Muhammad were among his pupils. Another among them was Ubaidullah Sindhi. While at Deoband, Sindhi also visited two cities of the United Provinces, Kanpur and Rampur, where he obtained an education from Maulana Ahmad Hasan and Maulvi Naaziruddin. In Deoband, Sindhi also studied the writings of Shah Waliullah and Muhammad Qasim Nanautvi. The works of the former consequently became Ubaidullah's lifelong passion, one he shared with his mentor, Mehmudul Hasan. It was under the intellectual tutelage of the latter that Sindhi, in the words of Aziz Ahmed, "evolved a curious political philosophy of his own, a kind of pseudo-Wali-Ullahi communism."[15]

In 1891, Sindhi graduated from Darul Ulum Deoband and went to Sukkur (Sindh) where he took up teaching under Taj Mahmud Amroti, who became his mentor after the demise of Maulana Sadiq. In 1901, Sindhi established the Darul Irshad in Goth Peer Jhanda in Sindh. He returned to Delhi in 1909, at the behest of his teacher Mehmudul Hasan and became the secretary of Jamayatul Ansar, which the Silk Letters report suggested

Modern Islamic Thought in a Radical Age: Religious Authority and Internal Criticism, Cambridge: Cambridge Univ. Press 2012, 283.

12 Metcalf, *Islamic Revival*, 108.

13 Ibid.

14 Ibid.

15 Aziz Ahmed, *Studies in Islamic Culture in the Indian Environment*, Oxford: Clarendon Press 1964, 269.

"may be called the Deoband Old Boys' Association".[16] There, he had the opportunity of meeting renowned scholar and Pan-Islamist Muḥammad Rashīd Riḍā.[17] However, Peter Hardy holds the view that Sindhi founded Jamayatul Ansar in 1910 purely of his own accord, aiming at forging a greater fraternity between the alumni of Deoband and Muhammadan Anglo Oriental College, which was established by Sir Syed Ahmad Khan in 1877 at Aligarh.[18] The object of Jamayatul Ansar was defined to be "preaching of Quran and hadith, to introduce reform in the faith and activities of the Muslims and to hold regular deliberations for preservation and propagation of Islamic sciences."[19]

Pan-Islamic sentiment was on the boil in India during the Balkan wars of 1911–1913, in which the Ottoman Empire ceded Macedonia and Tripolitania. Indian Muslims saw Britain lending support to Turkey's enemies and "were galvanized into action by anticolonial sentiment."[20] The issue triggered anti-British agitation which soon became religious in character, because of the famous Kanpur Mosque controversy in 1913. This led to a massive uproar and agitation which resulted in indiscriminate firing by police at demonstrators. This was when, according to Dietrich Reetz, "the three Deobandi clerics Mahmud al-Hasan, Husain Ahmed Madani, and Ubaidullah Sindhi pulled the seminary [Deoband] in the direction of international political activism."[21] In 1912, Sindhi took over a "Deobandi af-

16 In order to popularize the programme of the Jamiyatul Ansar (Assembly of Helpers), Mehmudul Hasan persuaded his colleagues in Darul Ulum to hold *Jalsa-i-Dastarbandi* (graduation ceremony) in 1910, which was attended by 30.000 Muslims of differing shades of opinion. Even the Aligarh delegation led by Sahibzada Aftab Ahmad Khan came to take part in that event. In one of the meetings the Sahibzada put forward a proposal of exchange of students between Deoband and Aligarh. The proposal was welcomed by Deoband authorities, but ironically the first batch of Aligarh students who came to Deoband turned out to be a British team of secret agents. Ziya-ul-Hasan Faruqi, *The Deoband School and the Demand for Pakistan*, London: Asia Publishing House 1963, 58.

17 Muhammad Qasim Zaman, *Modern Islamic Thought in a Radical Age: Religious Authority and Internal Criticism*, Cambridge: Cambridge Univ. Press 2012, 11. Muḥammad Rashīd Riḍā was an early Islamic reformer, whose ideas would later influence 20th-century Islamist thinkers in developing a political philosophy of an 'Islamic state'. Riḍā is said to have been one of the most influential and controversial scholars of his generation and was deeply influenced by the early Salafi Movement and the movement for Islamic Modernism founded in Cairo by Muḥammad 'Abduh (1849–1905). For biographical accounts of Riḍā and 'Abduh, see Alber H. Hourani, *Arabic Thought in the Liberal Age: 1798–1939*, Cambridge: Cambridge Univ. Press 2012, 222–224, 161–192.

18 Peter Hardy, *The Muslims of British India*, Cambridge: Cambridge Univ. 1972, 181.

19 Perwez, *Deobandi Movement*, 116.

20 Dietrich Reetz, "The Deoband Universe: What Makes a Transcultural and Transnational Educational Movement of Islam?", *Comparative Studies of South Asia, Africa and the Middle East* 27: 1 (2007), 5.

21 Ibid.

filiate in Delhi" where he pleaded in favour of the synthesis of Aligarh's modernism and Deoband's traditionalism, and therefore not only introduced English-educated instructors but also put into circulation newspapers with advanced political views.

Far too political for the Deoband high command, he had to resign in 1913 and founded his own madrassa in Delhi, the *Nizarat al-Mu'arif al-Quraniyya* (Academy of Quranic Learning) in order to acquaint Western-educated Muslim youth with Islamic knowledge. He found Nawab Viqarul Mulk (1841–1917), Hakim Ajmal Khan (1864–1927) and Dr Mukhtar Ansari (1880–1936) as his patrons. It was here that Sindhi was introduced to Muhammad Ali Jauhar (1878–1931) and Abul Kalam Azad (1888–1958).[22] He now began to toe a militant line in his teaching and his books. *Talim-i-Quran* and *Khalid-i-Quran,* published in 1914 and 1915 respectively, clearly elucidated Sindhi's militant streak. It is pertinent to state here that Sindhi's social thoughts were anchored in the work of Shah Waliullah, who figures conspicuously in the intellectual genealogy of Deoband.

Kabul Sojourn

In June 1915, Sindhi covertly established a network of contacts among the frontier tribes throughout Sindh and the Peshawar district with the aim of kindling an insurgency in the North West Frontier and the tribal areas. This was an opportune moment, because the First World War was occupying much of British attention. Thus, Mehmudul Hasan and Ubaidullah Sindhi thought it was an opportunity to rid India of the colonial yoke by organising the frontier tribesmen. They also thought seeking assistance from Afghanistan, the Ottoman Empire and Germany in liberating India from the British as the best option. As Qasim Zaman states, "a grander scheme was to forge an alliance that would enable the Indian revolutionaries to also join forces with the Ottomans and the Germans in evicting the British from India."[23] Thus, along with Maulana Fazal Rabbi of Lahore and Maulana Fazal Mahmud of Peshawar, Sindhi was supposed to launch a movement in *Yaghistan*–the name attributed to the Tribal Areas by the Jamaat-i-Mujahidin, to mean land of the free Afghan tribes.[24] Sindhi started re-establishing Sayyid Ahmed of Rai Bareilly's old military bases of Chamarkand in the Bajaur and Asmas (the latter means 'cave') in Buner, as new political and military centres for the organisations of religious warriors. The Intelli-

22 Ayesha Jalal, *Partisans of Allah: Jihad in South Asia*, Ranikhet: Permanent Black 2008, 204.

23 Zaman, *Modern Islamic Thought*, 12.

24 Sana Haroon, *Frontier of Faith: Islam in the Indo-Afghan Borderland*, London: Hurst & Company 2007, 30–31.

gence Bureau noted Chamarkand's strategic location as a "nodal point" for the anti-British struggle:

> Chamarkand is especially adapted as a centre of intrigue... [It has] close touch with Extremist leaders in India; equally close touch, through Jelalabad which is only 42 miles distant with Kabul and is situated practically on the undemarcated portion of the Durand Line and in a tract which is neither under Afghan [control] and direct political relations with the Indian Government. Moreover, Chamarkand is accessible from Tashkent via eastern Bokhara, the Badakhashan-Pamir border and the Kumar Valley. A route which could be freely used by individuals without exciting any comment in Kabul...[25]

Importantly, Mujahidin came to the Frontier region in the late 1820s led by Sayyid Ahmed to wage a jihad against the Sikh regime of Maharaja Ranjit Singh (1780–1839). That campaign ended in a disaster as the Sikhs defeated the Mujahidin and Sayyid Ahmed, along with his close companion Shah Ismael, died a martyr's death in 1831 at the battle of Balakot. "Sayyid Ahmed's surviving followers retreated into the mountains of Swat and established a colony near a village called Sitana on the Indus River in Buner."[26] The Mujahidin maintained links with like-minded people in North India, with Patna (in Bihar) serving as a hub which provided funds and recruits mostly from the poor sections of Bengal and Bihar. The 'Hindustani Fanatics', as the British had started calling them from 1840 onwards, established a mutuality with the local tribesmen "through a combination of political manoeuvring and the maintenance of a low profile."[27] Throughout these years the British were not bothered about them as they mostly challenged Sikh rule by periodic raiding or kidnapping, mainly of Hindu *bania* (a term used mainly by Muslims for Hindu merchants in a derogatory sense), for ransom.[28] In that particular context, Ubaidullah Sindhi decided to make his base in Buner and restored connections with 'The Hindustani Fanatics'.

Shortly afterwards, a handful of disenchanted students from Government College Lahore, such as Iqbal Shaidai, Abdul Karim Chamarkandi and Muhammad Ali Kasuri, moved to Chamarkand and joined the dissidents.[29] Talbot and Kamran's recent work provides quite important details about the backgrounds of the students who absconded to Northern areas:

---

25 Intelligence Bureau Note. NWFP Bolshevik Intrigues and Participation of the Amir of Afghanistan in anti-British Intrigues along the Frontier. 3 November 1921.L/P&S/11/201 1921 P3901.4500 IOR BL. Cited in Ian Talbot and Tahir Kamran, *Colonial Lahore: History of the City and Beyond,* London: Hurst & Company 2017, 160.

26 Benjamin D. Hopkins and Magnus Marsden, *Fragments of the Afghan Frontier,* London, Hurst& Company 2011, 78.

27 Ibid.

28 Ibid.

29 Haroon, *Frontier of Faith,* 102–103. Also see Talbot and Kamran, *Colonial Lahore,* 163–166.

> Abdul Haq, one of the absconding Lahore students, later on revealed in a statement to the Intelligence Bureau that fifteen students absconded, seven of them came from Government College Lahore. Four of them were in their third year at Lahore medical School, including Shaikh Khushi Muhammad, Khoja Shuja Ullah, who was the relative of a prominent Lahore doctor, Allah Jawaya and Rahmat Ali, whose father worked in the Commissioner's office, Lahore. Abdul Haq's father was a village cloth merchant in the Shahpur district, and Muhammad Hassan, a student of Islamia College, Lahore whose father worked in the Paisa Akhbar Office. Later two students had the most ordinary backgrounds among the absconders.[30]

Funds were funnelled from India to the Chamarkand base for the purchase of arms, a printing press and other paraphernalia, primarily to upstage the British in India. They founded a newspaper by the name of *Al-Mujahid* which was initially in Persian, but later was published in Pashto as well. In that paper, articles decried British atrocities. The tone and tenor of *Al-Mujahid* was supportive of the Afghan government and it informed the readership of events in the wider world.[31] It is important to mention here the simmering discontent that occasionally spurred the people of the region to rise against the British.

Interestingly, Deoband and particularly Mehmudul Hasan wielded considerable influence here, simply because a large number of Deobandi graduates belonged to the area, most of whom were Mehmudul Hasan's students. One of them was Haji of Turangzai. Haji of Turangzai's real name was Fazal Wahid (1842–1937), and he hailed from the Utmanzai area, a town in Charsadda District in the Khyber Pakhtunkhwa of Pakistan. It is one of the eight main villages of Hashtnagar, one of the two constituent parts of Charsadda District. That was also the birthplace of Khan Abdul Ghaffar Khan (1890–1988), the founder of the *Khudai Khidmat Gar* movement (Servants in the name of God, founded in 1929). Haji Turangzai went to Deoband in 1878 to seek Islamic instruction and came under the influence of Mehmudul Hasan. He lived there for an extended period and struck up a friendship with his teacher, Mehmudul Hasan. While travelling to Mecca to perform Hajj with Mehmudul Hasan, he became a disciple of Imdadullah Muhajir Makki (1817–1899),[32] an alim known for his puritanical views. He took an oath of allegiance to Imdadullah in Mecca and "promised that he would take up Sayyid Ahmed of Bareilly's mission, kept alive until that time by Haji Imadadullah, and promote revivalism and opposition to the British among

30 Ibid., 158.

31 Hopkins and Marsden, *Fragments of the Afghan Frontier*, 96.

32 For Haji Imdadullah, see Seema Alvi, *Muslim Cosmopolitanism in the Age of Empire*, Massachusetts: Harvard Univ. Press 2015, 222–266.

the Pakhtuns."[33] On his return to the northwest he took up instruction at the hands of Mulla Najumuddin, known as Mulla Hadda, committing himself to the revivalist mission of Shah Walliullah and its dissemination to the Pakhtun tribes. Haji Turangzai, having been inspired by Sayyid Ahmed's movement, kept the situation in the tribal areas on the boil, although with varying intensity. On top of this, the Ottoman Empire joined Germany in the First World War (1914–1918) and the Pan-Islamic impulse of the Indian Muslims in general and those trained and instructed at Deoband seminary in particular, moved them to act decisively against the British. Yaghistan was also affected by these events. Mehmudul Hasan, wielding his influence to stoke anti-British sentiments among Pakhtun tribes and to persuade them to wage jihad, which made his arrest imminent. At the suggestion of Dr Mukhtar A. Ansari, Mehmudul Hasan decided to proceed to Arabia in September 1915 primarily to escape arrest. In Mecca he was supported by another zealot of Sayyid Ahmed of Rai Bareilly, Hafiz Abdul Jabbar, a person of considerable influence. It was through Jabbar that Mehmudul Hasan managed to meet the Turkish Governor of Hijaz, Ghalib Pasha. Ziya-ul-Hasan Faruqi reports that Ghalib Pasha had "made all the necessary arrangements for his travel to the Ottoman capital; but in the meantime Anwar Pasha, the Turkish War minister himself arrived there and met him."[34] In a couple of meetings, Mehmudul Hasan was successful in convincing him of the sincerity of the intent underlying the mission. Consequently, Ghalib Pasha issued a proclamation of Jihad. The document known as *Ghalibnama* was widely distributed in India and also in Yaghistan.

Ubaidullah Sindhi proceeded to Afghanistan in October 1915, after having spent a short time establishing "a presence at Chamarkand and Asma" along with Maulana Abdur Raziq and Maulana Saifur Rahman (an Afghan Deobandi scholar, who was the head of the Fatehpuri mosque-madrasa in Delhi), to secure the favour and financial assistance of the Amir of Afghanistan, Habibullah Khan (1872–1919) and to prepare for a Turkish mobilization through the former. Despite its neutrality, Afghanistan was a centre of German and Turkish intrigues. Sana Haroon underscores the historic as well as strategic significance of Afghanistan as "the most obvious place in which to politically organise because of its strong historic connections to Muslim rule in India, to Islamic nationalist and pan-Islamic movements in Turkey and Iran, and as the only contemporary sovereign Muslim state."[35]

33 Aziz Javed, *Haji Sahib Turangzai*, Lahore: Idara-e-Tahqeq-o-Tasneef Pakistan 1981, 42–43, quoted from Haroon, *Frontier of Faith*, 55.

34 Faruqi, *Deoband School*, 61.

35 Muhammad Hussain Khan, *Afghan Badshah Alihazrat Amanullah Khan Khalladullah Malka va Hukma Ki Azimulishan Chasham Deed Dastan*, Lahore 1924, 190–251, quoted from Haroon, *Frontier of Faith*, 102.

Hakumat-i-Moagita-i-Hind or The Provisional Government in Exile

While in Kabul, Sindhi tried to forge a military compact between the Turks, Germans and Afghans. In this endeavour he worked alongside Maulana Barkatullah Bhopali (1854–1927) and Raja Mahendra Pratab (1886–1979), members of the Indian National Party who had also come to Afghanistan to make it their base for anti-British activity. Here a reference to the Indian National Party and its relation with the establishment of the Kabul-based Indian Provisional Government seems warranted. A number of revolutionaries originally belonging to the Ghadar Party (established in 1913 in San Francisco) had been operating in Berlin while the clouds of the First World War were looming large. It was in Berlin that the Indian National Party came into existence under the leadership of Lala Hardayal, Mahendra Partab and M. Barkatullah. In Germany they worked hard to mobilise public opinion against Britain and eventually succeeded in forging a Turco-German alliance,[36] by which the German government assured the Ottoman Empire of its support. That development emboldened the members of the Indian National Party. At the behest of German officials, the Ottoman Sultan and Enver Pasha granted them audience and promised support. Along with Mahendra Partab and Barkatullah, Dr Fawn Bentick, Captain Qasim Bey and Captain Hayns travelled to Kabul, equipped with letters from the German Kaiser, the Ottoman Sultan and Germany's Chancellor, for a meeting with Amir Habibullah. Over the course of a number of meetings, they presented and discussed the proposed establishment of an independent Indian Government in Kabul. Amir Habibullah was not convinced at the beginning, but German members Bentick and Hayns gave him assurance that the provisional Indian Government would be recognised by Germany and would be given assistance in arms, ammunition and finance. In the case of invasion on the part of the British Government of India, the governments of Germany and the Ottoman Empire would lend all possible support to Afghanistan. These assurances must have helped Amir Habibullah to grant permission to the Indian revolutionaries to form the Provisional Indian Government in Kabul. Thus, on 29th October 1915 the Indian Revolutionary Council was convened at the residence of Abdul Razzak Khan, where the final decision to form the Provisional Indian Government was taken.[37] On 1st December 1915, its formation was proclaimed. The Afghan Government facilitated the provisional Government by allotting office space and providing other lo-

36 M. Abdul Rahman, *Tehrik Reshmi Rumal*, Lahore: n.p. 1966, 171. Vinod Kumar Saxena, *Muslims and the Indian National Congress: 1885–1924*, Delhi: Discovery 1985, 160.

37 Hafiz Babar Khan, *Barr-i-Saghir Pak-o-Hind ki Siyasat Mein Ulama ka Kirdar*, Islamabad: n.p. 1985, 120.

gistic support. Within this context it becomes easy to make sense of the options available to Ubaidullah Sindhi.

The interface with the Indian National Party's communist outlook profoundly influenced Sindhi's interests.[38] The bond with these stalwarts persuaded Sindhi to join the Provisional Indian government. Sindhi was assigned the portfolio of Home Minister, whereas Barkatullah Bhopali was named Prime Minister.[39]

The Provisional Government dealt directly with the Afghan Government and sent emissaries to various governments to solicit their assistance in their bid to evict the British from India. It contacted Russia, the Ottoman Empire and Japan, but those efforts bore no fruit. As a representative of the Provisional Government, Sindhi wrote to different heads of state in order to persuade them to wage war against the British. The governor of Russian Turkistan and the Czar of Russia were the most conspicuous of them. He urged the Czar to rescind his alliance with the British and "assist in the overthrow of British rule in India."[40] On 9th July 1916, he also wrote a letter to Mehmudul Hasan and proposed an alliance with the Turkish Government. He also referred to the Army of God or Hizbollah,[41] which was to draw recruits from India. At the same time, Maulana Muhammad Miyan Mansoor Ansari also wrote to Mehmudul Hasan in a similar vein. Both the letters of Sindhi and Ansari were "neatly and clearly written on [a] yellow silken handkerchief to escape detection by Afghan and British intelligence."[42] Sindhi deputed Shaikh Abdul Haq, a new convert to Islam, to hand the letter over to Shaikh Abdur Rahim. He also enclosed a cover note for Abdur Rahim, asking him to entrust the responsibility of delivering those letters to Mehmudul Hasan in the Hijaz to a reliable haji (pilgrim). Instead of handing those letters to Abdur Rahim, Abdul Haq gave them to his employer, Allah Nawaz Khan, whose father was Multan's Honorary Magistrate Khan Bahadur Rab Nawaz Khan. Thus, the silken letters reached the British Commissioner in Multan and were subsequently transmitted to the Lieutenant-Governor of the Punjab, Michael O' Dwyer.[43]

---

38 Haroon, *Frontier of Faith*, 103.

39 Mahendra Pratab, *My Life Story of Fifty-Five Years*, World Federation: Dehradun 1947, 113.

40 Aijaz Ahmad, "Silken Handkerchief Letters Conspiracy: Maulana Mahmudul Hasan", *International Journal of Allied Practice, Research and Review* 1: 2 (2014), 54.

41 Ibid.

42 Ibid.

43 Muhammad Miyan, *Silk Letter Movement: Accounts of 'Silk Letter Conspiracy Case' from British Records: With Introduction to the Revolutionary Movement of Shaikhul Hind Moulana Mahmood Hasan for the Freedom of India*, Delhi: Shaikhul Hind Academy in association with Manak Publications 2013, 49.

When the letters reached the hands of the British, Mehmudul Hasan was still in the Hijaz and after having performed Hajj, proceeded to Medina to meet Turkish diplomats (Anwar Pasha and Jamal Pasha). The British approached their ally Sharif Hussain of Mecca who detained Mehmudul Hasan along with his four 'accomplices' Hussain Ahmad Madni, Ozair Gul, Hakim Nusrat Hussain and Waheed Ahmad and deported them to Jeddah on 19th December 1916. The prisoners were handed over to the British on 22 February 1917 and transported to Egypt and from there to Malta in the Mediterranean Sea where they remained imprisoned for three years and seven months. They were eventually released on 8 June 1920.[44] The Silken Letters Movement (*Tehreek-i Reshmi Roomal*) did not yield the desired result, but its importance as an anti-colonial episode can hardly be denied.

As Home Minister of an Indian government-in-exile, Sindhi tried to pursue his Pan-Islamic aims, but the Arab uprising in 1916 forced him to move in a more nationalist direction. He was convinced that the interests of Indian Muslims could best be served by forging a sense of Indian Muslim identity, instead of seeking cultural authenticity and religious guidance. He asserted that Indian Muslims ought to strengthen their ties with Indians from other communities through shared economic interests. Interestingly, Sindhi's willingness to work with a Hindu (Mahendra Partab) and readiness to forge close contacts with non-Muslim governments point to his cosmopolitan outlook, which distinguishes him from other Deobandi scholars.

The year 1919 was quite eventful. In that year the government-in-exile was dissolved as a result of British diplomatic pressure. In the same year Sindhi founded a militia, *Junud Allah* or *Junud-i Rabbaniyya* (The Muslim Salvation Army but its literal translation is The Army of Allah), for which he reached out to the pirs and successfully persuaded them not only to join its ranks but also to support it materially and to help him in recruitment. Eventually he succeeded in raising an army of 100.000 strong.[45] As Zaman states, it included English-educated Indian Muslims who had come to Afghanistan to pursue anti-British campaigns. Not only for them but also for those "associated with anti-British militancy in the tribal areas of the north-western Frontier" Afghanistan was a "relative safe haven".[46] Ayesha Jalal, while drawing on Zafar Hasan Aibak's book *Khatrat: Ap Biti*,[47] answers the question of why the militia was organised as a Salvation Army:

44 Ibid, 50; Jalal, *Partisans of Allah*, 208.

45 Tanvir Anjum, "A Voice from the Margins: An Appraisal of Ubaid-Allah Sindhi's Mahabharat Sarvrajia Party and its Constitution", *Journal of Political Studies* 20: 1 (2013), 159–177, 162.

46 Zaman, *Modern Islamic Thought*, 282.

47 Zafar Hasan Aibak, *Khatrat: Ap Biti*, Vol.1, Lahore n. d. Also see Zaman, *Modern Islamic Thought*.

> He (Sindhi) set up an organisation called Junud Allah, patterned on the Salvation Army, to collect the skins of animals slaughtered in the *Hejaz* on Eid. The hides would be processed in a leather factory and exported to Muslim countries. The profits were to be managed by a transnational Islamic company based in the Hijaz, and an Islamic bank was to be established to finance the project.[48]

The primary aim of the army (Junud Allah), according to Maia Ramnath, was to bring about "a union between Islamic kings" with Mehmudul Hasan as its General or *Al-Qaid*. Secondary centres were to be established in Istanbul, Tehran and Kabul and "third class" centres in countries which were under the influence of the colonial masters. Africa, India and central Asia were its potential "Spheres of Influence".[49] Ramnath provides graphic details of the movement's organisation:

> At the apex of this army's chain of command were the Ottoman sultan-caliph, the sultan of Persia and the Amir of Afghanistan, followed by field marshals, including Enver Pasha, Khedive Abbas Hilmi Pasha of Egypt, the Sharif of Mecca, Nasrullah Khan of Kabul, the Nizam of Hyderabad and the Nawabs of Rampur, Bhopal, and Bahawalpur. There are also twenty-one generals, nineteen major generals, twenty-nine colonels, ten lieutenant colonels, five majors, two captains and a lieutenant.[50]

The entire effort went wasted, however, because Amir Habibullah Khan was not favourably disposed to the scheme. Instead, he persuaded Sindhi to seek the support of Hindus in ridding India of British colonialism. It was at the suggestion of Habibullah Khan that Sindhi not only became a member of the Indian National Congress in 1919, but also established an independent Congress Committee of Kabul in 1922 and became its President.[51] In the same year (1922), through the efforts of Dr Mukhtar Ahmad Ansari, he managed to get the Kabul Congress affiliated with the Indian National Congress in its Gaya (Bihar) session, meaning that it became the first foreign branch of the Congress movement.[52] It is pertinent to note here that Sindhi, despite being a staunch supporter of Congress, was very critical of Gandhiism and lamented the fact that Gandhi was both a political and a religious leader.[53]

In 1919 during the Third Afghan War, Sindhi sent a public letter to his Indian compatriots urging them not to support the British Indian government, but rather to "kill the English in every possible way, don't help them

48 Ayesha Jalal, *Partisans of Allah*, 207.
49 Maia Ramnath, *Haj to Utopia: How The Ghadar Movement Charted Global Radicalism and Attempted to Overthrow the British Empire*, Berkeley: University of California Press 2011, 187–188.
50 Ibid, 188.
51 Perwez, *Deobandi Movement*, 138.
52 Anjum, "A Voice from the Margins", 162–163.
53 Faruqi, *Deoband School*, 57.

with men and money, and continue to destroy rails and telegraph wires." Ubaidullah Sindhi stayed in Afghanistan for nearly seven years, leaving after the Third Anglo-Afghan War. Habibullah was killed in 1919, and his brother King Amanullah stepped into his shoes as Kabul's next Amir. In 1921 he signed a treaty with Britain which recognised Afghanistan's sovereignty. Thus, King Amanullah no longer felt the need of Indian revolutionaries "to undermine British interests".[54] Within a year of the signing of the treaty, Sindhi was forced to leave Afghanistan.

Sindhi's Movement across Russia, Turkey and Arabia

While in Kabul, Ubaidullah Sindhi observed with great interest what was unfolding in Russia. Among his comrades was Muhammad Shafiq, later to be the Secretary of the Indian Communist Committee in Tashkent. Shafiq, supported by the Bolsheviks and their allies, organised revolutionary propaganda in India and linked it to Sindhi's group in Kabul.

Subsequent to his stay in Afghanistan, Ubaidullah travelled extensively. From Afghanistan he undertook a journey to Russia, entering the country on 15th October 1922, where he was accorded the status of a state guest. Zafar Hasan, Khushi Muhammad, Iqbal Shaidai, Umar Zafar Masud, Abdul Rashid, Abdul Aziz and Somnath Bannerji accompanied him to Bukhara, which was their first port of call.[55] After staying in Bukhara for a few days, they proceeded to Tashkent and eventually reached Moscow on 10th November 1922 where they lodged in the Deluxe Hotel. Their lodging and food were provided for by the Russian government.[56] Sindhi stayed in Russia for about seven months.

Here he studied the ideology of socialism and found many lacunae in it. Nevertheless, Sindhi was profoundly impressed by the overall improvement that socialism had brought in the lot of the people. Zaman contents that, "although he would anchor his social thought in the work of ... Shah Wali Allah (d. 1762), who figures prominently in the genealogy of Deoband, the experience of living in the Soviet Union shortly after the Russian revolution undoubtedly had a significant effect on his thinking."[57] Sindhi himself said later that the study of socialism "enabled him to defend his religious movement, which was a branch of the philosophy of Shah Wali-Allah, against the onslaught of atheism and anti-religious trend of time".[58] He is

54 Zaman, *Modern Islamic Thought*, 282.
55 Perwez, *Deobandi Movement*, 188.
56 Ibid., 189.
57 Zaman, *Modern Islamic Thought*, 13.
58 Shaikh Muhammad Hajan, "The Political Thought of Maulana Ubaidullah Sindhi", in: *The Quest of Identity* (Proceedings of the First Congress of Pakistan History and

reported to have debated with the Soviet high command, trying to expound the veracity of Islam, as opposed to communism which he argued was merely "a reaction to oppression". In the capacity of president of the Congress Committee in Kabul, he also had the occasion to meet Soviet Foreign Minister Chicherin and sought assistance in ousting the British from India. Zafar Hasan maintains in his memoirs that Sindhi had four meetings with Georgy Vasilyevich Chicherin (1918–1923), and eventually the latter agreed to provide assistance against the British. Hasan also revealed that the Russian government urged Sindhi to go to Istanbul and assured him that the Russian Council there would provide him with the necessary wherewithal.[59]

He went to Turkey in July 1923 and stayed for three years in Istanbul. There he watched with an analytical eye events unfolding under the charismatic leadership of Mustafa Kemal Atatürk (1881–1938). During that time, Turkey was undergoing an extraordinary transition from a monarchy epitomising tradition to a secular country aiming to embrace modernity. For a firebrand revolutionary and an anti-colonial Pan-Islamist as Sindhi was, it must have been a great disappointment. As Zaman states, gradually his thoughts began drifting away from Pan-Islamism, and the political future of India became his major concern.[60] During the course of his stay in Turkey he met various leaders including the Prime Minister Ismet Pasha [Inönü] (1884–1973),[61] although the outcome of those meetings are shrouded in mystery. It was during his stay in Turkey that his 'political ideology' took a definitive shape, when he founded the *Mahabharat Sarwrajia Party* (MSP) in 1924, under the aegis of the Congress Committee of Kabul. This development will be dealt with later in this chapter.[62]

From Turkey Sindhi went to Mecca in 1927 and lived there for thirteen long years. During this period he remained politically inactive, dedicating himself to scholarship and introspection. While in Hijaz, he spent most of his time studying and interpreting the teachings of the Quran in the light of Shah Waliullah's works, particularly *Hujjat al-Allah al-Balighah.*[63] He also wrote a few books and articles on the thoughts of Shah Waliullah. Besides this, he gave lectures on Quran's tafsir (exegesis), hadith (the traditions of the Prophet) and the teachings of Shah Waliullah. He returned to India in December 1939 after a quarter of a century and began teaching Shah Waliullah's books. He also founded another party by the name of *Jamna Narbada Sind Sagar Party* (JNSSP) in December 1939.

Culture, held at the University of Islamabad, April 1973), vol. III, Waheed uz Zaman and A H Dani, eds., Islamabad: Univ. of Islamabad Press 1974, 117–129, 127.

59 Aibak, *Ap Biti*, 15.

60 Zaman, *Modern Islamic Thought*, 14.

61 Anjum, "A Voice from the Margins", 163.

62 Ibid.

63 Ibid.

There had been several similarities in the objectives of *Jamna Narbada Sind Sagar Party* and MSP. However, by looking closely at the provisions of the JNSSP, Sindhi seemed to have gone soft on his unequivocal commitment to Indian nationalism and particularly its embeddedness in Indian tradition.[64] *Jamna Narbada Sind Sagar Party*'s membership was open to all irrespective of religious or ethnic specificity. However, the major focus was riveted on "Sind, the valley of the Indus, its tributaries controlled from Lahore, and the Gangetic Jamna Plain, including Ajmer and Benares, with Delhi as the centre."[65] The principal aim that the JNSSP would strive for was "Indian independence within British Commonwealth", until the time the Indian federation had become functional. The socio-economic amelioration of the lives of the general masses was the central objective that the party's leadership had set for itself to achieve. Unequivocal commitment to the advancement of democracy and working to end the discrimination on the basis of racial and religious difference was succinctly articulated. The adoption of the European mode of living was deemed necessary in order to introduce modern industry. The inclusion of 'Europeanism' in the party's program was to lure the Western-educated Muslims who "Sindhi believed held out more promise for the future than did the products of madrassas."[66] Quite contrary to his previous stance that did not endorse "Indians' becoming Europeanized",[67] now he was all for instilling "Europeanization" of the peasantry strictly in a technical sense, "so that they could benefit from modern knowledge and improve agricultural productivity."[68] In that context, Sindhi recommended that Urdu be written in the Roman alphabet, "which was easier to read and learn than the Arabic script."[69] However, the ethical dimension of JNSSP was embedded in Waliullah's philosophy. In Sindhi's view, Waliullah's thought epitomized the synthesis of intellectual pursuits undertaken by Indian Muslim thinkers since the sixteenth century "to perfect the philosophy of Ibn al-'Arabi, which Sindhi equated with Vedantism" and considered capable of "laying the political foundation for a united India."[70]

Ubaidullah Sindhi died in August 1944 in Lahore, while visiting his daughter. At the end of his life, Ziya-ul-Hasan Faruqi argues, his political

64 Much of the information regarding JNSSP that is furnished below has been gleaned from Ayesha Jalal's book *Partisans of Allah*, 223–224.
65 Ibid., 223.
66 Ibid., 224.
67 Ibid.
68 Ibid.
69 Ibid.
70 Ibid.

views had been transformed and he had virtually become a "nationalist-secularist".[71]

Radicalism in Sindhi's Ideology

Despite his criticism of the material foundations of the Soviet system, Sindhi's own thoughts regarding society's decline were informed by socialism. The reasons for the decline of any society founded on ideology (*nazariyya*), according to Sindhi, are two-fold. First, the concentration of wealth in the hands of a small elite and the impoverishment of the general populace mean that the masses are always busy making ends meet and lack the opportunity to attend to their moral or religious development. Second, the exclusion of the general population from knowledge of value to society, is the sole preserve of the elite. This exclusion, Sindhi avers, leads ordinary people to suspect the moral foundations on which the community supposedly rests. These thoughts of Sindhi, some scholars suggest, were gleaned from Shah Waliullah's classic *Hujjat Allah al-Baligha,* but the socialistic ring of his discourse can hardly be disputed. That socialist ring is particularly apparent in the constitution of the *Mahabharat Sarwrajia Party,* which was titled *The Constitution of the Federated Republics of India.* That Constitution encompassed the political and socio-economic vision of Sindhi.[72] The main features of the constitution were:

A) Securing complete Indian Independence from the Colonial yoke.
B) Establishment of a confederal system of governance in Free India.
C) Providing security to Islam, the Muslims and other minorities.
D) Doing away with feudal and capitalist dispensation(s).
E) Bringing about an Asiatic Federation to ward off any possibility of imperialism and colonialism.
F) The Government of Free India must be comprised of members of the peasantry, labour and the intelligentsia.[73]

As *The Constitution of the Federated Republics of India* succinctly states, Ubaidullah Sindhi's political ideals did not espouse India's status as a single country, but his ideology was inclusive and his nationalism had a pluralistic

71 Faruqi, *Deoband School,* 57.
72 It must be clarified here that the writer has benefited immensely from Tanvir Anjum's article "A Voice from the Margins" and a detailed chapter entitled "Bar-i-Saghir ka Dastoori Khaka, 15 September 1924" from Ubaidullah Sindhi's own *Khutbat wa Maqalat* (*Letters and Articles*), *Tahreek-i-Azadi key Tanazur mein tehrir kiye jane waley Siasi, Iqtasadi, dastoori wa Tarikhi Khutbat wa Maqalat,* Lahore: Darul Tehqiq wa Isha'at 2002.
73 Aibak, *Ap Biti,* 101–102.

resonance. Given the geographical, linguistic and cultural diversity of India, he proposed to divide India into three distinct zones: north-western, eastern and southern. Each zone would have the status of a democratic republic. Sindhi proposed the North-Western Indian Republic, which would comprise the regions of Punjab, the North West Frontier Province, Kashmir, Sindh, Baluchistan and Gujrat. For these republics, he proposed universal adult franchise with all adult men and women granted the right to vote. The people representing peasantry, labour/manual workers and intelligentsia would constitute the majority in the parliaments. Sindhi proposed proportional representation, with each social stratum electing its own representatives. How the social strata would be defined remained unclear.[74]

Nationalisation of all public utilities, restricted ownership of property, excessive taxation of the affluent and wealthy, doing away with feudalism, abolition of usury, free accommodation and medical facilities for all, compulsory education up to grade eight and the establishment of labour unions and their empowerment were the principal features of the MSP's constitution. Every republic would be able to have its religion, professed by the majority. Nevertheless, it would be made sure that economic and social realities held precedence over the religion. As regards the division of power between the republics and the central government, the constitution of the MSP proposed that foreign policy, defence and international trade and commerce would fall under the purview of the Central Government.[75]

Whereas Ubaidullah Sindhi embraced communist ideals, he was nevertheless constrained to keep his idealism within the larger framework of Indian Muslim identity. It would appear that he could not reconcile the various influences prevalent at the time–a hatred for British colonial rule manifested in violent resistance against the feudal system, an Indian Muslim identity shaped by Jamalud Din Afghani's Pan-Islamism, and Sindhi's own attempt to introduce inclusionary politics in the larger exclusionary schema of Deobandi thought. Thus, his well-meaning but vain attempts at creating a synthesised version of communism acceptable to Muslim religious sentiments contain various contradictions.

Membership in the MSP was open to all, irrespective of caste, creed or gender. Economic and social equality was a cornerstone of the party. Sindhi himself states that in the proposed political dispensation the possibility of capitalism's revival would cease. He was cognisant of India's multicultural ethos and he therefore strongly advocated against cow-slaughter so that Hindu sensitivities were not offended.[76]

---

74 Ubaidullah Sindhi, *Khutbat wa Maqalat*, 131–191.

75 Ibid.

76 Anjum, "A Voice from the Margins", 166.

To conclude this study, Ubaidullah Sindhi was markedly different from the rest of Muslim political thinkers in modern South Asia. He tried to be inclusive and pluralistic despite his Pan-Islamist tendency at the outset. An interesting aspect of Ubaidullah Sindhi was his endeavour to bring about a synthesis between socialism and Islam, which was, to say the least, quite a novel initiative in the second decade of twentieth century. Another remarkable feature of his personality was his nationalism. Having said all this, Sindhi's inability to translate his rather grandiose ideas into practice was far too conspicuous to be ignored. It was also noticeable that he embarked on action before giving proper attention to details. There is an increasing academic interest in the eventful life of Ubaidullah Sindhi and his attempts to re-interpret Islamic teachings in the light of the revolutionary currents of his own age. One may hope that the academic circles of Pakistan also reassess his role in history.

Part Three:
Social Justice and Anti-Capitalism

"... So That It May Not Circulate Solely between the Wealthy among You."

The Critique of Capitalism and the Vision of a "Balanced Society" (*mujtamaʿ mutawāzin*) in the Writings of Sayyid Quṭb (1906–1966)

Sabine Damir-Geilsdorf

Introduction: From a Poet and Literary Critic to an Islamist Writer

The Egyptian Sayyid Quṭb (1906–1966) is often regarded as one of the most inspiring authors for radical Islamist movements. Particularly his latest book, the manifesto *Milestones* (*Maʿālim fī l-ṭarīq*), published in 1964 and translated into several languages, has often been described as a standard reference for various jihadist groups worldwide, ranging from the Egyptian Jamaʿat al-Jihad which was responsible for the assassination of the Egyptian president Anwar al-Sadat in 1981 to current transnational Jihadi networks like al-Qa'ida.[1] His influence on these groups is, above all, related to 1) Quṭb's concept of God's *ḥākimiyya* (sovereignty on earth by the rule of Islamic laws) as a necessity for a 'real' Muslim society; 2) his description of Muslim rulers who consciously refuse to implement the Sharia as well as those who accept these rulers, as apostates; 3) Quṭb's call for establishing God's sovereignty by abolishing all human government and man-made laws, described as a jihad for the liberation of mankind. It is, however, contested whether Quṭb himself called for a jihad with violent means against current rulers, or if readers of his work (mis)understood his writings as a legitimation for militant action.

His numerous writings address diverse political and societal issues and mirror (in part fundamental) ideological shifts in his thoughts. Before he turned to Islam and was increasingly radicalized, he first became prominent as a poet and liberal literary critic and later through his socially critical articles.

Born in 1906 in Mūshā, a small village in Upper Egypt, as the oldest son of a privileged landowner family, Sayyid Quṭb experienced in his youth how his family's wealth dwindled gradually, like that of many farmers in

1 See for example John L. Esposito, *The Future of Islam*, New York: Oxford Univ. Press 2010, 67; Peter Wichmann, *Al-Qaida und der globale Djihad. Eine vergleichende Betrachtung des transnationalen Terrorismus*, Wiesbaden: Springer VS 2014, 166; John C. Zimmermann, "Sayyid Quṭb's Influence on the 11 September Attacks", *Terrorism and Political Violence* 16: 2 (2004), 222–252.

those days, and how his father was forced to sell land to pay back debts.[2] At the age of 15 he was sent to live with his uncle in Cairo and to continue his secondary education. He enrolled in *Dār al-ʿUlūm*, a teacher training school. After graduating, he worked as a teacher and later, until the early 1950s, as an inspector of elementary education for the Ministry of Education.[3] In his early years in Cairo, Quṭb's uncle introduced him to members of the nationalist party *al-Wafd* and to literary circles, to both of which he was soon drawn. In 1933, while still a student, he published his first work on poetry and literary criticism[4] and soon made a name for himself as a literary critic whose essays appeared in various magazines and newspapers. At the same time, he published poems in newspapers and journals, and in 1935 he published his first volume of poetry.[5] Most of these poems express feelings of uprootedness in a big city, restlessness, disorientation, and a strong longing to overcome the boundaries of human existence.[6] At the beginning of the 1940s, the issue of social justice became a major theme in Quṭb's articles. He called for substantial reforms in society, such as the setting of a minimum wage, governmental health insurance for everybody, and income-dependent taxes like in Britain. Having been a supporter of the nationalist parties, Quṭb now became increasingly disillusioned with the contemporary political system and leadership in Egypt. In 1945, Quṭb withdrew from all political parties with the impression that they did not offer any real solutions to Egypt's political and societal problems.[7] He now started to attack various sectors of the privileged upper classes. In his increasingly sharp-tongued articles, he accused the politicians of not speaking the language of the majorly poor people of Egypt, surrendering to the Britons. He even labelled the elites "cockroaches"[8].

It was only in 1949 that Quṭb wrote his first Islamist book *Social Justice in Islam* (*al-ʿAdāla al-ijtimāʿiyya fī l-Islām*) in which he described Islam as a system

2 For details on the economic transformations see Sayyid Quṭb's autobiography *Ṭifl min al-qarya* [*Child from a Village*], Beirut/Cairo: Dār al-Shurūq n.d. [orig. 1946], 18ff., 30, 179–180.

3 See ʿAbd al-Bāqī Muḥammad Ḥusayn, *Sayyid Quṭb. Ḥayātuhū wa-adabuhū* [*Sayyid Quṭb. His Life and his Literature*], Mansurah: Dār al-Wafāʾ li-l-ṭibāʿa wa-l-nashr wa-l-tawzīʿ 1993 [orig. 1986], 28–48.

4 Sayyid Quṭb, *Muhimmat al-shāʿir fī l-ḥayāt wa-shiʿr al-jīl al-ḥāḍir* [*The Task of the Poet in Life and the Poetry of the Present Generation*], Beirut: Dār al-Shurūq n.d. [orig. 1933].

5 Sayyid Quṭb, *Al-Shāṭiʾ al-majhūl* [*The Unknown Shore*], El-Minya: Maṭbaʿat al-Ṣādiq n.d. [orig. 1935].

6 See also Sayyid Quṭb, "Fī l-tīh" ["In the Desert"], in: *al-Risāla* (6.12.1943), 972–973; Sayyid Quṭb, *Kutub wa-shakhṣiyyāt* [*Books and Personalities*], Cairo: Maṭbaʿat al-Risāla 1946.

7 See Sabine Damir-Geilsdorf, *Herrschaft und Gesellschaft. Der islamistische Wegbereiter Sayyid Quṭb und seine Rezeption*, Würzburg: Ergon Verlag 2003, 28–35.

8 Sayyid Quṭb, "Ṣarāṣīr" ["Cockroaches!"], in: *al-Risāla* (6.8.1946), 756.

embracing all aspects of life. When the book was published in Egypt, Quṭb was abroad for a two-year visit in the United States, having been sent there by the Egyptian government to study English and the American educational curricula.[9] There, he experienced a cultural shock, and his anti-Western resentment increased.[10] When he returned to Egypt in 1951, he quit his job in the ministry and dedicated himself solely to writing. In 1953 he joined the Muslim Brotherhood. One year later an assassination attempt against Nasser was carried out by members of the secret apparatus of the Muslim Brotherhood. As a result, several thousand people were arrested, among them Sayyid Quṭb who spent most of the time of his incarceration in a military hospital due to a heart condition. In prison he wrote some of his most well-known books, which manifest a continuous radicalization, most probably influenced by the torture he himself endured, and that of other inmates. In 1964, Quṭb was released from prison, but a few months later arrested again. He was accused of being the spiritual leader and supervisor of a clandestine Islamist group which had planned to overthrow the Egyptian government. He was sentenced to death and executed in August 1966.

Quṭb's writings comprise several hundred articles in various journals and newspapers and more than 30 books, including his prominent six-volume commentary on the Quran. While his concepts of God's sovereignty, 'true belief' versus apostasy, and jihad have gained much scholarly attention, his critique of capitalism and theory of social justice in Islam, which can be found in both Quṭb's early and later writings, has been largely neglected by academics. This is in part understandable due to the obvious and serious influence of Quṭb's criteria for pronouncing that someone is an unbeliever and no longer a Muslim (*takfir*) and his ideas of jihad on current militant Islamist individuals and movements. At the same time, Quṭb's writings cannot be reduced to the topic of jihad and his call to abolish man-made laws and establish God's Sharia on earth. Furthermore, these ideas stem from and are based on his criticism of social and economic inequalities in society and the entanglement he perceived between capitalism, colonialism, and communism which also have had an influence on later Islamist move-

9 See Gilles Kepel, *Der Prophet und der Pharao. Das Beispiel Ägypten: Die Entwicklung des muslimischen Extremismus*, München: Piper 1995 [French orig. *Le prophète et le pharao. Les mouvements Islamistes dans l'Égypte contemporaine*, Paris: Éditions de Seuil 1983], 40. Sayyid Quṭb himself wrote later that friends from the education ministry sent him to the USA to protect him from his impetuosity after having been cautioned. See Sayyid Quṭb, "Wizārat al-maʿārif wa-fikrat al-thawra" ["The Ministry of Education and the Idea of Revolution"], in: *al-Risāla* (20.10.1952), 15.

10 For further details see John Calvert, *Sayyid Qutb and the Origins of Radical Islam*, London: Hurst 2010, 139–155. Some articles of Sayyid Quṭb on his experiences in the USA are collected in Ṣalāḥ ʿAbd al-Fattāḥ al-Khālidī, *Amrīkā min al-dākhil bi-minẓār Sayyid Quṭb*, Cairo: Dār al-Wafāʾ 1987.

ments. Therefore, the following sections of this contribution aim to shed light on Quṭb's line of arguments against capitalism and his vision of an Islamic governance in the form of a new "balanced society" (*mujtamaʿ mutawāzin*), established by a revolutionary liberation movement as a "new birth" (*milād jadīd*) of mankind, expressed in his early Islamist writings, and taken up in his later ones as well.

Capitalism and Colonialism

From the end of the 1940s onwards, Quṭb fiercely criticized both the Egyptian political elites and Western politics, which he contrasted with an Islamic way of governance. In particular after his return from the USA, he addressed in his writings capitalism as the underlying reason for social and political failures in Egyptian society. In 1951 Quṭb published his work *The Struggle between Islam and Capitalism* (*Maʿrakat al-Islām wa-l-raʾsmāliyya*) in which he portrays Egypt as a country whose resources are distributed among the few, who exploit it at the expense of the many, supported by a government eager to guarantee the interests of capitalists.[11] He elaborates that Egyptian politicians cannot represent the masses, because anyone entering the parliament has to pay a fee of 150 Egyptian Pounds and later several thousand Pounds for running an electoral campaign, thus making political participation a privilege of the rich.[12] In conformity with socialist rhetoric, he accuses political elites in an article entitled "Bread and Freedom" (*Khubz wa-ḥurriyya*), published in 1951 in the Journal *Socialism* (*al-Ishtirākiyya*), of not acknowledging the right of the masses to either bread or to inner freedom and therefore being unable to acknowledge their right to political independence.[13] A political change would demand firstly the removal of social grievances, because the constitution, parliament or laws cannot guarantee freedom to someone who suffers from hunger: "First of all, he has to be freed from hunger to feel that he is a human being, so that he can keep his head unbowed and optain his rights which are guaranteed by constitution and laws."[14]

For Quṭb, the injustice in contemporary social conditions manifests in the lack of rewards for the working poor's efforts and the lack of equal

11 Sayyid Quṭb, *Maʿrakat al-Islām wa-l-raʾsmāliyya* [*The Struggle between Islam and Capitalism*], 12th edition, Cairo/Beirut 1993 [1951], 113–114; see also Sayyid Quṭb, *Al-Salām al-ʿālamī wa-l-Islām* [*Universal Peace and Islam*] 6th edition, Beirut/Cairo: Dār al-shurūq 1982 [1951], 8.

12 Quṭb, *Maʿraka*, 162.

13 Sayyid Quṭb, "Al-Khubz wa-l-ḥurriyya" ["Bread and Freedom"], *al-Ishtirākiyya* (27.4.1951), 7–9, 9.

14 Ibid., 8.

chances for everyone, mirrored in the fact that the social status of the parents decides future positions in society.[15]

Moreover, he laments in *The Struggle between Islam and Capitalism* that miserable social conditions "ruin human dignity, spoil the character and the conscience, destroy all forms of justice, kill the necessary confidence in society and the state, spread concerns and destroy serenity".[16] In polemical words he describes how the political rights of the poor are suppressed in order to keep them obedient and calm:

> Who dares to say that the million hungry, naked and barefooted farmers whose intestines are eaten by the worms that snatch the inner corner of their eyes, and whose blood is sucked by vermin are people equipped with human dignity and human rights? [...] Who dares to say that the millions of domestic workers and day labourers in offices whom the law forbids to form trade unions because their masters reject this right for them to prevent slaves outbraving against masters [...] are people with human rights and human dignity?[17]

Quṭb's criticism of the imbalance in the distribution of wealth was shared by many other contemporaries at the time. In the 1940s social injustice was broadly discussed in the Egyptian public. Waves of (illegal) strikes flared up; many of them were violently suppressed and accompanied by violent outbreaks of discontent, such as peasant uprisings against landlords between 1944 and 1952, and assassinations of public figures.[18]

During the 1950s and 1960s in Egypt, many intellectuals and publicists with left-wing as well as anti-Western and anti-colonial tendencies based socialist views on Islamic principles by reading Islamic history as a repository of historical examples for social (redistributive) justice.[19] After the July 23 revolution in Egypt in which the Free Officers movement seized power by a military coup d'etat, Arab Socialism became one of the key elements in Nasserist official ideology.

According to Quṭb, the political grievances he perceived on the local Egyptian level are strongly connected to global capitalism and similar to other countries. Capitalist states' claims of free elections to parliament in

---

15 Quṭb, *Maʿraka*, 16–17.

16 Ibid., 5.

17 Ibid., 10–11.

18 See Adnan A. Musallam, *From Secularism to Jihad. Sayyid Qutb and the Foundations of Radical Islamism*, Westport: Praeger 2005, 15; Selma Botman, *Egypt from Independence to Revolution, 1919–1952*, Syracuse: Syracuse Univ. Press.

19 See Menahem Merhavy, "Arab Socialism and Ecumenical Tendencies in Egypt 1962-1970", *British Journal of Middle Eastern Studies* 43: 4 (2016), 472–485; Yvonne Yazbeck Haddad, *Contemporary Islam and the Challenge of History*, Albany: State Univ. of New York Press 1982, 24–42. Among these publications are for example Maḥmūd Shalabī, *Ishtirākiyya Muḥammad* [*The Socialism of Islam*], Cairo: Maktabat al-Qāhira al-ḥaditha 1962; Muṣṭafā al-Sibāʿī, *Ishtirākiyyat al-Islām* [*The Socialism of Islam*], second revised edition, Dimashq: Muʾassasat al-Maṭbūʿāt al-ʿArabiyya 1960.

general, are a "fairy tale" spun for the masses, by members of parliament who belong to a certain social class and enact laws merely for the interests of capitalists.[20] Likewise, he describes the slogan "people are the source of power" as a "fairy tale", because the majority of people are excluded from any political participation anyhow and their hard labour would prevent them from even thinking of their right to vote and free elections.[21]

From his point of view not only are global capitalism in the West and in the East closely intertwined, but also regional capitalism and colonialism seem to be inseparable.[22] For him, it was colonialism which had built the "ruling capitalist class" in Egypt, in order to control the country by systemically starving out the masses to prevent their rebellion.[23] Therefore, he describes in his work *Islamic Studies* (*Dirāsāt Islāmiyya*), published in 1953, with sarcasm how Britain, France, and the USA call themselves "the free world" at the same time they are busy destroying attempts to achieve freedom in Tunis, Marrakesh, Kenya, Vietnam and elsewhere. He concludes: "... the mission of the 'free world' is to kill freedom whenever it wants to do so".[24] When the work was published (with several chapters which appeared a year earlier in Egyptian journals), the brutal, so-called "First Indochina War" was going on. Resistance movements in Morocco–a divided Spanish and French protectorate from 1912 to 1956–, in Algeria which became independent from the French only in 1962, and the Mau Mau Rebellion in Kenya (1952–1960) against the British colonial state were brutally suppressed by the colonists. Quṭb warns that the so-called free world commits crimes "that make human conscience shudder" in their mission to bring principles of Western civilization to the perceived "dark continent" and "backward people". From his point of view, even more dangerous than violent colonialism which inevitably leads to opposition, are modern neo-colonial tactics with "words and tongues" and the ideological "soft colonialism" (*istiʿmār nāʿim layyin*) which nowadays use organizations with innocent names like UNESCO or educational institutions to fight the masses in suppressed countries and pursue the interests of the 'free world'.[25]

---

[20] Quṭb, *Salām ʿālamī*, 161–162.
[21] Quṭb, *Maʿraka*, 11–12.
[22] Ibid., 120.
[23] Ibid., 120–121.
[24] Sayyid Quṭb, *Dirāsāt islāmiyya*, 9th edition, Cairo: Dār al-shurūq 1993 [1953], 159.
[25] Ibid., 161–163.

Islam as a "Third Way" beside Communism and Capitalism

Quṭb warned not only of capitalism, but also of communism which he increasingly considered two sides of the same coin. In 1953, in the middle of the Cold War, he stated that both the Western bloc, based on colonialism, and the Eastern bloc, based on doctrinal grounds, "compete for the prey which is what we are" in order to "devour and swallow us".[26] Considering Arabic nationalism as a means to serve the imperial interests of either the Eastern or the Western bloc,[27] and the attempts of some Asian and African states to form a neutral bloc as too weak,[28] he called, at the end of the 1940s, for Islam as a third bloc, independent and at the same time superior to the contesting great powers. Quṭb advocated this third bloc, on the one hand as a "natural bloc" of the people of the wider region[29] and on the other hand, also as the solution for mankind in general. In contrast to the "narrow idea of nationalism in which Europe believes", Islam would be a "liberation power" considering all people as people, "regardless of nationality, colour, language or territory".[30]

The implementation of his political utopia would take place by returning to 'true' Islam, which would be achieved by accepting Islam as the first generations of Muslims had done. In *Social Justice in Islam* (*al-ʿAdāla al-ijtimāʿiyya fi l-Islām*), published in 1949 and revised five times until 1964,[31] he propagated Islam as a superior third bloc. An all-embracing solution for diverse societal, economic and political grievances would be achieved by referring to–selective–examples from the history of Islam, in particular to the role models of the first generations of Muslims. He described Islam as a solution for the contemporary weakness of Muslims who would regain power, and at the same time, it would not be restricted only to Muslims but be a solution for the adversities suffered by mankind in general. He praises his vision of an Islamic system in *Social Justice in Islam* for instance as "an elevation of the whole of humanity, impelling it to freedom and upward advancement, toward creation and innovation. Along this way it will deal with class bondage

26 Ibid., 100.
27 Ibid.
28 Ibid., 164.
29 Ibid., 103–105.
30 Quṭb, *Salām ʿālamī*, 174.
31 The changes are considered in the excellent translation and analysis of William E. Shephard, *Sayyid Quṭb and Islamic Activism: A Translation and Critical Analysis of Social Justice in Islam*, Leiden: Brill 1996. In this article, I take verbatim quotations from *al-ʿAdāla al-ijtimāʿiyya fi l-Islām* from Shepard's translation. All other direct citations of Quṭb's works are translated into English by the author.

and suffering and will destroy this bondage and end this suffering."[32] From Quṭb's point of view, Western hegemony had failed completely:

> Among the facts worth noting in this connection is that contemporary Western civilization has led the world to two comprehensive wars and since the second war has led it to the division between Eastern and Western blocs and to the ever-present threat of a third war, to disturbances everywhere and to hunger, destitution and misery in three-quarters of the globe. The whole world order today is in a state of convulsion and disturbance, seeking for new foundations and searching for spiritual sustenance that will give back to the human race its trust in humane principles.[33]

Citing the convert Muhamad Asad who described life in Europe as the sacralization of a life lacking any values and meaning, he continues:

> The ordinary European, whether democrat or fascist or Bolshevik, worker or intellectual, knows only one positive religion and that is the *worship of material progress*, that is the belief that there is no other goal in life than to make this life itself more and more comfortable. ... The inescapable result of this situation is that people toil for power and pleasure and this creates quarrelling communities armed to the teeth that insist on destroying each other whenever their opposing interests conflict. As for the cultural dimension, the result is the creation of a human type whose ethical philosophy is limited to useful and pragmatic matters and for whom the highest criterion of good and evil is material progress.[34]

Quṭb does not see much difference between capitalism and communism, because for him, both have a materialistic notion of life and banish the spiritual factor. According to him, their materialism only takes different forms, based on differences in economic and social circumstances: "We should not be deceived by the fact that we see a strong and violent struggle between the Eastern and Western blocs, for both of them have a materialistic notion of life, each is similar to the other in its thinking, and neither struggles for ideas and principles but only for influence in the world and profit in the markets."[35] Therefore, he states, the real struggle in the future will not be between capitalism and communism, but between materialism, visible throughout the world, and Islam.[36]

---

32 Quṭb, *ʿAdāla ijtimāʿiyya* (Shepard 1996, 311).
33 Ibid., 290.
34 Ibid., 292.
35 Ibid., 350.
36 Ibid. See also Sayyid Quṭb, *Fī Ẓilāl al-Qurʾān* [*In the Shadow of the Quran*], vol. 3, 16th edition Cairo/Beirut: Dār al-shurūq 1996 [1951–1965], 1652.

Islam as a Revolutionary Liberation Movement: Preaching and Jihad

In his later writings, from the mid-1950s onwards, Quṭb still reiterates his criticism of both capitalism and communism as well as the presentation of Islam as a system which rescues mankind, but he has given up the idea of a third bloc. From now on, he delineates an Islamic mode of governance in his increasingly radical writings as a requirement for believers and its establishment as an act of liberation, achieved by the jihad of a Muslim vanguard, which eliminates all human governance and man-made laws. The concept of Islam as a revolutionary liberation from injustice and all forms of exploitation is already expressed in Quṭb's 1951 published book *Universal Peace and Islam* (*al-Salām al-ʿālamī wa-l-Islām*):

> [The Islamic system] is the biggest liberating revolution known by mankind. It is a revolution against the lordship of God's servants for other servants of God. It is a revolution against all kinds of injustice: a revolution against systems, regimes and rules which are based on injustice, in order to give an advantage to an individual–such as a ruler or an exploiter–at the expense of the community, or an advantage of a certain class at the expense of other classes by feudal lords, capitalists and criminals. It is a revolution against unjust advantages of a certain state at the expense of another state by occupation and colonialism.[37]

In his later writings, he stresses the idea that not only capitalism and communism, but also all man-made ideologies inevitably divide mankind into masters and servants.[38] This firstly hinders mankind from achieving equality and liberation, and secondly forces people to adore human beings instead of God. Based on this assumption, he now makes a twofold argument: Man-made laws, passed on the grounds of autonomous human considerations would usurp the divine prerogative and God's sovereignty, because only God has the privilege to give mankind values, rules and laws for their life. Attacking God's sovereignty in turn is, according to Quṭb, also an attack on mankind and the dignity which they received from God, because all man-made laws inevitably oppress people. He claims for example in *Milestones* that "the oppression of individuals and nations by the predominance of capitalists and colonialism under the capitalist systems are nothing else than a sign of the attack against God's power and authority (*sulṭān*) and the dignity which he assigned to humans."[39]

Since from Quṭb's point of view only Islam could release mankind from the servitude and eliminate inequality, he accuses all those who prefer a differ-

37 Quṭb, *Salām ʿālamī*, 171.
38 See Quṭb, *Maʿālim fī l-ṭarīq*, 8 and 60.
39 Ibid., 8.

ent system to an Islamic system, "whether it be based on nation, race, territory or class or other principles", of being "truly enemies of mankind".[40] It is his radical conclusion that Islam is a "general declaration to liberate mankind on earth from the servitude to God's servants and … a complete revolution against the sovereignty and dominion (*ḥākimiyya*) of human beings in all its forms and appearances",[41] which means "the destruction of the kingdom of humanity to establish God's kingdom on earth".[42] For Quṭb, this cannot be achieved by preaching alone. He claims that convictions and ideas should be confronted through preaching, but that material obstacles such as political powers must be confronted with power and force to overturn obstacles in establishing the Islamic system on earth.[43] Jihad as a means to achieve this would be the right of all humanity, and at the same time the religious duty of the revolutionary Muslim vanguard.[44] After abolishing hindrances to Islam, in the form of governments based on human dominion, and establishing the Islamic system with its rules of governance, people would be free to choose if they want to accept the Islamic belief.[45] According to Quṭb, the Islamic order comes into existence by itself when people accept 'true' Islam, because "the creed (*ʿaqīda*) cannot bear passivity and transforms itself inside Muslims into movement and action (*ḥaraka wa-ʿamal*) in the world of reality".[46]

Among his key terms in this context is that of the "inner liberation of the soul" (*al-taḥarrur al-wijdānī*)[47] and the "new birth" or rebirth of an individual (*milād jadīd*)[48] with a substantial change in their personalities. In his Quran commentary, he describes this rebirth of the Prophet's companions as a "total recreation of the personalities and a substantial reconfiguration of one's atoms, like electro shocks which bring everything into a new order".[49]

---

40 Ibid., 54.

41 Ibid., 59.

42 Ibid., 60.

43 See ibid, 60–61; Quṭb, *Ẓilāl*, vol. 3, 1433 and 1737; Quṭb, *ʿAdāla ijtimāʿiyya*, 147.

44 See Quṭb, *Ẓilāl*, vol. 1, 186.

45 See Quṭb, *Maʿālim fī l-ṭarīq*, 57–58 and 82.

46 Quṭb, *Ẓilāl*, vol. 4, 2525. See also for instance Quṭb, *Ẓilāl*, vol. 5, 3165–3166; Quṭb, *Fī l-taʾrīkh: Fikra wa-minhāj* [*On Historiography: Concept and Method*]. 6th edition, Cairo: Dār al-shurūq 1991 [published first (posthumous) at Dār al-saʿūdiyya li-l-nashr 1968 with articles which were published from 1951 onwards], 22–24; Sayyid Quṭb, *Muqawwimāt al-taṣawwur al-islāmī* [Fundamental Bases of the Islamic Concept], Cairo et al.: Dār al-shurūq 1995 [first edition 1987; ed. by his brother Muḥammad Quṭb], 22.

47 See in detail for example Quṭb, *Adāla ijtimāʿiyya*, 32–44.

48 See for example Quṭb, *Ẓilāl*, vol. 2, 758 and 685; Sayyid Quṭb, *Khaṣāʾiṣ al-taṣawwur al-islāmī wa-muqawwimātuhu* [*Characteristics of the Islamic Concept and its Fundamental Bases*], 13th edition, Cairo et al.: Dār al-shurūq 1995 [first edition 1962], 206–207. In *Muqawwimāt* he also described it as birth of the "new real mankind" (*al-insān al-ḥaqīqī al-jadīd*) (Quṭb, *Muqawwimāt*, 194).

49 Quṭb, *Ẓilāl*, vol. 1, 149.

The „Balanced Society" (al-mujtamaʿ al-mutawāzin) *between Eternal Principles and Concrete Rules*

According to Quṭb, the Islamic system, which covers all aspects of life, in particular politics, economics and the societal order, consists of eternal God-given principles. These can be derived from the religious sources Quran and hadith and also from the transmitted acts and statements of the first Muslims, based on the idea of the Early Muslim community being the most authentic. It is quite obvious that the eternal principals Quṭb derives from these sources and often contrasts with 'western' capitalism, are strongly influenced by his perspectives and personal experiences, and mirror public debates on social grievances in Egypt by various contemporary political and intellectual actors. In the 1940s and 1950s, a number of political parties in Egypt called for reforms in order to abolish fundamental social inequalities, to fight corruption, and to gain political independence from Western interferences. Quṭb projects terms like 'unity', 'mutual social responsibility' and 'social balance' back into the past as characteristics of the first Muslim community and as counter images to the present. In contrast to the enormous financial privileges of leading politicians at his time (and today, too), Quṭb portrays all the first caliphs as humble, decent, and equipped with a high sense of morality. He stresses that they had neither more money than other members of society nor more privileges, citing for example an episode in Islamic historiography when Caliph Ali bowed to a judge's decision without claiming special treatment.[50] Based on–selective–examples of Muslim historiography, he claims that 'true' Islam guarantees a minimum standard of living and social insurance for medical treatment and unemployment, which he had already advocated before his turn to Islam and afterwards declared as authentic Islamic principles.[51] The same principle applies to his call for reforms in agricultural property, a much disputed issue at his time. From the mid-1940s onwards, both communists and Muslim Brothers demanded the redistribution of agricultural property, because as a result of drastically increased rentals, urbanization and the exodus from rural areas, the situation of peasants had dramatically deteriorated. While 33% of the land was owned by 94% of the farmers which were considered poor, the remaining 67% of agricultural property was owned by the 6% of rich landowners. As a result, half of the landowners possessed less than half a hectare which was only around a tenth of the agricultural land needed to secure the subsistence level.[52]

---

50 See Quṭb, *ʿAdāla ijtimāʿiyya*, 150–181.

51 See Damir-Geilsdorf, *Herrschaft*, 37.

52 For instance, see Helmut Mejcher, „Die Auswirkungen des Zweiten Weltkriegs auf Wirtschaft und Gesellschaft Ägyptens", in: *Die ägyptische Gesellschaft im 20. Jahrhundert*,

Quṭb developed a theory of justice in Islam in particular in his book *Social Justice in Islam* where he described the "eternal principles" for the organization of politics, economics and society as well as concrete rules for their implementation. In his last revision of the book (1962), he removed some passages on concrete measurements. This can be traced back to his idea that the Sharia as the God-given eternal law can meet all historical and cultural circumstances and conditions, because it comprises only a few detailed provisions and primarily unchangeable "universal principles" (*mabādiʾ kulliyya*) and "general maxims" (*qawāʿid ʿāmma*).[53] While the application of these principles and maxims would always be mandatory, the way they are put into practice could take place in numerous and varying forms. Especially from the mid-1950s onwards, he argues in his writings, the "jurisprudence of dynamism" (*fiqh al-ḥaraka*)[54] in Islam should provide concrete rules only in connection with concrete challenges and situations within a concrete Islamic state instead of theorizing without applicability.[55]

Private Property: Legitimacy and Limitations

According to Quṭb, the basis of Islamic economic theory is the right to individual ownership. For him this is clearly indicated in the Quran by the harsh penalty for theft, detailed inheritance regulations and also expressed in Quran 4:32 which states "To the men a share from what they have earned and to the women a share from what they have earned."[56] At the same time, Quṭb stresses that Islam also sets limitations for private property such as specific ways for increasing, spending and circulating wealth. First and foremost in Islam, the right to private property should come only from legal work.[57] He argues that this is a source which provides a necessary balance between effort and reward to the individual. Furthermore, a reward for work correlates with the welfare of the community, because it encourages the individual to expend his utmost effort for the advancement of life.[58]

Another limitation on private property is for Quṭb set in the Quran through the description of human beings as stewards (*khulafāʾ*) on earth. In

Alexander Schölch and Helmut Mejcher, eds., Hamburg: Deutsches Orient-Institut 1992, 94–147, 113–114; Ṭāriq al-Bishrī, *Al-Ḥaraka al-siyāsiyya fī Miṣr: 1945–1952. Murājaʿa wa-taqdīm jadīd*, Cairo: Dār al-shurūq 1983, 88–91.

53 For instance, see Sayyid Quṭb, *Naḥwa mujtamaʿ islāmī* [*Towards a Muslim Society*], 11th edition, Cairo/Beirut: Dār al-shurūq 1987 [first edition 1962; the booklet entails articles of Quṭb, published between 1952 and 1954].

54 Quṭb, *Ẓilāl*, vol. 3, 1743.

55 For instance, see ibid., 1518–1519 and 1634; Quṭb, *Ẓilāl*, vol. 5, 3166.

56 See Quṭb, *ʿAdāla ijtimāʿiyya* (Shepard 1996, 125–127).

57 Quṭb, *ʿAdāla ijtimāʿiyya* (Shepard 1996, 136–141).

58 See ibid., 126–127. See also Quṭb, *Ẓilāl*, vol. 1, 316 and 364.

this context he considers private property in Islam as completely different from private property in capitalist systems:

> .... the individual is virtually the community's agent in relation to his property and his tenure is more like employment than ownership, and that ownership in general is fundamentally the right of the community and that the community has this as a delegation from God, who is the only owner of anything. Private property arises from the particular effort expended by the individual to acquire title to part of the general property over which God has delegated stewardship to the human race.[59]

Based on this prerequisite, he argues:

> ... when the individual is aware that he is merely an employee in relation to this wealth that is in his hands and that it is basically the property of the community, this makes him accept the obligations that the system places upon his shoulders and the restrictions by which it limits his freedom of action. Likewise, when the community is aware of its basic right to this wealth, this makes it bolder to impose the obligations and set the limits.[60]

Therefore, he calls private property in his Quran commentary "restricted private property" (*milkiyya farḍiyya muqayyada*).[61] From his point of view the right to individual property goes along with the right as well as the duty of control. Spending one's wealth on illegal matters, for instance, would be a sign of not fulfilling one's duties of controlling one's property. This would be a misuse of power and the ruler in an Islamic state could declare this person legally incompetent and deprive him of the right to control his property.[62] In this case the property should go to the ruler, which Quṭb traces back to his transfer of a common legal opinion of Sunni schools of law, that the ruler is the heir of anyone who has no heir.

Quṭb derives another limit for private property from Quran 59:7: "... so that it may not circulate solely between the wealthy among you." His interpretation of the Quranic verse allows far-reaching limitations of private ownership: "The meaning of this [verse] is that some wealth should be taken from the rich since it really belongs to the poor."[63] He underlines that in contrast to capitalist societies, the principle of taking from the rich would prevent the hatred and jealousy of those deprived, who in the face of the power of money must either hate or break down and feel valueless because they are only satisfying the people of wealth and power.[64]

59 Quṭb, *ʿAdāla ijtimāʿiyya* (Shepard 1996, 129).
60 Ibid., 130.
61 Quṭb, *Ẓilāl*, vol. 1, 319.
62 See Quṭb, *ʿAdāla ijtimāʿiyya* (Shepard 1996, 130.)
63 Ibid., 131. See also Quṭb, *Salām ʿālamī*, 144–145.
64 See Quṭb, *ʿAdāla ijtimāʿiyya* (Shepard 1996, 133).

Mutual Social Responsibility (al-takāful al-ijtimāʿī) and Authority of the Ruler

Quṭb stresses in many of his writings "mutual social responsibility" (*al-takāful al-ijtimāʿī*) as an eternal Islamic principle which he derives from Quranic verses and other sources, such as the following hadith, transmitted by Ibn Hanbal: "If a person goes hungry all night, those living around him lose the protection of God." Or he refers to the fatwa of the Andalusian Ibn Ḥazm (died 1064) who states that if a man dies of hunger in a town its people are considered killers and liable to pay bloodwite for the dead man.[65] According to Quṭb, the application of mutual social responsibility should not be only the concern of the individual but also the duty of the lawmaker.[66] Here, he refers to a statement of the Caliph Umar b. al-Khattab: "If I had as much time ahead of me as I have behind me, I would take from the rich their excess wealth and return it to the poor."[67] Quṭb concludes: "The ruler may impose taxes until he achieves an equilibrium in society and relieves the masses of the nation (*umma*) from hardship and distress."[68] Important in this context are the concepts *sadd al-dharāʾiʿ* ("blocking the means") as a source of law, applied especially by the Maliki and Shafi'i school of law, *al-maṣlaḥa al-ʿāmma* ("public welfare") and *al-maṣlaḥa al-mursala* ("public interests not mentioned in authoritative sources") to which Quṭb frequently refers. He states: "Everything that leads to the public welfare and avoids harm to the public is incumbent upon the ruler and everything that leads to what is forbidden is itself forbidden."[69]

The ruler's obligation should be to provide jobs and enable each individual in the society to have enough money from his own income to take care of his medical needs and education without any difference in the quality of the medical treatment or education for the poorer and richer members of society.[70] According to Quṭb, applying the principle of mutual social responsibility requires a number of measures by the ruler, giving him a wide-ranging authority to ensure the public welfare in all times and places.

He refers for example to Malik b. Anas who had the opinion that if the treasury of a state is empty or the needs of the army increase, the ruler may tax the property of the wealthy to the extent needed.[71] For Quṭb, other needs of the state such as the "repair of public facilities, the reclamation of

---

65 See Quṭb, *ʿAdāla ijtimāʿiyya* (Shepard 1996, 163, 264 and 321).
66 See Damir-Geilsdorf, *Herrschaft*, 236–247.
67 See Quṭb, *ʿAdāla ijtimāʿiyya* (Shepard 1996, 340).
68 Ibid., 340.
69 Ibid., 342.
70 See ibid., 340, 342.
71 See ibid, 172 and 341.

wasteland, the teaching of the people and provision of medical care for the indigent"[72] are comparable to the needs of the army. "Taking the excess wealth from the hands of the extremely rich capitalists",[73] should also be the ruler's task, because excess wealth leads to a multitude of evils, such as luxury which Quṭb defines as exceeding "the average which is permitted by the national wealth in relation to the population".[74] Therefore, the ruler could go beyond the obligation of zakat and impose any other taxes in order to achieve a balance, provided that he does not violate an authoritative text of Quran or Hadith or a basic Islamic principle. He suggests for example in the first five editions of *Social Justice in Islam* that the ruler could "give the poor access to parcels of private land without any rent or with minimal rent so that they can have a livelihood"[75] or could make "the wage of the worker in the factory or the field a fixed proportion of the production or the crop. The minimum amount should be what is sufficient for food, drink, clothing and medical treatment within a reasonable limit, according to the average living standard permitted by the general wealth in relation to the population of the country."[76] From the hadith "People are partners in three things: water, pasture, and fire"[77], Quṭb concludes that it is forbidden to monopolize public resources and facilities necessary for the life of the community. For Quṭb necessities are not fixed, but vary depending on place and time. Therefore, he argues in the first five editions of *Social Justice in Islam* that the "general Islamic principle" of prohibition of monopoly on necessary public resources requires nowadays the nationalization of public resources, such as electricity, coal, oil, water, fuel, and public transport, which must not be "in the hand of individuals or companies who can run them as monopolies, charge the masses whatever they want, and exploit them in the horrible ways that we see today"[78]. Instead, the ruler should ensure that all these are the property of the state and put their rents and prices within the reach of the poorest people.

At the same time, Quṭb warns that the redistribution of wealth should not strip individuals entirely of their private property "so that they become parts of the state machine. In that case, the state can subjugate and enslave them even worse than can individual wealthy people, because it joins financial power to political power."[79]

---

72 Ibid., 341.
73 Ibid., 342.
74 Ibid.
75 Ibid., 340.
76 Ibid., 341, 340.
77 See Abū Daʾūd, *Buyūʿ*, 60.
78 Quṭb, *ʿAdāla ijtimāʿiyya* (Shepard 1996, 342). See also ibid., 133–134.
79 Ibid., 134. See likewise Sayyid Quṭb, *al-Islām wa-mushkilāt al-ḥaḍāra* [*Islam and the Problems of Civilization*], Cairo: Dār al-shurūq 1995 [1962], 108.

Conclusion

Quṭb's critique of capitalism and his vision of an Islamic system were embedded in the frame of the Cold War. Although he describes principles for the economic order and measures to implement them as authentic Islamic, derived from examples of early Muslims, Quran and Sunna, they often resemble popular socialist visions during that time, which Quṭb had also advocated before his turn to Islam. Among concepts with obviously socialist references is for example the redistribution of wealth and income by the state via measures like the expropriation of farmland and confiscation of wealth that exceeds the necessities of individual needs and consequently contributes to a luxurious life-style. This has to be understood firstly in the frame of the *zeitgeist* in his time and region, when socialist ideas were very popular against the background of extreme, unequal distribution of wealth and access to it, and secondly, against the background that liberal capitalism was perceived as a paradigm of colonialist Western societies. Therefore, Quṭb's ideas of an Islamic state in the first editions of *Social Justice in Islam* and others of his early Islamist works can also be regarded as an attempt, based on an anticolonial legacy, to offer a third way for decolonized Muslim states. He presented his vision of an Islamic state as a way of life, derived from Islamic principles and distinct from and superior to capitalism, communism as well as socialism which he increasingly saw as being alike. As the article has demonstrated, he argued particularly in his later writings such as in his manifesto *Milestones* that these ideologies are not only the means of Western hegemony over countries in the Global South and their suppression but also inevitably divide mankind into masters and servants and attack like all man-made laws both God's sovereignty and mankind's dignity.

Although Quṭb wrote his critique of capitalism more than 50 years ago, some of his ideas are still relevant for contemporary Jihadist groups. Quṭb's notion that all forms of exploitation, injustice and oppression are an inevitable result of man-made laws which at the same time are a usurpation of God's sovereignty and his authority, still has a strong impact and has become part of a common repertoire in the rhetorics of several Jihadist movements. This is displayed, for instance, in some articles in al-Qaida's English language magazine *Resurgence* which address in its issue from 2014 the fight against capitalism. Similar to Quṭb, one of its authors perceives the entanglement between capitalism and colonialism/imperialism and states that capitalism in Muslim regions has been enforced by "imperialist powers".[80]

---

80 Javed Akbar Ansari, "Islamization of a Declining System?", *Resurgence* 1 (2014), 83–89, 84.

Based on his assumption that capital is not only an "unjust use of wealth"[81] but also the usurpation of God's authority he concludes:

> While we believe in *La ilaha ilallah* (There is no God but Allah), modernist epistemology raises man to the status of the divine. Since capitalism, as a system, seeks to realize modernism's ideals, therefore, it would not be incorrect to state that the catch-phrase of capitalism is none other than *La ilaha ilal Insaan* (There is no God but the 'human'). Capitalism is thus a revolt against God, the Prophets, and all Abrahamic religions.[82]

Other articles in this issue call for a jihad against capitalist symbols and companies, presented as a religious duty for the liberation of the oppressed and exploited, which is for example expressed in the following statement of the cover story: "Major Western companies and multinational corporations like Walmart, MacDonald's, Proctor and Gamble, Microsoft, Nestle and Unilever are symbols of the rampant Crusader globalization which is characterized by the exploitation of the weak and impoverished, and the destruction of local economies. It is our duty as Muslims and as Mujahideen to stop this at all costs."[83]

Likewise, Usama Bin Laden stated 2007 in a video message that the essence of man-made positive laws is "to serve the interests of those with the capital, and thus, make the rich richer and the poor poorer."[84]

Similarities to the writings of Quṭb are obvious. Like in the writing of Quṭb, jihad is here presented as both a religious duty to restore power to God alone and as a liberation movement. This can have a mobilizing effect by providing the valorizing notion of being on the right side in a fight for a twofold higher cause, e.g. obeying God and liberating the impoverished and suppressed.[85] It is not sure whether current militant Islamists who argue in similar ways as Quṭb did and use some of his repertoire have derived their ideas from his writings. Usually groups such as al-Qaida or IS do not refer directly to Quṭb. This can be traced back, among other reasons, to the fact that he belonged to the Muslim Brotherhood, e.g. a movement which they do not acknowledge as being 'true' Muslim. However, since Quṭb's books are widely spread and well-known in Muslim contexts and ideas, and conceptualized as floating signifiers, they can be transmitted to various

81 Ibid., 83.

82 Ibid., 84.

83 Adam Yahiye Gadahn, "Besiege them!", *Resurgence* 1 (2014), 47–55, 53.

84 "Transcript of Osama Bin Laden Video", in: *Daily News* (08.09.2007), www.nydailynews.com/news/world/transcript-osama-bin-laden-video-article-1.244130, accessed 25.03.2018.

85 For details on the mobilization of transnational Jihadist groups by the perception of fighting imperialism see also Olivier Roy, *Globalized Islam. The Search for a New Ummah*, New York: Columbia Univ. Press 2004, 44–49.

contexts of time and space, where they can be re-conceptualized, adopted and further developed, independently of their origin.

A Shiite Economic Model. From Bāqir al-Ṣadr to Contemporary Iraq

Elisheva Machlis

Introduction

A contemporary Shiite discussion of Islamic economics evolved in the late twentieth century, drawing on the traditional Shiite emphasis on *ʿadl.* The notion of *ʿadl,* or justice, is not unique to Shiism, yet it holds significant ramifications for this persecuted community. In the Sunni world, *ʿadl* has a direct political implication–*dār al-Islām* would become *dār al-ʿadl,* if the community were to be ruled by a righteous Islamic government that would uphold the moral virtues of God's law. The sultan has an obligation to act in a moral way to implement Divine justice on Earth, although man cannot necessarily fully comprehend God's justice.[1]

Similarly to Sunnis, Shiites also revered God's justice and even included *'adl* as one of the five pillars of religion. Both also provided a political reading of the notion of justice. Nevertheless, in Sunni understanding implementing justice was the prerogative of a leader elected by humans, while Shiites linked justice to the divinely designated Imams.[2]

Consequently, Shiite historiography portrayed the historical injustice against the chosen family of the Prophet Muḥammad, the *ahl al-bayt,* as a human decision to go against God's will. This began with the rule of the early caliphate that usurped ʿAlī's legitimate quest for leadership. It continued with the Sunni persecution of Shiites throughout Muslim history, 'when the Muslim community was ruled by tyrannical and unjust caliphs'.

According to the traditional Shiite perception, Muslim kingship was illegitimate, since authority was invested in the divinely designated Imams. As a result, justice will prevail only at the end of days with the return of the awaited Imam. This unique Shiite discourse on justice, injustice, authority and human reason was further reshaped in the modern era, within a new debate on religion, politics and socio-economic change. The following pa-

---

1 See Ann Katherine Lambton, "Changing Concept of Justice and Injustice from the $5^{th}/11^{th}$ Century to the $8^{th}/14^{th}$ Century in Persia: The Saljuk Empire and the Ilkhanate", *Studia Islamica* 68 (1988), 27–60.

2 On the Shiite concept of justice see Shaykh Abū Jaʿfar Muḥammad ibn ʿAlī ibn Ḥusayn ibn Mūsā (known as Ibn Bābawayh al-Qummī), *Essence of Shia Faith,* transl. by Dr. Safi Hassan, n.p.: Createspace Independent Publishing 2012, 320–324; Najam Haider, *Shīʿī Islām: An Introduction,* Cambridge: Cambridge Univ. Press 2014, 18–30.

per will provide a unique angle on the question of Islamic economics, with its rising significance in the Muslim world and the West.

Looking into the case study of Iraq, the current study will contribute to an understanding of the contemporary challenges facing the new Shiite-led regime. The overall majority of the Shiite parties established within the new drive towards democratization in post-2003 Iraq claimed allegiance to the original Daʿwa Party and its chief ideologist Muḥammad Bāqir al-Ṣadr (1935–1980). Shedding further light on this linkage, this article will assess the extent to which al-Ṣadr's economic vision had an impact on the Shiite-led government following the fall of the Baath regime.

On the other hand, perhaps the new Shiite drive towards democratization actually contributed to a more capitalist orientation. Scholarship provides some support for the linkage between capitalism and democracy since similar social forces are behind both democracy and capitalism. They also share core values and historically tended to evolve together. Yet, there are also some contradictions between these two models, since a free market can undermine equality and provide true opportunity only for a bourgeois minority.[3] The following discussion will explore this relationship, focusing on the post-2003 period.

The creation of the new nation-state of Iraq in the aftermath of World War I led to significant changes in the orientation of the local Shiite community. Following the disintegration of the Ottoman Empire, the Shiites of southern Iraq began to gradually integrate into this new state-system. State education, mobility and social change led to the rise of an educated Shiite elite that began challenging the traditional authority of the *mujtahid*s (senior Shiite clerics who have the authority to infer legal precepts from the sources).

Responding to this leadership challenge, several reform-oriented *mujtahid*s from Iraq and Lebanon began introducing new topics into the religious discourse following their own exposure to modern knowledge. They sought to make Shiism more relevant to the contemporary needs of the community while offering a more active reading of religion and politics.

Thus, for example, Muḥammad Ḥusayn Kāshif al-Ghiṭāʾ, a leading *mujtahid* from Iraq, called Muslims to join the struggle for Palestine. In Kāshif al-Ghiṭāʾ's view, justice was no longer within the exclusive domain of the awaited Imam, as Kāshif al-Ghiṭāʾ called Muslims to unite in a joint struggle against imperialist control of the region.[4] Similarly, Muḥammad al-

---

3 See Gabriel Abraham Almond, "Capitalism and Democracy", *Political Science and Politics* 24: 3 (1991), 467–474; Walter Lafeber, "The Tension between Democracy and Capitalism during the American Century", *Diplomatic History* 23: 2 (1991), 263–284.

4 Muḥammad Ḥusayn Kāshif al-Ghiṭāʾ was a leading Shiite cleric from Iraq (b. 1876/1877). He contributed to the reform of Shia Islam in his engagement with a

Khāliṣī, another leading reformist of Iraqi origins, held the banner of Muslim unity in an effort to bring prosperity to the entire Muslim nation.[5]

The politicization of Islam, which began in the middle of the 19th century with Muslim reformists in the Sunni world, went hand in hand with a new social conscience. The Egyptian scholar and journalist Muḥammad ʿAbduh (d. 1905) spoke about the cohesion and prosperity of society, emphasizing the significance of *maṣlaḥa*, or the common good. In the following decades, the Muslim Brotherhood (*al-Ikhwān al-Muslimūn*) began advancing this dual aim of political Islam and social equality. This influential movement, established in Egypt in 1928, adopted the cause of the poor, expressing its dismay at 'the oppressive actions of the wealthy and the powerful'. Under the leadership of Ḥasan al-Bannā[6] the Ikhwān advanced the call for Islam (*daʿwa*) by providing much needed services in education and welfare, stressing the value of family and community cohesiveness.

Sunni reformists and Arab intellectuals expressed criticism against capitalism, presenting this model as a materialist, individualist and immoral system. Thus, for example, Sayyid Abu al-Aʿlā Mawdūdī (1903–1979), argued that the revival of Islam must go hand in hand with the value of brotherhood to provide material prosperity for all. This renowned Muslim reformist of South Asia would later have an impact on the Islamic Revolution of Iran and its leading ideologists.[7]

Already in the first half of the twentieth century, Shiite clerics from Iraq and Lebanon expressed an affinity with Sunni reformist ideas. This included the compatibility of Islam and science, the politicization of religion, an emphasis on orthodoxy, and a comprehensive notion of Islam. In the following generation, Muḥammad Bāqir al-Ṣadr joined this revivalist agenda. He called for an Islamic state, adding his voice to a new discourse on Islamic economics. Bāqir al-Ṣadr's contribution was in providing an all-inclusive theory, placing his Islamic model as a middle way between communism and capitalism. His aim was to stem the threat of secularism in Iraq with the growing attraction of Shiite youth to Marxism.[8]

---

new political discourse and in his call for Muslim unity. On Kāshif al-Ghiṭā's biography see Elisheva Machlis, "A Shiʿa Debate on Arabism", *British Journal of Middle Eastern Studies* 40: 20 (2013), 95–114.

5 For an elaborate analysis see Elisheva Machlis, *Shi'i Sectarianism in the Middle East: Modernization and the Quest for Islamic Universalism*, London: I.B. Tauris 2014.

6 See Charles Tripp, *Islam and the Moral Economy: The Challenge of Capitalism*, Cambridge: Cambridge Univ. Press 2006, 13–76.

7 M. Umer Chapra, "Mawlana Mawdūdī's Contribution to Islamic Economics", *The Muslim World* 94: 4 (2004), 163–180; Seyyed Vali Nasr, *Mawdudi and the Making of Islamic Revivalism*, New York, Oxford: Oxford Univ. Press 1996.

8 See Chapra, "Mawlana Mawdūdī's Contribution"; Seyyed Vali Nasr, *Mawdudi and the Making of Islamic Revivalism*, New York, Oxford: Oxford Univ. Press 1996.

In his *Iqtiṣādunā* (Our Economy), Bāqir al-Ṣadr described four social models: capitalist-democratic, socialist, communist, and Islamic. For Bāqir al-Ṣadr, the democratic-capitalist system had its merits since it provided freedoms for its people in the political, economic and intellectual spheres. Yet, he was also highly critical of this model, for its 'lack of morality and its materialistic and individualist basis'.[9] Islam alone can overcome self-love, Bāqir al-Ṣadr stressed, as he cautioned about the pitfalls of human indulgence and materialism.

On the other hand, Bāqir al-Ṣadr was also highly scornful of socialism and communism for rejecting private ownership. Classical Islamic teaching provided protection for private property and emphasized the right of ownership. Furthermore, trade was an important mark of Arabian traditional culture, from the pre-Islamic era and through centuries of Muslim history.[10] Nevertheless, Bāqir al-Ṣadr did not rely on this Arab and Islamic legacy to support private ownership, and instead employed a more modern discourse of human rights. Appealing to the secularized Shiite youth of Iraq, Bāqir al-Ṣadr attacked socialism and Marxism 'for abolishing individual freedoms, and disregarding natural rights'.

In his understanding, Islam provides the most suitable economic structure, thus contributing to the creation of a healthy society. The individual is no longer merely a mechanical tool, nor does society exist to serve the individual. Instead, Islam insures spiritual and material dignity, righteousness, goodness and justice.[11] Within this vision, Bāqir al-Ṣadr provided the state with an important role in instilling God's satisfaction (*riḍā*).[12] In this context, Bāqir al-Ṣadr lauded the Islamic tax of *zakāh* (alms) and *khums* (fifth) as a mechanism for ensuring social equality, stressing that the head of the state holds authority to exact these religious taxes, to raise the standard of living of the poor.

Silvia Naef, "Shi'i-shuyu'i or: How to become a Communist in a Holy City", in: Silvia Naef, Rainer Brunner and Werner Ende, eds., *The Twelver Shia in Modern Times: Religious, Culture and Political History*, Leiden: Brill 2001.

9 For a full description of his economic theory see Muḥammad Bāqir aṣ-Ṣadr, *Iqtiṣādunā: dirāsah mawḍūʿīyah tatanāwalu bi-al-naqd wa-al-baḥth al-madhāhib al-iqtiṣādīyah li-al-mārkisīyah wa-al-raʾsmālīyah wa-al-Islām fī usūsihā al-fikrīyah wa-tafāṣīlihā*, Bairūt: Dār al-kitāb al-lubnānī 1977, 2 vols.

10 See Saba Habachy, "Property, Right, and Contract in Muslim Law", *Columbia Law Review* 450 (1962), 450–473; Steven D. Jamar, "Protection of Intellectual Property under Islamic Law", *Capital University Law Review* 21 (1992), 1079–1106; Patricia Risso, *Merchants and Faith: Muslim Commerce and Culture in the Indian Ocean*, Westview Press 1995.

11 See Muḥammad Bāqir aṣ-Ṣadr, *Falsafatunā*, Bayrūt: Dār al-taʿāruf li-al-maṭbūʿāt 1399/1979, 27, 81–82.

12 Ibid., 32.

Bāqir al-Ṣadr here added another dimension to the embryonic politicization of Shiism, which began in the early twentieth century. Going beyond these early theoretical discussions, Bāqir al-Ṣadr called for the actual realization of an Islamic state. The state was to be given control over the socio-political domain, including the collection and allocation of religious taxes, with its important contribution to the welfare of the poor.[13]

In the area of Iraq with its important Shiite centres of Najaf and Karbalāʾ the religious dues of the *zakāh* and the *khums* were a critical source of income for the *mujtahid*s since they did not enjoy support from the Sunni state.[14] In the course of history, following the disappearance of the twelfth Imam, Shiite clerics began obtaining some of the functions of the awaited Imam, including the collection of religious taxes. Bāqir al-Ṣadr's contribution was in providing the envisioned Islamic state with the right to control these taxes.[15]

Nevertheless, Bāqir al-Ṣadr did not provide the state with exclusive rights to implement divine justice, but spoke instead about multiple forms of ownership. He did not dismiss private property, but he supplied it with a moral framework. Emphasizing the significance of social balance (*tawāzun ijtimāʿī*), Bāqir al-Ṣadr legitimized private property, but also called for a better distribution of wealth. In his understanding, Islam ensures the implementation of social justice through the prohibition of interest and hoarding, through its inheritance laws and through public ownership of natural resources.

Bāqir al-Ṣadr's multiple forms of ownership and his concept of social balance presented a utopian model. This was a very vague socio-political theory, which did not include a clear mechanism of implementation, and was left to human discretion. Bāqir al-Ṣadr did not define the scope of private, public, and state ownership and the relationship between these three entities. Man's goodwill was to determine social balance. Shiite control of the state after 2003 provided an opportunity to explore the feasibility of implementing this ideal vision in a new political context.

---

13 Aṣ-Ṣadr, *Iqtiṣādunā*, vol. 2. no. 2, 138–143.

14 See Meir Litvak, *Shiʿi Scholars of Nineteenth-Century Iraq: The 'Ulama' of Najaf and Karbala'*, Cambridge: Cambridge Univ. Press 2007, 12, 15, 35, and 180; and his article, "Money, Religion, and Politics: The Oudh Bequest in Najaf and Karbala' 1850–1903", *International Journal of Middle East Studies*, 33 (2001), 1–21. See also Yitzhak Nakash, *The Shiʿis of Iraq*, Princeton, Oxford: Princeton Univ. Press 2003, 205–237.

15 See Said Amir Arjomand, *The Shadow of God and the Hidden Imam: Religion, Political Order, and Society Change in Shiʿite Iran from the Beginning to 1890*, Chicago: Univ. of Chicago Press 1984.

The Economic Vision of Post-2003 Iraq

From Bāqir al-Ṣadr to Iranian revolutionaries, Shiites provided the state with power to implement justice. Yet, in the long term, this model did not survive. The democratization process in Iraq, which followed the US-led invasion, led to the emergence of several Shiite parties all stressing their link with the original Da'wa movement. This included the al-Ḥakīm wing which was among the founders and leaders of the Daʿwa movement. Other powerful forces were the newly claimed Daʿwa party, which differed from the historical Daʿwa movement in its more lay orientation. Another group was the Jaysh al-Mahdī militia led by Muqtadā al-Ṣadr, a family member of the late Bāqir al-Ṣadr. Ṣādiq al-Ṣadr, Muqtadā al-Ṣadr's father, studied under his cousin Bāqir al-Ṣadr, and the two were imprisoned together during the 1970s, under Ṣaddām's rule with his crackdown on the party.[16]

To what extent did the Shiite leadership that gained control in post-2003 Iraq endorse Bāqir al-Ṣadr's economic vision; and to what extent was this middle way between capitalism and communism appropriate for the socio-political conditions of this new era in Iraq? The process of institution-building which began following the ousting of Ṣaddām Ḥusayn was marked by a heated debate between Arab Sunnis, Shiites and Kurds on the nature of the new regime. Consequently, Iraq's new constitution of 2005 combined contradictory clauses on the relationship between Islam and state. It also reflected ambiguity over questions of authority, leadership, sovereignty, law and representation.

Thus, for example, Article 2 of the constitution stated that Islam is a fundamental source of legislation and that no law can contradict the principles of Islam. It also guaranteed the Islamic identity of the majority of the Iraqi people. Further provisions emphasized the Islamic character of the state. This included recognizing the importance of religious leaders, affirming Iraq's membership in the Islamic world and providing protection to holy shrines and religious sites. Concurrently, the constitution also affirmed that the law should not contradict the principles of democracy, and the basic rights and freedoms stipulated in the constitution.[17]

The draft of the constitution spoke about social justice as the basis for building society, by cooperation between public and private activity. It also

---

16 See Nimrod Raphaeli, "Understanding Muqtada al-Sadr", *Middle East Quarterly* 11: 4 (2004), 33–42. See also Patrick Cockburn, *Muqtada: Muqtada al-Sadr, the Shia Revival, and the Struggle for Iraq*, New York: Scribner 2008, 80–96.

17 Noah Feldman and Roman Martinez, "Constitutional Politics and Text in the New Iraq: An Experiment in Islamic Democracy", *Fordham Law Review* 75: 2 (2006), 883–920; Nathan J. Brown, "Debating Islam in Post-Baathist Iraq", *Democracy & Rule of Law Project, Carnegie Endowment for International Peace*, March 2005, 1–10, http://cabinet.iq/PageViewer.aspx?id=2.

stressed that Iraq's natural resources should be owned collectively by the Iraqi people. The constitution provided the state with broad responsibilities to promote growth, development, production and services. Its mission was to provide employment opportunities for every able citizen.

In post-2003 Iraq, the Shiites no longer had to wait until the end of days to achieve true justice for the community. The historical notion of *ʿadl* received a contemporary understanding, in the form of social justice, implemented through the power of the state. This draft constitution provided the state with broad responsibilities but did not eliminate private activity calling for collaboration between the public and private spheres. Political empowerment held the promise of *'adl* for the marginalized Shiite majority, and the Shiites were keen on advancing this notion through the new constitution.

Concurrently, the constitution's emphasis on a centralized socio-political model, may have actually reflected the continued legacy of the Baath Party. After decades of tight state control, the Shiites could not totally detach themselves from the political culture of Ṣaddām's oppressive dictatorship, and particularly from the ingrained notions of centralization and socialism. Iraq's democratization process was promoted by the US as a model for pluralism in the region. Yet, true democracy did not take root in Iraq. The Shiite-led governments which were established in the following years demonstrated the continued legacy of cronyism, favoritism and corruption, within a problematic legacy of minority-majority relations.

Furthermore, while the draft constitution embraced a centralized model, the final constitution represented a private-centred model, based on private property, private ownership and market forces.[18] As American forces became entrenched in the country, the vision of social justice expressed in the draft constitution, was now largely limited to Shiite political empowerment.

The draft signaled that Shiites of Iraq were indeed interested in providing the state with significant power to implement social justice. Yet, in the end of the day, Iraq did not adopt any form of socialism–or even a multiple ownership model–similar to Bāqir al-Ṣadr's vision.

While this shift can be attributed to pressure from US neo-liberal forces, within the Shiite scholarly leadership there was also a tendency to support an open-market model. In particular, Āyatullāh ʿAlī al-Sīstānī (b. 1930), the current most revered Shiite cleric in Iraq, endorsed private enterprise.[19]

---

18 Herbert Docena, "Iraq's Neoliberal Constitution: The Bush Administration's Shaping of the New Iraqi Constitution", *Foreign Policy in Focus* (02.09.2005), http://fpif.org/iraqs_neoliberal_constitution/.

19 For Sīstānī's background see, "Biography – The Official Website of the office of His Eminence Al-Sayyid Ali Al-Husseini Al-Sistani", http://www.sistani.org/english/data/2/.

Sīstānī, who is acknowledged as the highest-ranking *mujtahid* in Iraq, reflects the traditional Islamic acceptance of trade, private property and wealth. In his view, the believer can participate in any economic activity that does not include transactions forbidden in the Sharia, such as the sale of pigs or handling alcohol.[20]

In addition, Sīstānī approved the purchase and sale of foreign currencies and the profits acquired by the banks in this process. He also authorized the option of payments in installments. Sīstānī sanctioned the activity of the stock exchange, as long as it does not include forbidden transactions. Concurrently, Sīstānī argued that the Islamic ban on interest, including transactions or loans, can be bypassed by incorporating the profit into the price. This is similar to the mechanism of *murābaḥa,* approved by Islamic banks, in which both the buyer and seller agree on the value of the profit, which is added to the price, in exchange for allowing the buyer to defer payment.[21]

Sīstānī's superior religious position and broad popularity provided him with significant power over the political process. Endorsed by the majority of the Shiite political players, Sīstānī remained beyond murky politics, thus, maintaining his highly respected position. Nevertheless, Sīstānī issued statements on current developments when he saw an acute need to intervene. For example, Sīstānī expressed strong criticism against state corruption, calling upon the government to work on diversifying the economy.[22]

His acceptance of capitalism, within the limits circumscribed by the Sharia, reflected Sīstānī's traditional background. During the 1950s, Sīstānī studied in Najaf under the Grand Āyatullāh Abū al-Qāsim al-Khuʾī (1899–1992) who represented the prevalent quietest tendency. Following the death of al-Khuʾī in 1992, Sīstānī was acknowledged as the new supreme *marjaʿ* in Iraq. He focused on the traditional role of the *mujtahid*s, providing religious guidance to his followers on Islamic law. He did not join the Daʿwa party, and only began expressing his views on politics following the empowerment of the Shiites in the post-2003 period.

Nevertheless, together with this new political activism, Sīstānī did not embrace Khomeinī's doctrine of *wilāyat-e faqīh* (the guardianship of the Supreme cleric). Reflecting a more traditional position, Sīstānī emphasized

---

20 See Ali al-Sistani, "Dialogue on Economic Activity", http://www.sistani.org/english/boo/49/2412/.

21 See for example Ali al-Sistani, "Al-Istiftāʾāt: al-ʿumalāt al-ʾajnabiyya", www.sistani.org/arabic/qa/0609/; "Al-Istiftāʾāt: al-būrṣa", www.sistani.org/arabic/qa/0365/. On the concept of *murābaḥa* see "Murabaha on Shari'ah Ruling", *Institute of Islamic Banking and Insurance*, www.islamic-banking.com/murabaha_sruling.aspx.

22 "Iraq's Top Shiʿite Cleric Calls for Corrupt Officials to be Prosecuted", *Asharq Al-Awsat* (07.09.2015), http://english.aawsat.com/2015/09/article55345037/iraqs-top-shiite-cleric-calls-for-corrupt-officials-to-be-prosecuted.

that the role of the clerics was to provide advice to the ruler but not to assume direct power.

Sīstānī's traditional tendency combined a quietist worldview with a market-oriented perspective. Due to his immense popularity, Sīstānī succeeded in building a vast enterprise of Islamic institutions in both Iraq and Iran. Enjoying financial contributions from Shiites worldwide, Sīstānī became the wealthiest *marjaʿ* in the Shiite world.

Another important Shiite scholar who also contributed to this discourse was Āyatullāh Muḥammad Isḥāq al-Fayyāḍ (b. 1930), who is of Afghani origins. Al-Fayyāḍ together with Sīstānī are among the four Grand Āyatullāhs in Iraq of today.[23] He engaged in the political discourse, perhaps even more than Sīstānī, although both rejected the doctrine of *wilāyat-e faqīh*.[24]

On the economic front, al-Fayyāḍ actually endorsed the notion of multiple ownership (*al-mulkiyya al-muzdawija*), similar to Bāqir al-Ṣadr's vision. Al-Fayyāḍ explained that Islamic economics accepts the principle of economic freedom, within the constraints of the Sharia. As a result, it differs from capitalism in protecting the weak and avoiding exploitation. The basis for implementing justice is through balancing diverse social classes, al-Fayyāḍ argued.[25]

On the other hand, al-Fayyāḍ also stressed that an Islamic economic system should take into account the existing conditions. He called his followers to follow the law of the land, while expressing criticism over the prevalence of corruption.[26] Nevertheless, while declaring his support of multiple ownership and a balanced and just socio-economic system, al-Fayyāḍ did not reject Iraq's capitalist system. He also provided religious justification for all types of trade including participating in the activities of international stock exchanges.[27]

The only political force that explicitly promoted the flag of social justice was that of Muqtadā al-Ṣadr and his Jaysh al-Mahdī. In contrast, other Shiite politicians saw the solution to Iraq's economic problems in promoting the private sector and diversifying the economy. Thus for example, ʿAmmār al-Ḥakīm of the Islamic Supreme Council of Iraq–one of the most influen-

---

23 On Najaf's religious leadership see Augustus Richard Norton, "Al-Najaf: Its Resurgence as a Religious and University Center", *Middle East Policy* 18: 1 (2011), 132–145.

24 See Haytham Mouzahem, "Iraqi Shiite Clerics Maintain Humility, Influence", *Al-Monitor* (07.03.2014). See also al-Fayyāḍ's personal website: http://alfayadh.org/ar/.

25 See al-Shaykh Muḥammad Isḥāq al-Fayyāḍ, *Al-Anmūdhaj fī manhaj al-ḥukūma al-islāmiyya al-qāʾima ʿalā asās al-ḥākimiyya Allāh taʿālā*, Najaf 1426/2005, 15–26, 47–55. Online available at http://alfayadh.org/ar/site/uploads/2013/03/Hokoomat-Islami-ar.pdf.

26 See, for example, Muḥammad Isḥāq al-Fayyāḍ, *Istiftāʾāt muwājaha li-maktab samāḥat Āyatullāh al-ʿuẓma al-Shaykh Muḥammad Isḥāq al-Fayyāḍ: masāʾil fī mukhālafat niẓām al-dawla*, http://www.almurtadha.net/pages/news.php?nid=590.

27 Ibid.

tial Shiite parties in the country–embraced a more capitalist vision, similarly to the other Grand Āyatullāh's in the country.[28]

Following the US-led invasion, Muqtadā al-Ṣadr distinguished himself from other Shiite leaders through his outspoken and violent opposition to the occupation. A charismatic and populist leader, Muqtadā al-Ṣadr also took up the cause of the downtrodden in Iraq. He gained increased support among the Shiites of Madinat al-Ṣadr, a poor suburb of Bagdad, and among the Shiite community in Baṣra. Relying on the scholarly fame of his uncle, Bāqir al-Ṣadr, and his father, Ṣādiq al-Ṣadr, Muqtadā al-Ṣadr began enjoying growing support among the impoverished Shiite population. In 2005, he entered the political process, gaining seats in the newly established parliament. Moreover, Muqtadā al-Ṣadr and his movement positioned themselves in socially influential ministries, such as health, transportation, and municipal governorates, enhancing their ability to provide material support for their followers.[29]

However, while taking a fiery stand with regard to social welfare, Islamic morals, and the occupation, Muqtadā al-Ṣadr did not provide any systematic vision of Islamic economics. Furthermore, he did not overtly reject private enterprise and even called for non-intervention in the activities of the central bank.

In the aftermath of the US-led invasion, the Shiite-led government itself was seeking to stimulate economic growth by reviving its rich energy resources. Private Western companies began entering the country's energy market. Iraq itself began reaching out to its Arab neighbors, as well as to Turkey, Iran, China and India.[30] Islamic banks in Asia and the Gulf also saw the potential in the Iraqi market and began opening branches in Bagdad.[31] Nevertheless, the lack of security, political infighting, instability and corruption overshadowed these economic opportunities.[32]

---

28 See "Al-Sayyid 'Ammār al-Ḥakim yantaqid al-siyāsa al-iqtiṣādiyya 'al-iḥādiyya' fi-al ᶜIrāq: mutābaᶜāt", *Wikāla Anbāʾ Burāthan* (5, 2011).

29 See Matthew J. Godwin, "Political Inclusion in Unstable Contexts: Muqtada al-Sadr and Iraq's Sadrist Movement", *Contemporary Arab Affairs* 5: 3 (2012), 448–456; Benjamin Isakhan, "Despots or Democrats?: Sistani, Sadr and Shia Politics in Post-Saddam Iraq", Paper presented at the Australasian Political Science Association (APSA) Conference, University of Melbourne, Australia (1990); Raphaeli, "Understanding Muqtada al-Sadr"; "Muqtadā al-Ṣadr: Tadakhkhul al-ḥukūma al-ᶜirāqiyya fi 'amal al-bank al-markazi yuhadid iqtiṣād", *al-Balad* (30.10.12).

30 Thus, in a $7 billion deal with the United Arab Emirates concluded in April 2012, Iraq receives 250 MW from UAE power-generating ships moored outside the port of Baṣra. See www.arabiangazette.com/uae-iraq-power-generating-ships/; www.ft.com/cms/s/0/84213d46-68a7-11e3-bb3e-00144feabdc0.html#axzz3xDkaGWNA.

31 See www.thenational.ae/business/industry-insights/finance/sharia-lenders-team-up-to-fund-iraqs-promising-food-sector; www.cbi.iq/index.php?pid=IraqFinancialInst.

32 Http://www.al-monitor.com/pulse/originals/2015/02/iraq-contracting-corruption-reconstruction-projects.html#; http://www.aljazeera.com/indepth/opinion/2015/08/end

The Iran-Iraq Connection

The Islamic Republic's populist orientation employed in the early days of the revolution in Iran could have provided a model for post-2003 Iraq. Following the revolution, the new regime established vast charity organization based on the confiscated property of the Shah. Peasants and revolutionary forces seized a vast amount of land from its previous owners, directing their grievances against imperialism and foreign capitalism associated with the Shah and his supporters. These populist measures were intended to advance the revolutionary notion of social justice while mobilizing the lower classes behind the new regime.[33]

A leftist-Islamic tendency was apparent among leading ideologists of the revolution, and particularly ʿAlī Sharīʿatī (1933–1977), an Iranian intellectual who gained a PhD degree in philology from the Sorbonne. Sharīʿatī argued that Islam was opposed to capitalism, private ownership and class exploitation. In his view, the Iranian intelligentsia was to lead this struggle towards Islamic justice.[34]

Upholding the cause of the downtrodden was one of the dominant mottos of the Islamic Republic in the first decade following the revolution. Under Khumaynī's rule when the revolutionary fervor was at its height, the Islamic republic promoted a populist agenda calling for social justice and the redistribution of wealth. The new regime took over the Shah's vast property. It nationalized the economy in a bid to implement an anti-Western and Third World revolutionary agenda. The new regime strove to create a utopian society that will fight oppression and strive for social justice. Nevertheless, together with this populist call to assist the downtrodden, Khumaynī did not reject private property, sanctioned in Islamic teaching. He rejected accumulation of wealth but also legitimized production through small and large industries.[35]

Yet, among the Islamic revolutionaries in Iran, there was also criticism against a class-centered worldview, which divided Muslims into oppressed and oppressors. Leading this opposition was Murtaḍā Moṭahharī, a cleric

---

less-battle-fighting-systemic-corruption-iraq-150811084000991.html; "Iraq's Economy: An Empty Chest", *The Economist* (21.03.2015).

33 See Vedran Obuina, "Social Populism and the Future of the Islamic Republic of Iran", *Croatian Political Science Review* 52: 4–5 (2015), 163–186; Shaul Bakhash, "The Politics of Land, Law, and Social Justice in Iran", *The Middle East Journal* 43: 2 (1989), 186–201.

34 Sohrab Behdad, "A Disputed Utopia: Islamic Economics in Revolutionary Iran", *Comparative Studies in Society and History* 36: 4 (1994), 775–813. See also, Val Moghadam, "Socialism or anti-Imperialism? The Left and Revolution in Iran", *New Left Review* I/166 (11–12, 1987).

35 See Sohrab Behdad, "A Disputed Utopia: Islamic Economics in Revolutionary Iran".

and philosopher, who rejected the leftist tendency within the revolutionary camp. Defining this idea as non-Islamic, Moṭahharī argued that Islam sanctioned private property and that material differences between people are natural.[36]

Nevertheless, Iran's conservative religious establishment gradually shifted the regime's focus from social justice to cultural purification. Furthermore, Iran's experiment with populism in the first decade under Khumaynī did not bring prosperity or justice to the Iranian people. Nationalization coupled with the high cost of the Iran-Iraq war pushed inflation to 23% in 1987 and unemployment to 13%. The need to rebuild the country after the costly war provided President Akbar Hāshimī Rafsanjānī (1989–1997) with a mandate to introduce a more open-market policy. His ascendency was due to a growing Iranian understanding that reconstruction of the country required a shift towards a more open economy.

Rafsanjānī and, later on, Muḥammad Khātamī (1997–2005) began opening up the Iranian market to foreign investment and to private enterprise. The focus on economic development strengthened the Iranian middle class, who supported Rafsanjānī's pragmatic policy and Khātamī's drive towards political reform. In a backlash against Rafsanjānī and Khātamī's constituency, Maḥmūd Aḥmadīnizhād (2005–2013), revived the anti-Western rhetoric of the early days of the revolution and the populist promise of social justice.[37] The new Shiite-led government in Iraq, which came to power two years after Aḥmadīnizhād became president, enjoyed the support of its American occupiers but also began establishing growing ties with Iran, at both formal and informal levels. The historical scholarly links between Shiites of Iraq and Iran and the current expanding ties between Bagdad and Tehrān made the economic vision of the Islamic Republic very relevant for contemporary Iraq.

In 2003, as Iraq was remodeling its system, neither the Baath's socialist legacy nor the Islamic Republic's populist tendency provided good examples for implementing social justice. Socialism was associated with Ṣaddām Ḥusayn's oppressive and corrupt regime. The Iraqi people suffered immensely under a decade of international sanctions, while Ṣaddām and his loyalist elite continued to enjoy the wealth of this oil-rich country. Furthermore, the Soviet Union, which backed the socialist pan-Arab regimes in Iraq, Egypt and Syria from the 1950s and onwards, had disintegrated a decade prior to the fall of Ṣaddām. On the other hand, the Islamic Republic

36 Ibid.

37 See Ali Ansari, "Iran under Ahmadinejad: Populism and its Malcontents", *International Affairs* 84: 4 (2008), 683–700.

began shifting towards market economy in the 1990s following the reconstruction of the country in the aftermath of the devastating Iran-Iraq war.[38]

Democracy and capitalism–represented by the US-led invaders–held more promise for the impoverished Shiite majority than socialism and populism. The idea of representation was not alien to Shiites in the region. In the course of the twentieth century there was a lively discourse on this topic in Iran, Iraq and other Shiite locations. Beginning with the Constitutional Revolution in Iran (1905–1911), intellectuals, bureaucrats, merchants and clerics were united in their opposition to the despotic rule of the Qajars and their growing ties with the British.[39]

Iran's brief experiment with constitutionalism in the early twentieth century inspired a renewed call for representation. This began in the 1940s following the Allied occupation of Iran and the return of constitutional politics, and continued with the activities of the national front of 1963. Mehdī Bāzargān and Maḥmūd Taliqanī, the leaders of this Islamic national movement, would later play a significant role in the Revolution, with its constitutional element.[40]

In Iraq, Bāqir al-Ṣadr also expressed a similar notion of representation. During the 1970s, Bāqir al-Ṣadr delivered six essays dealing with the structure of the Islamic state. These essays, which were later bound under the title of *al-Islām yaqūd al-ḥayāt* (Islam governs life), played an important role in shaping the constitution of the Islamic Republic of Iran.

While Bāqir al-Ṣadr supported the concept of an Islamic state, he did not embrace the totality of Khumaynī's *wilāyat-e faqīh*, proposing instead a broader notion of authority. As an individualist source of authority (*marjaʿiyya al-dhātiyya*), Bāqir al-Ṣadr argued that the principle of *wilāyat-e faqīh* could lead to uninformed decisions. Therefore, the best model would be some form of group authority within an institutional framework, with clear-

38 See Massoud Karshenas, Mohammad Hashem Pesaran, "Economic Reform and the Reconstruction of the Iranian Economy", *The Middle East Journal* 49: 1 (1995), 89–111.

39 See Abrahamian, *Iran between two Revolutions*, 62–88; Mangol Bayat, *Iran's First Revolution: Shi'ism and the Constitutional Revolution of 1905–1909*, Oxford, New York: Oxford Univ. Press 1991, 106–138, 260–67. See also Said Amir Arjomand, "The Ulama's Traditionalist Opposition to Parliamentarianism: 1907–1909", *Middle Eastern Studies* 17: 2 (1981), 174–190; Vanessa Martin, *Islam and Modernism: The Iranian Revolution of 1906*, Syracuse, New York: Syracuse Univ. Press 1989; Fereshteh M. Nourai, "The Constitutional Ideas of a Shiʿite Mujtahid: Muhammad Husyan Na'ini", *Iranian Studies* 8 (1975), 234–247.

40 See Houchang Esfandiar Chehabi, "Religion and Politics in Iran: How Theocratic is the Islamic Republic?", *Daedalus* 120: 3 (1991), 69–91; Hamid Dabashi, *Theology of Discontent: The Ideological Foundations of the Islamic Revolution in Iran*, New York, London: New York Univ. Press 1993; Ann K. S. Lambton, "A Reconsideration of the Position of the Marja' Al-Taqlīd and the Religious Institution", *Studia Islamica* 20 (1964), 115–135.

ly defined functions that would include both jurists and laymen. This expanded *marjaʿiyya* –defined by Bāqir al-Ṣadr as an objective authority (*marjaʿiyya al-madʿiyya*)–would include various departments that would be responsible for the wide-ranging affairs of the Islamic nation.[41]

Bāqir al-Ṣadr's broad notion of authority corresponded with his concept of *ḥukm al-shūrā* (rule of *shura*) or *ḥukm al-umma* (the rule of the *umma*, the Muslim community of Islam). He argued that the idea of an Islamic state is rooted in the Islamic notion of *shūrā*, or consultation, in correspondence with the Muslim community's right to rule. In his understanding, people can choose the specific structure or form of the state as long as it does not contradict the Sharia.[42]

Following the fall of Ṣaddām, the newly appointed Shiite government began reviving this legacy of popular representation. Iraq began a process of democratization, establishing political parties, inaugurating a parliament and drafting a constitution. For the Shiites in the Arab world, democracy provided a means for empowerment. The opportunity presented in democracy for the marginalized Shiites may also have contributed to their embracing of the US liberal model in the economic domain.

Āyatullāh ʿAlī al-Sīstānī himself issued many statements supporting representation and the rule of law. While rejecting direct clerical involvement in power, this highly revered cleric demonstrated a clear shift from his former quietist position. Sīstānī began expressing his opinions on the politics of the day, becoming the kingmaker of Iraqi politics.[43]

Within this drive towards Shiite empowerment, the new regime rejected the former socialist system linked with Ṣaddām's oppressive rule. The Islamic Republic's model of populism also did not hold much promise for the Shiites of Iraq as it was overturned by the Iranians themselves over the years. As a result, Shiite politicians and clerics tended to support a more democratic and capitalist framework, due to the opportunities presented by

41 See Talib Aziz, "Baqir al-Sadr's Quest for the Marja'iya" in: *The Most Learned of the Shi'a: The Institution of the Marja' Taqlid*, Linda S. Walbridge, ed., Oxford: Oxford Univ. Press 2001, 140–148; Rodger Shanahan, "Shi'a Political Development in Iraq: The Case of the Islamic Da'wa Party", *Third World Quarterly* 25: 5 (2004), 943–954; Mallat, *The Renewal of Islamic law*, 67–69; T.M. Aziz, "The Role of Muhammad Baqir al-Sadr in Shi'i Political Activism in Iraq from 1958 to 1980", *International Journal of Middle East Studies* 25 (1993), 207–222.

42 See Jaffar Al-Rikabi, "Baqir al-Sadr and the Islamic State: A Theory for 'Islamic Democracy'", *Journal of Shi'a Islamic Studies* 5: 3 (2012), 249–275.

43 Raidar Visser, "Sistani, the United States and Politics in Iraq: from Quietism to Machiavellianism?", *Norwegian Institute of International Affairs* 700 (2006); Babak Rahimi, "Ayatollah Sistani and the Democratization of Post-Ba'thist Iraq", *United States Institute of Peace, Special Report 187* (6, 2007); Isakhan, "Despots or Democrats?". See also www.al-monitor.com/pulse/iw/originals/2014/06/iraq-isis-crisis-sistani-avoid-sectarianism.html#ixzz3U9q12vdO; www.youtube.com/watch?v=-9XR43YFdl4.

the American invaders. In addition, this more open political and socio-economic framework fits the notion of *shura* on one hand, and classical Islamic support for private ownership and trade on the other. Nevertheless, the implementation of both democracy and capitalism remained fragile with the political and socio-economic challenges that weakened the Iraqi state in the post-2003 period.

Conclusion

Certainly, from the Constitutional Revolution until today, Shiite scholars from Iran, Iraq and Bahrain found a way to reconcile representation with an Islamic political system. This was similar to other contemporary issues that were resolved in the modern era.[44] While none of these scholars fully endorsed democracy, they demonstrated an understanding of the merits of popular participation. Nevertheless, Iran did not produce a full-fledged democracy, either. Throughout the twentieth century, Shiites in the region expressed their support for representation. Yet, they also promoted diverse economic visions, supporting capitalism, socialism or Bāqir al-Ṣadr's combined model.

From a theoretical point of view, while there is a clear link between democracy and capitalism, the two systems may also clash or evolve separately. As a result, the fact that Shiites in the region supported representation does not necessarily entail their endorsement of capitalism. Concurrently, the Gulf provides an example of an Islamic tendency toward market economy without necessarily endorsing true representation.

In contemporary Iraq, any form of social responsibility necessitated a joint vision of the state. However, in the unstable and fragmented situation which emerged following the US-led invasion, Sunnis, Shiites and Kurds could not agree on a unified vision of the nation, inclusive of these three diverse groups. Iraq's embryonic democracy was threatened by a range of challenges, including a problematic legacy of minority-majority relations, deteriorating security conditions, and clashes between the regime's Islamic, democratic and federative elements. The political culture of favoritism and

---

44 Also in Bahrain, the largest Shiite party, the al-Wifāq Islamic Society (established in 2001), endorses some elements of democracy. Its discourse on democratization is particularly relevant today following the Shiite revolt in Bahrain which began in 2011. On its platform al-Wifāq speaks about civil rights, equality, freedom of religion, and the rule of law. Shaykh Qāsim, the party's spiritual leader, on the other hand, presents a narrower notion of democracy. He focuses on the people's right to choose their leaders, the rule of the majority, and free speech. See Elisheva Machlis, "Al-Wefaq and the February 14 Uprising: Islam, Nationalism and Democracy – the Shiʿi-Bahraini Discourse", *Middle Eastern Studies* 52:6 (2016), 978–995.

fear passed down by Ṣaddām's authoritarian regime further impeded the ability to create a viable democracy in Iraq, inclusive of its Sunni minority.[45]

With the growing fragmentation of Iraq in the post-2003 period and the challenge of Sunni Jihadists, the Shiite state was fighting for survival. The state became less democratic, and any form of social justice became at this stage irrelevant for the political vision of Iraq.

45 See Amnon Cohen and Noga Egrati, eds., *Post-Saddam Iraq: New Realities, Old Identities, Changing Patterns*, East Sussex, UK: Sussex Academic Press 2011.

Between Islamism and Human Rights

Mazlumder as a Third Way within Turkish Islamism?*

*Fabio Vicini***

Scholarly literature on Islamism in Turkey has generally focused on the two main drives of the Islamic revival of the last twenty years, the Justice and Development Party (*Adalet ve Kalkınma Partisi*, henceforth AKP) on the one hand and what today has become its fiercest nemesis, the Gülen community, on the other. By operating in the two distinct but complementary domains of party-politics and society respectively, these two actors have reconfigured the face of Turkey from a country still under the grasp of secular forces to one now promoting a religious outlook. Especially in the last ten years, they have been able to overturn the socio-political balance to their advantage by undermining the hold that the secularists had historically maintained on institutions (in particular the judiciary and the military) since the foundation of the Turkish Republic in 1923. While this scholarship has offered an important contribution, it has overshadowed parallel underground developments within Turkish Islamism, which have thus received relatively limited attention. New Islamic organizations have emerged and developed in the same period which can be seen as offering an alternative "third way" within Turkish Islamism with regard to the organization of the relationship between politics and society. These actors, indeed, often see themselves as distinct from and opposed to the theological views and patterns of social, civic and political transformation proposed by mainstream Islamic forces.

This chapter explores the particular case of *Mazlumder* (the Organization for Human Rights and Solidarity for Oppressed People), an Islamist Human Rights organization that began operating in the country in 1991. *Mazlumder* is one of the first of its kind. It operates within the framework of civil-society organizations by gathering younger and older Muslims around the common goal of improving human rights standards in the country. To this aim, over the last twenty-five years it has organized workshops, sit-ins and protests and released public statements to condemn abuses of power by

* The research that is presented in this work was supported for one year (2013–2014) by the Scientific and Technological Research Council of Turkey (Tübitak) with a one-year scholarship (2013–2014) [Grant No. 2216].

** Department of Political Science and International Relations, Istanbul 29 Mayis University, Istanbul, Turkey. İnkılap Mahallesi, Dr. Fazıl Küçük Cd. No:6, 34764 Ümraniye/Istanbul. Email: fvicini@29mayis.edu.tr

the state or by particular groups within society. Other Islamically-inspired associations have used the banner of human rights in these last two decades, but while they have generally focused on issues of religious discrimination, since its foundation *Mazlumder* has embraced a more open perspective on rights, including those of other religious and ethnic minorities in the country.[1]

Being loyal to more conventional Islamist positions that are critical of Westernization and that reject capitalism's principles and hedonistic values, many people at *Mazlumder* have often disapproved of the AKP administration's compliance with neoliberal policies.[2] In this regard, the organization can be partly seen as a precursor to more recent developments and realignments within the Islamist field that have led to the emergence of Islamically-inspired critical movements such as the Anti-capitalist Muslims (*Antikapitalist Müslümanlar*) and other left-leaning groups such as the Labor and Justice Coalition (*Emek ve Adalet Platformu*), which have lately come into the limelight for their participation in the Gezi protests of 2013. These movements are the expression of a new generation of Islamist youth disillusioned with the AKP administration, and especially with its more recent ideological alignment with conservatism and nationalism.[3] One should not, however, attribute a clear left-leaning inclination to *Mazlumder* or to these other

1 For example, *Özgür-Der* (*Özgür Düşünce ve Eğitim Hakları Derneği*, Association for the Freedom of Thought and Educational Rights) and *Ak-der* (*Ayrımcılığa Karşı Kadın Hakları Derneği*, Association against Discrimination and for Women's Rights) have traditionally prioritized the defence of Muslims' religious rights such as, in particular, the right to veil in public institutions following the emergence of the veil issue in the 1990s. For a comparison see Ayşe Kadıoğlu, "Civil Society, Islam and Democracy in Turkey: A Study of Three Islamic Non-Governmental Organizations", *The Muslim World* 95: 1 (2005), 23–41.

2 The recent swift turn toward positions much more sympathetic to the AKP administration is briefly discussed in the conclusion.

3 For an exploration of these two movements see respectively the article of Bayram Koca, "The Emergence of Anti-Capitalist Muslims in Turkey: 'God, Bread, Freedom'" in this volume, and Halil İbrahim Yenigün, "The New Antinomies of the Islamic Movement in Post-Gezi Turkey: Islamism vs. Muslimism", *Turkish Studies* 18: 2 (2017), 229–250. Given the prominent role that the Anti-capitalist Muslims had during the Gezi protests, this group has drawn great attention in the media and in the academic literature. See Mustafa Akyol, "Why Turkey Has 'Anti-Capitalist Muslims'", *Al-Monitor* 18 July 2013 (accessed 25 August 2017); Nilüfer Göle, "Gezi–Anatomy of a Public Square Movement", *Insight Turkey* 15: 3 (2013), 7–14; Erdem Damar, "Complexities of the Secular/Islamic Divide and Multiple Secularisms in Turkey: The Anti-Capitalist Muslims in the 'Gezi Park' Protests", *Studia Sociologia* 6: 1 (2014), 110–125; Ayşe Dursun, "Muslim Groups in the Gezi Park Protests: Identity Politics and Contentious Politics Under Authoritarian Neoliberalism", in: *Contentious Politics in the Middle East*, Fawaz A. Gerges, ed., New York: Palgrave Macmillan 2015, 373–390; Erdem Damar, "Radicalisation of Politics and Production of New Alternatives: Rethinking the Secular/Islamic Divide after the Gezi Park Protests in Turkey", *Journal of Contemporary European Studies* 24: 2 (2016), 207–222.

groups. Their members would indeed refuse the label "leftist"[4] Rather, *Malzumder* and these other associations, share a criticism of mainstream Islamic movements, for their ambiguous relationship with capitalism and neoliberalism.

Based on research conducted between 2013 and 2014 within the Istanbul branch of the organization (henceforth *Malzumder-Istanbul*),[5] the chapter illustrates how activists of the organization rely on Muslim views of social justice to question the modern political and economic order. In this light, it sheds light on the inherent criticism that before the Gezi protests people at *Malzumder-Istanbul* levelled at mainstream Turkish Islamic movements on the basis of their understanding of Islamic notions of justice.[6] Tackling the issue more from a theoretical perspective than an ethnographic one, the chapter will also point out some common traits in the views of my interlocutors and those of leftist thought with particular regard to a critique of capitalism. As it will be argued, my interlocutors' criticisms go even deeper and strike at the heart of the modern language of rights, in ways that are similar to those of twentieth century Islamist thinkers such as Said Qutb, but also of Western political philosophers such as Hannah Arendt and Giorgio Agamben.[7] After drawing these parallels, the chapter concludes by assessing whether this "third way" (and hence a new wave of Islamic movements that uphold social justice and human rights) has already reached maturity in Turkey. The answer is mostly negative, though the possibility of future positive developments is not ruled out.

---

4 All these groups claim, indeed, that they are first of all Muslim groups having as their main source of reference the Quran and the Islamic tradition in general. With particular regard to the case of *Mazlumder*, moreover, such a stance would be even more out of place if one considers the fact that following the recent clash between the AKP administration and the Gülen community, and the rising polarization between the Islamists and the secularists in the country after Gezi, *Mazlumder* has progressively taken a more "self-enclosed" approach to human rights and become less critical of the administration (see also below).

5 Although most of the ethnographic excerpts quoted in this study are from one single interview, they reflect widespread views within the Istanbul branch of the organization. For more ethnographic details see Fabio Vicini, "Turkish Islamism, Conservatism and Human Rights before and after Gezi: the Case of Mazlumder", *British Journal of Middle Eastern Studies* 2017, DOI: 10.1080/13530194.2017.1343124.

6 Between 2015 and 2016 a conflict emerged within *Mazlumder* between those who took a critical stance on the new military intervention in the South-East, and those who had a more sympathetic approach towards it. See below and Vicini, "Turkish Islamism".

7 See Jenna Reinbold, "Radical Islam and Human Rights Values: A 'Religious-Minded' Critique of Secular Liberty, Equality, and Brotherhood", *Journal of the American Academy of Religion* 78: 2 (2010), 449–476.

Disputing the State

Mazlumder was established in January 1991 by a group of 54 journalists, editors, lawyers and businessmen known to be close to Turkish Islamist circles. Their goal was to open an association operating in defense of human rights independently of both the state and political parties. According to its maxim, the organization aspires to defend the rights of the oppressed (*mazlum*) from *any* oppressor 'whoever the oppressed are' (*kim olursa olsun*), that is, regardless of what their religion, culture, ethnicity or political views are. The kind of organizational structure and rhetoric that *Mazlumder* has embraced since its foundation is the reflex of larger global transformations that followed the fall of the Soviet Union, when new national economic policies oriented towards the liberalization of the market were promoted across the world in the name of "democratization" under the protective shadow of US dominance. In line with modern liberal views, democratization had to stand on the flourishing of a strong "civil society" which had to function as a counterweight to the state by both spurring and sustaining it in the promotion of policies respectful of "human rights." The gusts of such liberal rhetoric were blowing with force in both the former Soviet Republics and the Middle East during the 1990s.[8] In Turkey this figuration of state-society relations was particularly suited to demands by Islamist groups, and conservatives in general, which had been repressed by the secularists dominating the institutions since 1923. Establishing a civil-society organization operating in the framework of the now globally accepted human rights discourse was for the Islamists one of the best possible ways to publicize their discontent with what they saw as the state's authoritarianism and monolithic view of Turkish identity.[9]

The founders of *Mazlumder* shared their concerns with other civic actors close to left-leaning circles which already controlled organizations such as the Association for Human Rights (*İnsan Hakları Derneği, İHD*) and the Turkey Human Rights Foundation (*Türkiye İnsan Hakları Vakfı, TİHV*). İHD and TİHV were dominated by Leftists and Kurdish nationalists who also

8 See Chris Hann, "Introduction: Political Society and Civil Anthropology", in: *Civil Society. Challenging Western Models*, Chris Hann and Elizabeth Dunn, eds., London and New York: Routledge 2005 (1996), 1–26; and Augustus Richard Norton, ed., *Civil Society in the Middle East*, vol. 1, Leiden: Brill 1994.

9 Amélie Barras, "A Rights-Based Discourse to Contest the Boundaries of State Secularism? The Case of the Headscarf Bans in France and Turkey", *Democratization* 16: 6 (2009), 1237–1260; İhsan Dağı, "Rethinking Human Rights, Democracy, and the West: Post-Islamist Intellectuals in Turkey", *Critique: Critical Middle Eastern Studies* 13: 2 (2004), 135–151; Jenny B. White. "The Islamist Movement in Turkey and Human Rights", *Human Rights Review* 3: 1 (2001), 17–26.

criticized state-promoted monolithic views of Turkish identity.[10] *Malzumder* was established as a Muslim counterpart to them, with the goal of sustaining the cause of faithful Muslims. The organization became particularly renowned for the stance it took in support of Islamic female students, organizations and communities that were subjected to media attack and police raids during the so-called "post-modern" coup of February 28, 1997, which led the first Islamist prime minister of Turkey, Necmettin Erbakan, to resign from office. For this reason, even today, *Mazlumder* is mostly known as an Islamist organization. However, in the first years after its foundation, it undertook common battles with İHD and TİHV by criticizing state repression and defending the rights of political opponents that were imprisoned in the 1990s because of their alleged affiliation with the Kurdistan Workers' Party (*Partiya Karkeren Kurdistan, PKK*). At least until recently (with limitations regarding some individual rights such as those concerning abortion and LGBT people) *Mazlumder* has fought against the state's violation of some basic rights, especially those of ethnic and religious minorities.[11]

The organization's disapproval of the old secularist hold on Turkish institutions is grounded in an even deeper feeling of dissatisfaction with the modern nation, its identity-based politics and its way of managing justice (see below). This inclination is related to a common critique within Islamist discourse in Turkey and beyond that sees the nation state as being primarily responsible for creating division within the worldwide Islamic community (*ummah*). For example, people I met at *Mazlumder-Istanbul* often recurred to common Biblical and Quranic narrations of the Pharaoh who oppressed Moses and his people. This is a widespread trope that in the eyes of Turkish Islamists epitomizes the unfaithful and authoritarian state and its unjust rule.[12] The secular reforms initiated by Mustafa Kemal Atatürk in the early decades of the Republic–which sanctioned the end of the Caliphate and the imposition of a European-like legal system–were seen by them as a top-down violent imposition that had culturally deprived the population.[13] For this reason, *Mazlumder* has in the past promoted several initiatives aimed at undermining the hegemony of secularist discourse in the country such as the campaign to abolish the oath of loyalty to the Turkish Republic that elementary-school students have until recently recited every morning before

---

10 Güneş Murat Tezcür, "Catholic and Muslim Human Rights Activism in Violent Internal Conflicts", *Politics and Religion* 8: 1 (2015), 111–134.

11 Although *Mazlumder* activists declared that they would defend LGBT people who had been victims of violence, they also said that they would never stand up for their sexual rights, just as they would not support the right to abortion.

12 As will be pointed out below, today it is more difficult for them to uphold this principle against the current administration given its ideological affinity with their own.

13 Vicini, "Turkish Islamism".

classes.[14] After all, the critique of the modern state put forward by *Mazlumder* is also the consequence of the way human rights discourse has been absorbed not only in Turkey but also in the broader Middle East. In these contexts, the discourse of human rights has been embraced by activists coming from a diversified ideological spectrum to denounce the abuses of monarchs and autocrats often operating in complicity with Western powers.[15] Yet, within *Mazlumder* and Islamist conservative circles in Turkey in general, the critique of the modern nation-state is rooted in an even deeper contention with some basic tenets of modernity and its political discourse that I explore below.

An Alternative View of Justice

Whereas by framing their activism in the language of human rights, people at *Mazlumder* are implicitly referring to the 1948 Universal Declaration of Human Rights (UDHR), they also claim that the West does not have the right to monopolize the discourse of rights. As written in the *Mazlumder* charter, several pertinent ancient sources pre-exist the UDHR, including those belonging to the Islamic civilization.[16] Among these, the organization attaches particular importance to the "Alliance of the Virtuous" (arab. *Ḥilf al-Fuḍūl*), a pact of honor signed by the chiefs of the most notable tribes of Mecca (including the Prophet Muḥammad and his father-in-law Abu Bakr) before Muḥammadian revelation. The pact was validated to solve a case of cheating that had been raised by a foreign trader and was functional to the reorganization of trade exchange among local tribes on the basis of shared views of justice. The principles that were agreed upon in the *Ḥilf al-Fuḍūl* were later ratified by Muhammad in one of his sayings as Prophet (hadith).[17] For this reason, similarly to other early episodes of Muslim history such as the covenant of Medina, the pact has been extensively examined by

14 The government passed a law prescribing the removal of the oath in 2013, but it was later rejected by the Supreme Court in 2014. In response, the government submitted the latter court's decision to a higher court for cancellation and the verdict has not been given yet.

15 Barras, "A Rights-Based Discourse".

16 Among those belonging to European tradition, *Mazlumder*'s charter lists: the Universal Declaration of Human Rights, the Ten Christian Commandments, the EU Human Rights Code, the *Magna Carta*, the French Declaration of the Rights of Man and of the Citizen that was issued during the French Revolution and the more recent European Convention on Human Rights. See http://world.mazlumder.org/en/main/pages/about-us-who-we-are/116 (accessed September 07, 2017).

17 *Sunan Al-Kubra*, hadith 12114; *al-Dalā'il fi Gharīb*, hadith 243.

Muslim liberal intellectuals and has become a source of inspiration for Muslim NGOs around the world.[18]

By referring to an Islamic precedent to human rights discourse, people at *Mazlumder* do not simply claim that Islam and human rights are compatible. They also openly question the philosophical assumptions upon which the Western understanding of such rights is based. Although not discussed in the charter, this aspect was raised by some of the activists I met in Istanbul. Take for example the following words by Cüneyt Sarıyaşar, the former president (2011–2015) of *Mazlumder-Istanbul*, in response to my question about what alternative understanding of freedom and justice they based their view of Western principles on:

> As Muslims we put the idea of justice in first place, but it is the principle of individual liberty that is prioritized in the West [...] For us, freedom is a concept that is related to justice. Once you violate the principle of justice, then both human nature and freedom are deformed. For us, creation and justice are important. Creation consists of the rules that have been fixed by God.

As he had just explained a few minutes before, indeed:

> We look at justice in this way. Any time an act that violates the attributes of human nature or that represses or attempts to annihilate them takes place, then justice has been eliminated. [...] [Because] in Islam justice does not simply consist of in the avoidance of exploitation. Rather, it consists in the rebellion against those who persecute. [...] For us freedom means helping somebody who is a servant's servant (*kula kulluk*) to escape from this condition. Where will he escape to? He will escape into service (*kulluk*) to God. All of us are equal as God's servants. All humanity is equal as God's servants (*Allah'ın kulu olarak eşittir*).[19]

Like other pious Muslims in Turkey, volunteers at *Mazlumder-Istanbul* understand sovereignty differently from the way it has been approached within European political discourse since modernity. As it has been argued by various voices within Western philosophical scholarship too, a notion of rights that is meant as a 'natural' and inalienable property of human life as such is a specific and intrinsic product of Western juridical tradition.[20] Ini-

---

18 For example see Rachid Ghannouchi, "The Participation of Islamists in a Non-Islamic Government", in: *Power-Sharing Islam*, Azzam Tamimi, ed., London: Liberty for Muslim World Publications 1993, 51–63. Tariq Ramadan, *In the Footsteps of the Prophet: Lessons from the Life of Muhammad*: Oxford Univ. Press 2006. For the use of the concept of *Ḥilf al-Fuḍūl* by Muslim NGOs see Mashood Baderin, "Islam and the Realization of Human Rights in the Muslim World: A Reflection on Two Essential Approaches and Two Divergent Perspectives", *Muslim World Journal of Human Rights* 4: 1 (2007). http://www.bepress.com/mwjhr/vol4/iss1/art5/.

19 Cüneyt Sarıyaşar, interviewed by author, fieldnotes, 4 July 2013, Istanbul.

20 See Giorgio Agamben, *Homo Sacer: Sovereign Power and Bare Life*, Stanford: Stanford University Press 1998; Hannah Arendt, *The Origins of Totalitarianism*, New York: Houghton Mifflin Harcourt 1973; Roberto Esposito, *The Third Person: Politics of Life and Philosophy of the Impersonal*, Cambridge: Polity 2012.

tiated in Greek antiquity, philosophical discussions around human 'natural rights' were later appropriated by European modern political philosophers and integrated within their theories of sovereignty and the state. Based on the key assumption that God's sovereignty had to be excluded from any serious formulation, modern European philosophers such as Thomas Hobbes advanced the idea that any discourse of legality and rights had to be based on a covenant between human beings, that is, on a pact of mutual human recognition independent of any reference to a transcendental principle. In the account of the Scottish philosopher, human beings were envisaged as rational individuals willing to devolve part of their sovereignty to the Leviathan ruler in exchange for protection under his aegis. They were thought of as the ideal signatories of a virtual social contract that they had subscribed together with other citizens to seal the social pact. In this configuration, the ruler immunized its subjects against the violence that dominated the state of nature, so granting them inalienable individual rights, including civil liberties and political rights.[21]

Without dwelling too much on politico-theological theory, it is important to highlight that it is in this modern liberal understanding of sovereignty that for the first time the individual is so clearly thought of as a subject entitled to some personal sacred rights *per se*.[22] This aspect has also been highlighted by Western critical thinkers who have questioned the secular and liberal foundations of political modernity in order to shed light on pre-modern ethical formulations and conceptualizations of social solidarity and justice.[23] According to these authors, during the Scottish Enlightenment an idea of the individual as the subject of his own freedom and as detached from any higher idea of God emerged. In this liberal configuration, the subject had to be "liberated" from any otherworldly constriction and encouraged to fully use his intellectual capacities to achieve the best for himself. It follows that justice was reduced to the regulation of inter-human relations on the basis of mutual recognition and, though only when possible and convenient, mutual help. As famously stated by the father of modern liberal political economy, by so doing, not only individual interest would be promoted, but the good of the collective would be automatically achieved thanks to the "invisible hand" of the market.[24]

---

21 Agamben, *Homo Sacer*, 35–36; Armando Salvatore, *The Public Sphere: Liberal Modernity, Catholicism, Islam*, New York: Macmillan 2007, 180.

22 Luca Mavelli, *Europe's Encounter with Islam: the Secular and the Postsecular*, London: Routledge 2013, 83; Salvatore, *The Public Sphere*, 179–180.

23 See Alasdair MacIntyre, *After Virtue*, Notre Dame: Univ. of Notre Dame Press 1986 (1984); Talal Asad, *Formations of the Secular: Christianity, Islam, Modernity*, Stanford: Stanford Univ. Press 2003; John Milbank, *Theology and Social Theory: Beyond Secular Reason*, Malden: Blackwell 2006 (1990); Salvatore, *The Public Sphere*.

24 Adam Smith, *The Wealth of Nations*, London: Everyman's Library 1964 (1776).

Similarly, according to Cüneyt, the Western understanding of rights gives excessive priority to the search for individual freedom over the search for forms of inter-human solidarity which, instead, prioritize justice. This aspect will become clearer below, where it is discussed in relation to my interlocutors' critique of capitalism. Yet, briefly, in line with a longstanding philosophical-theological tradition in Islam, Cüneyt raised the point that a system that relies excessively on human rational faculties risks bringing forth a conception of rights whose main focus is the satisfaction of each person's individual interests (at least as long as this search does not clash with other people's rights). Within such a formulation, a more genuine conception that prioritizes the search for inter-subjective understanding and solidarity is stymied from the start. In contrast, Cüneyt underlines the centrality of God and His sovereign power as the guarantor of an inter-human pact of fraternity, equality and justice. In this Islamically-grounded framework, it is only under God's aegis that inter-human relations, and hence also the functioning of social justice, can effectively work. Social justice can be achieved only when all people agree that regardless of their social status or class, they are equal as brothers in religion, and as such, subjects to the same and unique God.

As it has been stressed with regard to pioneer Islamist thinkers such as Said Qutb, it is the issue of the moral responsibility of the individual that is upheld in Islamic tradition in opposition to the excessive formalism that underlies Western accounts of human rights.[25] Echoing "the anxieties of certain 'Western' philosophers engaged in the work of postmodern self-criticism,"[26] in *Milestones* (*Maʿālim fī l-ṭarīq*, 1964) Qutb argued that the imperative of "moral choice" had to be at the basis of every formulation of justice. On the contrary, in a view of justice based on "inherent" and "inalienable" natural rights like those contemplated by modern liberal thinkers, the dimensions of agency and responsibility (which should be implicit in human commitment to a project for recreating social cohesion and justice) are obscured. Once rights are perceived to be inalienable parts of one's nature, the human contribution to establishing such a system is compromised from the outset. Although Islamist accounts may sound utopian, if not naïve, they bring to the fore some of the possible limits of modern liberal discourse, above all its "legalist" excesses. At the same time, inasmuch as they highlight collective interest and uphold a discourse that prioritizes people's responsibility over individual claims to rights, they are remindful of alterna-

---

25 Jenna Reinbold, "Radical Islam and Human Rights Values: A 'Religious-Minded' Critique of Secular Liberty, Equality, and Brotherhood", *Journal of the American Academy of Religion* 78: 2 (2010), 449–476.

26 Reinbold, "Radical Islam and Human Rights Values", 471.

tive understandings of modernity such as leftists' views–though, as it will be shown, their ontological premises remain different.

Towards a Dynamic View of Islam

Views of responsibility and justice of people at *Mazlumder* intersect with a critique of liberal modernity that, though expressed in different terms, has always been present within the West as well. Despite the monolithic view of Western history that is often reproduced in scholarship (and that my interlocutors seem to share), as an established tradition of studies has solidly argued, alternative and competing paths to modernity have coexisted within and outside the Western world.[27] With regard to the West, most notable is the opposition between libertarian and socialist views, which has dominated most of the twentieth century in Europe. Although people at *Mazlumder* were lukewarm about admitting to any closeness to leftist thought, this has to be seen as dependent on how Marxist doctrine has been implemented in concrete historical and geographical settings rather than as a total lack of affinity between leftist views and those expressed by my interlocutors. This is especially true with regard to their critique of capitalism.

The analysis of possible links between widespread formulations of Islamic justice and leftist views has indeed generally been obstructed by the fact that Muslim actors have always outrightly rejected Marxist critique of religion. During the first half of the twentieth century Muslims were already struggling against hedonist and materialist scientific doctrines that were coming from Europe. Communism, however, was seen as being potentially even more dangerous and threatening than these doctrines. It was not a coincidence that later, during the 1980s, mainstream Islamic movements opted for an alliance with the Turkish state and the market-driven liberal forces of capitalism against this common enemy–an implicit partnership that, as mentioned above, endures today within mainstream Turkish Islamic movements.[28]

---

27 Shmuel N. Eisenstadt, "Multiple Modernities", *Daedalus* 129: 1 (2000), 1–29; Peter Wagner, "Successive Modernities and the Idea of Progress: A First Attempt", *Distinktion* 11: 2 (2010), 9–24; Peter Wagner, *Modernity: Understanding the Present*, Cambridge: Polity 2012.

28 During this time national official ideology was reconfigured along the lines delineated by the Turkish-Islamic synthesis, a discourse about national history originating in conservative circles in the 1960s that reconciled the national and religious elements of Turkish identity by tracing their coupling far back in time to the very beginning of national history. For the contemporary alliance between Islam and capital see Cihan Tuğal, "Islamism in Turkey: Beyond Instrument and Meaning", *Economy and Society* 31: 1 (2002), 85–111; Cihan Tuğal, *Passive Revolution: Absorbing the Islamic Challenge to Capitalism*, Stanford: Stanford Univ. Press 2009.

Lately, however, a new generation of Turkish Muslims have advocated reconciliation between Islamic and left-leaning ideologies, with special regard to a critique of capitalism. This is the case with new movements such as the Anti-capitalist Muslims and the Labor and Justice Coalition. Brought to public attention by the Gezi protests of June 2013, these groups have repeatedly pointed to the fact that Islamic tradition shares what could be termed a common collectivistic basis with leftist thought. During the protests, for example, the Anti-capitalist Muslims launched slogans such as "Property belongs to God" (*Mülk Allah'ındır*) to claim that capitalism's defense of private property is contrary to basic Quranic injunctions predicating equality, solidarity and sharing among brothers in religion.[29] In those days, even *Mazlumder* took a stance in partial defense of the protesters. Some prominent members of *Mazlumder-Istanbul*, including the former president Cüneyt Sarıyaşar, released a joint declaration together with the Labor and Justice Coalition in which they partially supported the Gezi cause by denouncing the neoliberal-leaning policies behind the AKP administration's decision to replace Gezi Park with a shopping mall. The organization itself later released a report in which, though with some ambiguity, it criticized the behavior of the police against the protestors.[30]

However, these two stances caused uproar within *Mazlumder*, with many members threatening to withdraw from the organization. In a relatively short time, these internal clashes mounted, resulting in a split between those who pledged alliance to the AKP administration and those who were critical of its policies. The situation worsened in 2015 when Cüneyt was replaced with a president more sympathetic to the conservative constituency of the organization. Meanwhile, most of the provincial branches of *Mazlumder* were shut down by the Istanbul branch on the grounds that they had taken sides with the PKK following the re-opening of the armed conflict with the Turkish military in June 2015.[31] However, rather than being the cause of the split, this divergence of views was the outcome of the rising polarization between the Islamists and the secularists that had been intensifying in the country since the events at Gezi. Since the 2013 protests the vast majority of the religious conservatives have indeed aligned with the views and policies of the AKP administration. This has happened because, beyond an ideological affinity with the latter, they share a strong common identity which is grounded in common fears, such as that a secularist back-

29 Anti-capitalist Muslims had first launched these slogans a few years earlier, during one of the May 1st protests, as together with other left-leaning groups, they pointlessly tried to overcome police resistance and enter the pedestrian zone next to Taksim Square, *İstiklal caddesi*.

30 Mazlumder (İstanbul Şubesi), *Taksim Gezi Parkı Olayları Raporu*, 2013.

31 Vicini, "Turkish Islamism".

lash, like that which happened on 28 February 1997 may reoccur, allowing the opposition to retake power.[32]

Yet, here I would like to dwell for a moment on the analysis of *Mazlumder*'s ideological tenets. Turkish Islamists affiliated with the organization have traditionally been critical of capitalism and, for this reason, they are close to more conventional Islamist Parties such as the Felicity Party (*Saadet Partisi*). They have usually seen capitalism as a system linked to the modern liberal views of the human agency exposed above and for this reason inherently contradicting their understanding of justice. As explained again to me by Cüneyt, when human freedom is understood as the satisfaction of individual desires as it is in Western modern liberal tradition, this is also when "exploitation takes place" (*zulüm oluyor*). Aimed at the creation of multiple desires to be satisfied by the individual/consumer, in the view of people at *Mazlumder*, the capitalist system is structured around an individual-centered logic. And when people's "desire" (*heva*) takes the upper hand over God's commands, this is when exploitation and social disorder take place.[33] Although Cüneyt's words are certainly a simplification of more complex dynamics, from an Islamically-informed perspective about how to build a just social order, they reflect an essential truth; namely, that capitalism's dominant logic is intrinsically *not* oriented to the achievement of the common well-being. Rather, it is based on the individual search for economic and personal achievement.

In this light, the passage above in which Cüneyt used the expression *kula kulluk* acquires new relevance. Translatable as "a servant's servant" the expression is a trope that is used within Muslim Islamist circles in Turkey to refer to the condition of dependence that some people may develop toward others, especially in the modern work market. Since in Islam only submission to God is contemplated, whenever the conditions that may generate a situation of inter-human submission become manifest, Muslims must refuse to conform to them. There are two main reasons for this. First, the existence of such a relationship would imply that the person in a position of power is exalted as a God (*Tanrılık olarak düşünmek*, or the more commonly used *şirk koşmak)*, which is one of the worst sins in Islam. Second, the subservient person would be perceived as being subordinated to his superiors.

---

32 On the way political life in Turkey is structured around the main cultural cleavage between "secular" and "religious" factions see Ersin Kalaycıoğlu, "*Kulturkampf* in Turkey: The Constitutional Referendum of 12 September 2010", *South European Society and Politics* 17: 1 (2012), 1–22. On how fear has long guided Turkish society and politics see Michelangelo Guida, "The Sevres Syndrome and 'Komplo' Theories in the Islamist and Secular Press", *Turkish Studies* 9: 1 (2008), 37–52; Michelanglo Guida, "Negotiating Values in the Islamist Press after 2013", *Middle East Critique* 27: 2 (2018), 193–206. See also Vicini, "Turkish Islamism".

33 Cüneyt Sarıyaşar, interviewed by author, fieldnotes, 4 July 2013, Istanbul.

Since in the view of people at *Mazlumder* the capitalist system is based on mechanisms that crystallize relationships of subordination between men, they judged it as contrary in principle to the sociopolitical order that God wishes for them.

From their perspective, because in Islam everything, including property, belongs to God alone and is part of His sovereign domain, human beings can never *own* it, but only benefit from it. Accordingly, just as they do not have any right to arrogate property, they cannot dispose of other people as they wish. In this sense, their avowal of God's sovereignty in Islam should not be understood as a blind act of devotion and total surrender into God's hands leading to relief from all responsibilities, as a secular means-to-ends understanding of social action would assume. Rather, it is the premise upon which a conception of human-to-human relations is constructed as based on a taken-for-granted relationship between equals, without regard to any distinction of class, race, political or religious view. In this sense, in Cüneyt's words, "All of us are equal as God's servants. All humanity is equal as God's servants (*Allah'ın kulu olarak eşittir*)." Moreover, he added, in an ideal Islamically-grounded system it should not be enough to repel any form of exploitation of other brothers in religion. It is also necessary to "rebel against those who persecute" and who want to impose their own will on others.[34]

With his words, Cüneyt is not only criticizing capitalism. He is also mounting a covert attack against other Islamic actors in Turkey. According to Cüneyt, *Mazlumder* rejects in principle any kind of human exploitation, and advocates an interpretation of Islamic tradition as a dynamic (*dinamik*) source for thinking and practicing social justice, something that, in his view, mainstream Islamic movements such as the AKP and the Gülen community failed to do. In Cüneyt's opinion, these two political actors have either proposed a mere ideologically and ethically empty attachment to Turkey's Muslim past or just been content with promoting formal adherence to an outwardly religious life respectively.[35] As highlighted by Cüneyt and by other people at *Mazlumder*, Muslims should rather strive to go back to the hidden civic potential of Islam, which is embedded in thoughts and practices for the common good that are grounded in relationships of equality and brotherhood in religion. They should be engaged in striving for the reestablishment of solidarity and justice on premises that are different from those that appear to them to belong to an inherently individualistic and hedonistic capitalist-oriented modernity.

34 Cüneyt Sarıyaşar, interviewed by author, fieldnotes, 4 July 2013, Istanbul.
35 Cüneyt Sarıyaşar, interviewed by author, fieldnotes, 4 July 2013, Istanbul.

The Islamic Quest for Rights in Polarized Turkish Society

This chapter has illustrated the political-theological premises upon which *Mazlumder* has built its discourse and practices of justice in opposition to liberal modernity and its rights discourse. Starting from these same premises, the organization has long differentiated itself from mainstream Islamic movements, questioning their ambiguous relationship with capitalism. In this way, *Mazlumder* has carved out for itself a niche within Turkish Islamism. As it has the potential of catalyzing both pious and conservative Muslims around a common criticism of both neoliberal policies and state authoritarianism, *Mazlumder* has until recently hovered in an in-between sociopolitical space, calling for a dynamic approach to interpreting the Islamic tradition. In this regard, the organization has the potential to be one of the major exponents of an alternative "third" way within Turkish Islamism; a trend that has lately been questioning the boundaries between Islamism and conservatism in the country. These new emerging actors of Turkish Islam suggest that a revitalization of Islam as a tradition of civic engagement should be based on retrieving Islamic founding principles of equality, solidarity and social justice.

Being one of the first organizations that called upon Muslims to develop a critical approach to issues of social justice, *Mazlumder* could lay claim to being a pioneer and having a leadership role in the construction of such an alternative movement. But has *Mazlumder* been able to keep up its own standards and to pose as the defender of a new way of articulating social justice in the face of the changed political conditions of the last fifteen years? The recent developments seem to suggest a negative reply to this question. The inner split of the organization originates indeed from a conservative resurgence of its constituency in reaction to the renewed polarization of society along the main secular/religious divide following Gezi, the reopening of the armed conflict between the Turkish military and the PKK in 2015, and the more recent coup attempt of July 15, 2016. In the last five years, Turkish conservatives and Islamists have been asked to take sides in the all-out war between the AKP administration and the Gülenists. In the name of national security, political stability, and fear of retaliation by the secularists should they regain institutional power, the conservatives have converged towards the former.

In this light, *Mazlumder* seems to have been unable to readjust its justice discourse to the new sociopolitical conditions. As illustrated, the critique of the authoritarian secularist nation-state had a cardinal role in the interpretation of human rights discourse by people at *Mazlumder*. Even if my interlocutors tried to deny it, following the rise to power of more sympathetic Islamic forces, their old anti-establishment rhetorical framework no longer seems to work, with the consequence that they have entered a discursive vacuum. Now that power is largely in the hands of leaders who defend the same religious rights that they have long fought for, how could they still juxtapose the state with the Pharaoh and accuse it of tyranny?

These considerations pose the question of whether and how the organization can still pose as the defender of universal justice without running into a contradiction. The potential for *Mazlumder* to present itself as the bearer of a new and alternative message of Islamic justice largely depends, indeed, on its capacity to overcome this impasse and remain immune from the contingency of radical political shifts. New generations of Islamists seem to have endorsed a more open critique of the status quo and be looking for ways of interpreting Islamic tradition that better respond to contemporary challenges.[36] *Mazlumder* appears to be, at least momentarily, more concerned with maintaining a stance in line with that taken by the majority of its conservative constituency than with welcoming the views of these new generations. However, the possibility for *Mazlumder* and other yet-to-emerge groups to succeed seems to be largely dependent on whether they will be able to integrate and express the views and expectations of these new generations, as well as those of the more educated among the conservatives. Although the realization of this possibility is for the moment complicated by the current tensions crisscrossing Turkish society, it must not be ruled out for the forthcoming future.

36 Also see Yenigün, "The new antinomies of the Islamic movement".

A Sufi Martyr and Harbinger of Anti-Capitalism

Şeyh Bedreddin as an Emblematic Figure in 'Progressive' Publications

Béatrice Hendrich

I love my country:
I've taken the girth of its plane trees in my arms,
I've slept in its prisons,
Nothing lifts my spirits like its songs and tobacco.

My country:
Bedreddin, Sinan, Yunus Emre, and Sakarya,
Lead domes and factory chimneys –
It's all the work of my people, whose drooping moustaches
Hide their smiles
Even from themselves.[1]

Introduction

Samavna kadısı oğlu Şeyh Bedreddin (1359–1416) is a historical figure with a rather exceptional biography: He was a learned and pious man who started his professional career as an honorable servant of the Ottoman state, served as military judge (*kazasker*), but turned into a popular peripatetic preacher and an outcast who ended his life at the gallows for inciting the masses. His biography provides all the elements which make up a fascinating story, and at the same time there are enough biographical lacunas and rumors–after all the sheikh lived in the 14th/15th century–that the historiographical, political and religious imagination finds ample space to fill with a variety of additional stories, explanations and justifications.

Today, Şeyh Bedreddin is still a popular figure in Turkey, and in other countries among migrants from Turkey respectively; once in a while new publications appear on the book market which provide fresh perspectives or support traditional approaches regarding the activities and significance of the sheikh. Throughout the centuries, historiographers and political authors have been creating different stories: While some authors see in him a god-fearing Sunni theologian, others hail him as the first prophet of a communist or post-capitalist commune.

---

1 Nazım Hikmet, *Poems of Nazim Hikmet*, transl. by Randy Blasing and Mutlu Konuk, New York: Persea Books 1994, 79.

This paper will focus on the second thread: the transformation of a pre-modern figure into a hero of the (post-)modern left in Turkey, including the narrative of Şeyh Bedreddin as an Alevi revolutionary or saint and as a martyr for anti-capitalist Muslims. In order to comprehend how Şeyh Bedreddin has reached his present position in these narratives of movements and communities which would characterize themselves as "progressive", it will be necessary to follow both the chain of authors who, throughout the centuries, handed down remarks and stories referring to the sheikh, and the historical context, respectively. By means of this search it will come to the fore that the location of this intriguing biography in a zone of governmental, religious and linguistic intersection has to be considered as a key factor in the longevity of the narratives related to Şeyh Bedreddin Simavne.

A careful reading of the relevant texts and references will also demonstrate how a quote first attributed to the rebel Börklüce Mustafa gains its own agenda and serves to justify a critique of capitalism by rather diverse movements:

> Everywhere
> all together
> in everything
> but the lover's cheek.[2]

Historical Background

Şeyh Bedreddin was a scholar who held different positions as a state servant and a prolific author of theological, jurisprudential and mystical treatises. For this reason, we possess a relatively large number of biographical details. However, we cannot ignore the fact that he is a figure of the $14^{th}/15^{th}$ century and that the major contemporary sources are the hagiography *Sımavna Kadısıoğlu Şeyh Bedreddin Menâkıbı* by his grandson,[3] on the one hand, and on the other hand the historiography *Tevârîh-i Âl-i Osman* by Aşıkpaşazade (d. about 1502), an Ottoman chronicler with his own agenda, which was certainly not in favor of a person who, to say the least, had fallen out with the state. Later texts referring to the sheikh continued this tendency to take sides, claiming he was either a saint or a traitor. Particularly the accounts related to the second part of his life–from the exile in Iznik, Western Anatolia, and his contact with rebellious movements until his execution–are prone to partisan distortions and omissions.

---

2 Nazım Hikmet, *The Epic of Sheik Bedreddin and Other Poems*, transl. by Randy Blasing and Mutlu Konuk, New York: Persea Books 1977, 46.

3 Cf. Hans Joachim Kissling, "Das Menaqybname Scheich Bedr ed-Din's, des Sohnes des Richters von Samavna", *Zeitschrift der Deutschen Morgenländischen Gesellschaft* 100 (1950), 112–176.

Şeyh Bedreddin, or Bedrettin, was born in 1359 A.D. in Simavne, near Edirne in Eastern Thrace, the most western corner of today's Turkey. His father was the judge Gazi İsrail, an early Ottoman frontier warrior; his mother, a Greek Orthodox convert to Islam called Melek Hatun. Edirne, the former Byzantine Hadrianopolis, became part of the early Ottoman Empire only in 1362. Bedreddin was brought up as a scholar of Islamic theology and law; in this capacity, hc visited the cities of Islamic learning such as Konya, Jerusalem, Cairo, and Tabriz, and travelled to Mecca in order to do the *hajj*. During this journey, he took lessons from some of the most important scholars of his time in a variety of disciplines, e.g. mathematics, astronomy, and philosophy. Cairo seems to have been of specific importance for his career: There he was appointed as tutor for the Mamluk Sultan Barkuk's son, and, what is even more important, began to develop a keen interest in Sufism after having rejected Sufi teachings in his earlier life. His interest in Ibn Arabi's (d. 638/1240) reading of *waḥdat al-wujūd*, the Unity of Being, is thought to have been aroused during his stay in Cairo. For some years, he even acted as the sheikh of his Sufi community before he left for missionary activities in Anatolia, arriving finally in the Rumeli province.[4] Back in Anatolia, he was for some years a traveling celebrity, obviously able to attract the attention of his audience and of people from different religious and social backgrounds, before he settled down in his hometown Edirne and withdrew from the public eye.

The historical period we are dealing with is one of continuous battles over Thrace and nearby areas between Byzantine and Ottoman rulers, on the one hand, and on the other, between–shifting–alliances of the Christian and Muslim powers of Anatolia and the Balkans, and the (usually victorious) Mongolians under Timur. At the battle of Ankara in 1402, the Ottoman Sultan Bayezid I. was defeated, captured and taken to Timur where he spent the rest of his life. The following eleven years are usually called *Fetret Devri*, the Interregnum, or the Ottoman Civil War,[5] since three of Bayezid's sons started to fight among themselves for the Ottoman throne. The political instability, causing famine and poverty during Bedreddin's lifetime, and the power struggle of the *Fetret Devri* were the decisive actors in determining Bedreddin's fate: It was one of Bayezid's sons, Prince Musa, who ruled the areas of Edirne and Serres. In need of qualified staff, in 1411 Musa forced the scholar Bedreddin to serve as a military judge, *kazasker*. Bedreddin's reasoning and the decisions he made during his short service

4 Hasan Karatas, "Badr al-Dīn b. Qāḍī Samāwnā", in: *Encyclopaedia of Islam*, THREE, Kate Fleet, Gudrun Krämer, Denis Matringe et al., eds., Leiden: Brill 2013. http://dx.doi.org/10.1163/1573-3912_ei3_COM_24496 (last access 13.03.2017).

5 Dimitris J. Kastritsis, *The Sons of Bayezid: Empire Building and Representation in the Ottoman Civil War of 1402–1413*, Leiden: Brill 2007.

for Musa are collected in his *Jāmiʿ al-fuṣūlayn*, "a compilation of his verdicts and jurisprudential opinions ... a major textbook taught in the Ottoman *madrasas*."[6] Musa's rule did not last for long: In 1413, Prince Mehmed put an end to the Interregnum and became the sole ruler of the Ottoman domains. As a consequence, Bedreddin and his family were exiled to Iznik in Western Anatolia, alimented by the state because of the sheikh's reputation.

From this time on, the sheikh's life took a both intriguing and inexplicable turn. He became part of a series of rebellions by impoverished peasants in 1415/16, "a massive social movement"[7] in Western Anatolia and Thrace. After some time in contact with the rebels in the Iznik area, Bedreddin moved via Sinop at the Black Sea to the Zagora-Region in present-day Bulgaria, where he seems to have played an important role in further rebellions. When the rebellions in Anatolia and Zagora had been crushed, the rebels were executed; Bedreddin was publicly hanged in Serres. Yet, even as a convicted rebel, the government obviously hesitated to deprive him of his personal honor. He was interred with all the rituals befitting a Muslim funeral, and his private possessions remained in the hands of his family.

Until today, Bedreddin's role in the rebellions is not clear. This is partly so because research on the social upheaval itself remains insufficient, and partly because the image of Şeyh Bedreddin has acquired a mysterious quality not without a certain impact even on academic research. The author of the entry "Badr al-Din b. Qadi Samawna" in the highly esteemed *Encyclopaedia of Islam* states: "Here (in Iznik) Badr al-Din began to correspond with Börklüce Mustafa and Torlaq Hu Kemal, who were the instigators of a rebellion ... in western Anatolia, based on the revolutionary ideas of Badr al-Din."[8] Saygın Salgırlı, however, provides in his article on the rebellions a completely different perspective: Şeyh Bedreddin and his comrades Börklüce and Torlak were only three of many other "agents involved in an intensified process of social change."[9] Salgırlı further argues that Bedreddin's works, even his *Wāridāt*[10] (*Intuitive Revelations*, turk. *Varidat*) which differs greatly in content from the rest of his writings and might be the product of his followers, never call for rebellion and heresy but include at times

6 Karatas, "Badr al-Dīn b. Qāḍī Samāwnā".

7 Saygın Salgırlı, "The Rebellion of 1416. Recontextualizing an Ottoman Social Movement", *Journal of the Economic and Social History of the Orient* 55: 1 (2012), 32–73, 55.

8 Karatas, "Badr al-Dīn b. Qāḍī Samāwnā".

9 Salgırlı, "The Rebellion of 1416", 56.

10 For the first translation of the Arabic text into Ottoman Turkish see Mehmed Serhan Tayşi, ed., *Simavna Kadısı Oğlu Şeyh Mahmud Bedreddin, Vâridât-ı Bedreddin*, transl. by Musa Kâzım Efendi, Istanbul: MVT 2010. Version in modern Turkish: Şeyh Bedreddin, *Varidat*, Istanbul: Midas Kitap 2013.

scholarly and at times more Sufic views and ponderings.[11] Salgırlı concludes that historical details are of lesser importance when it comes to the emergence of the image as we know it today. It was the Ottoman government which created the immortal hero when they hanged him. "Regardless of what or who he might have been before, Bedreddin was, from that moment on, an icon, historically and historiographically."[12]

Bedreddin was interred in Serres which is today part of Northern Greece. Since this region was affected by the forced population exchange between Turkey and Greece in 1923/1924, Bedreddin's remains were exhumed in 1924, taken to Istanbul and later reinterred in the Conqueror's Mosque (Fatih Camii).[13]

Bedreddin, the Saint of the Poor and Oppressed

> Şeyh Bedreddin is a great Muslim scholar .... As we know, Nazım Hikmet wrote an epic. Nazım Hikmet, in his book *The Epic of Şeyh Bedreddin*, portrays the Sufi as someone who burns down and destroys in order to protest against the established order. Nazım and other leftists have even tried to depict Şeyh Bedreddin as an Anatolian communist. When the leftists tried to appropriate Şeyh Bedreddin for their own cause, they created a distance between the Muslims and him.[14]

This quote by Durali Yılmaz, a Turkish scholar of Turkish literature with a religious-nationalist political stance and author of a Bedreddin novel,[15] is a paradigmatic example of those who defend the 'true' Şeyh Bedreddin, the Islamic scholar and judge. It is easy to find many further examples of publications with a similar message throughout the 20th century, while after the millennium the number of (academic) papers in the same vein has almost exploded.[16] The proponents of the revolutionary sheikh, however, have not ceased for their part either, to celebrate his everlasting power and significance for today's Turkey, or to condemn him for his seditious nature. Thus we are confronted with basically three categories of Bedreddin narratives: Bedreddin the scholar, only falsely accused as an instigator; Bedreddin the instigator and villain, or in modern publications the communist, in an equally negative sense; and finally Bedreddin the (mystically inspired) rebel

11 Salgırlı, "The Rebellion of 1416", 56.

12 Ibid., 68–69.

13 Franz Babinger, "Das Grabmal des Schejchs Bedr ed-Din zu Serres", *Der Islam* 17: 1 (1928), 100–102.

14 N. a., „Şeyh Bedreddin'in sol ile ilgisi yok", *Vakit* (2 November 2002), www.davetci.com/d_soylesi/rop_dyilmaz.htm (last access 23.01.2018). Unless stated otherwise, all translations are mine.

15 Durali Yılmaz, *Şeyh Bedrettin. Sufinin İsyanı*, Istanbul: Ataç 2001.

16 To give just one recent example: Filiz Duman, "İslam İnancını Şeyhlerle Tahrif Etmek: Şeyh Bedreddin Örneği", *Eleştirel Bakış Dergisi* 1 (2016), 45–72.

for the just cause. I will focus in the following on those publications which declare the sheikh a communard, a leftist leader in the widest sense, and/or a fighter for economic justice out of religious conviction, be it Alevi or Sunni.

Narratives and Texts prior to Nazım Hikmet's Epic

Simavne kadısı oğlu Şeyh Bedreddin Destanı

In 1936, the Turkish poet Nazım Hikmet (1902–1963) published his fifty-page poem on Şeyh Bedreddin, *Simavne kadısı oğlu Şeyh Bedreddin Destanı.*[17] The Turkish literary critic Talat Halman calls it "one of the master poems of this century",[18] and Salgırlı sees the poem as "the turning point" in the reception of the sheikh since it made him an "ideological battleground ... from one end of the political spectrum to the other".[19]

Nazım Hikmet, the "Romantic Communist",[20] was obviously fascinated by Bedreddin's story: Not only in the *Epic* but in many other cases the poet mentions the rebel's name, often in the same line with other exemplary figures of the–from Nazım Hikmet's perspective–*national* Anatolian history, such as the Sufi poet Yunus Emre (13th/14th c.), or the Ottoman architect Sinan (1490–1588). One may wonder why *the* communist author of the early Turkish Republic was so intrigued by the life of an Ottoman state servant and religious scholar with a tendency towards heretic readings of the Quran and Sufi teachings. The answers to this question are manifold. In the following paragraphs, I will touch on Nazım Hikmet's own literary and political answers as well as on sources which most probably had inspired the poet. The analysis of these earlier texts and discourses will show that even if the *Epic* was indeed a masterpiece and a turning point, Nazım Hikmet had not created an entirely new topic but rather taken up a story which had emerged in its basic form in the late 19th century and which owes much of its content to both the emerging socialist discourse in the Ottoman Empire and the interest in the Bedreddin story of academics, politicians and romantic poets writing in German.

Nazım Hikmet created the *Epic,* which consists of different text sorts such as poetry, prose and theatrical scenes, and includes folkloric subjects as well

17 Nâzım Hikmet, *Simavne Kadısı Oğlu Şeyh Bedreddin Destanı,* illustr. by Suavi Sonar, Istanbul: Yeni Kitabcı 1936.

18 Talât Sait Halman, *The Turkish Muse: Views & Reviews, 1960s–1990s,* Syracuse: Syracuse Univ. Press 2006, 92.

19 Salgırlı, "The Rebellion of 1416", 35.

20 Saime Göksu and Edward Timms, *Romantic Communist: The Life and Work of Nazım Hikmet,* Basingstoke: Palgrave Macmillan 1999.

as socialist statements, during his detention in the prison of Bursa from 1933 to 1935. The dire conditions in the prison, the hope for a better, communist tomorrow and the poet's interest in historical subjects intersect in the text. The fictional author, afflicted by migraine and the suffering of his co-inmates, enters into a dream-like mood, which transports him to the time of Bedreddin's revolt and allows him to narrate the events as an eyewitness. The pride, power and pain of the medieval revolutionaries are constantly re-connected to the 'present' situation. When the narrator awakes from his dream and tells his inmates what he has experienced, a discussion emerges as to whether this was reality or fantasy. It is fascinating to see that the author Nazım Hikmet, as early as 1935, ridicules the quest for *reality* of modern, and particularly leftist-realist, literature: At the end of the text, the riddle remains unsolved. Creative fantasy appears to be as productive as proletarian action.

The *Epic* is framed by a "self-reflexive"[21] prose introduction which provides a fictional, literary explanation regarding the choice of the topic–the *Schreibanlass*–and the circumstances of the writing process. "I was reading 'The Simavne Governor's Son Bedreddin,' a treatise written by Mehmet Sherefeddin Effendi, Professor of Scripture at the University's School of Theology ..."[22]

The book mentioned had indeed been published in 1924/25 by the said person,[23] and this intertextuality allows the first-person-narrator not only to immediately make fun of two religious scholars, a Christian monk and a Byzantine historiographer, Dukas and his Muslim counterpart, Mehmed Şerafeddin, both described as neither handsome nor pleasant; but it also allows the author to present his key ideas in the text's second paragraph. This second paragraph of the *Epic* is a quote from the historiography of Dukas (1400–1462), repeated in Şerafeddin's treaty:

> In those days there appeared ... to the east opposite Chios, a simple-minded Turkish peasant. He taught the Turks that they must own no property and decreed that, with the exception of women, everything must be shared in common–provisions, clothing, yokes of beasts, and fields. "I shall have access to your house as though it were mine and you shall have access to my house as though it were yours, with the exception of the female members."[24]

It is important to note that this quote which inspired and angered so many authors originates from Dukas' chronic, not from an Ottoman source. While Aşıkpaşa focuses on Börklüce's claim to be the righteous ruler and

21 Göksu, Timms, *Romantic Communist*, 128.

22 Nazım Hikmet, *The Epic of Sheik Bedreddin*, 26.

23 Mehmed Şerefüddin [Yaltkaya], *Simavne Kadısıoğlu Şeyh Bedreddin*, Istanbul: Evkaf-ı İslamiyye Matbaası 1924.

24 [Michaēl] Dukas, *Byzantinoturkike historia: metaphrase - eisagoge – scholia*, Brasidas Karalēs, ed., Athens: Kanakes 1997. Doukas, *Decline and Fall of Byzantium to the Ottoman Turks*, transl. by Harry J. Magoulias, Detroit: Wayne State Univ. Press 1975, 120.

on the messianic hope of his followers, the author of the *Menakıbname* concentrates on Bedredddin's miracles and denies any relation between the same and the instigators.[25] Thus, Dukas is the source and blueprint for the probably best-known quatrain of the *Epic*, quoted earlier.

What is ignored in most interpretations of the *Epic*, is Nazım Hikmet's emphasis on the deplorable attitudes of both Islam and the bourgeoisie towards women, right at the beginning of the text. He not only asks rhetorically "Is not a woman in the eyes of Islamic theology a commodity?" but also quotes "two sentences of Marx and Engels": "The bourgeois sees his wife a mere instrument of production. He hears that the instruments of production are to be exploited in common, and, naturally, can come to no other conclusion that the lot of being common to all will likewise fall to the women."[26] The poet turns to this topic because of the Muslim scholar Şerafeddin's critique of Dukas' statement that the rebels excluded women from common possessions. This, according to Şerafeddin, is nothing but a willful deception (*takiyye*), since it is very unlikely that a follower of (the heretic concept) of the Unity of the Existing (*vahdeti mevcud*)[27] as Börklüce Mustafa was, would ever propose such a rule.

The introduction of the *Epic of Sheik Bedreddin* provides a first hint at the degree of popularity the Bedreddin story obviously enjoyed in those years. Mehmed Şerafeddin Efendi [Yaltkaya] was not just *a* theologian. He was one of those who represented the new Islam of the young Turkish Republic: He taught at the newly established Faculty of Theology at what would later become the Istanbul University, he led the funeral service for Mustafa Kemal Atatürk, and he became the second president of the likewise newly created Presidency of Religious Affairs (*Diyanet İşleri Başkanlığı*), the body which was to control religious life in Turkey and propagate a state-supporting Turkish Islam. In this capacity, he not only wrote the aforementioned article but also later became the author of the entry on Şeyh Bedreddin in the Turkish ver-

---

25 Friedrich Giese, *Die altosmanische Chronik des ʿĀšıḳpašazāde auf Grund mehrerer neuentdeckter Handschriften*, Leipzig: Otto Harrassowitz 1929, 81–82; Kissling, "Das Menaqybname", 169.

26 Karl Marx, Frederick Engels, *Manifesto of the Communist Party*, authorized translation, New York: Labor News Co. 1908. The Turkish Islamist-nationalist author Necip Fazıl Kısakürek (1905–1983) plods his way through the same passage in his *Batı Tefekkürü ve Islâm Tasâvvufu* [Western Thinking and Islamic Mysticism], a collection of talks from 1962 (Istanbul: Büyük Doğu Yayınları 1982, 71–72). In the same volume, Kısakürek mentions the *Epic of Sheik Bedreddin*, saying that "the misguidance of Şeyh Bedreddin is (not a question of being a communist but) a completely different matter" (ibid., 49).

27 While most sources mention the influence of *vahdeti vücud* (*waḥdat al-wujūd*) as it was taught by Ibn Arabi (1165–1240) on Bedreddin, Şerafeddin uses *vahdeti mevcut* (*waḥdat al-mawjūd*) in a pejorative sense with implicit reference to other "unruly" (Ahmet T. Karamustafa) Sufis such as Manṣūr al-Ḥallādj (858–922).

sion of the *Encyclopaedia of Islam*[28] and set the tone of the modernist-theological Bedreddin reception for the following decades. Şerafeddin Efendi describes the sheikh as both an outstanding scholar and a revolutionary with pseudo-Sufic concepts and tendencies towards high treason, who had made common cause with the Mongols and the non-Turkish non-Muslims in the region. Şerafeddin's perspective would deserve an analysis of its own.

The encyclopedic entry from 1949 no longer mentions the matter of "common possession". This circumstance deserves all the more attention as the narrative on shared possession and its use in Şerafeddin's treaty had caused a little plagiarism dispute inside the Ottomanist community. The German Ottomanist Franz Babinger (1891–1967) had presented a lengthy study on Bedreddin and his time in 1921[29] including a translation of the notorious Dukas quote. The article was partly translated into Turkish the same year.[30] Şerafeddin Efendi, however, never mentions Babinger's name although he clearly copied the lines of Dukas from Köprülüzade's translation of Babinger's text. (In the encyclopedic entry, Şerafeddin Efendi gives exclusively his own Bedreddin study as secondary source.) Among the later scholars touching on the affair[31], Hans Joachim Kissling (1912–1985) calls Şerafeddin's behavior "monopolization of a subject and a case of scientific chauvinism"[32]. This short sketch of Bedreddin studies in the 1920s enables us to better understand how much competition there must have been between the Turkish and the foreign scholars in this field. If one was further to ponder the reasons for this intensive interest in Bedreddin, the timeframe–the end of the First World War, the Turkish Liberation war and the early years of the Republic–would certainly have to be taken into account.

From Dukas to Navshirvano

With regard to the focus of this article, it was important to show that Nazım Hikmet took up a very popular topic and, almost more important, that there was a close exchange between scholars writing in Turkish and German. This gains more significance if we continue our backward journey to even earlier modern publications. Prior to the Turkish novelists of the 20th century, German authors with a romantic interest in the Ottoman Em-

28 Mehmed Şerafeddin Yaltkaya, "Bedreddin Simavi", *İslam Ansiklopedisi*, vol. 2, Istanbul: Millî Eğitim Basımevi 1949, 444–446.

29 Franz Babinger, "Bedr ed-din, der Sohn des Richters von Simaw", *Der Islam. Zeitschrift für Geschichte und Kultur des Islamischen Orients* 1: 11 (1921), 1–106.

30 Köprülüzade Ahmed Cemal, *Dergah Mecmuası* 24 (1921), 183–185.

31 So İsmet Sungurbey in his introduction („Önsöz") to Abdülbâki Gölpınarlı, *Sımavna Kadısıoğlu Şeyh Bedreddin*, Istanbul: Eti Yayınevi 1966, I–IX, II–III.

32 Kissling, "Das Menaqybname", 112.

pire and mysterious movements had discovered the story of Şeyh Bedreddin, Börklüce and Torlak.[33] Johannes Scherr, who bases his historiographical fiction on Dukas' chronic, appears to be the first author who characterized Börklüce's alleged preaching of shared possession as "Communism".[34] "We can see," writes Scherr, "that in addition to the dire conditions of that time, a muddle of Islamic-Persian, Jewish and Christian Mysticism triggered the emergence of an at least memorable attempt at a religious and social revolution."[35] Beyond that, he continues, Börklüce's communism features a higher morality than Jacobinical or other forms of communism because it holds matrimony in high esteem.[36]

A further example of German authors' interest in Börklüce's instigation is "Böreklidsche Mustapha, ein muhamedanischer Kommunist" from 1900 by I. Schiraki.[37] "I. Schiraki" is the pseudonym of Friedrich Schrader (1865–1922) and a–somewhat awkward–pun: Schrader was a Social Democrat and journalist who spent more than 20 years of his life in Istanbul.[38] His pseudonym alludes to the Arabic and Ottoman word for socialist, *ishtirākī*. The political aim of Schrader's article which was published in a newspaper of the Social Democratic Party is manifest. He describes Islamic mysticism as a continuation of neo-Platonism–an "old heathen spirit" which does not allow an individual to rise above the other. Bedreddin is a Mevlevi Sufi master and Börklüce's teacher, while Börklüce's movement is "aimed at social and religious reform".[39] Börklüce is a heroic figure fighting for Christian and Muslim peasants alike: It was his firm conviction that only the abrogation of private property would stop humankind from destroying each other.[40] Schrader, who mastered the Ottoman language so well that he was able

33 Leopold Schefer, *Der Gekreuzigte, oder: Nichts Neues unter der Sonne*, Berlin: Veit und Comp. 1857; Johannes Scherr, „Ein türkischer Heiland", in: *Dämonen*, Johannes Scherr, Leipzig: Otto Wigand 1871, 69–129.

34 From the perspective of national romanticism in the 19th century, Philhellenism and Orient romantic are easily conflated. So Schefer and Scherr are obviously attracted by the 'Hellenic heritage' in the form of Dukas' account, and by the multicultural setting of Western Anatolia and Thrace.

35 Scherr, "Türkischer Heiland", 99.

36 Ibid., 100.

37 I. Schiraki <Friedrich Schrader> (1900), "Böreklidsche Mustapha, ein muhamedanischer Kommunist", *Volksstimme. Sozialdemokratisches Organ für Magdeburg und Umgegend. Die neue Welt. Illustrierte Unterhaltungsbeilage*, 104: 11 (6. Mai 1900), 139–140; 110: 11 (13. Mai 1900), 147–150.

38 Ceyda Nurtsch provides a short biography of Schrader ("Porträt des deutschen Orientalisten Friedrich Schrader. Der Chronist vom Bosporus", *Qantara* 22.6.2018, https://de.qantara.de/inhalt/portraet-des-deutschen-orientalisten-friedrich-schrader-der-chronist-vom-bosporus, last access 26.06.2018).

39 Ibid., 139.

40 Ibid., 150.

to translate an Ottoman novel into German,[41] includes in his article not only the familiar ideas of Dukas but also refers to Ottoman sources. He even criticizes Johannes Scherr for writing "buffoonery" ("Hanswurstiade") for a particular readership, the "liberal-democratic Philistines", since the author allegedly used the Italian translation of a chronicle by Hoca Sadeddin (d. 1599),[42] an Ottoman scholar, and in this capacity, in Schrader's opinion, not a suitable source for neutral and just historiography.[43] We cannot say who or which publication had finally inspired Schrader to make use of this subject; but we can argue it was likely that someone who was so active in the intellectual scene of Istanbul would take up and disseminate popular topoi and narratives of his time. It is further important to note that despite Schrader's awareness of Ottoman sources, he still focuses on Börklüce, as Dukas did, and not on Bedreddin, as Nazım Hikmet would do some thirty years later.

At present, we do not possess sufficient documents in order to understand how the Ottoman (proto-)socialists[44] themselves used Bedreddin or Börklüce in their political activities. Mete Tunçay states, however, that "long before [1927], some persons had traced the pedigree of Turkey's left back to Bedreddin"[45]. In 1927, still a decade earlier than Nazım Hikmet, Tunçay continues, a Turkish communist who was well acquainted with the poet published an article on the situation of the peasantry where he referred to Şeyh Bedreddin's movement as being based on economic and social equality and inclined to communism.[46]

As Tunçay correctly claims, during the late Ottoman era and in the early Turkish Republic, Islamic and socialist movements were not necessarily adversaries. While socialist politicians would express respect for Muslim ritu-

41 Halide Edib [Adıvar]'s *Yeni Turan*, 1912, transl. as *Das Neue Turan. Ein türkisches Frauenschicksal*, Weimar: Kiepenheuer 1916.

42 Hoca Sadeddin, *Tac-ü Tevarih*. Schrader hints at a different source which includes the German chronicler Johannes Löwenklau's (1541–1596) *Neue Chronica türkischer Nation von Türken selbst beschrieben*, Frankfurt 1595. The analysis of the relation between the said texts would constitute a separate research. For a first impression see Johannes Heinrich Mordtmann, „Notiz über den türkischen Kalender der Heilbronner Gymnasialbibliothek", *Der Islam* 10 (1920), 157–160.

43 Schiraki, „Böreklidsche Mustapha", 147.

44 The first Socialist Party in the Ottoman Empire was founded in 1910 (*Osmanlı Sosyalist Fırkası*). For the earlier political discourse, beginning in the 19th century, see Christoph Neumann, "Mazdak, nicht Marx: Frühe osmanische Wahrnehmungen von Kommunismus und Sozialismus", in: *Türkische Wirtschafts- und Sozialgeschichte von 1071 bis 1920*, Hans Georg Majer, Raoul Motika, eds., Wiesbaden: Otto Harrassowitz 1995, 211–225.

45 Mete Tunçay, *Türkiye'de Sol Akımlar 1925–1936*, Istanbul: İletişim Yayınları 2009 (1978), 55.

46 Ibid.

als and faith,[47] movements based on a religious identity were often inclined to adopt discourses of (economic) justice or to openly support socialist principles.

An example of a socialist approach which is based on Muslim history is the activity of the Navshirvanos, a Volga Tatar couple that supported the establishment of a communist party in the early Turkish Republic.[48] In their opinion, anti-feudal and communist trends can be detected throughout Muslim history while Bedreddin's upheaval constituted the peak of such trends. Bedreddin's "disciples led peasant rebellions against Ottoman rule and set up what the Navshirvanovs called the 'first revolutionary government of Anatolia'".[49]

From a primarily Muslim and Ottoman but emphatically reformist point of view, the historiographer Mizancı Mehmed Murad (1854–1917) regards Bedreddin as an exemplary fighter for the greatly needed reform of the Ottoman state and its religious class.[50] Mizancı Mehmed Murad was a newspaper journalist, the founder of his own newspaper *Mizan* (*Balance*) and the author of numerous volumes dealing with the past and the future of the Ottoman Empire. The programmatic approach of his historiographical publication *Tarih-i Ebül Faruk* is discernible from its subtitle: "An endeavor to analyze the proper meaning of Ottoman history with regard to politics and civilization". By means of an analytical look back, political mistakes and future reforms would become observable. The Ottoman State needed, Murad argued, a fundamental religious reform–a return to the genuine teachings and practices of the early days of Islam–and some kind of political democratization with equality among the citizens and parliamentary representation. Şeyh Bedreddin and his–rather extreme–comrades Börklüce and Kemal Torlak had been fighting for equality among Christians, Jews, and Muslims, and for the protection of God's creation. Since God had given the world as a gift to humankind, everybody was entitled to a just share of possessions and the harvest.[51] In his work on the reception of the Bedreddin subject, Ahmet Cerrahoğlu concludes that although Mizancı Mehmed Murad did not nourish sympathy for socialism, he believed in the congruence of Quranic and communist principles such as shared possessions, so-

---

47 Mete Tunçay, *Türkiye'de Sol Akımlar 1908–1925*, Ankara: Ankara Üniversitesi 1978³, 44.

48 Michael Kemper, "The Soviet Discourse on the Origin and Class Character of Islam, 1923–1933", *Die Welt des Islams* 49: 1 (2009), 1–48, 6–7. See also Manfred Sing, "The Tempestuous Affair between Marxism and Islam: Attraction, Hostility, and Accommodation since 1917", in this volume.

49 Kemper, "The Soviet Discourse on the Origin and Class Character of Islam", 7.

50 Mizancı Mehmed Murad, *Tarih-i Ebül Faruk*, vol. 1, Istanbul: Maṭba'a-sı Āmedī 1907, 237.

51 Ibid.

cial equality and love of peace.[52] The influence of Murad's ideas can be discerned in the writings of later religious authors, e.g. the Bektashi dervish (Baba) Ahmet Rıfkı (1884–1935). With reference to Murad, Ahmet Rıfkı calls Bedreddin "a martyr for truth" while Börklüce's *tarikat* (mystic community) promised equality, collective ownership, the unity of all religions and denominations, and freedom.[53]

From the examples given up to this point, it has become obvious that at least from the beginning of the 20th century on, the narrative of Bedreddin and Börklüce as exemplary fighters for freedom, peace and equality has been a very popular and productive one in political discourse. When Nazım Hikmet published his artistic version of the account, he could trust on his readers' familiarity with the topic, and on the image Bedreddin already had among the progressive readership. To mention Mehmed Şerafeddin Efendi's *Simavne Kadısı oğlu Bedreddin* at the beginning of his *Şeyh Bedreddin Epic* was not necessary in the sense of providing needed information to the readers. It can be regarded as a literary strategy with the aim to put the readers' expectations on the right track. The subtext is that the *Epic* will praise Bedreddin the worldly revolutionary, and not the distorted figure of Islamic chroniclers.

Narratives and Texts after the Epic

In the decades after Nazım Hikmet's *Epic*, the academic and literary production on Şeyh Bedreddin once again increased. Today, there exists a countless number of novels, dramas, films, and popular and academic research publications. The engagement with the 'true nature' of Şeyh Bedreddin, however, had been obstructing serious historical research on the upheavals as such and the political and economic background, including Börklüce Mustafa and Torlak Hu Kemal for a long time. Only recently has this lacuna started to attract due attention in academic research and publications.[54]

From the 1960s onwards, the literary engagement with Bedreddin as the savior of the poor and the oppressed increased. However, the twofold character of Bedreddin as a religious, sometimes messianic, and worldly revolutionary character fueled the emergence of rather diverse readings, even

52 Ahmet N. Cerrahoğlu, *Şeyh Bedreddin ve Türkiye'de Sosyalizm Hareketleri*, Istanbul: Gün Matbaası 1966, 25.
53 Ibid., 31–32.
54 Salgırlı, "The Rebellion of 1416"; Alp Yücel Kaya, Mehmet Kuyurtar, Saygın Salgırlı et al., eds., *Uluslararası Börklüce Mustafa Sempozyumu [2–5 Haziran 2016]. Bildiriler*, Izmir: Egeus Matbaacılık 2017.

within the 'progressive' sector. Nazım Hikmet alluded, tongue-in-cheek, to this irresolvable tension when his first-person-narrator of the *Epic* reflects:

> Now, years later, as I write these lines, I think of the theology professor. ... if he's alive and reads what I write, he'll say: 'What a fake! He claims to be a materialist and then, like the Cretan monk, goes on–and centuries after the event!–about talking with [Börklüce] Mustafa's disciple who silently crosses seas.'[55]

For this reason, it is not astonishing that authors with both religious and progressive agenda are attracted to the Bedreddin story as a historical exemplar. Before examining these, I would like first to introduce two authors who see themselves as materialists in the political sense. I do this, because certain interrelations in the reception perspective can be seen.

Şeyh Bedreddin as Materialist

An edited volume–*History, Utopia, Upheaval. Şeyh Bedreddin*–demonstrates the breadth of the progressive spectrum which appropriates Bedreddin as their representative, while only a careful reading of the respective articles reveals the interpretative differences.[56] Ernst Werner (1920–1993), to start with, was a medievalist, head of the University of Leipzig and member of the Socialist Unity Party of Germany (Sozialistische Einheitspartei Deutschlands, SED) and in this capacity a representative of socialism as it was understood in Eastern Germany. The German original version of his publication on Bedreddin[57] demonstrates his political message more clearly than the here-and-there 'softened' version in Çoban's collection[58]. Werner's approach is characterized by a sometimes anti-Ottoman sometimes anti-Turkish bias. Bedreddin's insurrection is seen as the last and failed chance to rescue Greeks and Slavs from the "despotic Turcocratia". Bedreddin himself was not interested in an abolition of the ruling class; that is why he escaped torture, unlike Börklüce, and his blood was not shed, but rather he was hanged, since he was still a member of the Muslim nobility.[59] Werner's description of the agricultural system and the solidarity between the peasants who adhered to Börklüce, reads like a description of an ideal communist society: The peasants work in "production communities" ("Produktionsgemeinschaften") in "spontaneous self-help". What

---

55 Nazım Hikmet, *The Epic of Sheik Bedreddin*, 33.

56 Barış Çoban, ed., *Tarih, Ütopya, İsyan. Şeyh Bedreddin: Yaşamı, Felsefesi, İsyanı*, Istanbul: Su Yayınları 2011.

57 Ernst Werner, *Ketzer und Weltverbesserer: zwei Beiträge zur Geschichte Südosteuropas im 13. und 15. Jahrhundert* (Sitzungsberichte der Sächsischen Akademie der Wissenschaften zu Leipzig, Philologisch-Historische Klasse; 116,5), Berlin: Akademie-Verlag 1974.

58 Ernst Werner, "Bedreddin Hareketi", in: Çoban, *Tarih*, 11–35.

59 Werner, *Ketzer*, 57.

Dukas describes can be called "consumer communism" ("Verbraucherkommunismus").[60] But most importantly, Bedreddin "transgressed the borders of theology and professed an atheist-materialist worldview, which makes him an outstanding thinker," although he could not openly propagate atheism, since the time had not yet come.[61]

A different viewpoint, that of an academic Marxist literary critic, is illustrated in Nedim Gürsel's (1951–) paper,[62] which reflects Gürsel's theoretical approach of the 1970s, an approach he had acquired during his Studies of Literature at the Sorbonne in Paris 1971–1979. During this time, he published a short monograph which is still the most profound analysis of the *Epic* of Nazım Hikmet.[63] Gürsel combined a historical contextualization both of Bedreddin's movement and Nazım Hikmet's epic, with, as he says, a linguistic approach. To write a Marxist critique of a text by a communist author means for Gürsel to analyze the *Epic* both as a poem and as an ideological field which reflects the class struggle to which Nazım Hikmet gave a concrete form based on the poet's reading of history.[64] With his cross-disciplinary and careful approach, Gürsel is able to identify the multiple layers of the *Epic*. Just one example: according to Gürsel, the *Epic* was published at a time when the idea of a 'class-less state' had already become an organic part of Kemalist ideology[65] and when, coincidently, the state power did not protect the peasantry but rather the private land owners. The insurrection of Bedreddin which can be considered an expression of the cleavage between the peasant class and the state, can be likened to the situation of 1936 when the state was a key player in an otherwise unrestricted capitalistic system, and the repeatedly promised land reform once again turned into an unreachable fata morgana.[66]

Gürsel's interest in Nazım Hikmet and the *Epic* seems at first glance to originate from Gürsel's identification with Hikmet's political stance and

60 Ibid., 50.

61 Ibid., 43–44.

62 Nedim Gürsel, "Thomas Münzer, Şeyh Bedreddin ve Nazım Hikmet", in: Çoban, *Tarih*, 55–67.

63 Nedim Gürsel, *Şeyh Bedreddin Destanı Üzerine*, Istanbul: Cem Yayınevi 1978.

64 Ibid., 9.

65 The concept of the Turkish Republic as a class-less state is usually equaled to the Kemalist principle of Populism (*halkçılık*). It can be considered however an approach fundamental to all other concepts and to the political practice of Turkey until today. It epitomizes the fear of any kind of differences in society and state, and rejects any attempt to articulate openly differing needs, expectations and ideals inside the 'Turkish' society.

66 Gürsel, *Şeyh Bedreddin*, 19. On the failure of the State Economy model (Etatism, turk. *devletçilik*) and the political power of the affluent class in Turkey of the 1930s see Basak Kus, "Weak States, Unruly Capitalists, and the Rise of Étatism in Late Developers: The Case of Turkey", *British Journal of Middle Eastern Studies* 42: 3 (2015), 358–374.

significance as *the* leftist poet. If we are to follow Gürsel's literary development and particularly his more recent novels such as *Allahın Kızları* (*The Daughters of Allah*) or *Yedi Dervişler* (*The Seven Dervishes*),[67] however, we will find a further interest the two authors have in common: While both would characterize themselves as decidedly atheistic authors, they display a keen interest in protagonists of religious history.

Bearing this aspect in mind, it should not surprize us that Gürsel in his monograph on the *Epic* also elaborated on an idea which had been discussed by earlier authors such as Ahmet Cerrahoğlu[68]: the similarity between the sheikh and Thomas Müntzer (1489–1525), the revolutionary plebeian among the religious reformists of the 14th/15th century. Based on his own and Nazım Hikmet's familiarity with Friedrich Engels' *Der deutsche Bauernkrieg*[69] (*The Peasant War in Germany*), and quotes from Şeyh Bedreddin's *Wāridāt*, Gürsel argues that neither Müntzer nor the sheikh believed in the afterworld. They located Hell and Paradise in the here and now, and aimed to overcome economic inequality. (On the same page, Gürsel mentions that both authors leaned towards messianic expectations while he does not bother to analyze or comment on the contradiction between a messianic hope and the rejection of a possible afterworld.)[70]

To equate Şeyh Bedreddin to Thomas Müntzer also means to reject any comparability between the sheikh and Martin Luther (1483–1546), the Catholic reformist whose aim had been "to establish the rule of his own class"[71]. This comparison had been made before by historiographers such as Mizancı Mehmed Murad.[72]

Alevi Authors on Şeyh Bedreddin

Çoban's edited volume on Bedreddin further includes two papers by *Alevi* authors. The Alevi community is the second largest religious community in Turkey after the Sunni Muslims, and is, grosso modo, a Muslim community. (Admittedly, this categorization finds more supporters inside Turkey than among the migrant communities elsewhere; there are also representatives of scriptural Islam who would strongly reject Alevi's *Islamity*.) To include Alevi authors in a collection of 'progressive' publications on Bedred-

67 Nedim Gürsel, *Allah'ın Kızları*, Istanbul: Doğan Kitap 2008; Nedim Gürsel, *Yedi Dervişler*, Istanbul: Doğan Kitap 2007.

68 Cerrahoğlu, *Şeyh Bedreddin*, 30.

69 Friedrich Engels, *Der deutsche Bauernkrieg*, Leipzig: Verlag der Expedition des „Volksstaat" 1870.

70 Gürsel, *Şeyh Bedreddin*, 94.

71 Ibid., 92.

72 Cerrahoğlu, *Şeyh Bedreddin*, 30.

din is justified, given the Alevi self-assessment as a fundamentally progressive community. How and why today's Alevi community/communities have come to locate themselves among the progressive and secular forces of Turkey which also defend social and religious equality, is a lengthy story which cannot be told here.[73] Yet, the two papers strikingly demonstrate the broad range of Alevi approaches to religious-political affairs: in this concrete case, the divergent readings of the Bedreddin story inside one 'religious current'.

Ali Yaman's paper[74] represents a major trend in the research on Alevism in Turkey which includes a long chain of renowned historians who have aimed to establish both a modern Turkish-national historiography and the embedding of religious currents other than mainstream-Sunni into Turkish (also pre-Ottoman and Republican) history.[75] Faithful to this tradition, but unlike his academic predecessors, Yaman, an Alevi himself, aims to rescue Bedreddin from ideological distortions of any kind.[76] To Yaman, Bedreddin is a significant and venerable member of this non-Sunni-mainstream current–"heterodox", as Yaman would say–and thus, he is a great master of Alevi history. His greatness is due to his learnedness and his readiness to die as a martyr for the cause of the oppressed, as has often been the fate of Alevi opposition. Yaman, however, is far from admiring any 'revolutionary' activities of Bedreddin. Yaman views the historical socio-economic circumstances as having made the peasantry look in despair for a messiah or any other savior; thus, they would follow unruly figures such as Börklüce for social rather than religious reasons. Bedreddin's activities were a part of the upheavals rather as a historical necessity, and the preaching of common possessions met his followers' hopes and expectations. Thus, according to Yaman, the story of Bedreddin demonstrates the weakness of the rulers during the Interregnum, including their negligence of the peasantry's hardship and the conflict between the "Orthodox Sufis and theologians"[77].

The popular publications on Alevi history and Alevi saints by the Turkish Archeologist and Byzantinist Ismail Kaygusuz, who is better known for his popular books on Alevism than for his academic oeuvre, can be character-

73 For the history of Alevism as a political and social movement see Elise Massicard, *The Alevis in Turkey and Europe: Identity and Managing Territorial Diversity*, London: Routledge 2013.

74 Ali Yaman, "Simavna Kadısı Oğlu Şeyh Bedreddin Üzerine", in: Çoban, *Tarih*, 69–92.

75 On the roots and effects of this historiographic current which includes names such as Paul Wittek (1894–1978) and Fuat Köprülü (1888–1966) see Markus Dreßler, *Writing Religion: The Making of Turkish Alevi Islam (Reflection and Theory in the Study of Religion)*, New York: Oxford University Press 2013; Rudi Paul Lindner, "Wittek and Köprülü", *Journal of the Royal Asiatic Society* 26: 1–2 (2016), 333–340.

76 Yaman, "Simavna Kadısı Oğlu", 69.

77 Ibid., 72.

ized by two main features: The first one is an eclectic approach to the history of religion combined with a rejection of the Turkish History Thesis.[78] Unlike in Ali Yaman's argumentation, it is not the Turkish and Anatolian history which provides the backdrop of Alevism but rather the religious history of the Middle East and the Thracian and Aegean borderlands with their numerous dissident, often esoteric and border-transgressing communities and beliefs throughout history. In this vein, he claims that Hacı Bektaş Veli, the eponym of the Bektaşi *tarikat*, was a missionary (*dāʿī*) for the so-called 'mysterious' Assassins, the Nizārī Ismāʿīlites of the 11th century, who had their center at the Alamut Castle in northern Persia.[79] The second feature is that Kaygusuz bases his *cause*, the spreading of *true* knowledge on Alevism on–in his own words–historical materialism, since only by this means can the immanent revolutionary character of Alevism be properly analyzed.[80] When it comes to Kaygusuz' reading of Şeyh Bedreddin, we will find the corresponding features. Kaygusuz enumerates a long list of historical personalities who had allegedly been in an exchange of ideas with Bedreddin. This list includes the 'usual' Sufi masters and historical figures with a Nizārī Ismāʿīlī background. What is more intriguing yet, is that Kaygusuz mentions Gemistos Plethon. In the middle of the 15th century, Plethon had founded a community or "sect" "as a means for attaining utopian sociopolitical ends"[81] in the Peloponnese. According to Kaygusuz, Plethon and Bedreddin who were both of Thracian origin, must have influenced each other in their writings and activities.[82] As far as I can see, Kaygusuz is the only Turkish, respectively Muslim author who refers specifically to this relation between the two outcasts, whereas other Turkish authors work with rather superficial terms such as "Christians", "Monks", "Greeks",[83] if they make reference to interreligious relations at all. Kaygusuz, however questionable his eclectic approach is accentuates, in this article, the supra-national and inter-religious character of his saints.

78 Markus Dreßler, *Die alevitische Religion. Traditionslinien und Neubestimmung*, Würzburg: Ergon 2002, 201.

79 İsmail Kaygusuz, "Kennen wir Hacı Bektaş Veli richtig? Hacı Bektaş Veli und das Hünkar Dergahı", in: *Ocak und Dedelik: Institutionen religiösen Spezialistentums bei den Aleviten*, Robert Langer, Hüseyin Ağuiçenoğlu, Janina Karolewski, eds., Frankfurt a.M.: Peter Lang 2013, 95–110.

80 İsmail Kaygusuz, *Görmediğim Tanrıya Tapmam. Alevilik ve Materyalizm*, Istanbul: Su Yayınları 2009.

81 Niketas Siniossoglou, "Sect and Utopia in Shifting Empires: Plethon, Elissaios, Bedreddin", *Byzantine and Modern Greek Studies* 36: 1 (2012), 38–55.

82 İsmail Kaygusuz, "Büyük Bilgin, Hukukçu ve Devrimci Simavna Kadısıoğlu Şeyh Bedreddin Mahmud", in: Çoban, *Tarih*, 93–130, 121.

83 E.g. Mehmet Yavuz, "Şeyh Bedreddin'in Alevi-Bektaşi Toplumundaki Yeri ve Alevi-Bektaşi Şairlerinde Şeyh Bedreddin Telmihi", *Civilacademy* 8: 3 (2010), 97–121, 101, 103.

Kaygusuz' "historical materialism" appears here as a defence of Bedreddin's indisputable but often neglected "communist" ("*komunistik*") worldview. Some of Beddredin's (alleged) writings contain an interpretative snare for Kaygusuz since they do not explicitly express what Bedreddin 'really believed'. Kaygusuz' solution to this conundrum is that those in power, worldly rulers and theologians, from time to time forced him to write certain treatises.[84] Even the *Wāridāt*, which is considered to be the most "anti" (anti-establishment, anti-ulema and anti-scripturalism) of Bedreddin's writings– and as mentioned at the beginning of this article, Bedreddin's authorship is not always recognized–does not mention the matter of "shared possessions". Never mind, argues Kaygusuz; the important point is that a broad variety of authors, the historiographer Dukas, the Ottoman judge Ebussuud Efendi (1490–1574) and many more, include the sermons by Bedreddin and Börklüce in their publications, and that is how we came to know eventually and despite all efforts of the establishment to veil the truth, that Bedreddin was a communist revolutionary.[85]

Kaygusuz ends his article with a reference to Thomas Müntzer. He quotes from Engels' *Peasant War*, and concludes: "We have presented the great theoretician of the German peasant wars, Thomas Münzer, [sic!] who Engels had discussed. But it became obvious that the social fights of the Esoteric Alevi peasants and the oppressed proletarians in Anatolia 270-280 years earlier are of a much greater significance. [If Engels had studied Bedreddin's thoughts], there is no doubt that, in that case Marxism and Marxist literature would have been far more developed than is the case today."[86]

Today, many Alevi publications and webpages mention Şeyh Bedreddin with divergent interpretations. What makes him attractive for the Alevi communities of today is the combination of several features which are also key elements of the Alevi umbrella narrative and which render him in turn an 'ideal Alevi': immortality resulting from his messianic character, his struggle and martyrdom for social and economic equality, his respect for all religions, and a morality which exceeds that of the powerful majority. What appeals to a younger Alevi generation is his *active* fight. While the traditional narrative describes the Alevi way as that of peaceful, quiet suffering, younger Alevis often criticize the glorification of that unsatisfying form of moral superiority, since it does not shelter the Alevis from atrocity and hate.[87] Bedreddin, the inspired fighter for a better world who nevertheless

---

84 Kaygusuz, "Büyük Bilgin, Hukukçu ve Devrimci", 97, 107.
85 Ibid., 100.
86 Ibid., 130.
87 One example of this enthusiasm among Alevi youngsters can be found at the webpage of the Alevi Youth Krefeld, "Yol Ustatları", www.aleviten-krefeld.de/Genclik.html (last access 21.12.2016).

ended up at the gallows seems to be a kind of compromise between the traditional and the revolutionary narratives.

Bedreddin and the New Anti-Capitalism

Since the turn of the millennium, democratization and reconciliation inside the society of Turkey and her political arena have seemed possible. Partly caused by the enhancement of EU-Turkey relations since 1999,[88] partly due to other internal conditions, the fierce societal cleavage between the secular Kemalist elite and 'the rest' began to lose its sharpness and exclusivist distinctiveness. Regarding religious affairs this meant that relations between hitherto as 'irreconcilable' imagined concepts such as 'Islam' and 'modernity', 'democracy' or 'plurality' obtained new qualities, and dialogue was no longer restricted to the representatives of kindred currents and worldviews. Moreover, new, transgressive conceptualizations appeared. One of these new concepts was that of Anti-capitalist Islam. İhsan Eliaçık (1961–), usually mentioned as its founding father,[89] started training at a faculty of Theology but left without graduating. Instead, he began a career as an independent journalist and publisher. From the beginning his books were devoted to religious issues and personalities, e.g. *İslam ve Sosyal Değişim* (*Islam and Social Change*) in 1994, or *Muhammed İkbal* in 2004.[90] His preaching went against the grain of an ever growing (Islamic) capitalism in Turkey, and his vivid and easy language obviously met the expectations of the readers. His increasing popularity peaked during the Gezi Park unrests in 2013 in Istanbul, when the banners of the Anti-capitalist Muslims were raised in the protest camp, and heralded the ideas of anti-capitalist Islam which were conveyed to other cities with the help of national and foreign broadcast channels. Irrespective of the fact stressed again and again by Anti-capitalist Muslims that Eliaçık is not the chairman of their movement, his fate and popularity have been directly related to the group's activities. For some, he should even be considered a link in the historical chain of Muslim fighters for social justice as the following quote demonstrates:

---

88 Atila Eralp, Asuman Göksel, Jakob Lindgaard, "Political Changes in Turkey and the Future of Turkey-EU Relations: From Convergence to Conflict?", FEUTURE Online Paper No. 12 (2017), www.feuture.uni-koeln.de/sites/feuture/pdf/D2.3_Online_Paper_No._12.pdf (last access 23.12.2017).

89 For more details on İhsan Eliaçık and the Anti-Capitalist Muslims see Bayram Koca's article "The Emergence of Anti-capitalist Muslims in Turkey: 'God, Bread, Freedom'" in this volume.

90 Whereas his first books were published at small publishing houses such as Bengisu, currently most of his books are (re-)printed at Doğu Yayınevi.

> Islamic movements today are not only pro-imperialist and pro-capitalist, but also antagonists of these phenomena. Throughout history, it has been observed that religion-based opposition to Western capitalism/imperialism could sometimes exist through religious movements such as liberation theology or religious fundamentalism... As the Karmatis opposed the Abbasid state in the 900s by establishing a system of common ownership, some other prominent figures of opposition appeared in the past, including *Sheikh Bedreddin* in the Ottoman Empire, Ali Shariati in Iran, Sayyid Qutb and Hassan Hanafi in Egypt, Mustafa al-Siba'i in Syria, Muhammad Baqir al-Sadr in Iraq, Mawdudi in Pakistan, and *Ihsan Eliacik* in Turkey. These prolific intellectuals produced a huge amount of work at the intersection of Islam and social justice.[91]

Eliaçık bases his entire work on the argument that the Quran has to be read as an anti-capitalist text: "Based on the teachings of the Qur'an, no social order founded on a monopoly of wealth and property can be regarded as Islamic or religious."[92] In his opinion, the Quran and hadiths do not allow the accumulation of wealth, and so Islam and Socialism are not antipodes but include the same values. The Turkish reception of Şeyh Bedreddin and his activities clearly mirrors, according to Eliaçık, the ideological misconceptions both of the Left and the Muslim establishment. Bedreddin was a socialist revolutionary as well as a high-ranking scholar of Islam and a true believer. The argument that Bedreddin criticized Islam and the ulema, and was therefore not a Muslim, ignores the fact that Bedreddin did not criticize Islam per se but "the Islam of the palace" (*saray İslamı*).[93] Bedreddin is part of the aforementioned chain of those who fought for social equality in Muslim history, beginning with Abū Ẕharr al-Ghifāri, 'the fourth convert to Islam'[94] and his "class character" cannot be doubted. His faith and his religious knowledge were so elevated that he could make those refrain from apostasy who had lost their faith because of Ottoman oppression and evildoing.[95] Eliaçık stresses that Bedreddin is *not* an Alevi saint but that he epitomizes the upheaval (*isyan*) of everybody who suffers from injustice, irrespective of religious or ethnic affiliation. In criticizing the Alevis' appropriation of Bedreddin as *their's*, Eliaçık's strategy is twofold: He speaks in the name of all groups who share his critical position against (Turkish) capitalism and the ruling establishment, in order to strengthen his own position

---

91 Emre Basci, "Islam and Capitalism: Current Islamist Modernities in Turkey", *International Journal of Scientific Research and Management* 5: 10 (2017), 7264–7269, 7265. The Italics are mine.

92 İhsan Eliaçık, "The Critique of Capitalism in the Light of Qur'anic Verses", *Studies in Christian Ethics* 28: 4 (2015), 391–401, 401.

93 Recep İhsan Eliaçık, *Şeyh Bedreddin*, Istanbul: Tekin 2017.

94 The significance of Abū Ẕarr in ʿAlī Sharīʿatī's concept is explored in Katajun Amirpur's article "Iranian Godfathers of Islamic Socialism – 'It Is the Marxists Who Have Learned It from Islam' " in this volume.

95 Eliaçık, *Şeyh Bedreddin*, 18.

(and indirectly that of the Anti-capitalist Muslims), while at the same time implying that his inclusivist reading of Şeyh Bedreddin is the only acceptable approach. Since both the Alevi community and the Anti-capitalist Muslims address, to some extent, the same segment of society, it is all the more important to justify the validity and singularity of his own position.

Eliaçık's reference to Nazım Hikmet and the *Epic* is of a peculiar sort: He quotes the famous line "… but the lover's cheek" without reference, but later he criticizes the poet saying that "You cannot learn about Şeyh Bedreddin from a classical atheist and leftist mouth. … I read … the epic, I learned about the uprising, but nothing about my faith; no, because it doesn't deal with (anything related to faith)."[96]

To sum up Eliaçık's position: *Bedreddin* was a revolutionary because of his faith; the roots of socialism, including the rejection of wealth accumulation, can be traced back to the values and thinkers of early Islam; Bedreddin is a revolutionary socialist Muslim.

A much more ambitious and learned Leftist-Muslim approach to Şeyh Bedreddin can be found in Tevfik Ziya's article "A Revolution against Chronological Time: Remembering Şeyh Bedreddin and Varidat" in a journal entitled *İştirakî* (*The Socialist*).[97] The article starts out with a quote from Walter Benjamin's *Theses on the Philosophy of History* (1940): "Nothing that has ever happened should be regarded as lost for history. To be sure, only a redeemed mankind receives the fullness of its past." While every ruler, in Tevfik's view, tries to build his hegemony on an imagined continuity of time–the timeframe of the ruler–, actually, as Benjamin said, events of the past are not lost in 'chronological time' but can reappear in the present. Revolutionary action needs to produce its own time, otherwise it is only reactive action.[98] Şeyh Bedreddin's upheaval 600 years ago, when the Ottoman ruler accumulated wealth and established a monopoly on political authority, has never lost its presence. Nazım Hikmet's *Epic* responds to this revolutionary timeline as it is structured in the form of a journey in time, while at the end of the text it is stated that Bedreddin will be resurrected with the breath of the peasants and the oppressed.[99] Şeyh Bedreddin and his comrades are making themselves heard even now. "Against the interpretation of time as a chronological continuity which rulers favor, one must pay attention to the added value of the revolutionary struggle which engenders ruptures reaching from now to the past and produces its own 'time'."[100]

96 Eliaçık, *Şeyh Bedreddin*, 15.
97 Tevfik Ziya, "Kronolojik Zamana Karşı Devrim: Şeyh Bedreddin ve Varidat'ı Hatırlamak", *İştirakî* 2: 10 (2016), 7–12.
98 Ziya, "Kronolojik Zamana Karşı Devrim", 7.
99 Ibid., 8.
100 Ibid., 12.

Conclusion

A quick search at the pages of a Turkish online-bookshop results in a list of 44–available!–books, not counting sold-out publications, related in one way or another to Şeyh Bedreddin. The result indicates that a scholar of Islamic law, sued and sent to the gallows in 1416, has become part of the cultural memory of Turkey. A short check of the book titles reveals that the story of Bedreddin cannot be considered the possession of one distinctive community or current; in fact, this story has been both shared and contested by a rather diverse readership throughout the last six centuries. Historiographers, established scholars of Muslim theology and scholars of Oriental Studies, philhellenes and 'orientophiles', socialists, leftist poets and anti-capitalist/establishment/inequality Muslims, have all managed to discover a Bedreddin who is *theirs*. The resonance and reverberations of these multiple voices constitute what I call here "the story of Bedreddin". The story includes diverse historical figures and landscapes, perspectives and foci; that is, differing narratives which cohere to form a story.

The article endeavored to track the evolution of the story of Bedreddin and the related narratives as they have been told among progressive authors, poets, and preachers. What connects the members of this group is the conviction that Şeyh Bedreddin was indeed a venerable revolutionary who fought for the poor and who propagated shared possession of all material goods as a remedy for poverty and political oppression. However, beyond this common conviction, there exists a broad range of opinions regarding the correct understanding of the sheikh, his activities, and the related circumstances, even within this progressive grouping. This is not so remarkable if one bears in mind how many currents, movements or communities in Turkey would identify themselves as progressive. There exist intersectional areas of moral values and ideals: the longing for a just world, the belief in a duty to change the world for the better, the demand for a democratic, pluralistic political system and a certain criticism of an (unrestricted) capitalist market–these basics could be detected among Alevis as well as among Non-Capitalist Muslims or leftist literary critics. The consensus ends however when it comes to the definition of the *true*, underlying identity, or even 'cultural roots', of Bedreddin. While Bedreddin is hailed for his respect and love towards all ethnicities and religions, the foundation of this respect is thought to be a distinctive and exclusivist identity.

What is more intriguing than the existence of 'different Bedreddins' is, in my opinion, the agency that a single thought, or a line, has developed throughout history. Dukas' words, "He taught the Turks that they must own no property and decreed that, with the exception of women, everything must be shared in common–provisions, clothing, yokes of beasts, and fields"[101] inspire later authors, for good or for bad, and find their poetic expression in Nazım Hikmet's formula "... but the lover's cheek!" Attention should be paid to at least two remarkable aspects of this matter. The first is that Dukas does not mention Bedreddin, but refers to Börklüce Mustafa, the "simple-minded Turkish peasant", and has him preach this message. In later texts, particularly those of Non-Muslim authors, the idea of collective ownership is again ascribed to Börklüce as he is the main figure of the upheavals. Nazım Hikmet eventually connects Şeyh Bedreddin and this quote inextricably when he calls his epic *Simavne kadısı oğlu Şeyh Bedreddin Destanı* and has an anonymous chorus say "yarin yanağından gayri her şeyde/her yerde/hep beraber!". From then on, "... but the lover's cheek!" has been Bedreddin's credo, be it in Nedim Gürsel's literary analysis or İhsan Eliaçık's sermon. Only recently have the social history of the numerous uprisings in Anatolia during the 14th/15th century and the historical background of Börklüce and the Torlaks started to attract fresh attention.[102]

The article introduced publications by several authors who covered one or the other narrative of the Bedreddin story. It is fascinating to realize that this story was written by authors of diverse historical, ethnic and religious backgrounds. As the examples of Gemistos Plethon or Thomas Müntzer as reference points have shown, the story produces a cultural map which connects the key cities of Muslim erudition with political hotspots of Christian history across the centuries. A major reason for this 'transnational' interest in Bedreddin can most certainly be found in the geography and historical period of the upheavals: Timurids, Ottomans, Byzantines, and Serbians fought for power in Western Anatolia, Thrace and the Southern Balkans, and they fought wars of succession and separatism inside their own dynasties. The historiographers of the related powers wrote down their perspectives in diverse languages, fascinated by the similarities of social movements at home and in the neighboring countries. Historiographical gazes across the border are more often than not a tool for criticizing the political circumstances at home. The issue of social justice which goes alongside political justice, and which is epitomized in the story of Bedreddin as it is told by progressive minstrels, is without a doubt a key issue for all societies, while in Turkey with the triumph of the hypercapitalism of a new Muslim elite, *wealth accumulation* has again obtained a quite topical explosiveness.

---

101 Doukas, *Decline and Fall of Byzantium to the Ottoman Turks*, 120.

102 Salgırlı, "The Rebellion of 1416"; Kaya, Kuyurtar and Salgırlı, *Uluslararası Börklüce Mustafa Sempozyumu*.

Part Four: Different Ways to Non-Capitalism

The Lure of Gold and Silver Dinars and Dirhams for the 21st Century*

Hans Visser

Islamic finance can be seen as a child of the Islamic revival that emerged at the end of the 19th century in the Middle East, in particular Egypt. Prominent names were Jamāl al-Dīn al-Afghānī (1839–1897), his pupil Muḥammad ʿAbdū (1849–1905), the mufti of Egypt, and Muḥammad Rashīd Riḍā (1865–1935), born in Lebanon but living in Egypt. This revival was fed by a deep-felt resentment towards the Western powers, which they felt had humiliated Islam, and as an answer Rashīd Riḍā developed the ideal of a modern Islamic state ruled by Islamic religious law. Among those who continued this work were the founder of the Muslim Brotherhood in Egypt, Ḥasan al-Bannā (1906–1949), another Egyptian Muslim Brother, Sayyid Quṭb (1906–1966), and Sayyid Abū l-Aʿlā Mawdūdī (1903–1979) in British India and after the 1947 Partition in Pakistan.[1] An important younger contributor was the Iraqi Shiite Muḥammad Bāqir al-Ṣadr (1935–1980). Mawdūdī was perhaps the first to develop, from the early 1940s, a programme for an Islamic economy, and Quṭb likewise set out, in 1949, what an Islamic society and an Islamic economy should look like, on what principles of ownership and what ethical rules it should be based.[2]

With the oil bonanza of the early 1970s the time was ripe to put some of these ideas into practice and the first explicitly Islamic banks saw the light of day. The Islamic finance industry as it has developed has, however, come under fire from critics who argue that it may be Sharia-*compliant*, obeying the letter of Sharia, but that it is not really Sharia-*based*, and that it is at odds with the spirit of Islam. Critics in particular complain that Islamic finance in large part forsakes the ideals of profit sharing and profit-and-loss

* NOTE: Earlier versions of this paper were presented at the conference on 'Non-capitalist Islam–Yesterday's Ideology or New Horizon?' at the Oriental Seminary, University of Cologne, 15–17 February, 2016, and at the XIIth ISINI conference, Groningen 25–26 August, 2016.

1 Ahmed Abdel-Fattah El-Ashker and Rodney Wilson, *Islamic Economics. A Short History*, Leiden and Boston: Brill 2006.

2 Syed Abul A'la Maududi, *Economic System of Islam*, ed. by Khurshid Ahmad, transl. into English by Riaz Husain, Fourth Edition, Lahore: Islamic Publications 1999; Sayyid Qutb, *Social Justice in Islam*, transl. by John Bruce Hardie, translation rev. and introduced by Hamid Algar, Oneonta: Islamic Publications International 2000. First Arabic ed. publ. in 1949 as *al-ʿAdāla al-iḏjtimāʿiyya fī 'l-Islām*.

sharing and embraces debt-based fractional-reserve banking.[3] This sentiment is shared by others, who are not motivated by religious convictions but are opposed to fractional-reserve banking on the grounds of the dangers it is alleged to represent to economic stability and justice. The focus here is on Muslim groups active during the last quarter of a century or so, including those that seek an alternative to fractional-reserve banking because of technical, not religious, objections. What unites them is a yearning for a stable, fully metallic gold or gold-and-silver currency.

In this article, first the ideas of these groups will be explained, starting with the Murabitun movement. This is followed by a survey of other proponents of a gold dinar and, at least as regards some of them, also a silver dirham. That includes the Indonesian group IMN-World Islamic Standard, Islamic State (*al-Dawlah al-Islāmīya*, IS), *Ḥizb ut-Taḥrīr* (Liberation Party) and the Minaret of Freedom Institute, plus a group that is more loosely interested in gold as a means to cement economic cooperation between Muslim-majority countries. After this rundown of projects and proposals the objections of these groups to the conventional monetary system and the prevailing Islamic finance industry are explained, as are the objectives of the groups themselves. After an analysis of the various projects and plans from a strictly economic point of view the paper winds up with an assessment.

The Murabitun Movement

No group has done more to introduce an Islamic metallic currency as an alternative to conventional fractional-reserve banking than the Murabitun Movement (not to be confused with al-Murābiṭūn, a group formed in 2013 by the merger of two former splinter groups of al-Qāʿidah in the Islamic Maghreb). The movement was founded in the 1980s by the converted Scotsman Shaykh Dr Abdalqadir as-Sufi (born 1930 as Ian Dallas), who, as stridently as Ezra Pound (1885–1972) did both in his poems (*Cantos* 45 and 51 in particular)[4], and in his fascist radio propaganda from Italy during the Second World War, fulminates against interest, or usury, as the greatest of the sins of liberal democratic states.[5] What as-Sufi calls "the psychosis of believing and obeying the impulses of market", or the capitalism of those

3 Tarek El Diwany, "Travelling the Wrong Road Patiently", *Banker Middle East* (November 2003), available on www.islamic-finance.com; Yusuf Jha, "Money Creation and Debt-Based Finance: A Fundamental Challenge to the Islamic Finance Industry", *New Horizon* 189 (2013), 28–30.

4 Ezra Loomis Pound, *The Cantos*, Second Impression, London: Faber & Faber 1968.

5 Khalid Noorshah, "The Islamic Gold Dinar Movement in Malaysia", paper for Seminar Penjanaan Ekonomi Melalui Transaksi Wang Dinar, Bandar Baru Bangi, Malaysia, 2009, http://muamalat.gov.my/sites/default/files/kertas_persidangan/2010/04/09_Khalid_Norshah.pdf (accessed 26.08.2015).

states, is the root cause of, in his words, vanishing species, globally fateful warming and genocide.[6] The Murabitun's political activist is Shaykh Umar Ibrahim Vadillo (born 1964), a Spanish Muslim. Ibrahim Vadillo has in effect taken over from as-Sufi, as as-Sufi has put his support for the introduction of Islamic coins on hold. He now thinks that prior to that introduction Muslims should first find ways to manage without the financial instruments and institutions of capitalism. This is because the Islamic coins are, in his view, inextricably wound up with a correct organisation of the collection of *zakāh* (alms-giving), which is not yet feasible.[7]

The Murabitun movement derives its name from the 11th and 12th-century Murābiṭūn, also known as Almoravids. This was a group made up of West Saharan tribes, Berber-speaking tribes prominent among them, who conquered large swathes of the Maghreb and strove to impose, or in their view restore, a pure form of Sunni Islam, untainted by the lax morals characteristic of luxurious city life. In 1086 they were invited by Muslim rulers in Spain to support them in their struggle against the Christian rulers, the Umayyad caliphate of Cordoba having been dissolved in 1032. The Murābiṭūn succeeded in reconquering a large part of the peninsula until uprisings and attacks by Christian Spanish rulers and Almohads from Morocco put an end to their rule.[8] As-Sufi apparently finds inspiration in the exploits of the historical Murābiṭūn. After the publication of the cartoons depicting the Prophet by the Danish daily *Jyllands-Posten* on 30 September, 2005, he thundered that "The idea that the dubious doctrine of Freedom of Speech should be defended over the scribbling of an insult revealed the quite nihilistic bankruptcy of the current world-view of corporation capitalism" and lamented the lack of leadership in Islam, in this case in Britain, that "produced that dreadful fringe that the BBC and Sky have a genius for finding–I mean those who inform the viewers that Islam means peace, tolerance and democracy, which is surely nonsense. Islam means submission to the Commands of Allah, glory be to Him. Allah commands, 'Love with the love of Allah and hate with the hatred of Allah'." Still, after a rambling discourse on the massacres suffered by Muslims in former Ottoman territo-

---

6 Shaykh Abdalqadir as-Sufi, "The Islamic Dinar–A Way-stage Passed", 2014, http://www.shaykhabdalqadir.com/2014/02/11/the-islamic-dinar-a-way-stage-passed (31.08.2015).

7 As-Sufi, "The Islamic Dinar".

8 Nazeer Ahmed, "The Murabitun in the Maghreb", http://historyofislam.com/murabitun/ n. d. (accessed 07.12.2015); Peter Bernard Clarke, "Moravids", in: *Encyclopedia of Islam and the Muslim world*, Richard C. Martin, ed., New York: Macmillan Reference USA 2004, 475. H.T. Norris and P. Chalmeta, "al-Murābiṭūn", in: *Encyclopaedia of Islam*, Second Edition, P. Bearman, Th. Bianquis, Clifford Edmund Bosworth, Emeri van Donzel and W.P. Heinrichs, eds., 2012, www.brillonline.nl/entries/encyclopaedia-of-islam-2/al-murabitun-COM_0798 (accessed 14.12.2015).

ries and on the un-Islamic character of Wahhabism, alternating with both vicious attacks on the Western countries and eulogies of their political constitutions in the past, a call to vote for Cameron rather than Blair (in order 'to protect the legal rights of the individual'), and the expression of regret at the loss of power of the British monarch (in line with his preference for a strong leader and rejection of democracy), he declares himself against terrorism.[9] His harking back to the Murābiṭūn suggests, however, that he would not reject using military force if victory were within reach.

The message of the Murabitun movement is the central role that *zakāh* should play. This role requires:

1. An appointed *amīr* (commander, leader);
2. that *amīr*'s appointment of *zakāh* collectors;
3. this resulting in a collected and assessed amount of *zakāh*;
4. the gathering of the *zakāh* in a *bayt al-māl* (central treasury);
5. the immediate distribution of the *zakāh* to the legally worthy recipients.[10]

First, this is not how *zakāh* collection and distribution is organised at present, and second, this is deemed incompatible with a monetary system based on *ribā* (surplus, excess, usually equated with interest), using money that is in fact no more than a promissory note–that is, debt–and can be created and destroyed by pressing a key on a computer keyboard. The task the Murabitun set themselves therefore is to reorganise both the collection and distribution of *zakāh* and the monetary system.

To further his aims, Shaykh Vadillo in 1993 founded an institution of which he is still the chairman, the World Islamic Mint, with its seat in Abu Dhabi. The Mint promotes the gold dinar and silver dirham and sets standards for those coins.[11] His missionary zeal bore fruit when on 20 September 2006 the Malaysian state of Kelantan, governed by the Pan-Malaysian Islamic Party, introduced gold dinar coins in three denominations. It was the next step in a process in which the youth organisation of that political party had also played an active role, having unveiled a gold dinar already at its annual general meeting in Kelantan on 3 May 1998. According to State Fi-

[9] Shaykh Abdalqadir as-Sufi, "On Terrorism", 2004, www.shaykhabdalqadir.com/2004/02/19/on-terrorism/ (accessed 04.01.2016); Shaykh Abdalqadir as-Sufi, "The Role of the Muslims of Britain", 2006, www.shaykhabdalqadir.com/2006/02/20/the-role-of-the-muslims-of-britain/, (accessed 04.01.2016); "Murabitun World Movement", *Wikipedia*, n.d. (accessed 07.12.2015).

[10] As-Sufi, "The Islamic Dinar".

[11] World Islamic Mint is a standard-setting body that checks whether the coins are manufactured in accordance with Islamic law. The coins produced following their standards receive a corresponding licence from World Islamic Mint and can be mutually exchanged without a fee, see "Gold Dinar and Silver Dirham", n.d., www.islamicmint.com/dinar-dirham.html (accessed 27.01.2016).

nancial Planning committee chairman Datuk Husam Musa the coins were meant as a means of saving.[12] They initially did not serve as legal tender or even as a means of payment, but the next step was that on 12 August 2010 the state government issued gold dinar and companion silver dirham coins that were explicitly meant to circulate as an alternative to the Malaysian *ringgit* and were touted as Sharia-compliant.[13] Then, scarcely a year later, in the presence of delegations from other countries the Kelantan government announced that henceforth gold dinar and silver dirham coins would be accepted in payment for *zakāt al-māl*, the annual Islamic wealth tax for social purposes.[14] At the time they were already widely accepted by shops and government agencies. Earlier in 2011, the Malaysian state of Perak had launched its own dinar and dirham.[15] Islamic Mint in Kelantan is supported by an organisation called Muamalah Council, which runs an online payment system and publishes directories of firms accepting payment in gold dinars and silver dirhams.[16]

A serious setback for the World Islamic Mint and the Kelantan state government was the refusal of Malaysian *zakāh* Collection Centres to accept *zakāh* payments in gold dinars, a Sharia requirement in the eyes of the Murabitun. Furthermore, the Kelantan state mufti Datuk Mohamad Shukri Mohamad stated that the division of power between the federal government and the states assigns the right to issue legal tender exclusively to the central bank, Bank Negara Malaysia.[17] It may be noted that Bank Negara Malaysia issues its own gold bullion coin, the Kijang Emas (golden deer), in three sizes, weighing respectively 1 Troy ounce, ½ Troy ounce, and ¼ Troy ounce. It is distributed by a commercial bank, Maybank Berhad, for investment purposes.[18] The coin is a far cry from the currency the Islamic Mint and the Kelantan state government have in mind.

---

12 "Kelantan to have gold coins with no legal tender", *The Star* 2006 (4 September), www.thestar.com.my (accessed 08.09.2015). Datuk is an official Malaysian honorific title.

13 "Kelantan makes dinar and dirham legal tender", *The New Straits Times* 2010 (August 14), http://news.asiaone.com/print/News/AsiaOne%2BNews/Malaysia/Story/A1Story20100814-232042.html (accessed 08.09.2015).

14 Ibrahim Abdulaev, "Malaysia: Kelantan collects Zakat in Shariah money", 2011 (August 26), www.islamdag.info/news/1348 (accessed 31.08.2015).

15 "Modern gold dinar", *Wikipedia* n. d. (accessed 07.01.2016).

16 Mumalah Council, www.muamalahcouncil.com.

17 Sulaiman Jaafar, "Kelantan dinar, dirham not legal", *The New Straits Times* 2012 (7 July), available on www.malaysianbar.org.my/legal/general_news/kelantan_dinar_dirham_not_legal.html.

18 For particulars, see www.bnm.gov.my.

Other Islamic Proponents of a Gold (and Silver) Currency

Along with the Murabitun, other groups are in favour of a gold dinar and silver dirham, or have introduced their version already. These include the IMN-World Islamic Standard in Indonesia, Islamic State and *Ḥizb ut-Taḥrīr*. The Minaret of Freedom Institute by contrast favours a metallic currency without specifically having a predilection for dinars and dirhams. One might, finally, discern a group that does not want to replace existing national systems with another one, but is in favour of some form of gold dinar for settling international payment imbalances between Muslim-majority countries. Former Malaysian Prime Minister Mahathir Muhammad was an outspoken representative of this group. We thus have the following line-up:

1. The Murabitun Movement.

2. The Malaysian initiative was enthusiastically followed in Indonesia. An organisation called Islamic Mint Nusantara,[19] now using the name IMN-World Islamic Standard, was set up in 2000 in order to mint gold dinars and silver dirhams. They run a mobile exchange system, Dinarfirst, fully backed by gold and silver coins, meant for saving purposes, *zakāh* payments, *mahr* (nuptial gifts) and "sundry financial transactions"–the last of which can only refer to money used as a medium of exchange.[20]

3. The Islamic State Caliphate announced, in a video released on 29 August 2015, that it was minting gold dinars and silver dirhams, supplemented by copper fulus for small denominations.[21] They are not only meant for circulation in the areas under Islamic State's rule, but are also offered to residents of other countries. Sets containing two gold dinars, three silver dirhams and two copper fulus could be ordered by paying US $950 into a bitcoin account.[22] It is rumoured, though, that the coins issued by Islamic State are not made of solid gold, but are only plated with gold.[23]

4. The British branch of *Ḥizb ut-Taḥrīr*, a group that is out to restore the Caliphate in the Muslim world (but not IS-style), propagates a full gold dinar and silver dirham currency for Muslims and similar fully metallic currencies

19 Nusantara is an Indonesian word denoting the Archipelago of Indonesia.

20 Dinarfirst, http://dinarfirst.org; Sunnah Money, http://www.sunnahmoney.com, http://gold-dinar-silver-dirham.

21 Gillian Mohney, "Islamic State Claims to Mint Gold Coins in Effort to Drive US to Financial Ruin", 2015, https://news.vice.com/article/islamic-state-claims-to-mint-gold-coins-in-effort-to-drive-us-to-financial-ruin (accessed 11.02.2016).

22 ISIS, http://isis-coins.com. The site is no longer active.

23 Ivan Plis, "ISIS' New Gold Coins Aren't Even Real", *Daily Caller News Foundation*, 2015 (9 April), http://dailycaller.com/2015/09/04/isis-new-gold-coins-arent-even-real/#ixzz3zt0OdGLP.

for other countries, arguing that such a currenct not only is required for a genuinely Islamic state but is also indispensable for economic stability and sustainable growth.[24]

5. The Minaret of Freedom Institute of Bethesda in the US, an Islamic think-tank close to the Austrian School of economics in its views on the economy, is, like *Ḥizb ut-Taḥrīr*, convinced that a truly Islamic society requires a metallic standard and argues that the rest of the world would be well-advised to adopt the gold standard as well, as it is seen as a prerequisite for a more just, inflation-free economy. Its President, Imad-ad-Dean Ahmad, states that "The case for following our Islamic heritage on these matters is moral as well as utilitarian".[25] Unlike *Ḥizb ut-Taḥrīr*, though, he sets little store by specifically Islamic dinars and dirhams. Like one strand of the Austrian school, what counts for him is to have a stable currency.[26] Ahmad even goes so far as to maintain that "A 100% reserve in a monetary commodity is not necessary if one has ample total collateral to maintain confidence". He does not pay any attention to silver.

6. The (unorganised) sixth group, like the last two, sees a gold dinar first of all as a safeguard for monetary stability–that is, a means to prevent inflation. Mahathir Muhammad, the then Prime Minister of Malaysia, proposed in 2001 to introduce a gold dinar equivalent to 1 ounce of gold that would serve for settlement of trade between Malaysia and the Muslim-majority countries with which it had a Bilateral Payment Arrangement. He placed much emphasis on such a gold dinar as an instrument to forge closer links between Islamic countries and give the *ummah*, the community of Muslims, a more prominent place in the sun.[27] It would be a supplement to the prevail-

---

24 "Gold Standard; The Future for a Stable Global Currency", 2011 (27 December), *Hizb ut-Tahrir Britain*, available on http://www.hizb.org.uk/solutions/gold-standard-the-future-for-a-stable-global-currency.

25 Imad-ad-Dean Ahmad, "The Dinar: Indispensibility of Hard Money to the Islamic Monetary Regime", 1998, paper presented to the American Muslim Social Scientists in Chicago on Oct. 30 (Abstract), http://www.minaret.org/OLD/MONETARY.HTM (accessed 02.10.2008).

26 Perhaps the most prominent Austrian School representative was Friedrich von Hayek (1899–1992). The Austrian School is focused on individual decision-making and is suspicious of macroeconomic analysis with its emphasis on aggregates such as aggregate consumption and aggregate investment. 'Austrian' economists favour free-market policies and share a fear that government intervention may prove a camel's nose. Hayek's *The Road to Serfdom* (1944) has cult status.

27 Abu Bakar Bin Mohd Yusuf, Nuradli Ridzwan Shah Bin Mohd Dali and Norhayati Mat Husin, "Implementation of the Gold Dinar: Is it the End of Speculative Measures?", *Journal of Economic Cooperation* 23: 3 (2012), 74; Noorshah, "The Islamic Gold Dinar Movement in Malaysia", 168; James Sinclair, "The Seriousness of the Gold Dinar–A Presentation Made in Kuala Lumpur Malaysia by the Honorable Dr. Mahathir Bin Mohammed Minister of Finance for Malaysia 'The Gold Dinar in

ing system rather than a full substitute, and should ensure first and foremost that the Islamic world could hold its own in a world payment system dominated by US dollars, euros, yen and, increasingly, yuan. The only country supporting his proposal was Iran, and the idea mainly lies dormant, but it crops up every now and then. At a summit of the Organisation of the Islamic Conference (OIC) in 2003 a proposal for an Islamic trade system denominated in gold dinars was discussed.[28] *The Economist* called it quixotic, which it surely was at the time, but it is probably not yet buried.

Former Libyan leader Muᶜammar al-Qadhāfi was taken with similar ideas. He dreamt of an alliance of Muslim states sharing the gold dinar and forcing the rest of the world to pay for oil in those dinars. The gold dinar should join the dollar and the euro as a dominant international money.[29]

We see groups and individuals with different views on what role a gold dinar and, in some cases, a silver dirham, should play, and why they should be introduced. Most, however, are opposed to both the conventional banking system and the Islamic finance industry in its present form. In the Introduction some of their objections were noted. The next section expands this discussion.

Objections to Conventional and Islamic Finance

It is widely felt by Muslims that conventional finance, including insurance, is not Sharia-compliant. This is because it is tainted with:

1. *ribā*,
2. *gharār* (avoidable risk and uncertainty) and *maysir* (gambling, speculation),
3. *harām* goods and services;

while furthermore the contract law it applies differs in some respects from Islamic contract law.[30]

Islamic finance claims to be free from these defects. However, critics note that Islamic finance essentially mimics conventional finance and is not fundamentally different.[31] There is one point these critics stress in par-

Multilateral Trade' ", 2002, www.gold-eagle.com/article/seriousness-gold-dinar-presentation-made-kuala-lumpur-malaysia (accessed 10.06.2016).

28 "Times are changing. Muslims see the world shifting–and aren't sure what to do about it", *The Economist*, 2003 (16 October).

29 "Modern gold dinar".

30 Hans Visser, *Islamic Finance: Principles and Practice*, Second Edition, Cheltenham: Edward Elgar 2013, 29–60, 94–103.

31 Mahmoud A. El-Gamal, " 'Interest' and the paradox of contemporary Islamic law and finance", *Fordham International Law Review* 27 (2003), available on https://ir.lawnet.fordham.edu/ilj/vol27/iss1/6.

ticular, namely the fact that Islamic finance preaches profit sharing and profit-and-loss sharing (PLS) but actually practices debt finance, which is inextricably bound up with fractional-reserve banking.[32] If conventional banks grant a loan, they credit the borrower's bank account, creating money in the processs.[33] This is also the principal mode of operation of Islamic banks. The money supply consequently is not fully backed by base money (gold or silver, but mainly central bank money and coins issued by the government or the central bank), let alone gold and silver. This fractional-reserve banking, the critics emphasise, is the source of many economic ills, such as inflation, speculative booms followed by disastrous busts, and an increasingly imbalanced distribution of wealth.[34] The power of governments and banks to create money is seen as benefiting the elite who control the financial institutions, and brings them wealth and increased power to the detriment of the not-so-fortunate. This, and the loss of purchasing power as a result of inflation, is deemed unacceptable to Muslims, as one of the *maqāṣid al-sharīʿa* (goals of the divine law) is the preservation of wealth.[35]

Some champions of gold dinars and silver dirhams are convinced that the fractional-reserve system is an instrument in the hands of the foes of Islam. One vocal activist, Imran N. Hosein, observes that "It is both strange and embarrassing that even at this late hour when enemies are about to weld into place the final iron gate of a financial Guantanamo, so many Muslims remain ignorant about the devilish nature of European-created money in the modern world."[36] He sounds the alarm bell because "There seems to be little understanding of the role that a European-created money-

32 El Diwany, "Travelling the wrong road patiently"; Salman Ahmed Shaikh, "An Ideal Islamic Economic System: A Gone Case?", *Journal of Islamic Economics, Banking and Finance*, 7: 3 (2011), 23–34; Bernardo Vizcaino, "Islamic financial products risk losing uniqueness", *Reuters* 2015 (21 May), https://af.reuters.com/article/africaTech/idAFL5N0YC04B20150521.

33 It is not only debt finance that may involve money creation. *Ijārah* or leasing is no different in this respect: if a bank buys a good for leasing out (or for that matter for any other purpose) it credits the seller's bank account with newly created money.

34 Tarek El Diwany, "Fractional reserve banking", *The New Straits Times*, 1997 (August), available on www.islamic-finance.com (accessed 01.09.2008); Abdul Halim, Abdul Hamid and Norizaton Azmin Mohd Nordin, "Islamic Banking with Dinar and Dirham: Meeting the Challenges to Uplift the Ummah Economy", paper for Seminar Penjanaan Ekonomi Melalui Transaksi Wang Dinar, Bandar Baru Bangi, Malaysia (27 August 2009), http://e-muamalat.gov.my/sites/default/files/kertas_persidangan/2010/04/03_Halim__Norizaton.pdf (accessed 02.09.2015); Jha, "Money Creation and Debt-Based Finance".

35 Ahamed Kameel Mydin Meera and Moussa Larbani, "Seigniorage of Fiat Money and the Maqasid al-Shari'ah: The Compatibility of the Gold Dinar with the Maqasid", *Jurnal Muamalat* 2 (2009), 93–116.

36 Imrān N. Hosein, *The Gold Dinār and Silver Dirham: Islam and the Future of Money*, San Fernando, Trinidad and Tobago: Masjid Jāmi'ah 2007, 6, available on https://asimiqbal2nd.files.wordpress.com/2009/06/dinardirham.pdf.

system has been playing in delivering to enemies of Islam the capacity to engage in massive legalised theft of the wealth of mankind. Nor is there realization that those enemies have designed a monetary system that would eventually deliver to them financial dictatorship over the whole world. They have already succeeded in enslaving millions of Muslims (as well as others amongst mankind) with slave wages and even destitution, while pursuing a sinister global agenda on behalf of the Euro-Jewish State of Israel. It is truly pathetic to listen to those who blame Pakistanis and Indonesians for miserable poverty in Pakistan and Indonesia."[37] The weapon of those enemies of Islam is the system of non-redeemable paper money. This money can be devalued, which entails a legalised theft of the holder's wealth and adds to the burden for borrowing countries of repaying loans taken on interest, in the end bankrupting them so that they are at the mercy of the lenders. That is what those lenders are after, all the time. They can now buy property, labour, goods and services from the indebted countries at low prices and live in luxury, leaving the debtors in poverty and in the process causing corruption in the countries they loot. Sure enough all this is meant to "pave the way for the Euro-Jewish State of Israel to become the ruling state in the world and, eventually, for a ruler of Israel to startle the world with the utterly fraudulent claim that he is the true Messiah." And why do governments in Muslim-majority countries not see the danger? Because of "the subservient role to which they must adhere as governments in their relations with the Judeo-Christian alliance that now rules the world."[38] A similar apocalyptic vision comes from Nik Mahani Mohamad, a former pupil of Imran Hosein and one-time executive director of Kelantan Golden Trade, the firm that mints the gold dinar and silver dirham. She holds that the fractional reserve banking system lies at the root of the rotten capitalist system spread by the Western powers. Like Hosein, she does not hesitate to see in this system the coming of the *Dajjāl*, the Jewish False Messiah.[39] She, too, prophesies about the dire role of Israel: "With the control over currencies and making it whether 'regional' or 'single' currencies; we now under-

37 Hosein, *The Gold Dinār and Silver Dirham*, 7.

38 Ibid., 8–12.

39 The *Dajjāl* is a creature featured in Islamic eschatology. He is the Antichrist who at the end of time will deceive the great majority of people into following him and will fight the few remaining Muslims, until Jesus descends and kills the *Dajjāl* (David B. Cook, "Dajjāl", in: *Encyclopaedia of Islam, THREE*, Kate Fleet, Gudrun Krämer, Denis Matringe, John Nawas and Everett Rowson, eds., Leiden: Brill 2012, http://referenceworks.brillonline.com/entries/encyclopaedia-of-islam-3/dajjal-COM_25826 [11.01.2016]). The *Dajjāl* is mentioned in a hadith that is not deemed very reliable. Cook notes that the contemporary Islamic apocalyptic literature blends stories of the *Dajjāl* with anti-Jewish elements from *The Protocols of the Elders of Zion*. The link with monetary developments is Imran Hosein's and Mahani Mohamad's own contribution. Apparently they believe that the end of the world is nigh.

stand that our each individual country 'sovereignty' is now slowly beginning to be passed into the hands of the Central Powers–call it IMF and the World Bank! Soon USD will be made to demise and so too the Ruling State Power will be shifted from USA to another Central Power–centered no doubt in Israel as prophesised by our Holy Prophet Muhammad SAW."[40] It is left to her readers to figure out how Israel could ever play such a pernicious role in international finance.

In the same vein, Islamic State wants its own currency "to prevent blind and tyrannical monetary system that was imposed on the Muslims and was a reason for their enslavement, impoverishment and the wasting of national wealth, making it easy prey in the hands of the Jews and Christians".[41]

Imran Hosein and Mahani Mohamad are frequently quoted, for instance in master theses written at Malaysian universities.[42] Though in the discussion on the subject the measured tone of the likes of El Diwany is more usual than the shrill voices of Hosein and Mahani Mohamad, many share the latters' conviction that fractional-reserve banking and fiat money serve to concentrate wealth and also sovereignty in the hands of those who control the system.[43] An interesting position is taken by Imad-ad-Dean Ahmad of the Minaret of Freedom Institute. Like many economists who follow the Austrian School, Ahmad is in favour of the gold standard because it makes for monetary stability and prevents both manipulation of the currency by the authorities and unjust benefits for the rich, who possess inflation-proof assets. A stable currency, not in danger of the erosion of its value by inflation, is a prerequisite for a just society, and therefore for an Islamic society, but no less for others.[44] Unlike most Muslim advocates of a gold currency, he does not equate interest with *ribā*[45] and he sees as one of the benefits of a gold standard that interest rates tend to be lower than under a managed currency. *Ḥizb ut-Taḥrīr* likewise puts the stability of the currency centre stage, but sticks to the rejection of interest common among Muslims.

A curious conviction among opponents of an interest-based system, which they seem to have borrowed from Bernard Lietaer, famous for his advocacy

---

40 Nik Mahani Mohamad, "The Real Implementation of the Gold Dinar Economy", paper for Seminar Penjanaan Ekonomi Melalui Transaksi Wang Dinar, Bandar Baru Bangi, Malaysia, 27.08.2009, available on http://e-muamalat.gov.my/sites/default/files/kertas_persidangan/2010/04/14_Nik_Mahani.pdf.

41 ISIS, http://isis-coins.com.

42 Her paper was accepted as a conference paper at a Malaysian state university and has been published on the Malaysian government internet portal.

43 Meera and Larbani, "Seigniorage of Fiat Money", 94.

44 Ahmad, "The Dinar".

45 Imad-ad-Dean Ahmad, *Riba and interest: Definitions and implications*, Minaret of Freedom Institute Preprint Series 96-5, Bethesda: Minaret of Freedom Institute 1996, paper delivered at the 22nd conference of American Muslim Social Scientists, Herndon, VA, 15–17 October 1993, available on www.minaret.org/riba.htm.

of alternative exchange systems, is that an interest-based bank system requires an ever-expanding fiduciary money circulation.[46] This is based on the belief that interest payments imply that money is taken out of circulation. But that would require that banks operate without incurring any costs, do not distribute profits and do not use retained profits for investments or deposits with other institutions. Another strand in Lietaer's crusade against interest, shared by many Muslim critics of fractional-reserve banking, is that interest payments are a major source of wealth concentration. In reality, interest appears to play at most a minor role in this respect. Other forms of capital income (rent, profits) and, perhaps more importantly, business acumen, monopolies, tax deals, tax evasion and political manipulation of the fiscal system are much more likely to be the driving forces.[47] The critics' complaint that the fiat money circulation shrinks during a recession, due to a fall in the volume of credit, making a bad situation worse, is better founded, though central banks do have instruments to counter such a fall in the money supply.

It appears that a gold dinar and a silver dirham find support across a broad spectrum of Islamic economists and political activists. They are united in their opposition to fiduciary money and fractional-reserve banking. Many are also motivated by a sense of frustration over the rules and practices that dominate financial systems in Muslim-majority countries, as everywhere else.[48] These are seen as a remnant of the colonial period, and an alternative to the Western financial system that is rooted in Islam is a heartfelt wish. But the proponents have different ideas about the design and purpose of such an alternative system.

What Are the Gold Dinar and the Silver Dirham for?

People have different ends in mind when propagating a gold dinar and a silver dirham. First are those who see the dinar and dirham as essential for obeying Islamic religous law, the Sharia. These include the Murabitun/World Islamic Mint, Islamic State and, presumably, IMN-World Islamic Standard.[49] It is asserted, with liberal quotes from the sources, that the Quran and the

---

46 Meera and Larbani, "Seigniorage of Fiat Money", 94; Bernard Lietaer, *The Future of Money*, London: Century 2001.

47 Hans Visser, "Is interest-free banking the answer to our prayers? Bernard Lietaer and Islamic Banking", 2013, *Elgarblog*, http://elgarblog.wordpress.com/2013/12/13/is-interest-free-banking-the-answer-to-our-prayers-bernard-lietaer-and-islamic-banking-by-hans-visser/#more-3241.

48 Mezbah Uddin Ahmed, "Riba, Bank Interest, and Islamic Banking: A Summarised Response to Fundamental Questions", *New Horizon* 191 (2014), 23–28.

49 There are precious few sources on IMN-World Islamic Standard other than in Bahasa Indonesia.

Hadith, when discussing money, are referring to gold and silver money.[50] It may be objected that it could hardly have been otherwise, because fiduciary money did not exist in the world known to the Prophet Muḥammad and his Companions. That argument, however, does not carry much weight with the Murabitun or Islamic State. Shaykh Vadillo stresses that *zakāh* cannot be paid in fiduciary money, which is no more than a debt: "Zakat in Islam must be paid in *ʿayn*, that is tangible merchandise and cannot be paid in *dayn*, that is, a debt, a liability or a promisory note."[51] And that is not all. The gold dinar and silver dirham should more generally help Muslims to better obey the Sharia. According to World Islamic Mint, paper money, or fiat money, again is not real money but no more than a promise to pay. It may, and is very likely to, lose value over time, whereas the gold and silver coins in use in the 14 centuries before the existence of "the new postcolonial national states created from the dismemberment of Dar al-Islam"[52] by and large retained their purchasing power over that period.[53] Gold and silver are no one else's liability but fiduciary money is. If a Muslim uses, say, the US dollar, the issuers hold the 'real' payment outside Muslim jurisdiction and 'paper money has been a permanent instrument of default and cheating the Muslims'. All this is not Sharia-compliant, because Muslims must not entrust wealth to non-Muslims and, furthermore, a promise of payment must not be used as a medium of exchange. Islamic Mint also states that not only *zakāh* payments, but also payments made in connection with marriages can only be Sharia-compliant if not made in fiduciary money. Both the Murabitun behind the World Islamic Mint, and Islamic State strive to unite Muslims behind a Sharia-compliant monetary system as part of a caliphate that unites Muslims and frees them from submission to the present economic order.

The Murabitun set great store by minting coins that have the same metallic content as the early dinar and dirham, though not exactly the same as the coins circulating at the time of the Prophet. Instead, they want to copy the early truly Islamic dinar and dirham. According to Ibn Khaldūn, it was the fifth Umayyad caliph, ʿAbd al-Malik (caliph 685–705), who founded a mint that supplied the first standardized Islamic coins, with Islamic inscriptions.[54] They were based on the coins in use at that time, the Byzantine gold solidus or bezant and the Persian silver drahm. *Dinar* stems from the Roman *denarius*, which had become synonymous with the solidus. Its

50 Meera and Larbani, "Seigniorage of Fiat Money", 102.

51 Shaykh Umar Ibrahim Vadillo, "Muamalaat: The Alternative to the Riba System Exists", 2013, available on https://umarvadillo.wordpress.com.

52 *Dār al-Islām* ('House of Islam'), a legal and political term to denote the territory under Muslim rule.

53 "Gold Dinar and Silver Dirham".

54 Ibn Khaldun, *The Muqaddimah*, chapter 3 section 34, written 1377, available on www.muslimphilosophy.com/ik/Muqaddimah/Chapter3/Ch_3_34.htm.

weight, however, was reduced by ʿAbd al-Malik from approximately 4.55 grams to 4.25 grams gold of between 96% and 98% purity. The word *dirham* derives, via the *drahm*, from the Greek *drachma*. Its weight was 2.97 grams, down from the Persian (Sassanid) weight of 4.11 to 4.15 grams. It follows that a dirham should have 7/10 of the weight of a dinar.[55] This harking back to the early period of Islam does not imply that the Murabitun want to renounce such modern achievements as electronic payments. Bank money is fully acceptable, but bank balances should be 100% backed by gold (they are silent with regard to silver in this respect).

With Islamic State it is different. They may embrace modern means of communcation, but in monetary matters they want to go back as far as possible to the time of the Prophet. Their coins are meant to be used as a physical means of payment, though it is not clear how far they have succeeded in bringing them into circulation. The gold dinar of Islamic State differs very slightly from the World Islamic Mint standard, having a weight of 4.27 grams (21 carat). Their silver dirham, though, only weighs 2 grams. The dinar of Islamic Mint Nusantara remains closer to the coins of the time of the Prophet, consisting of 4.44 grams of gold (presumably of greater purity). Its dirham weighs 3.11 gram, again between the original dirham and ʿAbd al-Malik's version.[56] A second group is made up of Minaret of Freedom and *Ḥizb ut-Taḥrīr*. They are in favour of a fully metallic currency for its alleged benefits to society in the first place. They differ in that *Ḥizb ut-Taḥrīr* favours a bimetallic currency, with both gold and silver coins, because of the higher monetary supply such a system will allow, whereas for Minaret of Freedom a gold-based currency, even without full 100% gold backing, would suffice.[57] Neither group expresses a wish to replicate a system from the seventh or eighth century, even if *Ḥizb ut-Taḥrīr*'s ideal is a caliphate.

The third group is made up of people like Mahathir and Qadhāfi, who saw a gold dinar as an anchor for monetary stability but most of all as a vehicle for uniting and strengthening the Muslim-majority part of the world, making it the equal of other world powers.

What unites the first and the third group seems to be a feeling of resentment about two centuries of Western dominance, and it is not only piety or the wish to create a better financial system that play a role, but also

---

55 G.C. Miles, "Dīnār", in: *Encyclopaedia of Islam*, Bearman et al., www.brillonline.nl/entries/encyclopaedia-of-islam-2/dinar-SIM_1865 (accessed 21.01.2016); G.C. Miles, "Dirham", in: *Encyclopaedia of Islam*, Bearman et al., www.brillonline.nl/entries/encyclopaedia-of-islam-2/dirham-SIM_1875 (accessed 21.01.2016); Ahamed Kameel Mydin Meera, n.d., "Islamic Gold Dinar: The Historical Standard", *Imam Reza (A.S.).Network*, www.imamreza.net/eng/imamreza.php?id=10683 (accessed 18.12.2015).

56 *Dinarfirst*, http://dinarfirst.org (accessed 10.06.2016).

57 "Gold Standard", 7.

the hope of recapturing something of the former glory of Islam. It is very much about identity.

At this point an analysis of how the proposed systems might work in practice is in order. The basic idea of the economics discipline is that 'there is no such thing as a free lunch', or, more prosaically, there is a presumption of positive opportunity costs. What problems might confront economies introducing the proposed currency systems?

The Functioning of a Gold Dinar and Silver Dirham Currency

Those who, like the Murabitun, wish to base *zakāh* payments on the arrangements in use in the early days of Islam, may run into difficulties when they take those arrangements too literally. If one follows the Hadith literally, *zakāh* should be levied starting from a *niṣāb* (minimum level of wealth) which is put at five camels, forty sheep, two hundred dirhams of silver, or five *wasq* of grain, fruits, or agricultural crops.[58] But what should the *niṣāb* be today, starting from those texts? Obviously, sheep and camels are often absent in an urban environment and price ratios have changed. Two hundred dirhams of silver will not always buy exactly five camels or some given volume of fruits, and if the *niṣāb* is left unchanged, people will if possible choose as a yardstick the good that offers the highest exemption. But it is not difficult to find a rationale behind the original *niṣāb*. Five *wasq* of grain would feed three people for a year, with something in reserve for emergencies. Likewise, two hundred dirhams is said to have been sufficient to keep body and soul together for three persons for a year.[59] At the price ratios prevailing at the time of the Prophet, the different yardsticks would probably have given similar outcomes in terms of purchasing power, which offers a solution to the problem but implies that the original *niṣāb* cannot be applied by those living now. To an outsider it looks as if the correct thing to do now is to establish a *niṣāb* corresponding to some amount of purchasing power, but this is too simple, because there is no end of discussion among Islamic scholars with regard not only to threshholds but also to the range of assets that should be subject to *zakāh*.[60] The question is whether one should only levy *zakāh* on assets mentioned in the Hadith, observing the thresholds mentioned there, and if not, to what extent *qiyās* (application of analogy), *ijtihād* (independent reasoning by a qualified jurist) and *istiḥsān* (juristic

58 Yusuf al-Qaradawi, *Fiqh al-zakat*, vol. I, Jeddah: King Abdulaziz University 2000, 64, available on http://iei.kau.edu.sa/Pages-E-EnglishPublications.aspx. *Wasq* is a measure of volume.

59 Al-Qaradawi, *Fiqh al-zakat*, 64–65.

60 For a brief survey, see Visser, *Islamic Finance*, 31–36.

preference, justifying exceptions to strict or literal legal interpretations) can be applied. The Murabitun are vague on this point. How would a bimetallic currency system as favoured by both the Murabitun and *Ḥizb ut-Taḥrīr* function? A system with a two standard coins made of different metals has to cope with problems peculiar to such a system. The price ratio between the metals will generally fluctuate over time, and given the prices of goods and services denominated in one of the standard coins, prices denominated in the other one will fluctuate as well. Users have more calculations to do when collecting and processing price information, which translates into higher transaction costs in the economy. A fixed price ratio between the two coins would require a constant price ratio between the two monetary metals on the metals market and that would be difficult to maintain. If the price ratio on the market for metals were to deviate from the official monetary price ratio, Gresham's Law, which says that 'bad' money drives out 'good' money from circulation, would come into operation. The 'good' money–that is, the coins made from the relatively underpriced money–would be driven from circulation by the coins made from the relatively overpriced metal, as it would be profitable to melt down the underpriced coins and sell them on the metals market. A given weight of metal made from the underpriced coins would fetch more coins made of the overpriced metal than a direct exchange of the coins at the official price ratio would. Admittedly, opinions differ on whether this really was a serious defect of the system as it functioned in the United States, France and a number of other countries in the 19th century. Some argue that free minting and deminting saw to it that market prices adjusted to the official price ratio. The coins made from the relatively overpriced metal would be preferred for making payments and, being legal tender, the receiving party could not refuse them. Market participants who needed large sums to amortise debt would find it profitable to buy the metal in question on the metals market and have it minted. The demand for that metal would increase and drive the market price up.[61] This is a moot point, but even if true, the weight of one or a couple of Islamic countries adopting a bimetallistic system would certainly not be enough to have such an effect on metal price ratios. So they would be stuck with two price systems and strong forces would be at work to stick to one standard metal for the payment system, as the Murabitun seem to accept.

The main economic argument for introducing a fully metallic standard, whether monometallistic or bimetallistic, is that it will function different-

61 Marc Flandreau, "The French Crime of 1873: An Essay on the Emergence of the International Gold Standard, 1870–1880", *The Journal of Economic History* 56: 4 (1996), 862–897.

ly–and better–than a fractional reserve system, or so their proponents claim. Some important distinguishing characterstics are:

1. The money supply in a country or currency area becomes rather inflexible, being limited by the domestic supply of gold, or silver and gold. If these are limited or cannot easily be converted into coins or be acquired by the authorities or institutions that offer gold- and silver-backed e-money, it can only increase through a positive balance on the current account of the balance of payments or through capital imports (foreign borrowing and investments from abroad).
2. Countries with gold or silver mines might be able to increase production, but the rate of production is bound to be very small relative to existing supplies and thus can only bring limited relief. A gold or gold-and-silver currency might therefore stymie economic growth or make deflation necessary. Deflation would take place because at a given price level the demand for money increases and economic agents will be willing to reduce their prices in order to get hold of money. The increased demand for money thus drives the relative price of the monetary metal up. Given that the monetary metal functions as the unit of account, nominal prices of other goods and services will fall.
3. A fully metallic money, without fractional-reserve banking, not only has implications for the money supply, but also for financial intermediation. Financing is no longer possible with newly created money. The banks, just like other financial institutions and financial markets, first must attract money by offering money holders other financial assets, such as time deposits, shares and participations in an investment fund, before they themselves can provide funds.

Only *Ḥizb ut-Taḥrīr* has adressed these issues seriously, demonstrating a much deeper understanding of monetary economics than, in particular, Islamic State and the Murabitun, who simply want to follow their interpretation of God's commands, with a cavalier disregard for the consequences. Let us run through the list:

1. A fully metallic currency is by nature left to market force and provides no place for monetary management, unless recourse is made to practices which the propagandists of fully metallic currencies will tend to see as fraudulent, in particular the clipping of coins or changing the metal volume of coins without corresponding changes in the denomination of the coins. The attractive feature of gold and silver coins, in their eyes, is precisely the price stability that is thrown overboard by tinkering with the denomination of the coins. Imad-ad-Dean Ahmad of the Minaret of Freedom agrees that circumstances may demand an expansion or con-

traction of the money supply at times, but market forces will see to it that this happens "naturally through additional mining or the meltdown of jewelry. It can contract through the diversion of coins into jewelry or other products. The difficulty involved in money supply adjustment is natural and controlled by God"[62]–who apparently acts through the market mechanism, and fast enough, which is no more than a pious hope.

2. The need, or even inevitability, of deflation is acknowledged by the proponents of the gold dinar and silver dirham, but they tend to downplay the associated problems. These, however, may be quite serious:

   a. Price ratios between goods, including services, constantly change, and an adjustment of relative prices is much easier when some nominal prices and wages can go up without others going down than when nominal reductions in prices and, even more, wage cuts have to be accepted. Resistance to nominal price reductions, and most of all wage cuts, may impair the functioning of the price mechanism and cause unemployment.

   b. A given nominal debt will increase in real terms (purchasing power) when the price level falls and thus become more onerous, increasing the risk of default.

   c. People have an incentive to postpone purchases if prices fall.

   Central banks are therefore allergic to deflation and instead favour a moderate rate of inflation. Proponents of a fully metallic currency, however, argue that the market will adjust to deflation and understand that lower wages and prices are not synonymous with a loss of purchasing power. *Ḥizb ut-Taḥrīr* in particular believes that in an Islamic economic environment people will not be subject to this money illusion and will thus not equate price with value.[63] People may indeed adjust their expectations after a transition period.

   As for the burden of debt, *Ḥizb ut-Taḥrīr* sees it as a welcome incentive to get rid of debt. They prefer funding of investment by savings. In their view, "the Islamic model is built on the premise of encouraging the market participant of the virtue of living within one's means and funding investment through savings and not unsustainable debt".[64] Funding by share capital would meet with their approval. It may be noted that if deflation becomes the normal state of affairs and people get rid of money illusion, debt would likely be indexed, or the nominal rate of interest will

62 Ahmad, "The Dinar".
63 "Gold Standard".
64 "Gold Standard".

be lowered. However, in a truly Islamic economy no interest is allowed in the first place, and indexation would also be problematic, because Sharia scholars generally maintain that debt can only be traded and amortised at face value. But as *Ḥizb ut-Taḥrīr* sees debt finance as inferior to profit sharing or profit-and-loss sharing, they would not bemoan its demise.

Then there is the issue of the incentive to postpone purchases. *Ḥizb ut-Taḥrīr* calls this a false dogma. If wages are flexible the incentive to delay a purchase will disappear, they think, as the price to wage ratio does not change. This neglects, however, that the ratio between future prices and present wages does change, still making it attractive to postpone purchases. This is because money holdings carry an implicit positive interest rate under deflation: the purchasing power of one nominal unit of money increases over time. That makes money more attractive vis-à-vis other assets, including financial assets such as shares and *ṣukūk* (Islamic certificates), to the detriment of financial intermediation and investment, and possibly leading to unemployment. Arguably such a positive implicit interest is at odds with the Islamic view of money, which resembles Aristotle's, and in his footsteps the Scholastics', view that money is first and foremost a means of exchange and a unit of account, and not an asset to be held.[65]

3. The Murabitun, *Ḥizb ut-Taḥrīr* and kindred spirits would surely push for pure forms of Islamic finance, PLS (Profit-and-Loss Sharing). As the development of the prevailing Islamic finance industry shows, however, the market has a strong need for debt finance. PLS makes up only a small part of total financing by Islamic banks.[66] Running the payment mechanism enables banks to monitor the cash flows of their clients and thus receive an early warning if their fortunes are in danger of taking a wrong turn. If they have granted credit they can intervene. Financiers without access to such monitoring may be tempted to charge higher rates or require a higher markup on funds supplied in order to make up for a higher perceived risk. Very likely, therefore, the economies of jurisdictions introducing a full-fledged gold dinar and silver dirham, with financial

65 Muhammad Taqi Usmani, *An Introduction to Islamic Finance*, 1998, 12, available on http://www.muftitaqiusmani.com; Aristotle, *The Politics*, transl. by T. A. Sinclair and rev. by Trevor J. Saunders, Harmondsworth: Penguin 1992, 85–87.

66 *Mushārakah* (shared ownership) and *muḍārabah* (sleeping partnership), the PLS forms of finance, for instance made up no more than 16.3% of outstanding financing by Pakistan's Islamic banks as per end March, 2017 (State Bank of Pakistan, *Islamic Banking Bulletin*, 08.03.2017, www.sbp.org.pk/ibd/Bulletin/2017/Mar.pdf). True, diminishing *mushārakah* held a share of 32.3%, but is in fact more akin to *ijārah*: the bank and the buyer jointly own real estate and the buyer pays rent plus a markup on the (diminishing) share owned by the bank.

intermediation decoupled from the payment mechanism, would have to face a less efficient functioning of financial intermediation, in particular if in addition debt finance is banned. For another thing, restrictions on debt finance would make financing of consumption extremely difficult–probably a good thing in the eyes of *Ḥizb ut-Taḥrīr*.

An Assessment

Advocates of the gold dinar and silver dirham act from various motives. Some prefer the monetary discipline of a fully metallic currency over the opportunities for monetary management offered by a fiduciary currency. Others want to go back to the early times of Islam. There is an element of arbitrariness in such a drive, as neither the Murabitun nor Islamic State intend to forgo the benefits of modern technology, in particular as regards communication and travel. The Murabitun in addition have no problem with accepting electronic payments mechanisms. Moreover, the case for adopting gold dinars and silver dirhams seems less compelling even for Muslims of a traditionalist bent if one realises that the Prophet probably accepted a fully metallic currency because that is what was in use in his time. It was simply the prevailing system and there does not seem to be any reason, according to Chapra, why later generations might not consider adopting a fiduciary currency. The second caliph, ʿUmar (caliph 634–644), even contemplated introducing camel skin coins. His advisers, however, warned him that money creation might get out of hand and result in a disastrously large-scale slaughter of camels.[67] Chapra also notes that Islamic jurists from later periods, such as Aḥmad ibn Ḥanbal (the inspirator of the Ḥanbalī *madhhab* or law school, died 855) and Ibn Taymiyyah (who is often regarded as a forerunner of the Salafi movement, died 1328) saw the acceptance of specific forms of money as depending on custom and usage. In Chapra's eyes the quasi-unanimous acceptance of fiduciary money by modern Islamic jurists and fiqh committees of the Organisation of the Islamic Conference (in October 1986) and others is tantamount to an *ijmāʿ* (consensus among the scholars, widely accepted as a source of law).

A full-blooded gold-and-silver currency would be very expensive and work as a straightjacket for the economy. That would be the price for what is seen as a prerequisite of an Islamic, just society, though Minaret of Freedom and *Ḥizb ut-Taḥrīr* tend to trivialise these downsides. The wish to use gold as a transaction currency in trade between Muslim-majority countries seems to lack religious foundations, or, for that matter, an economic ra-

67 Muhammad Umer Chapra, "Monetary Management in an Islamic Economy", *Islamic Economic Studies* 4: 1 (1996), 1–36.

tionale. It is first and foremost a drive to club together as Muslim countries. The Murabitun movement is a very special case, with their fixation on Sharia-compliant *zakāh* payments. The various movements differ in their rejection of what is perceived as a Western-dominated world order, Minaret of Freedom being markedly less critical than Islamic State, *Ḥizb ut-Taḥrīr* and the Murabitun.

Three Images of Anti-authoritarian Socialism within Islamic Contexts: Isabelle Eberhardt/Mahmoud Essadi, Muammar Qaddafi's *Green Book*, and Heba Raouf Ezzat

Anthony T. Fiscella

Introduction

This chapter aims to present three contrasting images of anti-authoritarian socialism that can be viewed as uneasy complements and/or revolutionary contrasts to global and regional capitalisms. In either case, they present a challenge of some sort in terms of how social and economic relations might be organized differently. The examples of Isabelle Eberhardt/Mahmoud Essadi, Muammar Qaddafi (specifically his *Green Book*), and Heba Raouf Ezzat both express their own unique articulations about what might be loosely described as *anti-authoritarian socialism* but also respectively recall precedents and echoes in both anarchist and Islamic contexts. Despite a long history of commonalities, exchanges, and overlapping concerns, Muslims are not typically identified with socialists or communists (preceding or subsequent to Marx). For example, even while examining egalitarian thought within Islamic contexts historian Louise Marlow assumed that, despite occasional rebellions inspired by Islamic egalitarian ideals, the oft-cited egalitarian principles in the Quran and Islamic tradition "probably never corresponded very closely to the social organizations of the communities in which they were produced"[1]. Whether or not her remark is historically justified, one could say the same about ancient Greek and early American egalitarians yet that has not hindered both from being perceived as having formed the ideological foundations of democratic equality. Ideas are valuable in themselves, when they point toward visions of organizing society differently.

This chapter works with three different conceptions of anti-authoritarian socialism: dervish socialism, minarchist socialism, and small-scale non-state-based socialism.[2] After outlining different approaches to studying socialist

---

1 Louise Marlow, *Hierarchy and Egalitarianism in Islamic Thought*, Cambridge: Cambridge Univ. Press 1997, 9.

2 For the purposes of this chapter, 'communism' refers to the collective sharing of resources in either a small community or broader societal sense. 'Capitalism', in contrast, refers to economic systems based on private domination of property and resources serving the desires of the few at the expense of the needs of the many. "Anti-capitalists" are united in opposition to this premise, as in the words of Malcolm X,

or non-capitalist elements within Islamic contexts within existing research, the cases of Eberhardt/Essadi, Muammar Qaddafi and *The Green Book*, and Ezzat are discussed in light of the three conceptions. It ought to be noted that the literature lists in this chapter are not exhaustive. Nor is it possible here to provide a proper overview even of all English-language research on Islamic socialism–to say nothing of other languages–but the few selections here ought to help frame the material while locating this work within a broader spectrum of research. Except for anarchist studies, most studies of non-capitalism within Islamic contexts are of philosophies that assume the state to be necessary. Subsequently, this chapter may be considered a contribution to the development of thinking about anti-authoritarian and non-state-based socialism within Islamic contexts. All history is a form of story-telling. How these stories are justified and received are then matters of method and consensus. One aim of this chapter is to highlight certain stories that have been relegated to scholarly sidelines. The core of the argument here is that there are different ways of conceiving blends of Islam and socialism and that differences may be complementary.

Imagining Islamic Socialisms

As the 'winners' tend to write and re-write history, even within Islamic contexts, communistic and syncretic socialist currents, such as the Khurramiyyah or the Babis, are typically written off as non-Muslims or heretics. Similarly, the Qaramatiyyah (or Qarmatians/Qaramites) established what has been called the "world's first enduring communistic society"[3] in eastern

"You can't operate a capitalistic system unless you are vulturistic; you have to have someone else's blood to suck to be a capitalist" (Malcolm X, *Malcolm X Speaks: Selected Speeches and Statements*, George Breitman, ed., New York: Pathfinder Press 1990, 121). Socialism often refers to worker ownership of the means of production and distribution yet shall here include both social democrats and grassroots mutual aid both of which, in very different ways, strive for more equal distribution of resources within capitalist contexts. Nearly all examples of 'Islamic socialism' are of this kind rather than either communistic or completely opposed to all aspects of capitalist economics.

3 For a journalistic overview, see Mohanned Rahman, "The Qarmatians: The World's First Enduring Communistic Society", *World Bulletin* (22 January 2014), www.worldbulletin.net/haber/127416/the-qarmatians-the-worlds-first-enduring-communistic-society. Possibly Ismailites or a related group, the Qaramatiyyah were notorious for having stolen the Black Stone of the Kaba (circa *317*/929–*340*/951). They had stolen it from Mecca in three pieces and taken it to their base in Hajar/al-Hasa. According to the Ottoman historian Qutb al-Din: "Qarmatian leader Abu Tahir al-Qarmati set the Black Stone up in his own mosque, the Masjid al-Dirar, with the intention of redirecting the Hajj away from Mecca" (Rahman, "The Qarmatians"). They resisted offers to pay them for its return. Approximately 22 years later, according to the historian al-Juwayni, they returned it in seven pieces with the statement: "By command we stole it, and by

Arabia from approximately *286*/899 to *470*/1077. In *The New Encyclopedia of Islam* they are described as "a movement of peasants and laborers [who] bear a strong resemblance to modern 'liberation armies'"[4]. With a 178-year span, the communistic state of the Qaramatiyyah lasted more than twice as long as the Soviet Union's 73-year reign.

Ever since the 1960s, the idea of Islamic socialism and self-proclaimed socialist governments or organizations in predominantly Muslim countries became common (however egalitarian or not) and there has already been a considerable amount of research in this area. Research in regard to socialist or anti-capitalist currents within Islamic contexts might be divided into the following primary categories:

(1) 'Islamic economics' and 'Islamic banking'[5];
(2) various self-proclaimed Islamic socialist governments such as Algeria[6], Egypt[7], Pakistan[8], or South Yemen and Afghanistan[9];
(3) case studies of resistance movements in places such as the Anti-capitalist Muslims and Alevis in Turkey[10], peasants in Egypt[11], the PKK

command we returned it" (Cyril Glassé, *The New Encyclopedia of Islam*: *Revised Edition of the Concise Encyclopedia of Islam*, Walnut Creek: AltaMira Press 2001, 369). Their society was a curious syncretism that put them at odds with Sunni and Shi'i-Muslims alike as well as an interest-free economy in which property and wealth was shared among citizens yet purportedly built upon the labor of 30,000 enslaved Ethiopians. Most details about their society are drawn from Nasiri Khusrow (1004–1088 CE) who visited al-Hasa in 1051. At their peak their reign stretched from what is modern-day Bahrain to Syria and Palestine. Although their rule seems to have waxed and waned, their base in Bahrain appears to have been ultimately defeated by *470*/1077 (for a more detailed account see "Decline of the Qarmatians" in: *Ismaili History*, drawn largely from Mumtaz Ali Tajjdin's *History of the Ismailis*: http://ismaili.net/histoire/history05/history511.html).

4 Glassé, *The New Encyclopedia of Islam*, 369.

5 Robert W. Hefner, "Islamic Economics and Global Capitalism", *Society* 44: 1 (2009), 16–22; Farhad Nomani and Ali Rahnema, *Islamic Economic Systems*, London and New Jersey: Zed Books 1994.

6 Jeffrey James Byrne, "Our Own Special Brand of Socialism: Algeria and the Contest of Modernities in the 1960s", *Diplomatic History* 33: 3 (2009), 427–447; John R. Nellis, "Algerian Socialism and Its Critics", *Canadian Journal of Political Science / Revue canadienne de science politique* 13: 3 (1980), 481–507.

7 Hamid Enayat, "Islam and Socialism in Egypt", *Middle Eastern Studies* 4: 2 (1968), 141–172.

8 Bidanda M. Chengappa, "Pakistan: Impact of Islamic Socialism", *Strategic Analysis* 26: 1 (2002), 27–47; Nasim A. Jawed, "Islamic Socialism: An Ideological Trend in Pakistan in the 1960s", *The Muslim World* 65: 3 (1975), 196–215.

9 John Ishiyama, "The Sickle and the Minaret: Communist Successor Parties in Yemen and Afghanistan after the Cold War", *Middle East Review of International Affairs* 9: 1 (2005), 7–29.

10 Güldem Baykal Büyüksaraç, "'All Dominion Belongs to Allah... Capital Get Out': The Issue of Social Justice and Muslim Anti-Capitalists in Turkey", *Cross Currents* 66: 2 (2016), 239–251; Omer Tekdemir, "Constructing a Social Space for Alevi Political Identity: Religion, Antagonism and Collective Passion", *National Identities* 20: 1 (2017), 1–21.

in Kurdistan[12], the Muslim Brotherhood in Syria[13], or the Mojahedin in Iran[14];

(4) relations between anti-socialist Muslims, Muslim socialists, Sufis, and Communist Party administrations during the Soviet-period[15] or (largely) Western socialists living in Muslim countries[16];

(5) theoretical work such as comparisons between Islam and Marxism[17] or development of Islamic Liberation Theology[18].

To these one might add secondary categories that are either:

(a) Indirectly related to socialism such as anti-colonialist/anti-imperialist struggles[19] and pan-Islamism[20]; or

(b) biographies of activists/thinkers such as 'Alī Sharī'atī in Iran[21], Faysal Al-'Attas in Yemen[22], and Meena Keshwar Kemal, the founder of Revolutionary Association of Women of Afghanistan[23].

---

11 Nathan J. Brown, *Peasant Politics in Modern Egypt: The Struggle against the State*, New Haven and London: Yale University Press 1990.

12 Abdullah Öcalan, *Democratic Confederalism*, transl. by International Initiative, London and Cologne: Transmedia Publishing 2011; Oso Sabio, *Rojava: An Alternative to Imperialism, Nationalism, and Islamism in the Middle East*, self-published 2015; Yagmur Savran, "The Rojava Revolution and British Solidarity", *Anarchist Studies* 24: 1 (2016), 7–12.

13 Joshua Teitelbaum, "The Muslim Brotherhood in Syria, 1945–1958: Founding, Social Origins, Ideology", *Middle East Journal* 65: 2 (2011), 213–233.

14 Ervand Abrahamian, *Radical Islam: The Iranian Mojahedin*, London: I. B. Tauris 1989.

15 Alexandre Bennigsen and S. Enders Wimbush, *Mystics and Commissars: Sufism in the Soviet Union*, London: C. Hurst 1985; Ben Fowkes and Bülent Gökay, "Unholy Alliance: Muslims and Communists. An Introduction", *Journal of Communist Studies and Transition Politics* 25: 1 (2009), 1–31; Adeeb Khalid, *Islam after Communism: Religion and Politics in Central Asia*, Berkeley and Los Angeles: Univ. of California Press 2007; Michael A. Reynolds, "Muslim Mobilization in Imperial Russia's Caucasus", in: *Islam and the European Empires*, David Motadel, ed., Oxford: Oxford University Press 2014, 187–212; Maxime Rodinson, *Marxism and the Muslim World*, London: Zed Press 1972.

16 Ilham Khuri-Makdisi, *The Eastern Mediterranean and the Making of Global Radicalism, 1860–194*, Berkeley and Los Angeles: University of California Press 2010; David Porter, *Eyes to the South: French Anarchists & Algeria*, Oakland and Edinburgh: AK Press 2011.

17 Ernest Gellner, "Islam and Marxism: Some Comparisons", in: *Islam: Critical Concepts in Sociology*, vol. 2, Bryan S. Turner, ed., London and New York: Routledge 2003, 24–30.

18 Asghar Ali Engineer, *Islam and Liberation Theology: Essays on Liberative Elements in Islam*, New Delhi: Sterling Publishers 1990; Hamid Dabashi, *Islamic Liberation Theology: Resisting the Empire*, London and New York: Routledge 2008.

19 Fait Muedini, "Sufism and Anti-Colonial Violent Resistance Movements: The Qadiriyya and Sanussi Orders in Algeria and Libya", *Open Theology* 1 (2015), 134–145.

20 Sami A. Hanna, "Al-Afghānī: A Pioneer of Islamic Socialism", *The Muslim World* 57: 1 (1967), 24–32.

21 Ali Rahnema, *An Islamic Utopian: A Political Biography of Ali Shari'ati*, London and New York: I. B. Tauris 1998.

22 Thanos Petouris, "Faysal Al-'Attas: The Maoist Sayyid", *British-Yemeni Society Journal* 21 (2014), 32–40.

Although the scope is too broad to allow for much detail, a few examples can be mentioned, in particular Muṣṭafā al-Sibāʿī of the Syrian Muslim Brotherhood, in order to exemplify three distinct manifestations of Islamic socialism conceived here as minarchist, dervish, and small-scale, non-state-based variants (not necessarily mutually exclusive in relation to one another).

In regard to Islamic economics, Islamic socialism, and Islamic banking, it is common to express Islam as a 'third way' that is spared from the excesses and materialism of both capitalism and 'secular' socialism. Yet 'Islamic banking' may tend to be closer to capitalism than socialism. As Robert Hefner wrote in his article "Islamic Economic and Global Capitalism":

> Although aspiring to provide a full-blown alternative to neoclassical economics, the programs recommended by Islamic economists are actually modest in scope. They focus on the effort to build two institutions: a system of Islamic banking that steers clear of charging interest, and a program of religiously mandated almsgiving, the *zakat*, the purpose of which is to purify wealth and redistribute some of its surplus to the needy. … Islamic jurisprudence did not develop laws for corporations, and, therefore, it did not develop a concept of banking or corporate finance. This is to say that the broader legal framework on which Islamic banking depends actually owes more to Western civil law than it does to classical Islamic precedents. [So] from the perspective of Western finance, the principles underlying Islamic banking are not in the least alien. On the contrary, they operate in the same manner as the venture capital industries that have financed some of the American economy's most dynamic enterprises, including Silicon Valley's software industries.[24]

To a large extent one might say something similar about Islamic socialism in relation to most of the governments who have self-identified as such. As with European social democracies, there are far more similarities to capitalist economics than differences. Perhaps more of a challenge to global capitalist economics might be found in resistance movements. One example is that of the Iranian Mojahedin, founded in the early 1960s, who wrote in an early pamphlet:

> Islam and Marxism teach the same lesson, for they both fight against injustice. Islam and Marxism contain the same message, for they both inspire martyrdom, struggle, and self-sacrifice. Who is closer to Islam: the Vietnamese who fight American imperialism or the Shah who collaborates with Zionism and imperialism?[25]

One of the clearest and most prominent examples of Islamic socialist resistance is that of Syrian Muslim Brotherhood leader Muṣṭafā al-Sibāʿī whose development of 'Islamic socialism' in his book *Ishtirakiyyah al-Islām*

23 Melody Ermachild Chavis, *Meena: Heroine of Afghanistan*, New York: St. Martin's Griffin 2003; Friba of Rawa, "Life Sketch of Martyred Meena, Founding Leader of RAWA", *Storia delle Donne* 4 (2008), 21–34.

24 Hefner, "Islamic Economics", 17–19.

25 Abrahamian, *Radical Islam*, 102.

(*Socialism of Islam*)[26] in the 1950s is thought to have influenced others in the region such as the socialism of Gamal Abdel Nasser even while he persecuted members of the Muslim Brotherhood in Egypt[27]. Al-Sibāʿī wrote:

> What socialism really aims at, in all its various ideologies, is to put a stop to the individual who would exploit capital to become rich at the expense of the misery and wretchedness of the masses; to provide state supervision over the individual's economic potential and to bring about social equality among all citizens so as to eliminate all manifestations of poverty and deprivation as well as the disproportionate divergence in which you have hunger, poverty, sickness and degradation on the one hand, and luxury, harshness and moral disintegration on the other. I do not believe that anyone who knows Islam and understands its spirit can properly deny that Islam clearly had these same goals in mind when legislating, and so legislated as to guarantee its realization in the best possible form.[28]

He also distinguished Islamic socialism from capitalism with which it had "nothing in common as economic systems go" and "no common meeting ground as far as politics are concerned, since Western capitalism is stained with people's blood and has imperialism"[29]. Nonetheless, his vision was to be inclusive: "Islamic Socialism takes in all citizens of the state, Muslims and non-Muslims alike, because its doctrines and rights do not exclude anyone."[30] Al-Sibāʿī also wanted to "rid society of poverty" wherein poverty meant not only hunger and disease but "a paucity of affluence, or rather inequality in comforts and living standards"[31]. Furthermore, among a person's basic needs which ought to be guaranteed by the state, al-Sibāʿī included a home, property, education, transportation, books, and weapons. Yet he also distinguished Islamic socialism from communism which leads to "class war" and forbids "individual ownership"[32]. Even political, social, and religious rights were important because they keep "government and governors dependent on the will of the people, unlike communist socialism where people are made to depend on the will of a small group of rulers"[33]. Interestingly, this combined with the idea of leaving some responsibilities for welfare up to citizenry. For example, relatives would be responsible for the care for elderly and sick family members though they would not receive compensation for their labor: "Islamic Socialism gives people a share in the govern-

---

26 *Ishtirakiyah,* usually translated as "socialism", literally means partaking or sharing (Mahmoud Ayoub, *Islam and the Third Universal Theory: The Religious Thought of Mu'ammar al-Qadhdhafi*, London: KPI 1987, 97).

27 Teitelbaum, "The Muslim Brotherhood in Syria", 220.

28 George H. Gardner and Sami A. Hanna, "Islamic Socialism", *The Muslim World* 56: 2 (1966), 71–86, 75–76.

29 Ibid., 79.

30 Ibid., 78.

31 Ibid., 76.

32 Ibid., 79–80.

33 Ibid., 78.

ment's social security scheme by letting them look after relatives. This has the advantage of relieving the state's budget, and keeping intact charity, friendship and family ties."[34]

This minimal approach to the state combined with socialism might be described as 'minarchist socialism'. This could also be detected in the work by Egyptian Muslim Brotherhood ideologue Sayyid Quṭb who wrote that Islam "strives from the beginning to abolish all those systems and governments which are based on the rule of man over men and the servitude of one human being to another"[35].

Notably, al-Sibāʿī clarified that Islamic socialism was not the socialism of "the Darwishes or of the ascetics; it is not that of the Sufis or of the Indian fakirs who shun money and possessions, fighting shy of life's burdens and responsibilities"[36]. This last version, what might be labeled here 'dervish socialism' is, as al-Sibāʿī noted, not aimed at providing a model for all of society but in maintaining an ideal within or outside of society in which economics is characterized by mutual aid, sharing, trust in God, rejection of money and property, and vagabondism. In a sense, the dervishes as described by Ahmet Karamustafa[37] and others manifested a type of social solidarity on the fringes of, or sometimes outside of, dominant Islamic society. It was not a path for all citizens but it was a path that rejected conventional economics. For example, one of the earliest Sufis, Rābiʿa al-ʿAdawiyya of Basra (ca. 717–801), is reported to have said that a servant of God "should possess nothing in this world or the next, save Him"[38] and the dervish Otman Baba (ca. 1378–1478) was "completely averse to owning property" while comparing money to feces.[39]

In contrast, some scholars have taken certain practices and traditions to manifest egalitarianism within Islamic societies (rather than Islamic societies as such) such as Jean Chesneaux who, drawing on French scholarship, wrote that in classical Muslim societies,

> [E]galitarian and community tendencies are manifested … in the form of groups and private or semi-private associations, some of which have survived up to the threshold of the modern world; village communities (*djemaa*), corporations (*sinf*),

34 Ibid.

35 Albert J. Bergesen, *The Sayyid Qutb Reader*, New York: Routledge 2008, 31.

36 Gardner and Hanna, "Islamic Socialism", 78.

37 Ahmet T. Karamustafa, *God's Unruly Friends: Dervish Groups in the Islamic Middle Period 1200–1550*, Oxford: Oneworld 2006 [1994].

38 Margaret Smith, *Rábiʿa the Mystic and Her Fellow-Saints in Islam*, Cambridge and New York: Cambridge Univ. Press 1984 [1928], 84.

39 Karamustafa, *God's Unruly Friends*, 48.

with their chivalrous oath of solidarity (*futuwwa*), and fraternal societies of mutual aid (*akhi*).[40]

To these Chesneaux also added *zakāh* (obligatory alms-giving), *ribā* (the ban on usury), and *waqf*, the principle of "property ... destined to foundations with a collective interest: hospitals, water adductions, drains, cemeterial spas, schools and various other charitable works."[41] Even in the example that might seem the least socialistic, the corporation, Chesneaux noted that it is possible that they developed in relation to the Qaramatiyyah: "Craftsmen lived a common life and divided the commissions they received..." and "they were bound" by an oath of solidarity with poor people.[42] The *akhi* mutual aid societies of Asia Minor in the 1200–1300s functioned similarly and also played roles in revolts against unpopular rule. Under the larger umbrella category of anti-authoritarian socialism, these tendencies, if manifest in a context such as the reign of the Qaramatiyyah (regardless of actual authoritarian or hierarchical practices), might be thought of as an ideal of totalistic socialism in which socialistic elements are coordinated together through the state or a similar central organization. These tendencies in non-communistic states might be thought of as 'small-scale non-state-based socialism'. In such cases, many parts can operate socialistically independent of the state.

Imagining Islamic Anarchisms

Closely related to anti-authoritarian socialisms is a research area, still in its infancy, concerned with anarchist elements of Muslim thinking, practice, and history.[43] Almost no research had been published in this area prior to

40 Jean Chesneaux, "Egalitarian and Utopian Traditions in the East", *Diogenes* 16 (1968), 76–102, 96.

41 Ibid., 98; see Adam Sabra, *Poverty and Charity in Medieval Islam: Mamluk Egypt, 1250–1517*, Cambridge and New York: Cambridge Univ. Press 2000 for a historical discussion of *waqf* in Egypt.

42 Chesneaux, "Egalitarian and Utopian Traditions", 97.

43 Harold Barclay, *People without Government: An Anthropology of Anarchism*, London: Kahn & Averill and Cienfuegos Press 1982; idem, "Islam, Muslim Societies, and Anarchy", *Anarchist Studies* 10: 2 (2002), 105–118; Patricia Crone, "Ninth-Century Muslim Anarchists", *Past and Present* 167 (2000); Anthony T. Fiscella, "Imagining an Islamic Anarchism: A New Field of Study is Ploughed", in: *Religious Anarchism: New Perspectives*, Alexandre Christoyannopoulos, ed., Newcastle upon Tyne: Cambridge Scholars Publishing 2009, 280–317; idem, *Varieties of Islamic Anarchism: A Brief Introduction*, Alpine Anarchist Productions 2014; Mohamed Abdou [Jean-Veneuse], *Anarca-Islam*, MA Thesis Queen's University, Kingston, Canada 2009, https://central.bac-lac.gc.ca/.item?id=MR65136&op=pdf&app=Library; Karamustafa, *God's Unruly Friends*; Peter Lamborn Wilson, *Sacred Drift: Essays on the Margins of Islam*, San Francisco: City Lights 1993.

1990 and there is no consensus about key terms such as 'anarchism' (Karamustafa and Wilson included antinomian Sufis whereas Barclay and Crone reserved the term for anti-statists such as the Najdiyyah). Furthermore, the retroactive application of terms such as 'socialism' and 'anarchism' to non-European contexts prior to the 1900s is hardly unproblematic. Karamustafa's dervishes would not be considered socialist in a Marxist sense and Crone denies that the subjects of her study were[44]. Often combined with a dearth of historical evidence, this can lead to enthusiastic speculation. For example, Peter Lamborn Wilson's description of the famous Assassins (the Nizari Ismailis who took over regions of Persia ca. 1088–1256):

> One might derive a great deal of enjoyment from contemplating–imagining–a contemporary version of the concept of social justice propagated at Alamut [their major stronghold]. ... the economic communism and the cooperation between autonomous strongholds which characterized Nizari society somewhat resembled certain ideas such as syndicalism and council communism. Altogether, a curious blend of individualist anarchism, Bakuninism, and antinomian mysticism sums up Alamut in modern political language.[45]

Wilson, who identifies with Sufism, syndicalism, anarchism, and a host of other traditions, imagines his own version of the Assassins. Similarly, this chapter is interested more in imagination and vision than determining what is 'true'. In contrast to Wilson's example, this chapter aims to present stories and visions by the actors themselves from within Islamic contexts in order to develop a broader vocabulary for understanding varieties of Islamic socialism.

All of these tendencies within Islamic contexts have relatively similar counter-parts within anarchist contexts. Dervish socialism is comparable to drop-out culture or anarcho-primitivism (with Peter Lamborn Wilson/Hakim Bey being a prominent figure who is associated with both). A notable difference however is the insistence among most Sufis upon the centrality of direct experience of the Divine as well as a lineage or tradition through which alternative institutions are based and through which dialogue with other believers is possible (even if they might be deemed heretical). Totalistic visions such as the Qaramatiyyah or al-Sibāʿī's Islamic socialism might be remotely comparable to anarcho-syndicalist visions of entire societies that are run with minimal or non-existent states (such as in Barcelona in 1936)[46] and primarily organized through numerous professional as-

44 "Mu'tazilite anarchism was not concerned with social reorganization at all, nor was it egalitarian, let alone communist" (Crone, "Ninth-Century Muslim Anarchists", 21).

45 Wilson, *Sacred Drift*, 74.

46 During the Spanish Civil War, Catalonia in general and Barcelona in particular were under anarcho-syndicalist control in which the economy (mills, mines, power companies, factories, theaters, transportation, etc.) was largely run by trade unions (pri-

sociations, committees, worker syndicates, and collectives. Small-scale non-state-based socialism within Islamic contexts also has corresponding counterparts within anarchist contexts such as the Catholic Worker Movement founded by Dorothy Day and Peter Maurin which emphasizes simple and collective living, serving the needy, anti-militarism, anti-imperialism, and following the example of Christ.

It can also be worth mentioning that recent years have seen the rise of persons who self-identify as Muslim anarchists. One such person is activist and scholar Mohamed Jean-Veneuse, whose *Anarca-Islam* has suggested various ways in which anarchism and Islam overlap and complement one another. In relation to economic questions of property, for example, Jean-Veneuse cited a verse from the Quran ("O believers, expend of the good things you have earned, and of what We have produced for you from the earth…" 2: 269) and developed thoughts on it:

> God ordains property as divinely possessed, to circumscribe the hoarding of property by Caretakers. No Caretaker may deprive another Caretaker from property, even if by force. … The role of a human being, as noted, is the temporary caretaking for or 'borrowing' of God's property. ... a Muslim community's economic system is decentralized. That is, it is a system structurally comprised of a multiplicity of decentralized small firms co-borrowed from God, with each small firm constituted by a group of Communal Caretakers in collective partnership. … In this interpretation of Islam, the ethico-political principles involve upholding anti-authoritarian and anti-capitalist commitments.[47]

In this vision property, a cornerstone of capitalist economics, is both limited (by virtue of it being on loan) and also constrained through obligations to counsel and cooperate with others as well as to take public interest (*maṣlaḥah*) into consideration in regard to economic engagements. While there are certain Quranic verses that many Muslim critics of capitalism return to, and observers may witness recurring themes, there is no one single vision of either Islamic anarchism or Islamic socialism.

Isabelle Eberhardt/Mahmoud Essadi and Anti-Economics

Isabelle Eberhardt/Mahmoud Essadi (1877–1904)[48] is most known for being a feminist without a movement, a white person who moved to Africa

marily the CNT and the UGT). See Antony Beevor, *Battle for Spain: The Spanish Civil War, 1936–1939*, New York: Penguin Books 2006.

47 Abdou [Jean-Veneuse], *Anarca-Islam*, 98–99.

48 The standard is to refer to her by her birth name but in other contexts (e.g., Malcolm X/El-Hajj Malik El-Shabazz, Muhammad Ali) the standard is to refer to a person by their chosen name that, in this case, would be Mahmoud Essadi. My deviation from the standard involves thus a compromise in which she is referred to here as Eberhardt/Essadi.

and dressed like an Arab, an anarchist who converted to Islam, a woman who dressed like a man, an aristocrat who lived as a pauper, a Sufi steeped in drug addiction, a European with racist views[49] who married a North African man, and a gifted writer whose work was primarily recognized after her death at the age of 27. Born to a Russian mother, she was raised in Geneva with several siblings and a (presumably biological) father named Alexandre Trophimowsky who was an ex-Orthodox priest from Armenia and an acquaintance of the well-known anarchist Mikhail Bakunin. Her journalistic and literary career was challenged in part by her lack of focus, continuing economic troubles, restless traveling, and her addiction to *kif*. She drowned in a flash flood in the Algerian desert before her most popular works–including her diaries–were published. Much of her writing (nearly all in French) was destroyed in the flood but much of it survived her and was translated into English in the 1980s. Today one can find short stories and journals by her[50] as well as biographies and scholarly work about her and her life.[51]

As far as I can tell (at least from the English literature), there is no research explicitly in regard to her thoughts and writing on economics. Indeed, some might find the very idea laughable as her life was riddled with economic woes, frequent debt, and financial chaos. Even when she had the potential to access her notable inheritance, she bungled it and continued to live in great debt. Furthermore, in 1899, she leaned out her second-story window in Batna and threw her money to the wind. She was subject to an assassination attempt in 1901 but miraculously survived. She received small amounts of money for her writing and a meager inheritance, yet she remained nearly destitute and often turned to her Muslim co-workers to bor-

49 This has been documented and discussed by, amongst others, Lynda Chouiten, *Isabelle Eberhardt and North Africa: Nomadism as a Carnivalesque Mirage*, London: Lexington Books 2015.

50 Isabelle Eberhardt, *The Oblivion Seekers*, San Francisco: City Lights 1975; idem, *Vagabond*, London: Hogarth Press 1988 [1922]; idem, *The Passionate Nomad: the Diary of Isabelle Eberhardt*, Boston: Beacon Press 1988; idem, *In the Shadow of Islam*, London and Chester Springs: Peter Owen 1993.

51 Emily Apter, *Continental Drift: From National Characters to Virtual Subjects*, Chicago: Univ. of Chicago Press 1999; Michelle Chilcoat, "Anticolonialism and Misogyny in the Writings of Isabelle Eberhardt", *The French Review* 77: 5 (2004), 949–957; Chouiten, *Isabelle Eberhardt*; Julie Ann Clancy-Smith, *Rebel and Saint: Muslim Notables, Populist Protest, Colonial Encounters (Algeria and Tunisia, 1800-1904)*, Berkeley: Univ. of California Press 1994; Kelsey DeForest, "Imperial Performativity: The Life, Transgressions, and Writings of Isabelle Eberhardt under the Lens of Queer Theory", *Undergraduate Research Awards*, Paper 6, Hollins University 2011, http://digitalcommons.hollins.edu/researchawards/6; Annette Kobak, *Isabelle: The Life of Isabelle Eberhardt*, New York: Alfred A. Knopf 1989; Patricia M. E. Lorcin, *Colonial Nostalgia: European Women's Narratives of Algeria and Kenya 1900–Present*, New York: Palgrave Macmillan 2012; Cecily Mackworth, *The Destiny of Isabelle Eberhardt: A Biography*, New York: The Ecco Press 1986.

row money or relied on the generosity of others including the Sufi order, the Qadiriyyah, to which she belonged. She occasionally tutored in Arabic and took odd jobs. For a short while she worked alongside a friend whose occupation was that of tax collector which gave her a grim view on a seldom seen side of national economics. Her trip to Algeria in 1900 had been financed by the wealthy American widow of the racist Marquis de Morès who enlisted Eberhardt to find the culprit who lay behind her husband's murder in the Algerian desert. In rather typical Eberhardt fashion, the money was spent but little, if any, effort was laid down in the criminal investigation. Although she spent a good part of her adult life scrounging off of others, it seems that when she did have money she frequently spent it on others in an embodiment of the spirit of mutual aid. Once, when she stumbled upon an impoverished and dying man who had been abandoned by his children, she put him on her horse, carried him to the hospital and paid for his care. This was not an isolated incident but reflected her attitude in general. It's reported that during the time she lived in Ténès she regularly applied her skills in language, medicine, and Quranic study to the benefit of the local population and spent her money–not only on tobacco and books–but on the sick or oppressed who came to her seeking help.

In this way, her economic troubles and personal inadequacy in regard to finances can help highlight her views that might be described as anti-economical yet not irrelevant to economics. For example, in 1904 she wrote in a short section of her journal titled "Saharan Theocracy":

> Thanks to the *zawiya* [sanctuary and home of the local Sufi leaders], misery is unknown in Kenadsa. No beggars in the streets of the *kasr*; all unfortunates take refuge in the *zawiya*'s protective shadow, and live there as long as they please. Most make themselves useful as servants, workers, or shepherds, but no one is compelled to work.[52]

For Eberhardt/Essadi who regarded herself as "a nomad who has no country besides Islam", this observation goes beyond a mere description and into the realm of the prescriptive[53]. Indeed, her ideal vision of economics was not intended to be a blueprint for all cultures or all of society but as a remedy for the gaps in current economics which tend to let so many people fall through the cracks and into destitution. It was both a vision of vagabond economics that allowed for impromptu exchanges where "you asked for soup and a bed in exchange for a helping hand or some small repair job," and also a vision of mystical transcendence which called for some section of society to occupy themselves with the intoxication of prayer, devotion,

[52] Eberhardt, *In the Shadow of Islam*, 68.
[53] Idem, *The Passionate Nomad*, 2.

and a constant preoccupation "with the quest for better selves".[54] It entailed, on the one hand, a committed resistance to worldly materialism where one could "sleep in the chilly silence of the night below stars that drop from great heights, with the sky's infinite expanse for a roof and the warm earth for a bed."[55] This was not a mere excursion but the ideal of a lifetime:

> Oh, to be alone, to be free, unknown, with no ties or attachments, treading the traveller's welcoming, soft earth! To fall asleep in some chance spot, possessing nothing, attached to nothing, and the next day to travel on into different surroundings, amongst other people ... and so on forever![56]

She had an ongoing debate with her dear friend Archivir about desire and this too relates to economics. While he felt that happiness was derived from pursuing one's many needs, Eberhardt/Essadi felt that "one should limit one's needs as much as one can to avoid disillusionment".[57] However, it is also interesting to note her own contradictions here as her actual lifestyle and dream of a stable life included having a servant tend to her needs (which seemed to contrast sharply with her desire for simplicity).

Foreshadowing Guy Debord's *Society of the Spectacle* (1967), she wrote in her 1900 piece entitled "The Age of the Void" (L'Age du Néant), against a civilization in which "[h]our by hour needs increase and are nearly always unsatisfied, peopling the earth with discontented rebels. The superfluous has become a necessity and luxuries indispensable." Atheism placed society "on its knees in front of the menacing spectre of nothingness." There is no longer a framework for people to relate to and strive within. Instead, humankind is consigned to a "void of which it believes itself to be a part."[58]

This rejection of materialism coincided with, in her words, "a boundless compassion for all who suffer injustice, all who are weak and oppressed."[59] In a description of a physical marketplace, Eberhardt/Essadi could just as well be describing the global market:

> Fights erupt over the slightest challenge, and one can guess what it must be like in the Moroccan bled-es-siba [Berber-controlled areas], far from any surveillance. There, in the even more tumultuous markets, gunpowder speaks, cadavers roll amid the merchandise, and blood flows on the beaten earth.[60]

---

54 Idem, *Vagabond*, 78; idem, *The Passionate Nomad*, 9.

55 Ibid., 2.

56 Eberhardt, *Vagabond*, 79. Notably, in one journal entry she expressed her desire to settle down in Ouargla/Wargla which happens to be an Ibadi town populated predominantly by Berber Mozabites whose own economic prosperity, thrift, and prudence stood in sharp contrast to her own life.

57 Idem, *The Passionate Nomad*, 11.

58 Kobak, *Isabelle*, 103.

59 Eberhardt, *The Passionate Nomad*, 1.

60 Chouiten, *Isabelle Eberhardt*, 19.

In contrast, her ideal was an embrace of mutual aid and rejection of bureaucracy and wealth. It was an ideal in which "no one is compelled to work" but wherein most contributed according to their abilities even when they failed to fall within the spectrum of mainstream work and lifestyle norms. This assessment does not mean to idealize or romanticize her views. In many cases she expressed cluttered and contradictory views. Her ambiguous relationship to French colonialism in Algeria and Morocco and her depictions of the racial Other as a "primitive animality" are problematic to say the least.[61] Yet this does not mean that her views on economics do not fall within longstanding traditions. In Northwest European contexts, it might be recognized as dropout culture or anarcho-primitivism. In Islamic contexts, it might be recognized as that which al-Sibāʿī pejoratively described as dervish socialism: a place for nomads, deviants, and mystics to support one another and others who had been excluded from (or reject) the broader society's economic system.

The Green Book and "Third Universal Theory" Economics

The Green Book (1982) is the ideological vision outlined by Colonel Muammar Qaddafi[62] (1942–2011) upon which Libyan society was to develop. This vision developed gradually from the beginning of the bloodless revolution on September 1, 1969 until its very bloody fall at the hands of NATO forces aligned with local rebels in 2011. In fact, while some of the proposals and practices outlined in *The Green Book* were implemented to some degree (such as worker-owned and run jobsites and housing for all), other aspects seemed to have been virtually ignored. For example, Qaddafi's own role as de facto dictator was not even mentioned in *The Green Book* which, in other respects, was described by himself as a socialist form of di-

61 Her own apparent misogyny toward other women (whether in Europe or Africa) was also problematic. She held a strong preference for male protagonists in her stories and seldom depicted women positively including in her first short story *Infernalia* (1895) which was about necrophilia. Michelle Chilcoat wrote, "Women are loathed in these texts, it seems, because they cannot tolerate solitude, and they always need to know things, like when their lover will be coming back, or what the future holds for them. Their deaths are often gruesome" (Chilcoat, "Anticolonialism and Misogyny", 953). In contrast, two people whom she maintained respect for in real life were women: Vera Popov, an anarchist friend, and Lalla Zaynab, a prominent Sufi leader and personal acquaintance. Regarding colonialism, Patricia Lorcin has noted that colonial power structures "were not binary" (Lorcin, *Colonial Nostalgia*, 8). Eberhardt/Essadi's position of privilege as a white person was complicated by her position of vulnerability and oppression as woman, nomad, convert to Islam, and cross-dressing outsider (ibid., 22).

62 His name is also spelled Gaddafi, al-Qathafi, Khadhafi, and al Qadhdhafi to mention a few of the various transliterations.

rect democracy (labeled *jamāhīriyyah*, or people's democracy) with family, tribe, and nation as the basis for social order.

The ideal presented, however far from reality it may have been, was that of a stateless society in which there were neither governments nor prisons. Instead, all citizens were to organize according to their profession (syndicates, unions, professional associations) and their location. They would gather every month in each neighborhood ("basic popular congress") to decide through direct voting all matters that could be decided at the local level. Those matters that addressed shared concerns of the region or nation would be dealt with by the same means, except that delegates (via "working committees" and "people's committees") would be sent to the higher levels of decision-making which would meet annually in the General People's Congress. Delegates would not be representatives capable of making independent decisions but were to be bound by the decisions of their constituency in all matters.

A great deal of literature is available both about Libya during the reign of Qaddafi in general[63] as well as works that discuss *The Green Book* and Qaddafi's ideology specifically.[64,65] This section is intended to provide both a brief overview and to locate the ideology of *The Green Book* within anarchist and Islamic contexts.[66] The primary concern here is not with actual practic-

63 John Davis, *Libyan Politics: Tribe and Revolution*, Berkeley and Los Angeles: Univ. of California Press 1987; Dirk Vandewalle, *A History of Modern Libya*, Cambridge: Cambridge Univ. 2006.

64 Ayoub, *Islam and the Third Universal Theory*; Alia Brahimi, "Libya's Revolution", *The Journal of North African Studies* 16: 4 (2011), 605–624; Mohamed A. El-Khawas, *Qaddafi: His Ideology in Theory and Practice*, Brattleboro: Amana Books 1986; Mansour O. El-Kikhia, *Libya's Qaddafi: The Politics of Contradiction*, Gainesville: Univ. Press of Florida 1997; Mattias Gardell, "Muhammar Al-Khadaffi och den Libyska Revolutionen", *Anarkistisk Tidskrift* 6–7 (1992), 11–34; Sami G. Hajjar, "The Jamahiriya Experiment in Libya: Qadhafi and Rousseau", *The Journal of Modern African Studies* 18: 2 (1980), 181–200; idem, "The Marxist Origins of Qadhafi's Economic Thought", *The Journal of Modern African Studies* 20: 3 (1982), 361–375; Raymond A. Hinnebusch, "Charisma, Revolution, and State Formation: Qaddafi and Libya", *Third World Quarterly* 6: 1 (1984), 59–73; Dirk Vandewalle, "Qadhafi's 'Perestroika': Economic and Political Liberalization in Libya", *Middle East Journal* 45: 2 (1991), 216–231.

65 It could be noted that at least one scholar has suggested that Qaddafi's ideology drew in large part upon (if not plagiarized) the thinking of Al-Sadiq al-Nayhum (Alberto Fernandez, "Liberating Islam from Bondage: The Radical Democratic Discourse of Al-Sadiq al-Nayhum", paper presented at the Seventh Annual Conference of the Center for the Study of Islam & Democracy (CSID), 5–6 May 2006 Washington, https://csidonline.org/7th-annual-conference-abstracts/).

66 While some have noted parallels in Qaddafi's thinking to anarchist Petr Kropotkin (Said Gafourov, "Social Philosophy of Russian Anarchism [Kropotkin] and of Muammar Al Qadhafi: An Essay in Comparison", *A-Infos News Service* 8 May 2003, www.ainfos.ca/03/may/ainfos00180.html [accessed 6 January 2008] or Jean-Jacques Rousseau [Hajjar, "The Jamahiriya Experiment"], and anarchist anthropologist Har-

es in Libya under Qaddafi but on the thoughts expressed in *The Green Book* in relation to economics that is discussed in one of the book's three main sections: "Part Two: The Solution of the Economic Problem 'Socialism' ".

First, as noted earlier, it has been common to portray 'Islamic socialism' as a third path alternative to Western materialistic capitalism and Soviet atheistic communism. *The Green Book* is no exception to this pattern. Qaddafi spent equal energy railing against capitalist parliamentary democracy and Soviet-style state socialism as he did promoting his own ostensibly more democratic vision. The book is strewn with slogans such as "The party system aborts democracy" and "No representation in lieu of the people". When it comes to the economy Qaddafi stated that "A person in need is a slave indeed" and socialism is the answer.[67] In other words, a system wherein all people's needs are met is a prerequisite to a just society. Furthermore, workers should be their own bosses since "the wage-worker is like a slave to the master that hires him"[68]. As a counter to those who would interpret the solution as something akin to Soviet state socialism he clarified that the wage-worker's slavery "lasts as long as he works for wages from the employer, whether the latter is an individual or a state"[69]. The solution then is to emancipate the worker from bosses altogether and let the worker personally own and manage production. Qaddafi provided an example of different scenarios in which a worker produces ten apples. In the first scenario (representing state socialism), the worker is given one apple for labor that produced ten apples. If the apple satisfies his[70] needs he will have no incentive to increase his production since he will anyways only get one apple. The same goes for the worker in such societies whose needs are not satisfied by one apple. In the second scenario (representing capitalism), the worker who produces ten apples receives a wage of less than the price of one apple. Since his wages are not enough to satisfy his needs he will either seek employment elsewhere or continue working just to survive (no mention is

old Barclay described Qaddafi's Third Universal Theory as a "decentralized syndicalist type of arrangement" (Barclay, "Islam, Muslim Societies, and Anarchy", 115), such influences have been denied on at least one occasion in which either Qaddafi, speaking of himself in the third person, or editor A. E. Murad wrote: "Muammar Qadhafi is a practical man. He did not research the orientation of his political action in books, but in the streets, learning from the people and from experience. Joseph de Maistre, Jean-Jacques Rousseau or Proudhon, one should realize, represent simply the reflection of what they encountered. It was never a question of Qadhafi being directly influenced by such thinkers" (A. E. Murad and R. Delorme, eds., *Testimonials*, Ottawa: Jerusalem International Publishing House 1982, 43).

67 Muammar Al Qathafi, *The Green Book*, Tripoli: Public Establishment for Publishing, Advertising, and Distribution 1982, 53.

68 Ibid., 45.

69 Ibid.

70 The text uses exclusively male pronouns here.

made of any potential incentive to produce more in order to receive higher wage). In the third scenario (representing the Third Universal Theory), the worker who produces ten apples keeps all ten apples for himself. It is only in this last scenario, according to Qaddafi, where production takes place "without apathy and without coercion".[71] The produced apples can then be traded with others for mutual benefit. At the same time, he did not mean that one person should have ten apples (beyond his needs) while other people go without enough to satisfy their own needs:

> Ultimately, all that is beyond the satisfaction of needs should remain the property of all the members of society ... because the hoarding of what exceeds their needs involves an encroachment on public wealth.[72]

This includes the rights of the physically and mentally disabled to as equal a share as everyone else. Not only should each person retain ownership of their vehicle (such as car) and their personal income (he even included food and clothing in the basic needs that he termed "sacred ownership"[73]), but each person should own their home. No one is allowed to rent out a home to someone else. Similarly, land is to be used by all for all: "Land is no one's property. But everyone has the right to use it, to benefit from it by *working, farming or pasturing*" (italics in original text[74]). The new socialist society will ultimately lead to the automatic disappearance of the wage system, profit, and money itself.

Unlike Eberhardt/Essadi, Qaddafi believed that "scientific development is an irreversible gain to humanity". Also unlike her, he explicitly declared domestic servants to be a form of enslavement to be abolished. However, he did provide a notable caveat to the equal sharing of resources by stating that "differences in individual wealth are only permissible for those who render a public service" and this disparity is to be in proportion to the degree of that service.[75] Such a curious caveat might explain how he could justify the massive wealth he accumulated in real life. As Leader of the Revolution the entire country was purportedly indebted to him. Although he philosophically rejected the types of servitude Eberhardt/Essadi cherished, the caveat enabled him to assume far more power, control, and domination than she could ever have dreamed of. In any case, the caveat need not eradicate the philosophical value of the original argument regarding excess and public needs.

71 Ibid., 59.
72 Ibid., 61–61.
73 Ibid., 64.
74 Ibid., 55.
75 Ibid., 61–63.

In "Part Three: The Social Basis of the Third Universal Theory" other issues related to economics were also addressed. Reminiscent of the Situationist critique of passive spectacle-based culture, Qaddafi critiqued masses for consuming public performances such as the arts and sports when they ought to instead be engaging in those activities directly:

> Sport is like praying, eating, and the feeling of warmth and coolness. It is stupid for crowds to enter a restaurant just to look at a person or a group of persons eating; it is stupid for people to let a person or a group of persons get warmed or enjoy ventilation on their behalf. … Public sport is a public need and the people should not be represented in its practice either physically or democratically. … The thousands who crowd stadiums to view, applaud and laugh are those foolish people who have failed to carry out the activity themselves. … The grandstand will disappear when no one is there to occupy it. … Those who direct the course of life for themselves do not need to watch it working through actors on the stage or in the cinemas.[76]

Such questions relate to economics in at least three senses: first, in relation to the production and/or sale of culture by the state or business sector; second, the consumption or production of culture by citizens; and third, in the interaction between state, market, and individual wherein the economic consequences of popular activity versus passivity play out in terms of subsequent mental and physical fitness, social habits, medical needs, etc.

Some have regarded Qaddafi's views as heretical for he has stated that *The Green Book* is a secular interpretation of Islamic principles.[77] Critical of the reliability of most hadiths, Qaddafi has emphasized the Quran and stated "The Qur'an is a guide to life for the entire world."[78] Yet *The Green Book* itself does not mention the Quran or Muḥammad. Qaddafi explained this omission as an attempt to retain interest for non-Muslims:

> It was not necessary to write… "The Prophet said 'all men are equal, like the teeth of a comb'." Nor…"Anyone who goes to sleep sated while his neighbor is hungry, is not one of us." Had we done this, *The Green Book* would have been simply a *hadith* book… Non-Muslims would see these references to the *hadith* and say, "This is a book for Muslims only".[79]

Interesting to note is that while U.S. Army War College professor Sami Hajjar saw Qaddafi's economic vision as directly influenced by Marxism,[80] Muslim anarcho-capitalist author Davi Barker found elements to appreciate in Qaddafi's economics writing that "one area where he was uncharacteristically lucid is monetary policy":

---

76 Ibid., 116–119.
77 Ayoub, *Islam and the Third Universal Theory*, 75.
78 Ibid., 77.
79 Ibid., 87.
80 Hajjar, "The Marxist Origins of Qadhafi's Economic Thought".

> Under Gaddafi, the Central Bank of Libya was completely state-run, funded by the country's vast oil wealth. It issued interest-free loans, and its own currency, the Libyan dinar, which was not controlled by international banks. … Before the US intervention in Libya, Gaddafi was on the verge of launching the Islamic Gold Dinar. The gold dinar would have transformed Libya into an economic powerhouse in the region. At the time Libya held an estimated 144 tons of gold. American press was almost completely silent about Gaddafi's gold dinar, but *Russia Today*, *Al Jazeera*, and the international press reported this as the reason for US intervention almost exclusively. Experts said the move had the potential to wreak havoc on the US economy as all those dollars flooded back to US shores.[81]

In at least some sense, Qaddafi's background as a Bedouin and Sufi enthusiast might place his vision of economics as a more detailed and totalistic version of Eberhardt's dervish socialism. However, aside from other distinctions, it is precisely the totalistic aspect that would place his vision more closely in line with that of anarcho-syndicalism in North-West European contexts and the Qaramatiyyah or, to some extent, the minarchist Islamic socialism of al-Sibāʿī in Islamic contexts.

Heba Raouf Ezzat and Anarcho-Islamist Economics

Heba Raouf Ezzat (b. 1965, also Hiba Ra'uf Izzat) is an Egyptian activist and Assistant Professor in political science at Cairo University. She has worked as editor of the women's of the Labour paper *al-Shaʿb*, co-run by the Muslim Brotherhood and the Labour Party and was co-founder of the popular website *IslamOnline*. Rejecting the label "feminist" she has emphasized women's issues from an Islamist perspective. Over the last 15 years she has received more attention outside of Egypt as a speaker at international conferences such as the World Economic Forum (Switzerland), World Social Forum (Brazil), and the State of the Union conference (Italy). She has previously studied or worked in Germany, London, Berkeley, and Georgetown (U.S.) and has been inspired by European social democratic and anarchist thought (though she identifies herself more as social democrat than anarchist). In Arabic she has authored several books (as well as an article in 2001 about anarchism). Her work in English consists mostly of chapters in various anthologies[82] and some interviews/debates.[83] In addi-

81 Davi Barker, *Voluntary Islam and Other Essays*, Free Press Publications 2013, 55.

82 Heba Raouf Ezzat, "The Silent Ayesha: An Egyptian Narrative", in: *Globalization, Gender, and Religion*, Jane H. Bayes and Nayereh Tohidi, eds., New York: Palgrave Macmillan 2001, 231–257; idem and Ahmed Mohammed Abdalla, "Towards an Islamically Democratic Secularism", in: *Faith and Secularism*, Rosemary Bechler, ed., London: The British Council 2004, 32–54; idem and Mary Kaldor, " 'Not Even a Tree': Delegitimising Violence and the Prospects for Pre-Emptive Civility", *Global Civil Society* 7 (2006), 36–37; idem, "The Umma: From Global Civil Society to Global Public Sphere", in: *Bottom-Up Politics: An Agency-Centred Approach to Globali-*

tion she has been the subject of some study within English language literature.[84] Ellen McLarney has described her as a "bright star in the Islamic movement", adding that she has "assumed a place of leadership in Islamic politics, both intellectually and politically" and is ranked the 39th "most influential Arab on Twitter, with over 100,000 followers."[85] In general Ezzat's vision has focused on polity, global civil society, and the family as a center for political activity. First of all, she completely rejects as false the typically assumed dichotomy between 'religion' and 'politics'. She does adopt the term 'secularism' however as something that can help inform democratic governance. In an interview, she stated,

> What we mean by "Islamic secularism" is not that Islam is subject to secular restructuring, but that through Islam, we can arrive at a form of secularism which suits us. We can decide where the power of the state should be minimal, where the power of the people should be maximised, where law enters, and where morality rather than law decides.[86]

In Ezzat's vision the main purpose of the state is to distribute the wealth and provide equal justice yet, beyond that, its power ought to be minimal and kept in check through a strong civil society of many organizations and institutions including the family unit, activist groups, unions, faith communities, and specifically the *waqf* system. The people of the world, the *umma*, are the focus of polities in Muslim philosophy she asserts, not the state: "In the Islamic paradigm, the relationship between the individual, group, nation, the globe and the cosmos is a relation of inclusion and not one of exclusion or dominance. In the Quran, the word Umma is used to describe all of those levels respectively."[87] This does not mean that the state is to be abolished. Rather she wants to reduce the centrality of the state in our political imagination and harness what remains toward humane ends:

---

zation, Denisa Kostovicova and Marlies Glasius, eds., London: Palgrave Macmillan 2011, 40–49; Khaled Mansour and Heba Raouf Ezzat, "Faith-Based Action in Development and Humanitarian Work", *Global Civil Society* 9 (2009), 118–146.

83 Rosemary Bechler, "Islam and Democracy: An Interview with Heba Ezzat", *Open Democracy* 11 May 2005, www.opendemocracy.net/faith-europe_islam/article_2501.jsp (accessed January 6, 2008); Karim El-Gawhary and Heba Ra'uf Ezzat, "An Interview with Heba Ra'uf Ezzat", *Middle East Report* 191 (1994), 26–27; Emran Qureshi and Heba Raouf Ezzat, "Are Sharia Laws and Human Rights Compatible?", *Qantara* 10 April 2004, http://en.qantara.de/content/emran-qureshi-heba-raouf-ezzat-are-sharia-laws-and-human-rights-compatible (accessed 11 January 2008).

84 Carolyn Barnett, "The Socialization of Female Islamists: Paternal and Educational Influence", *Journal of Women of the Middle East and the Islamic World* 7 (2009), 57–87; Ellen Anne McLarney, *Soft Force: Women in Egypt's Islamic Awakening*, Princeton and Oxford: Princeton Univ. Press 2015; Yusuf Sidani, "Women, Work, and Islam in Arab Societies", *Women in Management Review* 20: 7 (2005), 498–512.

85 McLarney, *Soft Force*, 219.

86 Bechler, "Islam and Democracy".

87 Ezzat, *The Umma*, 43.

> If we can put the debate about faith and politics on a new footing, we can look forward to a third-way Islam that could embark on a pacifist struggle for civil *jihad*, a *jihad* that would target neither the state nor the Other, but aim to win the fight over poverty and discrimination by expanding and empowering religion in a more civilised public sphere.[88]

The market violates human rights and dignity not merely through economic exploitation but also through the manufacture of lifestyles and personal choices. She has asserted: "When people decide for themselves, I want the effect of the market to be as minimal as possible. This, not that the authority of the state should be reduced, is my primary concern."[89] When women discard the veil, expose their bodies, or pierce their noses, she questions whether these are independent decisions or corporately manufactured commands "just like any dictatorial regime" designed to make people "consume more, and focus on their bodies and on consumption itself" (ibid.). It is in this battle between the forces of the market and the ability of people to organize their own lives and desires that she sees the crux of social struggle:

> The question, then, is not how can we best enforce democracy on people from above, but how can people enforce democracy on their states, make their presence felt and exert their influence from beneath, when this probably entails civil disobedience?[90]

The question then of democratizing economies and states begins at home where women are the primary social force. McLarney observed how (despite Ezzat's aversion to the term 'feminist') "Ezzat stresses the family as the site of women's political participation", emphasizes the etymological connotations of the Arabic word for mother (*umm*) at the base of nation (*umma*), and essentially concurs with one of feminism's core tenets, "the personal is political".[91] Ezzat, a mother herself, has described women's work to be manifest in *tarbiyah* (defined by McLarney as "discipline, childrearing, education, pedagogy") as a "women's jihad" and a pillar of a nation's polity.[92] By centering an economic vision of society on women's unpaid labor, informal exchanges and voluntary service are also highlighted as critical (non)economic forms of social relations. As McLarney observed:

> Women are the crux of this biopower, as its very levers, mechanism, and controls. Wielding this power, they contest the governmentality of the state through an Islamic politics of self-cultivation at the level of the body, soul, family, and com-

88 Ezzat and Abdalla, "Towards an Islamically Democratic Secularism", 53.
89 Bechler, "Islam and Democracy".
90 Ibid.
91 McLarney, *Soft Force*, 222, 251.
92 Ibid., 223.

> munity. Islamic *adab* (discipline) becomes a mechanism for challenging state control over the bodies of the population.[93]

In relation to the personal being political (as well as economical), some personal notes can be added here in regard to Ezzat. When I was organizing her visit to Scandinavia in 2008 for the European Social Forum (a trip she later had to cancel, unfortunately) she happily accepted the chance to speak at no charge ("I do not charge anything when I am among fellow socialists"). When she was subsequently offered the opportunity to receive payment for speaking at Copenhagen University during the same trip, she politely declined, writing: "I am grateful, but I do not want to spoil my '*neyya*' which means in Arabic religious intention. This is a trip devoted to my socialist passion so I do not want to be distracted by any other circles" (personal communications 28 and 29 May 2008). When I later asked her about economic exchange she responded:

> As for your question on exchange and development I think what matters more is restoring the *human scale*–there needs to be a way we can deal with big numbers and organize without cementing that in new forms of big organizational structures of power (personal communication 8 April 2017).

Her brief response (along with the recollection that she had previously referenced Christian anarchist and technology critic Jacques Ellul) seemed significant. It alerted me to a theme underlying her general approach to economics that I felt could be seen as resonating with the ideas of E. F. Schumacher, author of *Small is Beautiful* (1973). In this classic collection that helped spark a movement, Schumacher's Buddhist-inspired "economics as if people mattered" is filled with pragmatic-oriented aphorisms such as "any activity which fails to recognise a self-limiting principle is of the devil", "the present consumer society is like a drug addict who, no matter how miserable he may feel, finds it extremely difficult to get off the hook", and "an ounce of practice is generally worth more than a ton of theory"[94], Schumacher insisted that for "every activity there is a certain appropriate scale", and that "[s]mall-scale operations … are always less likely to be harmful to the natural environment than large-scale ones, simply because their individual force is small in relation to the recuperative forces of nature."[95] According to Schumacher, the misunderstanding that 'bigger is better' has helped create violent and ineffective systems of production such as nuclear power and weapons industries that both misuse human and natural resources while burdening socie-

93 Ibid., 5–6.

94 E. F. Schumacher, *Small is Beautiful: A Study of Economics as if People Mattered*, London: Vintage Books 1993 [1973], 127, 25.

95 Ibid., 50, 22.

ties and habitats with war and pollution. In contrast, Buddhist economics, according to Schumacher, emphasizes simplicity and non-violence.

When I re-read Schumacher's work after corresponding with Ezzat, I felt as if I could hear her spirit in his vision of "self-help technology, … democratic or people's technology" wherein "everybody can gain admittance and which is not reserved to those already rich and powerful."[96] Indeed, Ezzat and Kaldor's delegitimization of violence through citing the first Caliph Abu Bakr's declaration that "not even a tree" ought to be unnecessarily cut down in war finds its complement in Schumacher's reminder that each follower of the Buddha "ought to plant a tree every few years and look after it until it is safely established".[97]

If Eberhardt/Essadi advocated a form of dervish socialism and the *Green Book* proposed a totalistic socialism, then Ezzat's vision seems to emphasize small-scale non-state-based socialism as the means to keep both state and capital in check. In North-West European contexts this might recall the simplicity, non-violence, and small-scale organization of Christian anarchists such as Jacques Ellul and the Catholic Workers Movement. Within Islamic contexts, her vision seems rooted in similar types of small-scale institutions that have held together tribal societies across North Africa and the Middle East for centuries.

Concluding Remarks

This chapter has outlined three different visions of anti-authoritarian socialism within Islamic contexts. While each of the three individuals whose thoughts were considered, Isabelle Eberhardt/Mahmoud Essadi, Muammar Qaddafi, and Heba Raouf Ezzat, were determined to exemplify distinct variants of Islamic socialism, they also shared common ground. In essence, all three of them (along with Schumacher) offer anti-capitalist critiques and simultaneously insisted that a new economics is neither sustainable nor meaningful without faith, without a personal relationship to the Divine (however one conceives it). In this sense, their views converge. Yet whereas Eberhardt/Essadi advocated deviance, anti-economics, and the mutual aid of vagabonds and Qaddafi, in sharp contrast, envisioned an orderly stateless society in which all political, economic, and social problems were resolved through adherence to his totalistic blueprint, Ezzat seems to be arguing for a third path amongst third paths: acceptance of the state but emphasis upon smaller-scale forms of economic and political action, namely, the family and civil society. As such, one might regard the three different

96 Ibid., 127.

97 Ezzat and Kaldor, "'Not Even a Tree'", 18; Schumacher, *Small is Beautiful*, 44.

visions as potentially complementary. Ezzat's vision is the most pragmatic for most people and addresses the direct concerns and potential of people in their everyday lives to affect change and fill their daily needs. Qaddafi's vision urges people to continue to dream of the possibility of abolishing the state and the money system altogether. Eberhardt/Essadi's vision, in turn, reminds people not to forget the lives of those who will never fit in the boxes of conventional society as well as the devoted few who organize real life sanctuaries and pragmatic utopias wherein people work and exchange without compulsion or deprivation.

While all three of these visions of anti-authoritarian socialism have some types of precedents within anarchist as well as Islamic contexts, their limitations, as manifest in the self-destruction of Eberhardt/Essadi and the de facto dictatorship of Qaddafi, also provide impetus to further consider the third potential path of moderation between the two as outlined by Ezzat: an imperfect world wherein capital is subordinate to the state, the state is subordinate to the non-violent pressure of the populace, and each family of believers is subordinate to God. Through these means both society and the individual might employ self-restraint and mutual respect in order to care for and share the limited resources on this planet, cutting down "not even a tree" unless necessary and planting many more.

Turkish Islamists' Enthusiasm for Versace: Islamism between Rejection and Adoption of the West

Michelangelo Guida

As rightly noticed by İbrahim Kaya, Turkish modernity, as a 'later' experience, imported the idea of modernity from the 'West' and, indeed, Westernized to a certain extent. However, the Western element in the Turkish experience does not suffice for Turkish modernity to be seen simply as the result of Westernization. Indeed, even Kemalist interpretation of modernity was different from that of the 'West', mainly because the historical, civilizational and political specific features of Turkish society were not completely undermined by Western values. Certainly, the 'West' has always provided a criterion for Turkey to check itself against in terms whether its goals have been achieved.[1] Consequently, in Turkey and elsewhere, state elites had the opportunity to learn from an already experienced modernity.

> However, when a state aims to follow that model it encounters a historical/contextual resistance to it. In other words, the historical/civilizational context makes it almost impossible for non-Western countries to imitate the Western model.[2]

Kaya adopted Eisenstadt's "multiple modernities" as starting point for his work.[3] Eisenstadt too highlighted that the process of modernization is inevitably influenced by historical and civilizational contexts. Indeed, he stressed the fact that modernization broke their patterns of development. New patterns were distinctively modern, though greatly influenced by specific cultural premises, traditions, and historical experiences. Moreover,

> One of the most important implications of the term 'multiple modernities' is that modernity and Westernization are not identical; Western patterns of modernity are not the only 'authentic' modernities, though they enjoy historical precedence and continue to be a basic reference point for others.[4]

Modernity, then, is not intended as inevitably synonymous with *Westernization*. However, 'multiple modernities' maintain a Eurocentric method of analysis and an apparent inevitability of modernization.

---

1 Ibrahim Kaya, *Social Theory and Later Modernities: The Turkish Experience*, Liverpool: Liverpool Univ. Press 2004.

2 Ibid., 38.

3 Shmuel Noah Eisenstadt, "Multiple Modernities", in: *Multiple Modernities*, Shmuel Noah Eisenstadt, ed., New Brunswick-London: Transaction Publishers 2002, 1–30.

4 Ibid., 2–3.

Moreover, before the rise of the West there were already some tangible conflicts in terms of interpreting the world and the self in some non-European societies.[5] For instance, Muslim cultural tradition–before the advent of press and public education–showed predilection for the spoken word that *continuously* interpreted and re-interpreted–according to the social, historical and political context–the written and immutable language: 'paradoxically, and at the same time therefore, texts are important, yet not so important.'[6] The institution of *tajdīd* in Islamic tradition constitutes another example of the capability of renewal and dynamism (at least intellectual and religious). *Tajdīd* must not be intended as a reform of an already 'perfect religion',[7] but as a tool to renew the relation between religion and contemporary society, as well as to legitimize a new condition (if it is not in open contradiction with religion).[8]

However, Western Europe as a model of reference should also be put in the framework of the asymmetric economic and political relations in the nineteenth-century and contemporary world. Here, Matin's adoption of Trotsky's "uneven and combined development"[9] may be particularly useful. A key aspect of 'uneven and combined development' is the fact that a society can adapt and adopt other societies' products without undergoing the developmental processes from which these products had originated in their host societies. Consequently, 'later modernities' pre-empts historical and developmental repetitions. These repetitions are avoided mainly because they enjoy 'the privilege of backwardness', which permits the adoption of whatever is ready in advance of any specified date (skipping a whole series of intermediate stages), and 'substitution', which involves the mobilization of various replacements, native or foreign, in 'backward' contexts. Inevitably these produce a 'historical reshuffling', the merger or reversal of economic and political movements in capitalist modernization. Moreover, Trotsky pointed to the 'whip of external necessity', namely the imposition that capitalism imposes on all non-capitalist polities. Western modernities, then, have undoubtedly preceded in time 'later modernities' (as Kaya names it) or 'uneven and combined development' (as Trotsky names it) in non-Western societies, and the 'West' has represented a model of reference, but it also imposed on developing societies an economic model as well as social and cultural models.

---

5 Kaya, *Social Theory and Later Modernities*, 6–7.

6 Edward Wadie Said, "The Text as Practice and as Idea", *Modern Language Notes* 88: 6 (1973), 1071–1101, 1074.

7 See Quran V: 3, *Sūra al-Māida*.

8 Tahsin Görgün, "Tecdîd", in: *İslâm Ansiklopedisi*, Mehmet Âkif Aydın, ed., Ankara: İSAM 2011, 239.

9 Kamran Matin, *Recasting Iranian Modernity: International Relations and Social Change*, London, New York: Routledge 2013, 1–23.

In the context of Turkish modernization, which started in late eighteenth-century, Islamism must be seen as one of the *modern* reactive movements that adopted a *post-oriented* approach, in which the past is idealized in comparison with problems faced in the present. Islamists' dream of a return to pristine Islam[10] is a modern *imagination* (in Anderson terms) of their identity and past, very frequently idealized and detached from historical reality. The return to the past was a nationalistic approach needed for the building of a discourse necessary for the shaping of a *new* Islamic identity and tradition, which would fit in the contemporary world made of nation states.[11]

The idea that Islamism is a modern ideology is in contrast with classical modernization theorists, who saw modernity and tradition as antithetical and wrongly perceived Islamism as an anomaly in the Muslim world. However, precisely because the idealized past is privileged under conditions and institutions of modernity, these movements cannot be understood as *anti*-modern movements. Islamism is indeed the result of late nineteenth-century modernity and operates within the institutions of modernity.[12] Islamism is essentially modern because it had to frame itself in a new framework of *later* modernity under the whip of Western political, economic and cultural hegemony. In this context, Turkish Islamism has acquired three key elements, which strongly influenced and shaped it and demonstrate how *modern* its ideology is.

Firstly, anti-Westernism and the reaction to Western imperialism have been wrongly taken to be synonymous with the rejection of modernity. However, as we will see in the examples that this paper will present, Islamists were not opposing modernity *per se*, but the classical understanding of the modernization theory, which assumed that all industrial societies would one day converge into the Western model and discard their own culture and tradition.

Even if Turkey was not directly under the imperialist *whip*, it was influenced by the consequences of unequal economic, political and cultural relations since the early nineteenth-century. Moreover, Imperialism encouraged the emergence of Westernized elites that upheld the 'civilizing mission' among Muslim societies. In Turkey (and similarly in other Middle Eastern countries), Westernized elites were perceived as alien to the local social fabric by the Islamists. Westernized elites gained power and imposed authoritarian regimes that marginalized those deviating from the project of

10 The *Asr-ı Saadet*, the 'happy era' when the Prophet and his followers were alive or to a glorious era of Muslim history such as the Ayyubid or, more recently, Ottoman eras.

11 Olivier Roy, *L'échec de l'islam politique*, Paris: Seuil 1992, 15–16.

12 Kaya, *Social Theory and Later Modernities*, 153.

Westernization/modernization of society, triggering even more resentment. Islamism has evolved in opposition of the Imperialist West as well as in opposition to the Westernized elites. However, these elites imposed a cultural and political hegemony, which tightly restricted the chances to frame an alternative discourse.

Secondly, Islamist intellectuals adopted the hegemonic modern scientific epistemology. This process was due to sociological changes that occurred both in the Empire and in the Republic. With the *Tanzimat*, a new class of intellectuals (*üdebâ*), trained in the modern education system or into the Ottoman bureaucracy, replaced the declining *ulema* class, trained in the unreformed *medrese* system. We have very few Islamist intellectuals who were members of the *ulema* class.[13] Inevitably their education and social position provided them with rationalist modes of thinking that appraised their own social position and Islamic culture in a critical and worldly manner.[14] In the early stages of the Republic the *ulema* class disappeared. The new *İlahiyat*, faculties created to train imams, were shaped in the framework of modern university, imposing textuality and a modern classification of Islamic science not following the classical Muslim understanding. Rather than *ilim*, the classical understanding of religious knowledge, Islamist intellectuals would aim at producing *bilgi*, modern, *Western* knowledge.

Finally, as an ideology, Islamism had to also frame an economic vision in the unequal contemporary global economy. As we will see in this chapter, in the post-colonial world, there were two opposite views among Islamists. The first one adopted a Third Worldism idea of state-guided national development focused on import substitution industrialization accompanied with anti-colonial nationalism and its efforts to mesh often highly romanticised interpretations of pre-colonial traditions and culture.[15] The other idea was a refusal *tout court* of Weberian modernity inspired also by Western romanticism.

To understand how modernity moulded Islamism in the Turkish context, this chapter will present two key figures of Turkish Islamism: Nurettin Topçu (1909–1975) and Necmettin Erbakan (1926–2011). On one side, Topçu, a public intellectual very influential in the development of Islamist ideas after the end of the one-party era, denounced industrialization as a morally destructive force. On the other side, Erbakan, a key figure for the establishment of the Islamist political movement in Republican Turkey, advocated for a

13 Bedri Gencer, *İslâm'da Modernleşme (1839–1939)* [Modernization in Islam (1839–1939)], Istanbul: Doğubatı 2012, 174–179.

14 Kemal Haşim Karpat, *The Politicization of Islam: Reconstructing Identity, State, Faith, and Community in the Late Ottoman State*, Oxford: Oxford Univ. Press 2001, 3.

15 Mark T. Berger, "After the Third World? History, Destiny and the Fate of Third Worldism", *Third World Quarterly* 25: 1 (2004).

Third Worldist economic development strategy. They, however, also shared some common features as they were both educated in Europe and were influenced by the same Sufi master. Moreover, both were influenced in similar ways by Turkish *later* modernity and present the three key elements of Islamist modernity. The two Islamist authors were paradoxically in antithesis with the West yet in conformity with Western epistemology, as you would expect from intellectuals raised in a 'uneven and combined development'.

Nurettin Topçu and French Intellectuals

Nurettin Topçu was born on 7 November 1909 in Istanbul in a family of small traders. In 1928 he graduated from high school and in the same year he moved to Aix-en-Provence, where he studied one more year at a secondary school and two years later he graduated in philosophy at the University of Strasbourg. In 1934, he gained the *Licence de lettres* from Paris University. He then returned to Turkey and accepted a position as professor of philosophy at the Galatasaray *lycée* and started a career as teacher. Despite his early attempts, his conservatism precluded a tenure in Turkish academy, which was at the time strongly dominated by Kemalism.

The time he spent in France was decisive for his intellectual orientation. Nurettin Topçu was deeply influenced by three French intellectuals: Maurice Blondel (1861–1949), Louis Massignon (1883–1962), and Henri Bergson (1859–1941). Henri Bergson was clearly the philosopher, the intellectual spokesman par excellence in the eyes of Europe's educated public in the first decades of the twentieth-century.[16] Bergson aimed to liberate French intellectual life from scientism, materialism, and positivism of the *Lumières* ideology. Bergson's aim was certainly shared by Turkish conservative authors in the early years of the Republic, who criticised the Kemalist model of modernization. World War I marked, in the former Ottoman Empire, the end of the utopian idea of the West as a rational civilization. The pro-modernist and pro-West Ottoman intellectuals were troubled by the dystopian potential of modern Western civilization and its imperialist motivations. Although they had taken the West as a civilizing reference model for almost half a century, the Ottoman intellectuals began to express their loss of faith in the West after the events of the war. A widespread sense of despair among intellectuals was coupled with heated debates about the future of the Empire, which, as an ally of the Central Powers was defeated and occupied. Consequently, "Bergsonian philosophy was the harbinger of a near and bright future in the spirits of young university students who were walking through Beyazıt Square full of foreign soldiers dressed in strange uni-

16 Leszek Kolakowski, *Bergson*, South Bend: St. Augustines 2001, 1.

forms".[17] Similarly, Mustafa Şekip (Tunç, 1886–1958)–probably the most distinguished follower of Bergson in early twentieth-century Turkey and highly esteemed by Topçu–remembered that rationality was insufficient to interpret his past and his nation's identity, which was shaped by thousands of feelings, dreams and memories.

Furthermore,

> Completely afar from my spirit, I remained hanged to thought [*mefkûre*] just from one point like a hanging chandelier. During the tensest moments of my condition, the infection of the World War affected us and the most treacherous weapons encircled our lives. These events demolished the dam between simple rationality and my ego as well as transformed me in a single power while my soul's entire past assaulted my mind.[18]

Bergsonism then found fertile ground and offered to conservative intellectuals a sort of alternative to Western modernization without losing 'Oriental' metaphysics. Moreover, Turkish Bergsonians shared the anti-clerical republican attitude (Topçu also had a strong anti-clerical approach) and were not politically different from the republicans who were committed to the formal Kemalist principles. However, Bergsonism soon clashed with Ziya Gökalp's (1876–1924) positivist sociology and his mechanical theories as well as Unionist–and consequently Kemalist–political theory and its positivist civilizing project.[19] What drew them away from the mainstream politics of the day was their challenge of the rationalist foundations of humanist secularism adopted by the positivist republican factions who dominated the single party. "Bergsonians tried to provide a new interpretation of the Turkish Revolution and the emerging republican project of modernity by establishing a new communication between the two worlds–the spiritual aspects of the West and the mystic essence of national culture."[20]

When Topçu arrived in France, he was already acquainted with Bergson's ideas, because the French philosopher was well known in Istanbul thanks to early conservative and Anatolian nationalist writers. For Topçu, however, Bergson represented a source of legitimacy and a sort of intellectual Trojan horse rather than a true source of inspiration. Indeed, Bergson's under-

---

17 Ziyaeddin Fahri Fındıkoğlu quoted in Nazım İrem, "Turkish Conservative Modernism: Birth of a Nationalist Quest for Cultural Renewal", *International Journal of Middle Eastern Studies* 34 (2002), 94.

18 Mustafa Şekip, *Bergson ve "Manevî Kudret"e Dair Birkaç Konferans* [Some Conferences on Bergson and "Spiritual Power"], Istanbul: Muallim Ahmet Halit Kitaphanesi 1934. Throughout the paper, the translations are, except where stated differently, mine.

19 İrem, "Turkish Conservative Modernism", 92–93.

20 Nazım İrem, "Undercurrents of European Modernity and the Foundations of Modern Turkish Conservatism: Bergsonism in Retrospect", *Middle Eastern Studies* 40: 4 (2004), 79–112, 6.

standing of God as not absolute and not omnipotent is difficult to be accepted by traditional Christianity, but also by mainstream Islam.[21] A Catholic author like Blondel and, as in the case of our author, an Islamist intellectual, who by definition places religion and God at the core of his thoughts and deeds, may be influenced only marginally by Bergson. Bergson's Jewish background also might have negatively influenced Topçu's opinion. Unfortunately, Topçu had strong anti-Semitic feelings.

It appears, though, that Bergson furnished a Western and scientific legitimacy to his ideas critical of the dominant positivist approaches; his choice to write a thesis for associate professorship on Bergson maybe originated from here.[22] Topçu, as many of the Islamist authors that followed, were committed to vindicating the superiority of Islam but to avoid exploiting 'the privilege of backwardness', they carefully selected authors and ideas. Because Western authors were considered (and are still considered) intellectually superior to Islamic references by the general public and academia, to lead readers to Islam he often instrumentally used Western authors to contest materialism and anti-religious feelings inside Turkey. Moreover, French literature was also much more accessible considering Topçu and his peers' poor language skills, the difficulty of accessing books in Arabic after the proclamation of the Republic, and a lack of traditional Islamic education.

Much more influential on the young Topçu were the teachings of Maurice Blondel. Turkish convert to Catholicism and Blondel's godchild, Paul Mulla (Mehmet Ali Mulla-zadé, 1882–1959), introduced him to the Catholic philosopher. Mulla and Topçu met in 1928, introduced by the cultural attaché of the Turkish Embassy in Paris.[23] Moreover, Mulla was a careful reader of Topçu's review *Hareket* (*Action*) and helped Topçu in several occasions, for instance introducing him to Louis Massignon, who Topçu frequented in Paris between 1933 and 1934.[24]

Moreover, Topçu shared Blondel's commitment to begin a scientific discussion in which religious questions could be aired on the level of ideas, even where oppositions are recognized, instead of just on a level of blind emotions.[25] Topçu imported to Turkey this approach and applied it with the circle of young conservatives gathered around his journal *Hareket*, and was later adopted by other Islamist circles. The name of the journal–which was published by Topçu between 1939 and 1975–is also redolent of Blondel's

21 Oliva Blanchette, *Maurice Blondel: A Philosophical Life*, Chicago: Wm. B. Eerdmans Publishing Company 2010, 354.

22 Nurettin Topçu, *Bergson*, İstanbul: Hareket 1968.

23 Tuncer Enginertan, "Çağdaş Bir Mistiğin Hayatına Dair Bazı Notlar", in: *Nurettin Topçu*, İsmail Kara, ed., Ankara: Kültür Bakanlığı 2009, 94.

24 Paul-Mehmet Mulla-Zade and Jean-Mohammed Abd-el-Jalil, *Deux frères en conversion du Coran à Jésus. Correspondance 1927–1957*, Paris: CERF 2009, 242–244.

25 Ibid., 22.

most famous book *L'Action*.[26] However, while Bergson was very popular in Turkey, Blondel was essentially ignored and has only recently been translated into Turkish. Topçu did not make any effort to render a so-important author more readable to the Turkish reader and apparently ignored his mentor's antifascist and anti-war stands strongly expressed just before World War II. Topçu, on his side, never made any effort to conceal his sympathies for Nazism; a photograph of Hitler hung on the walls of his home.

Nevertheless, Blondel's *L'Action*, as well as the edited work *Qu'est-ce que la mystique*[27], had a huge influence on Topçu's doctorate thesis, which presents the fundamental ideas of the Turkish author's philosophy. On one side, Topçu seems to accept Blondel's Catholic dimension that God is immanent within man and that human action is directed beyond the phenomenal order. Moreover, it is in action that we apprehend God. On the other side, Topçu concentrated himself on one aspect of *action*–rebellion. God instigates in us an act of rebellion (*révolte/isyan*) against ourselves and against social serfdom to free us from insufficiency and infirmity owed by our attachment to the material, "True liberty, then, belongs to God; it is the divine liberty realized in us and in a certain measure realized by us. Rebellion is nothing but the affirmation of liberty in our action."[28] Rebellion brings us to *conform* ourselves to the divinity. This conformism (*conformisme/uysallık*) has been labelled as fatalism, yet "in reality is the greatest power of mysticism".[29]

Topçu's mystical model here is the mystic theologian al-Ḥallāǧ (857–922), who advocated God's immanence within man and a personal fight to recognize human imperfection and to rebel to this imperfection ascending towards God. However, Topçu became acquainted with al-Ḥallāǧ only through the works of Massignon,[30] he did not have the linguistic skills to read al-Ḥallāǧ by himself, nor did he quote in his work any literature in languages other than French. Also in later publications, Islamic sources would always be neglected or read superficially.

Nevertheless, Massignon, more than other authors, made progress on the study of Islamic mysticism. He also showed how Sufism is essentially of Islamic origin, contrary to many others that tried to prove non-Islamic sources of Sufism. However, the choice of al-Ḥallāǧ for his masterwork was

26 Maurice Blondel, *L'Action: Essai d'une critique de la vie et d'une science de la pratique*, Paris: Presses universitaires de France 1950.

27 Maurice Blondel, *Qu'est-ce que la mystique? Quelques aspects historiques et philosophiques du problème*, Paris: Bloud & Gay 1925.

28 Nurettin Ahmet [Topçu], *Conformisme et révolte: esquisse d'une psychologie de la croyance*, Paris: Les Press Modernes 1934, 129.

29 Ibid., 152.

30 Mainly Louis Massignon, *La Passion d'al-Hallâj*, Paris: P. Geuthner 1921. Massignon will recognize Topçu's admiration for al-Ḥallāǧ adding his thesis in the *bibliographie hallagienne* in the fourth volume of the new edition of *La Passion d'al-Hallâj*.

due not only to the relevance in Islamic philosophy of the Sufi master, but also to the conviction that al-Ḥallāğ represented the extreme convergence between Islam and Christianity.[31] For this reason, Edward Said criticizes "the disproportionate importance accorded al-Hallaj" and noticed that "Massignon's al-Hallaj was intended literally to embody, to incarnate, values essentially outlawed by the main doctrinal system of Islam, a system that Massignon himself described mainly in order to circumvent it with al-Hallaj."[32] Elsewhere, Said noticed that Massignon really represents an example of an erudite scholar where his personal, even his intimate, problems, concerns, and predilections are very much a part of his public work and position as an orientalist. That produces, however, an Orientalism blinded by what it perceives, "They [Massignon and Ernest Renan] grasp Islam, they also lose it."[33] Topçu may have not perceived Massignon's 'malicious' approach, but he must have been charmed by Massignon's courageous and devoted life, a true model of *action*.

After being influenced by Massignon, back in Istanbul Topçu found spiritual sustenance in the teachings of a Sufi master, Abdülaziz Bekkine (1885–1952) in 1943. Bekkine was a Nakşibendi sheikh inviting his adepts to conduct a modest life of involvement in society. With his charisma, Bekkine influenced an entire generation of well-educated likeminded conservatives who eventually became bureaucrats and prominent politicians. Moreover, Topçu's affiliation to Bekkine appears perfectly in harmony with his interest for mysticism, which was aroused by Massignon's research. Indeed, in the last pages of his PhD thesis, Topçu states that returning to the spirit of early Sufism–which goes from Muḥammad to Manṣūr al-Ḥallāğ – will help the sons of Anatolia to end their material and moral crisis.[34]
Interwar French cultural debates helped him in framing an opposition to the Kemalist idea of modernization. Something, however, which Topçu contested ontologically:

> Here [in Istanbul] Turkish-Islamic spirits fight with Western technology, which long ago overcame its romanticism. Everywhere the big industry's spiritless empire has flattened Muslim Turk's delicate spirit and taste. In Istanbul, the only masterpiece that has not been touched by the West is the Topkapı Palace. The House of Osman has built this sanctuary of Islam with the fringed flag made of silver thread

31 Pierre Rocalve, *Louis Massignon et l'Islam*, Damas: Institut Française de Damas 1993.

32 Edward Wadie Said, *Orientalism*, New York: Penguin 1979, 272.

33 Edward Wadie Said, "Islam, the Philological Vocation, and French Culture: Renan and Massignon", in: *Studies: A Tradition and Its Problems*, Malcolm Hooper Kerr, ed., Undena: Malibu 1980, 60.

34 [Topçu], *Conformisme et révolte*, 126. Here Topçu accepted Massignon's opinion that Islamic spirituality after al-Ḥallāğ never recovered and entered a period of protracted and unrelieved decline. Later, the Turkish author departed from this opinion to harmonize it with his nationalistic ideas and included late 'Turkish' mystics such as Rūmī and Yunus Emre.

> from Domaniç [the fatherland of the Ottoman rule] to the shores of the Marmara Sea. Here dominating the city silhouette the palace stands with the nobleness of a *Ka'aba* stone, which avoids harming others with its pain, against the barbarians' attack to the city coming from the West. Under this peak of nobility, the life strengths of the entire city apparently joined in the market in search of profit. The profit set two posts at the two extremes of the Galata Bridge as it was ready for an ambush.
>
> The leaders of these two posts are the Jews–the owners of big trades–, the Greeks, the Armenians and some of the men from the shores of the Black Sea. They poured here after they acquired for themselves all existences and strengths of this great nation, which is represented by the people of Anatolia who own not only this city but its history.[35]

These words were published by Topçu in early 1948 on the pages of his journal and summarize the author's image of Europe and modernity. In the quotation, Topçu strongly criticizes modernity as represented by mechanization and a capitalist economy. The Turkish author's ideal was a moral society without the inhumanity of machines: "Our era will be the era when hymns [*ilâhi*] will silence machines' creaks."[36] Moreover, he stresses the prominence of Anatolians who, despite the fact that they have a week national identity, are the people with finest and noblest characters, though polluted by the presence of profit led non-Turkish minorities and by those who misunderstood the nationalism introduced by great Turkish-Muslim leaders like Mehmed II.

Topçu was strongly influenced by the European Romantics' vision of modernity and pointed to it as one of the main reasons behind the decadence of humanity: "Think what kind of suffering beings you are! In this city mosquitoes and engines without soul are freer than humans. All aggressive powers are free, are free as much as they want; only men have no freedoms."[37] On the other side, Istanbul and Anatolia represent a symbol of Turkish history's greatness, but at the same time, they represent decadence in not only beggars in the streets, but also modern industry that attracts and dehumanizes poor immigrants from Anatolia. The capitalist continuous research for profit has also brought a loss of spirituality and morality. Istanbul was now representing the Turkish model of modernization, with all its injustice and inequalities. In the short stories written by Topçu and then collected in the volume *Taşralı* (*The Provincial*), Anatolian peasants escaping from their villages and pouring into the big city think that

35 Nurettin Topçu, *Amerikan Mektupları. Düşünen Adam Aramızda* [*American Letters. The Man Who Thinks Is Among Us*], Istanbul: Dergâh 2004, 15.

36 Nurettin Topçu, *Ahlâk Nizamı* [*The Moral Order*], Istanbul: Dergâh 2008, 28.

37 Topçu, *Amerikan Mektupları*, 28.

> Istanbul is a Hell and everyone here is a *zebâni*.[38] This is the grave of Anatolia. Destiny drags here the slaves that shall receive their punishment. Suddenly, she tried to find again the path of the light, which the reading of the call to prayer [*ezan*] opens; yet she could not find it.[39]

In reading Topçu's image of urbanization, we should also remember that Turkey had just started to experience a dramatic process of urbanization, which would change the social geography profoundly.

Taşralı was one of the two literary attempts of Topçu. The novel *Reha*, written before his departure for France and completed after his return but published only posthumous, is the expression of spiritual unrest and disapproval of the results of modernity, very similar to contemporary European works like *La coscienza di Zeno* by Italo Svevo (1923). Topçu's language, though, is too awkward and his sentences too long to give him fame as a novelist. *Taşralı*, published in 1959 (written between 1952 and 1958), shows not only the condition of underdevelopment of the Turkish provinces, but the loss of morality of the peasants and the abuse of religion by greedy imams and mystics. Again, the corruption of the peasants was brought to Anatolia by the new modes of production introduced by non-Turkish elements. Indeed, in many stories perversion and oppression is brought by Muslim Bosnians immigrated from the Balkans as the Empire retreated. Non-Muslim minorities and particularly the Jews that dominated big trade and the banking system were seen as the most important source of corruption.

Despite his hostility towards capitalism and mechanization, Topçu did not sustain anti-European feelings. European societies with their materialism attacked and colonized the Muslim world and Islam, but the 'real Europe' was represented by the Romantic intellectuals that searched for spirituality. Turkish elites that, since the *Tanzimat* era, have rushed to imitate Europe, Topçu argued, are neglecting the true Europe and forgetting the great Turkish past and identity.

Necmettin Erbakan and the Automobile Made in Turkey

As we already noticed, Nurettin Topçu was deeply influenced from his encounter with the Nakqshibendi shaykh Abdülaziz Bekkine and became a member of his Sufi order (*tarika*). Topçu eventually distanced himself from the confraternity because he did not recognize the authority of Bekkine's successor (*postnişin*), Mehmet Zahid Kotku (1897–1980). Topçu believed that Kotku was not the successor chosen by Bekkine and was brought from Bursa to Istanbul by the circle of the entrepreneur (and later, politician) Necmettin

38 A demon of Hell.

39 Nurettin Topçu, *Taşralı* [*The Provincial*], Istanbul: Dergâh 2006, 19.

Erbakan.[40] However, Kotku would become extremely influential among the Islamist intellectuals and politicians who emerged in the 1970s, and he actively encouraged believers' involvement in the economic and intellectual domains, as well as in religious practices. The *İskender Paşa Dergâhı*–the lodge created around the mosque of Istanbul where Kotku was appointed–constructed a web of economic activities, believed by his followers to be a religious duty. However, Kotku's economic vision and his idea of industrialization of the country was something that probably appeared outrageous to Topçu, who strenuously condemned modernity and any attachment to material interests: "You remember there is a shaykh effendi [a religious authority, Kotku is probably intending here] who opens factories; he even gives religious names to chimneys. This perversion, these bewilderments are opposed to the Islamic cause."[41]

Mehmet Zahit Kotku eagerly advocated the need to promote a simultaneously moral and material development of Turkey. In his speeches, Kotku promoted 'national industry'; in front of the lodge he showed to the followers the parked cars saying: "Instead of importing these automobiles from foreign countries, I wish we could establish manufactures, we could provide employment for our country's starving people."[42] In another more incisive version:

> Do not buy cars from the giaour (*gavur*). When I see the cars made by the giaours in front of the mosque I feel sad. In search of a modest livelihood, our people go abroad as guestworkers. This makes me sad. Instead of buying a car, set up a workshop, set up an engine factory. On the one hand you'll give chances to workers to live in a Muslim country; on the other hand, we'll free ourselves from being slaves of the giaours.[43]

Kotku's successor, Esad Coşan (1938–2001), also promoted industrialization. He condemned the use of violence and stressed that jihad was not to be intended exclusively as a personal struggle to control passions (as you would expect from a mystic), but also as progress:

> [The enemy…] does not want our development. Did you ever think how much a military airplane costs? Billions… [The enemy] provides you with a plane or medical device with a value equivalent to all Konya plateau's wheat crop. Thus you have to commit, be patient and build yourself that device… This is a form of jihad.[44]

---

40 Interview with İsmail Kara (Istanbul, 7 June 2011).

41 "Nurettin Topçu'nun 'Vaizlar Semineri'ndeki Konuşması", *Hece* 109 (Nurettin Topçu Özel Sayısı) (2006), 401–432, 426.

42 Necmettin Erbakan, *Davam: Ne Yaptıysam Allah Rızası İçin Yaptım* [*My Cause: What I Have Done I Did for the Sake of God*], Ankara: MGV 2014, 9.

43 Sedat Özgür, *Necmettin Erbakan Ve Gümüş Motor* [*Necmettin Erbakan and Gümüş Motor*], Istanbul: İlke 2014, 56.

44 Mahmud Esad Coşan, *İslam Dergisi Makaleleri*, Istanbul: Server 2007, vol. I, 19.

Erbakan shared this idea of *Islamic* modernization. In 1956, Kotku promoted the establishment of an engine factory–*Gümüş Motor*–as a stimulus for the Turkish (Muslim) economy. He named it *Gümüş* (namely 'silver') to recall the *Gümüşhanevî Dergâhı*, the Nakqshibendi lodge established by Gümüşhanevî Ahmet Ziyaüddin (literaly Ahmet Ziyaüddin 'from Gümüşhane', a city on the Turkish Black Sea region, 1813–1893) to which he belonged.

Gümüş Motor was directed by Necmettin Erbakan, an engineer with a PhD obtained from Aachen University with research on diesel engines. Before winning a scholarship to Germany, Erbakan graduated in 1948 from Istanbul Technical University, where he was approached by Bekkine. In Germany, he was impressed by the devastation of World War II, but at the same time by the discipline and motivation in rebuilding the country and its remarkable heavy industry. He also had the chance to work at the engine research unit of *Deutz*, a German engine manufacturer based in Cologne. The details of his contribution there are sketchy. However, his biographies emphasise his decisive role in developing a diesel engine for the tank Leopard.

Back in Turkey, he had a very rapid academic career. In 1957, he became associate professor and, in 1965, he became one of the youngest professors in Turkey. Erbakan, however, very soon preferred to dedicate himself to the engine factory and to politics. The factory led by Erbakan was established as the first step towards the production of a family automobile. However, its first products were engines for water pumps for irrigation and was established by the Czechoslovakian car maker *Škoda*. The contribution from a communist country was preferred because they were providing licences to produce all parts needed for the engines, whereas Western companies were only helping in the establishment of assembly lines with components produced in Europe, which would increase economic dependency.[45] Moreover, the company was set up with the clear aim of making only interest-free operations and with a capital collected among different businessmen, no shareholder would hold the majority or a position of dominance inside the company. Serial production of engines actually started in March 1960, two months before the overthrow of the *Demokrat Parti*'s government by the generals. The opening ceremony of the factory was attended by the Ministry of Finance, Hasan Polatkan, who expressed the interest of the government in the enterprise. Unfortunately, Polatkan was among the political figures hanged in 1960 coup.

Nevertheless, Erbakan also presented his work to the generals who took power. They remained impressed by Erbakan's efforts to create a national industry. In the presentation, Erbakan expressed to the generals that heavy industry was necessary to reach "the Great Turkey again" (*Yeniden Büyük Tür-*

45 Özgür, *Necmettin Erbakan Ve Gümüş Motor*, 65–66.

kiye) and spoke about the importance for Turkey in designing and producing its own automobile.[46] Erbakan was convinced that Islamic and Turkish civilization was not only superior to Western societies, but was also materially powerful. Imperialism, as well as wrong policies in the early republican era, brought the collapse of local industry and "great Anatolia remained deprived from industrialization."[47]

Erbakan, in an attempt of 'substitution', but in contrast with Topçu, also defended the possibility of an economic and material development beside a moral development:

> First of all morality and spirituality is the fundament of industrialization. If people do not have the same zeal of worshiping when working, the development that we expect is impossible. The presence of this flambeau in people's hearts is the necessary amulet. We say: competition with the West. In what we rely to compete? We will rely on our faith, we will rely on our spirituality; we will rely on our history.[48]

The leader of the military junta–Cemal Gürses–was so impressed by Erbakan's factory that on 15 May 1961 he made a fervent speech at the first Car Industry Congress, which Erbakan contributed to organizing. Also Erbakan was among the delegation who presented the final report of the congress to Gürsel.[49] A few days later, Gürsel ordered the state railways atelier of Eskişehir to produce the first prototype of a *national* automobile by the date of the Republic Day. The incredible effort to produce two prototypes has been staged in the film *Devrim Arabaları* (Cars of the Revolution).[50]

As the film shows, the 25 engineers were successful in realizing two prototypes in time for the Republic Day and presented them to General Gürsel in front of the members of the Turkish Parliament and the press in Ankara. However, because they did not have time to fill the fuel tank in Ankara, the first prototype stopped without completing the General's unscheduled test-drive. Forced to move to the second car, the leader of the military junta concluded that "we made the car with a Western head but we forgot to fill the tank with an Eastern head."[51] Despite General Gürsel's commitment, the press and the bureaucrats used the mishap to ridicule the project and, eventually, to terminate it. The reason behind it was a general mistrust in the capabilities of the local industry and of its engineers; as one of the characters

46 Erbakan, *Davam*, 15.

47 Necmeddin Erbakan, *Türkiye'de Sanayileşme Meselesi* [*The Issue of Industrialization in Turkey*], Istanbul: Aydınlar Ocağı 1975, 18.

48 Ibid., 37.

49 Muhittin Şimşek, *Yarım Kalan Devrim Rüyası: Cumhuriyet Dönemi Endüstrileşme Maceramız* [*The Dream of 'Devrim' Abandoned Halfway through: Our Industrialization Adventure in the Republican Era*], Istanbul: Alfa Yayıncılık 2008, 35, 48.

50 *Devrim Arabaları*, Dir. Tolga Örnek, Pinema 2008.

51 Şimşek, *Yarım Kalan Devrim Rüyası*, 86.

of the film affirms dishearteningly: "My son! In Turkey no achievement remains unpunished" [*Türkiye'de hiçbir başarı cezasız kalmaz, evladım!*].[52]

Erbakan, in all his speeches, attempted to fight this general defeatism, but his engine factory was also short-lived. The bumpy economic conditions delayed the project. Then the shareholders' structure of *Gümüş Motor* was too idealistic and small shareholders very soon sold theirs to a sugar state company and cooperatives of sugar beet producers, which under the *Demokrat Parti* government bought some of the shares to finance the enterprise. Under a new administration the company changed the name of the company into *Pancar Motor* and in 1965 started to produce engines under the licence of German and, later, Italian firms. Under the new administration the company had lost its ideal of producing 'Turkish engines' and to develop a local automobile industry. Erbakan then left the factory in 1964 but continued along his long political career to advocate the importance of industrialization and particularly of realizing a national automobile industry.

His enterprise's failure convinced him to run for politics. Initially, in May 1969, Erbakan was elected chairman of *Türkiye Odalar ve Borsalar Birliği* (Union of Chambers and Commodity Exchanges of Turkey, TOBB), which represented the small and middle size economic activities against the big economic corporations. However, the Justice Party (*Adalet Partisi*, AP) led by another engineer from Istanbul Technical University–Süleyman Demirel–challenged the elections and obtained its invalidation. Because Demirel also vetoed his candidacy to Parliament in the ranks of his party, Erbakan chose to run as an independent in the district of Konya, a stronghold of conservatism. Throughout his political carrier Erbakan defended the necessity of a policy of industrialization to reduce unemployment, reduce technological dependence, cure the scarcity of foreign currency, and gain national strength and prosperity.[53] These ideas were in line with Third Worldism, he was convinced that technological and economic dependence from the developed nations inevitably brought political dependence.

Finally, Erbakan's political career ended in 2002 when another Islamist party–the Justice and Development Party (*Ak Parti*, AKP)–emerged from the ashes of his party, once again banned by Kemalist bureaucracy. His political career was made difficult by his personal rivalry with Demirel–and later with Turgut Özal. However, taboos and legal restrictions of the political scene confined his actions and discourse. Four parties established by Erbakan were shut down by the courts or military junta and he was banned from politics between 1980 and 1987 and again between 1998 and 2003. However, many members of *AK Parti*'s echelon came from Erbakan's

52 *Devrim Arabaları*, 48:00.

53 M. Mustafa Uzun, *Ağır Sanayi Davası* [*The Cause for Heavy Industry*], Istanbul: Ravza 2014, 36–37.

movement and promoted a very similar economic model and 'Greater Turkey' has become the political mantra. They also promoted the project to realize an autarkic automobile, as well as a Turkish plane, helicopter, and drone. All projects developed by state agencies are now producing significant results.

Conclusions

Erbakan's dream of a Turkish automobile has failed to produce a result even if, in 2016, Turkey was the fourteenth in the world and fifth in Europe for the number of car and commercial vehicles produced.[54] However, those vehicles are designed and built by prestigious foreign firms (such as Hyundai, Toyota, FIAT or Renault) with the emergence of satellite activities. However, his model of modernization has been influential among Islamist circles. Erbakan's idea of industrialization is a *later* modernity, formally against European imposed modernity but at the same time an attempt to reach modernity without intermediate stages and presented in line with national culture. Nevertheless, even so, with the advantages of 'the privilege of backwardness' and 'substitution', his modernity is based on the same European epistemology of competition for technological and economic development. His attitude can be symbolized by his passion for Versace's ties. Some specify that those colourful ties were styled by a Turkish fashion designer and not by the famous Italian designer.[55] Nevertheless ties were not an attempt at a new conceptualization closer to Islamic and Turkish civilizations, but the reproduction of Western epistemology presented with a *native* narrative.

On the contrary, Topçu abhorred the Kemalist interpretation of development and European modernity based on industrialization, progress and urbanization. However, his critique of modernity was once again influenced by the cultural circles of interwar France and in the framework of the Western epistemology.

Certainly, Turkish Islamism is the result of modernization and both Topçu and Erbakan had to operate in the academic and political environment strictly limited by Kemalist cultural and political hegemony. Nevertheless, Islamism has failed in breaking the paradoxical dichotomy between passion for the West and repulsion of Western modernity. The result has been that Islamism is Turkish modernity strongly influenced by the histori-

---

54 OICA (International Organization of Motor Vehicle Manufacturers), http://www.oica.net/category/production-statistics/ (accessed 31/04/2017).

55 "Erbakan'nın Kravatlarını Versace Değil Ben Tasarladım," *Yeni Şafak* (01/01/2012), http://www.yenisafak.com/yenisafakpazar/erbakannin-kravatlarini-versace-degil-ben-tasarladim-359659.

cal and civilizational context, yet Islamism has been advocating an ontological critique of modernity outside the Western model that never materialized.

These two important examples of Turkish Islamism verify the premises of 'multiple' and 'later modernities', which assume historical precedence, but also the fact that Western patterns of modernity are the basic and inescapable reference point. From our examples we may even say that Islamism has introduced a lexicon apparently traditional, but epistemologically inside the pattern of Western modernity.

The Authors

Katajun Amirpur is a Professor of Iranian Studies at the University of Cologne. Her doctoral thesis and postdoctoral habilitation were on Iranian reformist thinkers. From 2011-2018, she served as a deputy director of the Academy of World Religions at Hamburg University. One of her most recognized publications is *New Thinking in Islam*, University of Chicago Press 2016. Her main research activity is Shi'i Islam and Iranian Intellectual history. She received her PhD in Iranian Studies from the University of Bamberg. Her Habilitation was on the Iranian scholar Mohammad Mojtahed Shabestari.

Sabine Damir-Geilsdorf is Professor of Islamic Studies at the University of Cologne. She obtained her PhD in Islamic Studies from the University of Gießen in 2001 with a thesis on the Egyptian Islamist Sayyid Quṭb (1906-1966) and received her postdoctoral qualification degree (Habilitation) from the University of Bonn in 2008 with a study on Palestinian narratives of the Arab-Israeli war 1948. Her current research projects are on salafism in Germany and on forced migration of Syrian refugees.

Anthony T. Fiscella has a PhD in the History and Anthropology of Religions from Lund University, Sweden. He is the author of articles such as "Imagining an Islamic Anarchism: A New Field of Study is Ploughed" (2009), "From Muslim Punks to Taqwacore: An Incomplete History of Punk Islam, " (2012), and "Removing MOVE: A Case Study of Intersectional Invisibility within Religious and Legal Studies" (2016). His dissertation, *Universal Burdens* (Lund University Press: Lund, 2015) focused on decolonizing conceptions of "freedom".

Leandros Fischer researches exile communities from the Middle East in Cyprus and teaches at the Department of Social and Political Sciences of the University of Cyprus in Nicosia. He previously taught at the University of Marburg's Center for Near and Middle Eastern Studies. His doctoral dissertation, *Zwischen Internationalismus und Staatsräson* (Wiesbaden: Springer VS, 2016), dealt with the German Left Party's positions on Palestine and Israel. He is a contributor for publications and media, such as *Jacobin Magazine*, *The Real News Network*, *Neues Deutschland* and others.

Michelangelo Guida is Professor at the Department of Political Science and International Relations at Istanbul 29 Mayıs University (Turkey). He has published several articles on Islamist intellectuals in Turkey in English, Turkish and Italian. The most recent ones in English are on İsmet Özel (*British Journal of Middle Eastern Studies*, 2014) and Nurettin Topçu and Necip Fazıl Kısakürek (*Journal for Islamic Studies*, 2014).

Béatrice Hendrich is Assistant Professor at the University of Cologne, Turkey Studies. Her main research area are the religious landscape of Turkey, Turkish literature, gender issues in Turkey Studies and the colonial history of the Turkish community in Cyprus. She is the author of articles such as "From Ottoman to Turkish Script in Cyprus: Conception and Implementation of a 'Kemalist Reform' against a Colonial Backdrop" (Nathalie Clayer, Fabio Giomi, Emmanuel Szurek (eds.), *Towards a Transnational History of Kemalism in the post-Ottoman Space beyond Turkey*, London: Tauris 2018).

Tahir Kamran is Professor of History at Government College University, Lahore, and affiliated scholar of Centre of South Asian Studies, Cambridge University. He is founding editor of *Pakistan Journal of Historical Studies* (Indiana University Press, Bloomington, US) and *The Historian* (Department of History, Government College University, Lahore). He has served on Iqbal Chair, Cambridge University, between 2010 and 2015. He writes on sectarianism and colonial Punjab. He has authored four books, his recent book is with Ian Talbot, entitled *Colonial Lahore: A History of the City and Beyond.*

Mouez Khalfaoui is Professor of Islamic Jurisprudence at the University of Tübingen. His main research fields are Islamic Law and its History, Minority Rights, Ethics and Education. He is member of several publishing, advising, social and political boards in Europe and worldwide. His last publication is: *Islam und Muslime in Europe*, Lit-Verlag, Berlin (2016).

Bayram Koca is Research Assistant at the Department of Political Science and Public Administration, Hacettepe University. He continues his PhD studies in Political Science at Hacettepe University, Ankara. He is the author of *Türkiye'de İslam ve Sol* (Vivo: İstanbul, 2014).

Elisheva Machlis is a lecturer at Tel Aviv University and a research fellow at the Truman Institute at Hebrew University. Her research focuses on modern Shiite trends and particularly on religion and state in Iran and Iraq. She has a PhD from the University of Cambridge Elisheva Machlis's publications include: *Shi'i Sectarianism in the Middle East: Modernisation and the Quest for Islamic Universalism*, I.B Tauris, London (2014).

Anas Malik is Associate Professor of Political Science at Xavier University and External Affiliated Faculty at the Vincent and Elinor Ostrom Workshop at Indiana University (Bloomington). He is the author of *Polycentricity, Islam, and Development: Potentials and Challenges in Pakistan* (Lexington, 2018) and *Political Survival in Pakistan: Beyond Ideology* (Routledge, 2011), and various articles, book chapters, and other publications related to the political economy of development and collective action in religious and interreligious contexts. Malik received his PhD in Political Science and Master's in Economics from Indiana University in Bloomington.

Manfred Sing is a Senior Researcher at the Leibniz Institute of European History in Mainz, Germany, interested in the history of Islam and Marxism in a transnational and transcultural perspective. He is author of "Arab Self-Criticism after 1967 Revisited: The Normative Turn in Marxist Thought and its Heuristic Fallacies," in: *Arab Studies Journal* 25, 2 (2017): 144–190; "New Approaches to Arab Left Histories," in: *Arab Studies Journal* 24, 1 (2016): 90–97 (with Sune Haugbolle); "The Specters of Marx in Edward Said's *Orientalism*," in: *Die Welt des Islams*, 53, 2 (2013): 149–191 (with Miriam Younes); and "Brothers in Arms. How Palestinian Maoists Turned Jihadists," in: *Die Welt des Islams* 51, 1 (2011): 1–44.

Fabio Vicini is Assistant Professor of Sociology and Anthropology at Istanbul 29 Mayıs University. Previously PhD fellow at Berlin Graduate School Muslim Cultures and Societies and *Zentrum Moderner Orient* (2011) and TÜBITAK post-doctoral fellow (2013-2014), he received his PhD in Anthropology and History (2013) from the Institute of Human and Social Sciences, Scuola Normale Superiore in Pisa. In 2013 he was awarded the Middle East Studies Association's (MESA) Malcolm H. Kerr Award in the Social Sciences. His work has appeared in journals such as *Anthropology & Education Quarterly, La Ricerca Folklorica, Sociology of Islam, Culture and Religion*, and the *British Journal of Middle Eastern Studies.*

Hans Visser is Professor Emeritus of Monetary Economics in the School of Business and Economics at the Vrije Universiteit Amsterdam. He is the author of *Islamic Finance: Principles and Practice*, Edward Elgar 2013. He lectures and publishes on Islamic finance and other money and banking topics.